FLORIDA STATE
UNIVERSITY LIBRARIES

FEB 13 1997

TALLAHASSEE, FLORIDA

United States-Third World Relations in the New World Order

UNITED STATES-THIRD WORLD RELATIONS IN THE NEW WORLD ORDER

Abbas P. Grammy and C. Kaye Bragg

Nova Science Publishers, Inc.
New York

Cover Design: Maria Ester Hawrys

Art Director: Maria Ester Hawrys
Assistant Director: Elenor Kallberg
Graphics: Eddie Fung, Barbara Minerd, and Kerri Pfister
Manuscript Coordinator: Gloria H. Piza
Book Production: Tammy Sauter, Gavin Aghamore, Christine Mathosian and Joanne Bennette
Circulation: Irene Kwartiroff and Annette Hellinger

Library of Congress Cataloging-in-Publication Data

Grammy, Abbas P.
    United States—Third World Relations in the New World Order / Abbas P. Grammy, C. Kaye Bragg.
      p.   cm.
    Includes index.
    ISBN 1-56072-350-5
    1. Developing countries—Foreign relations—United States.
    2. United States—Foreign relations—Developing countries.
I. P. Bragg, C. Kaye.   II. Title
D888.U6G73   1996
327.73017'24—dc20   996-20518
                                                                                       CIP

© 1996 by Nova Science Publishers, Inc.
6080 Jericho Turnpike, Suite 207
Commack, New York 11725
Tele. 516-499-3103   Fax 516-499-3146
E Mail Novascil@aol.com

All rights reserved. No part of this book may be reproduced, stored in a retrieval system or transmitted in any form or by any means: electronic, electrostatic, magnetic, tape, mechanical photocopying, recording or otherwise without permission from the publishers

Printed in the United States of America

Contents

Preface ix
   Abbas P. Grammy and C. Kaye Bragg

Introduction: The Grass Suffers Equally 1
   Steven W. Hook

Section 1: United States and Third World

A Policeman's Lot is Not (Always) a Happy One 9
   Murray Wolfson

The Political Economy of Oil: United States and Middle East Post World War II Relations 23
   Behrooz Fattahi and Omid Fattahi

The American Doctrine on Low Intensity Conflict in the New World Order 49
   Beau Grosscup

Section 2: United States and Latin America

AIDS in Latin America and the Caribbean: New Challenges for United States Foreign Policy 65
   Robert McNamara

Cultural Barriers to Effective Trade between the United States and Latin America 87
   Joanne Schmidt and Janis Ruiz

Relations Among Neighboring Nations in South America 101
  Freeman J. Wright

Post-Devaluation Mexico in the New World Order 123
  Mark A. Martinez

SECTION 3: UNITED STATES AND ASIA

United States-East Asian Trade in the New World Order 149
  Margaret M. Malixi and Mohsen Bahmani-Oskooee

United States-ASEAN Economic Relations 169
  Robert L. Curry, Jr.

Strategic Economic Development: Singapore Style 191
  Robert G. Fletcher and Brenda J. Moscove

The Vietnam Crucible:
The Political Economy of Normalization 207
  M. Kent Bolton

Indian-United States Relations in the New World Order:
Restructuring of Indian Foreign Policy 231
  C. Kaye Bragg

SECTION 4: UNITED STATES AND THE MIDDLE EAST

United States-Middle East Policy in the Aftermath of
the Cold War and Persian Gulf War 249
  David H. Johns

Economic Development in Muslim Countries:
A Comparative Empirical Analysis 265
  Abbas P. Grammy

The Peace Process and the Palestinian Refugees 279
   Elias H. Tuma

The Geo-Economics of Iraq-Kuwait Conflict:
A Retrospective Comparative Analysis 297
   Abbas P. Grammy and Richard G. Quiring

SECTION 5: UNITED STATES AND AFRICA

Orthodox Strategies in a "Disenabling" Environment:
Politico-economic Decline in Sub-Saharan Africa 313
   Marlyn A. Madison

Market Reforms and Structural Adjustments in
the New World Order: The Case of Côte d'Ivoire 333
   Abel Konan and Djeto Assane

SECTION 6: THE POLITICAL ECONOMY OF DEVELOPMENT

The Economics of Political Change 347
   Abbas P. Grammy

Factors Affecting the Development of Fossil Energy
Resources of Developing Countries 361
   Muhammad Sahimi

The Role of Political Risk in Foreign Direct Investment:
The Case of Eight Asian Countries 391
   Harinder Singh

The Macroeconomic Effects of Oil Price Shocks 411
   Mohsen Bahmani-Oskooee and Margaret M. Malixi

Index 431

PREFACE

From World War II to the late 1980s, the Cold War between the United States and the Soviet Union defined the tone and direction of the United States-Third World relations. Tension between the two superpowers affected the scope of choices available to Third World development. Yet in the 1990s, the collapse of the Soviet Union brought an end to this bipolar arrangement and a beginning to political reconstruction. Economically, the transition from central planning to free market system, growth of transnational corporations, and consolidation of regional economic associations promoted greater integration of the world economy. Politically, conflicting forces of nationalism in Eastern Europe, the Middle East, and Africa challenged traditional patterns of nation-state behavior. All of these changes demanded restructuring of international relations. By the end of the Persian Gulf War, the principle of collective security and economic interdependence enabled President Bush to declare a "New World Order."

For United States-Third World relations, increased cooperation requires the recognition not only of economic and military interdependence, but also the "mutual dependence" among nations in addressing transnational issues of culture, environment, and health. Meanwhile, growing political and economic instability in the developing countries has raised concerns about issues of human rights, democratization, and social justice. In this context of insecurity and interdependency, a new set of principles and institutions are shaping international relations.

This book explores the primary issues and organizing principles that define the United States-Third World relations in the New World Order. It consists of twenty-two chapters on the political economy of the New World Order. Of the twenty-six scholars who have contributed to this volume, sixteen are faculty members of eight universities in the California State University System: Bakersfield (eight), Chico (one), Fullerton (two), Fresno (one), Sacramento (one), San Diego (one), San Marcos (one), and Sonoma (one). The remaining ten scholars belong to a private company (CalResources LLC), a research organization (East-West Center), and eight educational institutions (University of Missouri-Columbia, Columbia University, Grand Valley State University, Highland High School, University of California-Davis, University of Nevada-Las Vegas, University of Southern California, and University of Wisconsin-Milwaukee).

This book consists of six sections. The first section includes three essays on the political economy of the United States-Third World relations and American political, economic, and military involvement in the developing countries. In section two, there are two chapters that address the political and cultural challenges facing the United States-Latin American relations in the post-Cold War era, followed by a regional and a country study. Section three devoted to the United States-Asia relations in the New World Order consists of two general essays and three case studies. In section four, we find a chapter that will focus on the relationship between the United States and the Middle East, an essay on economic development, and two case studies. Section five consists of one general essay on the economic decline of countries in Sub-Saharan Africa in the post-Cold War era, followed by a case study of structural adjustments in an African country. The final section of the book is comprised of four general chapters on the political economy of development in the New World Order.

The completion of this research project took nearly two years of inquiry of interest from potential contributors, review and approval of the submitted research abstracts, referee and review of the submitted chapters, first, second, and (sometimes) third revisions of the accepted chapters, word-processing and editing of the accepted chapters, and submission of the volume for publication. In completing this time-consuming and sometimes exhausting process, we benefited from an award from the University Research Council and a grant form the Division of Graduate Studies and Research of California State University, Bakersfield for which we are indebted to Edwin Sasaki and Nancy Myers. We are thankful to

Tina Giblin for helpful secretarial assistance and Sylvia O'Brien for skillful word-processing services. We are grateful to all of our contributors who enabled us to publish their research. While they bear full responsibility for their results and views, we remain responsible for any errors. The completion of this challenging project has been rewarding, nonetheless.

Abbas P. Grammy
C. Kaye Bragg

INTRODUCTION: THE GRASS SUFFERS EQUALLY

Steven W. Hook
Department of Political Science
University of Missouri - Columbia
113 Professional Building
Columbia, MI 65211

According to a popular African aphorism, "When elephants fight, the grass suffers."

These words were often used to describe the Cold War's pernicious effects on less-developed countries (LDCs) in Africa, Latin America, and southern Asia, many of which served as surrogate battlegrounds for the United States and the Soviet Union during their nearly half-century of competition.

In the late 1990s, a corollary to this aphorism has gained widespread currency: "When elephants make love, the grass suffers equally."

Such is the ironic fate of many impoverished states which escaped from the shadow of the Cold War superpowers, only to find themselves in equally distressed circumstances in the late 1990s. Far from the "New World Order" envisioned by U.S. President George Bush in 1991 -- which anticipated collective action by affluent states to redress long-neglected transnational problems -- the post-Cold War era has instead witnessed the revival of parochial self-interests among the great powers and general *malaise* toward the developing world, where most of the world's 5.7 billion people live and where population growth rates are by far the most rapid.

For many LDCs -- still suffering from acute malnutrition, overcrowding, and political repression -- hegemonic meddling by the superpowers has been replaced by indifference and neglect, with tragic consequences for them and, in the long run, for the industrialized North as well.

I. THE COLD WAR AND THIRD WORLD DEVELOPMENT

In assessing the status of U.S.-Third World relations in the late 1990s, one must first consider the Cold War experience and its omnipresent legacy. The Soviet rivalry dictated U.S. policy toward many parts of the developing world, much of which was emerging from colonial rule. The U.S. government's dominant role in the Bretton Woods regime, which through the World Bank and International Monetary Fund supported economic development in LDCs based on linear Western models (see Rostow, 1971), overshadowed the processes of indigenous social, political, and economic development. Both superpowers sought the allegiance of LDCs through varying combinations of political propaganda, military coercion, and material incentives, effectively drawing Third World elites and mass publics into their regional and global designs.[1]

The transparent self-interests of these aid donors aside, more than $1 trillion in bilateral and multilateral aid flowed to LDCs between 1945 and 1990 which contributed to demonstrable improvements in living standards.[2] Annual economic growth rates in the 1960s averaged 6.2 percent, well above the United Nations' target of 5 percent for the first "Development Decade." Average life expectancy among low-income states increased from 43 to 59 years; literacy rate grew from 33 to 59 percent; and the rate of child mortality fell by more than two-thirds (World Bank, 1991; see also OECD, 1985). Gradually, as the perils of rapid population

---

[1] Western European states, meanwhile, concentrated aid flows among their former colonies in Africa and southern Asia, further complicating the process of "state building" in these areas.

[2] The U.S. served as the primary donor of foreign aid during most of the Cold War, transferring more than $500 billion in bilateral economic and military assistance to nearly every pro-Western LDC in the international system (see USAID, 1993). Japan overtook the United States as the world's leading aid donor in the 1990s, followed by France, Germany, and Great Britain.

growth were widely understood, education and family-planning programs were established which led to declining birth rates in many areas by the 1990s.

Thus the superpower rivalry served, paradoxically, to benefit LDCs in many tangible ways. Its overall effects, of course, were far more complex, and in many respects more insidious. In its effort to "contain" communism, the United States encouraged and rewarded authoritarian regimes across the Third World, particularly in Latin America, which it had claimed as its sphere of influence since the Monroe Doctrine was expounded in 1823. Ideological divisions which were transplanted to fragile LDCs polarized their societies into hostile and militarized factions, marginalized moderate groups, and provoked civil unrest and constant insurgencies. Regional conflicts in Korea, Indochina, southern Africa, Central America, and other areas were inflamed by the superpowers, which equated the security of their Third World clients with their own "vital interests."

For the United States, which broadened its activities well beyond Latin America during the decolonization period, the Cold War produced intimate ties between Washington and remote capitals from Buenos Aires to Monrovia, Mogadishu, and Djakarta. Many Third World dictators -- Marcos in the Philippines, Somoza in Nicaragua, Mobutu in Zaire, the Shah of Iran -- owed their longevity in large part to U.S. material and political support. Given that a direct confrontation with the Soviet Union was effectively precluded in the midst of the nuclear arms race, Third World states assumed the front lines of the Cold War and bore its consequences.

In these multiple ways the "Third World" -- a dubious analytic concept borne of the Cold War -- was profoundly shaped by the superpower struggle. It was for this reason that many in the North and South longed for a resolution of this protracted struggle, assuming that its conclusion would lead to more cooperative efforts which would ease the widespread suffering in the LDCs.

II. DIMINISHED EXPECTATIONS SINCE THE COLD WAR

As noted above, the great expectations for a harmonious New World Order have not materialized. Amid a cascade of unforeseen crises abroad, the world's affluent states have largely forsaken the transnational objectives they previously embraced and have turned inward, attending to domestic problems neglected throughout the Cold War and pursuing more narrowly defined national interests. As they have done so, a wide range of developments -- the revival of nationalist tensions, genocidal ethnic warfare, and massive refugee migrations -- have further distracted world leaders from the cooperative transnationalism of the New World Order.

In the United States, social problems and a burgeoning national debt became the primary focus of attention upon the Cold War's abrupt conclusion. Newly elected President Bill Clinton, who had promised to emphasize domestic priorities rather than foreign policy, remained true to his word upon taking office. His pursuit of "geoeconomics," including expanded trade with Pacific Rim states, hemispheric economic integration, and a strong World Trade Organization, represented his few early achievements in a foreign policy that was otherwise characterized by indecision and vacillation.

The Clinton administration initially joined the multilateral campaign to promote "sustainable development" within LDCs, an effort initiated at the 1992 United Nations Conference on Environment and Development (UNCED). The U.S. Agency for International Development (USAID) pledged larger flows of aid to LDCs in the pursuit of social, environmental, political, and economic reforms. The State Department revived Jimmy Carter's campaign to make human rights a central concern of the United States and to condition future U.S. relations upon the "enlargement of democracy" in the Third World.

These efforts were disrupted, however, after the Congressional elections of November 1994 brought control by the opposition Republican Party to the U.S. Senate and the House of Representatives. In pressing their foreign-policy agenda, Republican leaders called for deep cuts in U.S. foreign aid programs and the abolition of USAID in its existing form. At the same time they proposed increases in U.S. defense spending -- to $262 billion in Fiscal Year 1996, an amount more than $10 billion higher than that requested by the Pentagon. Finally, the Congress voted to restrict U.S. participation in U.N.-sponsored peacekeeping efforts and to reduce U.S. contributions to transnational efforts for environmental protection, population control, and democratic development in the Third World.

These events, coupled with Congressional attacks on Clinton's domestic agenda, undermined the president's ability to support the U.N.'s sustainable development initiatives. But the United States was not alone among industrialized states in finding the New World Order less than hospitable to improved North-South relations. Domestic strains provoked a resurgence of nationalist uprisings in Germany, Great Britain, and France, where sluggish regional economic growth was often blamed on immigrants and political refugees (see Fenske, 1991). Scandinavian countries, traditionally the most generous in supporting LDCs, also scaled back aid commitments as conservative parties demanded reductions in government spending. Even the government of Japan, the world's largest foreign aid donor after 1989, struggled to overcome a prolonged recession and political crisis that hindered its effort to support LDCs (see Rix, 1989-1990).

As these events unfolded, another less conspicuous development occurred in the aftermath of the Cold War which would have ominous implications for development. In 1992, private financial flows from North to South -- including foreign direct investment, transnational bank loans, and the expansion of multinational corporations -- exceeded government flows for the first time. Unlike foreign aid programs, which were guided in part by considerations of human need in the LDCs, private loans and investments were driven exclusively by profit motives. Thus most private capital was directed toward newly industrialized countries in the Pacific Rim, along with some middle-income regions in Latin America, which had already established a track record of economic expansion.

This trend toward private capital flows was felt within the foreign aid regime as well, which adopted a "new development paradigm based on markets, competition, and private initiative and enterprise" (OECD, 1995: 12). As in the case of private flows, economic aid flows were increasingly predicated upon the ability of recipients to convert the resources into sustained economic growth, a process which not only benefited recipient states but created export markets and investment opportunities for donors. Under strong domestic pressure to reduce public spending and diminish the state's role in many sectors of economic activity, political leaders in wealthy states were forced to defend aid packages on the basis of their own economic self-interests.[3]

For much of the Third World, these trends served collectively to widen the gaps between rich and poor. As private capital poured into the Newly Industrialized Countries (NICs), the remaining pool of foreign aid was redirected to Eastern Europe and the former Soviet Union, the Middle East, and middle-income states. Left out of both the private and public capital flows were most peoples in least developed countries (LLDCs), who were increasingly marginalized in the post-Cold War era. As the OECD (1995: 2) acknowledged, "The implications of these trends for longer-term development efforts are obviously enormous."

As a result, citizens in the most distressed regions (the so-called "Fourth World") continue to endure economic stagnation, social and political unrest, and ongoing dependence on affluent states. In the absence of private investment their needs for foreign aid steadily grows as their populations swell and as the availability of arable farmland diminishes. With their leaders barely able to retain power, and then only through coercive practices, the conditions in these regions are hardly favorable for a recreation of the East Asian economic "miracle" heralded by the World Bank (1993).

III. PROSPECTS FOR U.S. FOREIGN POLICY

As with other aspects of its foreign relations, U.S. policy toward the Third World has lacked a common orienting principle in the post-Cold War era, shifting spasmodically across regions and issue areas in an *ad hoc* manner (see Spanier and Hook, 1995). The failed relief effort in Somalia, an area of diminished concern to the United States in the 1990s, has come to symbolize the pitfalls of humanitarian intervention in the Third World. Notably, the widely criticized U.S. effort to "restore democracy" in Haiti was justified on the basis of securing U.S. borders rather than humanitarian concerns.

---

[3] The global volume of development assistance increased steadily between 1973 and 1992, but for the first time in 1993 aid commitments fell in absolute terms, from $61 billion to $56 billion (OECD, 1994).

For President Clinton, who campaigned on a platform of domestic renewal, foreign policy has been largely reduced to foreign *economic* policy, and in this regard most LDCs figure only indirectly. The U.S. government has in the post-Cold War period been preoccupied with trade issues, opening markets in Eastern Europe, and securing peace -- and oil supplies -- in the Middle East. If foreign policy is indeed a "zero-sum game," as it tends to be with an embattled administration that has more pressing domestic priorities at stake, these efforts effectively crowd out transnational concerns which have less tangible short-term benefits for the United States.

If the past is any guide, U.S. policies toward the Third World will likely continue to reflect its emerging geopolitical priorities -- or more correctly in the post-Cold War era, its geoeconomic interests. In this sense the United States will likely continue to support only those LDCs which provide some return to U.S. domestic constituencies -- farmers, manufacturers, investors, and multinational corporations. Other LDCs, particularly those of "collapsed" states in remote areas, will likely receive little attention from Washington, as they have from other Northern capitals in the 1990s.

For a brief but fleeting moment, the New World Order promised to focus U.S. foreign policy on the realities of an interdependent world, in which not only the global economy but its ecological fortunes were wedded across national borders in ways that demanded cooperation by nation-states. U.S. national interests were, correctly, identified with regional and global interests, and concerns over global population growth, environmental destruction, epidemics, and arms proliferation were seen as pressing threats to U.S. national security. Given that such transnational problems demand transnational solutions, U.S. foreign policy seemed directed toward new and hopeful directions.

Instead, unilateralism has instead resumed its central place in U.S. foreign policy, as exemplified by the cutbacks in U.N. funding and simultaneous increases in the U.S. defense budget. Further troubling for the South, the United States has committed itself to a costly NATO commitment in the former Yugoslavia, along with ongoing aid to Russia, Eastern Europe, and middle- and upper-income states in the Middle East. Thus the U.S. foreign-policy agenda, already shrunken under the leadership of a "domestic president," has moved ever distant from the needs of the world's most distressed populations in the Third World.

As subsequent chapters of this volume demonstrate, U.S. foreign policy toward the Third World continues to cast a long shadow over its political and economic development. It is for this reason that the Cold War's conclusion was so widely welcomed, and for this reason that the subsequent performance of the United States is of such great concern.

REFERENCES

Fenske, John, "France's Uncertain Progress Toward European Union," *Current History*, November, 1991, 90, 358-362.

Hook, Steven W., *National Interest and Foreign Aid*, (Boulder, CO: Lynne Rienner Publishers, Inc., 1985).

Organization for Economic Cooperation and Development, *Development Cooperation: Efforts and Policies of the Members of the Development Assistance Committee*, (Paris: OECD, 1994, 1985).

Rix, Alan., "Japan's Foreign Aid: A Capacity for Leadership?", *Pacific Affairs*, Winter 1989-1990, 62, 463-464.

Rostow, W.W., *Politics and the Stages of Growth*, (New York: Cambridge University Press, 1971).

Schraeder, Peter J., "'It's the Third World Stupid!' Why the Third World Should be the Priority of the Clinton Administration," *Third World Quarterly*, 1993, 14(2), 215-237.

Spanier, John, and Steven W. Hook, *American Foreign Policy Since World War II*, 13th ed., (Washington, DC: Congressional Quarterly, 1995).

U.S. Agency for International Development, *U.S. Overseas Loans and Grants, and Assistance from International Organizations*, (Washington, D.C.: U.S. Government Printing Office, 1993).

World Bank, *The East Asian Economic Miracle*, (New York: Oxford University Press, 1993).

World Bank, *World Development Report*, (New York: Oxford University Press, 1991).

A POLICEMAN'S LOT IS NOT (ALWAYS) A HAPPY ONE

Murray Wolfson
Department of Economics
California State University, Fullerton
Fullerton, CA 92634

Abstract—With the end of the Cold War, the United States has increasingly taken on the role of world policeman. A policeman's lot is to deter as well as punish crime. This paper studies the aspects of the U.S. interest: the difficulties of deterrence with special reference to the case of Iraq and Kuwait, and the costs and benefits to the domestic economy of the United States.

I. INTRODUCTION

As the remaining superpower in the post-Cold War world, the United States is increasingly taking on the role of world policeman. Television drama notwithstanding, most of the time the police manage to deter criminal acts without violence. They apprehend criminals with a minimum of force, and thus also deter the rest of us who might be tempted to step over the line. But in the Gulf War, why did the U.S. policeman fail to convince Iraq to retreat from Kuwait by the threat of force?[1] Why did the

---

1. We are starting our exercise after the Iraqi attack on Kuwait was a fait accompli rather than before. Within this exposition, Iraqi attack means staying in Kuwait. This makes the problem symmetrical in time, and is consistent with the notion that Saddam Hussein chose not to believe that the US policeman would show up on the Gulf beat.

U.S. implement its threat and actually lauch its offensive against Iraq after the occupation of Kuwait?

To search for answers, let us pursue the policeman analogy. Fearful though we are of crime, we only maintain a limited police force. Police cost money. Devoting a very much larger portion of public expenditures to crime deterrence would imply a weakened capacity to deal with other dangers such as fire and flood. It would also reduce our investment in the sources of growth in civilian economic activity such as investment in human and physical capital. As a result we might not be able to sustain the level of deterrence in the future. Finally, as some critics say of the "war on drugs," excessive stress on enforcement would divert funds from other programs designed to mitigate its economic roots. Carried to an extreme, excessive enforcement might lead to more crime rather than less.

Therefore we must ask: What are the future consequences of the policeman's role for the safety and welfare of the United States?

II. LIMITS TO DETERRENCE

In an earlier stage of the Cold War, Michael Intriligator and Dagobert Brito (1975, 1984) offered an intriguing model of an open ended nuclear arms race in which they argued that high levels of arms actually preserve the peace as long as the trajectory of the arms race remains within a "cone of deterrence." In this region both parties deter one another by credibly threatening to inflict unacceptable casualties on each other even after an exchange of fire has destroyed some of their missiles. An arms reduction agreement might result in insufficient casualties to deter, with the result that the arms trajectory would enter a "cone of initiation" in which one or both parties would attack.

In the context of the Gulf War, let the two parties be indexed by i, j such that i,j=I,U. Let us generalize the concept of missiles to include all military instruments aggregated as M_i.[2] Generalizing the Intriligator-Brito concept of maximum acceptable casualties, let K_i represent the maximum acceptable human and economic destruction from attack. Let f_i stand for

---

2. In light of the fact that both sides used missiles, it might be interesting to apply the model in the original sense in which Intriligator and Brito propounded it. Given the peripheral military use of Iraqi SCUD missiles, I do not pursue this approach here.

the "counter-force" effectiveness of M_i in destroying M_j, and v_i be their effectiveness in inflicting the K_i losses.

The model shows that U would deter I if:

$$M_U \geq f_I M_U + K_I/v_U \tag{1}$$
$$M_I \geq f_U M_I + K_U/v_I$$

or more compactly $M_i \geq f_j M_i + K_j/v_i$. The regions of deterrence and war initiation are portrayed in Figure 1. For sufficiently large military build-up the confrontation should have been in the cone of deterrence in which Iraq withdraws peacefully from Kuwait and the United States does not attack.

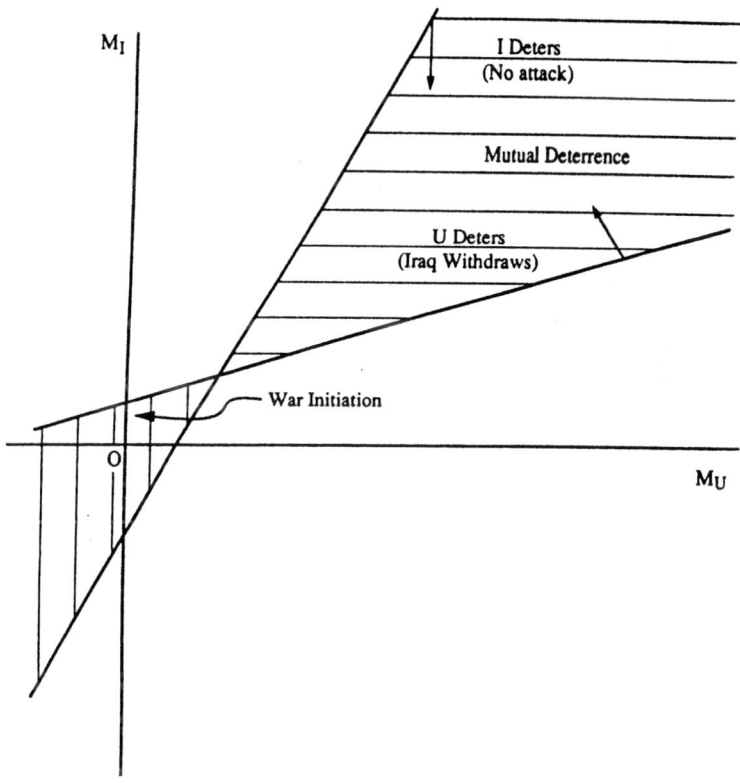

Figure 1. Deterence in the Gulf

There are two assumptions implicit in the model which did not apply to the Gulf War: (i) Each party correctly assessed the coefficients of capability and stocks of weapons of its opponent. (ii) The coefficients were such that the M_i required for mutual deterrence would be non-negative as shown in Figure 1. However, if the slopes of the deterrence boundaries as perceived by the two countries were chosen as shown in Figure 2, they would cross in the negative quadrant. Then the cone of deterrence would not exist for positive arms, and much of the positive quadrant would be occupied by the cone of war initiation.

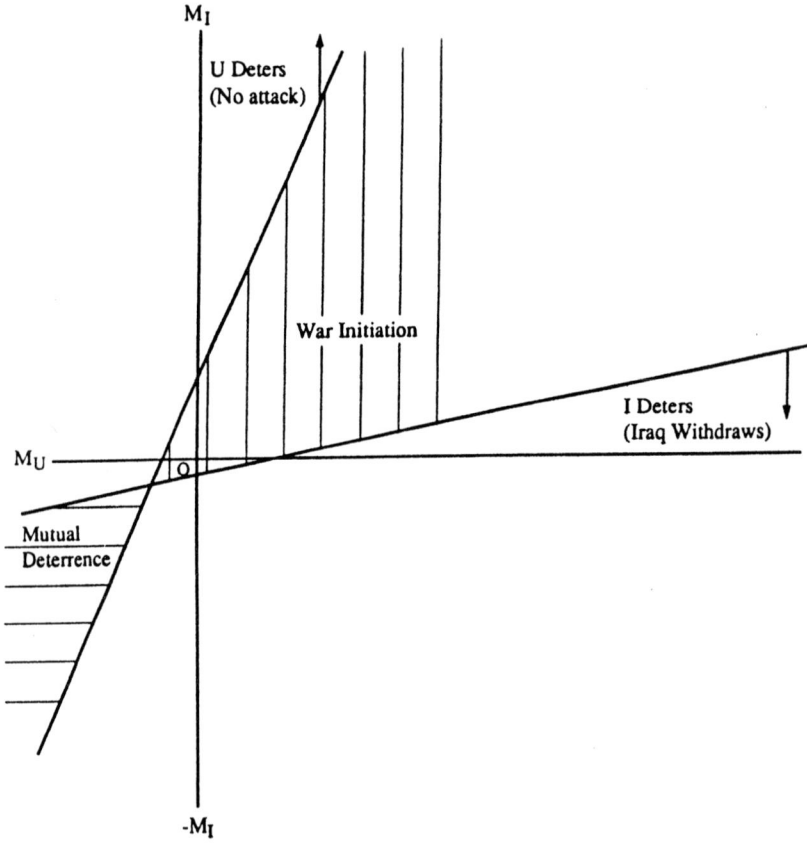

Figure 2. War Breaks Out in the Gulf

Mathematically, the necessary and sufficient conditions for the existence of a non-negative solution to equations (1) with positive terms on the right hand side is given by the Hawkins-Simons condition that the determinant inequality:

$$\begin{vmatrix} 1 & -f_I \\ -f_U & 1 \end{vmatrix} > 0 \qquad (2)$$

or that $1-f_I f_U > 0$ (Wolfson, 1987, 1992). The possibility of deterrence--although not the bringing of it about if it is possible--depends entirely on the slope of the two bounding lines. If both are large, the product of the two is not likely to be less than unity, and deterrence will be impossible. In Figure 2, the I-deters inequality shown by the solid line is very steeply sloped and the U-deters inequality will be sloped very little so the curves cross in the negative quadrant. Neither party deters the other and war ensues.

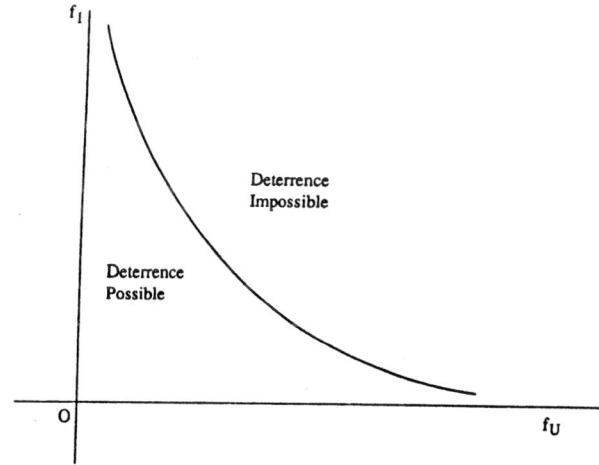

Figure 3. Counter-force Efficiecy and War Initiation

The possibility--again not the actual realization--of mutual deterrence depends on the perceived counter-force effectiveness of each party in destroying the arms of the other. Possibility does not depend on the level of acceptable casualties or the effectiveness of weapons in inflicting them.

The more effective the weapons in destroying other weapons, the less likely it is that deterrence is possible.[3] In Figure 3, the graph of equation (2) is the rectangular hyperbola $f_u f_i = 1$ which the boundary between the combinations of counter-force weapon effectiveness that are consistent with peace and those that are not.

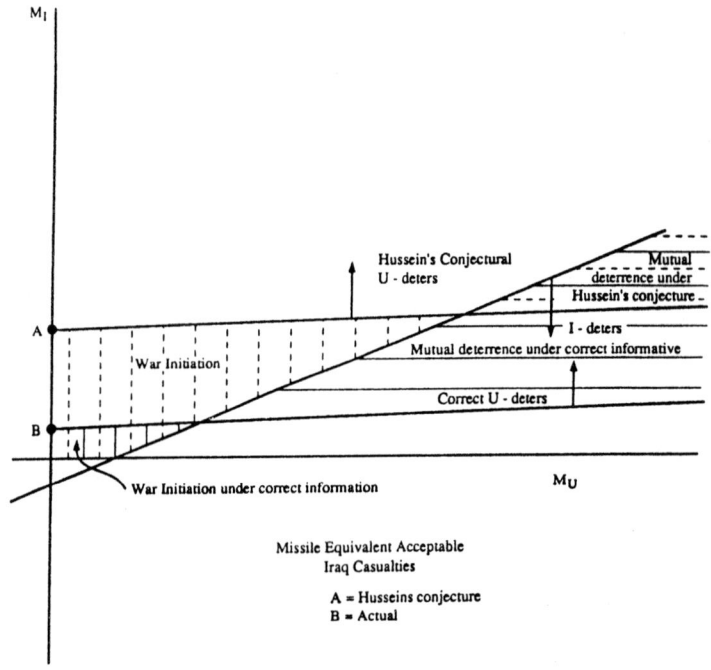

Figure 4. Conjectures and Reality in Deterrence

One hypothesis for the onset of the war was that Saddam Hussein overestimated the capacity of his forces to destroy U.N. forces, and was not deterred from remaining in Kuwait. His high expected counter-force efficiency combined with that of the U.S. made the conflict inevitable.

---

3. This condition becomes more stringent when three or more parties are involved, making it increasingly implausible that each nation could deter any possible combination against it without at the same time threatening any one of them. This is the case for the need for nuclear non-proliferation and more generally the spread of military power to many nations [Wolfson, 1987, 1992].

There is another related possibility illustrated in Figure 4 that has to do with the realization of the peace possibility. The hyperbola in Figure 3 suggests that peace is made possible by one party having a sufficiently low f to compensate for the high value of the other. Suppose Hussein had a somewhat more realistic view of his own counter-force capability shown by a slightly sloped I-deters line, but suppose he believed that its intercept was substantially the same as in Figure 2. This would be the case if the ratio K_I/v_U were such that the greater effectiveness of U.S. capacity to inflict damage were matched by the equally great willingness of the Iraqi army and populace to absorb those losses. Then a positive cone of deterrence would exist, but it would be realized only after the U.S. had expended a very large effort which Hussein calculated would be unbearable to it. The result was that the relevant portions of the quadrant would be dominated by the region of war initiation.

In fact the willingness of the Iraqi army itself to absorb that punishment turned out to be very low, despite Hussein's willingness to have them endure losses. In the course of the conflict, their own low intercept term of the I-deters line was the relevant one and Hussein notwithstanding they entered the cone of deterrence. That is to say they abandoned Kuwait and surrendered.

III. THE ECONOMICS OF A WORLD POLICEMAN

The most important element of the preceding analysis is what is missing: there is no apparent economic constraint on the actions of the decision makers on both sides. This was not the case during the Cold War, where it is reasonable to believe that the essential weapon was not nuclear missiles but GNP. By focussing on the guns-vs-butter production possibility frontier facing the clumsy Soviet economy, Farrell (1987) and I (1992) were able to show that the open ended arms race envisioned by Intriligator and Brito amounted to economic warfare. The Soviet Union attempted military parity with the U.S., and as the Reagan administration launched an arms build up, the Soviets were required to divert an unbearable amount of resources from civilian purposes. The Cold War arms race was not innocuous mutual deterrence at all, but economic warfare which the U.S. won.

Sanctions rather than war would have been the corresponding strategy in the Gulf. Using the OMB report on the incremental cost of the war, my students and I (Wolfson et al (1992), (Wolfson and Smith, 1993), Wolfson (1994)) studied the marginal costs of the war to the United States and compared them to various estimates of the Value of Statistical Life. We found the marginal costs to the United States to be extremely low--perhaps even negative--because much of the variable costs were covered by contributions from the allies, and because of the high proportion of fixed and sunk costs in the operation. The large fixed-sunk costs component came about because much of the weaponry was either obsolescent or redundant in light of the end of the Cold War.[4]

Insofar as the U.S. was concerned it is reasonable to say that the brief war was fought out of stocks rather than flows.[5] Ordinary economic reasoning reveals the reason why President Bush opted for a lightning war rather than slow sanctions. It was costless in an opportunity cost sense and almost certain in its outcome. The low cost of weaponry and the relatively high cost of human life made it possible to conserve on U.S. casualties by waging capital intensive war. A long military or economic war, might have "weakened the alliance" which may be read as a reduction in the willingness of the allies to bear the remaining marginal cost in the form of commitments to subsidize the U.S. effort.

Were the U.S. not able to fight out of stocks, it would have had to confront the guns-vs-butter flow problem and its willingness to play policeman might have been much reduced. Certainly this expectation formed the basis for Saddam Hussein's strategy.

There is a down-side to the dynamics of this sort of situation. Since weaponry, trained troops and by extension alliances with other countries are based on expenditures made in the previous period, they will at any discrete period appear as a sunk and fixed costs. This effect will be reinforced during periods of rapid technological change in the instruments of

---

4. The OMB evaluates the cost of the war in terms of the destruction or expenditure of inventories of these weapons and bills the allies accordingly. While that might be sound business practice--after all they were the US's weapons--the market cost of implements not to be replaced does not enter into marginal opportunity costs. The United States was therefore able to earn a rent on the transaction.

5. Certainly other nations and various groups within the US had different valuations depending on their contributions and anticipated gains. These marginal costs and benefits as well as the Iraqi evaluations are discussed in the paper cited.

war. Taking a myopic view, therefore, war will appear to be very cheap and attractive, especially if they are short and capital intensive.

That is to say, if the U.S. arms itself to take on the role of policeman, it is very likely that it will be frequently called out to war by the rest of the world and will frequently respond. The analogy with the police force is exact. If citizens collectively hire policemen on a fixed salary rather than a fee-for-service basis, citizens will have no hesitation in dialing 911 whenever they hear a rustle under their bedroom window. Eventually, when it is clear that this is an ongoing process, the over-use and mis-allocation of police services, results in a collective refusal to provide as much police protection in the future. Nevertheless, at an instant of time, police protection is free to users, and they can be expected to react accordingly. This aspect of the problem is independent of the additional free-rider issue of individual versus collective provision of a municipal police force.

Consequently, the proper policy for the United States is to prepare only for those wars it thinks it will be willing to fight in the future as if they were currently financed out of flows of real product.[6] It should not provide the capacity to fight the Gulf war again unless it thinks it is willing to do so again.

IV. ANALYTICS OF A WORLD POLICEMAN

Let us formalize the policy conclusion by modifying a model of social choice and defense which Shabahang (1991) and I (1992) developed. In Figure 5, let us imagine a four quadrant diagram in which the Intriligator-Brito relation between the military acquisitions of the U.S. (M_u) and those of a potential large-country adversary (M_e) appear in the fourth quadrant. Let the U.S. guns-vs-butter production possibility frontier in year t be shown in the first quadrant. C_u measured vertically stands for civilian income. The first quadrant also displays various possible indifference curves encapsulating the social choices the U.S. is willing to make between military and civilian goods. The second quadrant shows a long term savings function out of civilian income. On the assumption that savings is equal to gross investment, a points in the third quadrant relates the military expenditure of a potential enemy of the U.S. to the U.S. gross invest-

---

6. Of course future uses must be discounted back to their present values.

ment. Assume for convenience that production possibility frontiers and utility functions are homogeneous of the first degree.

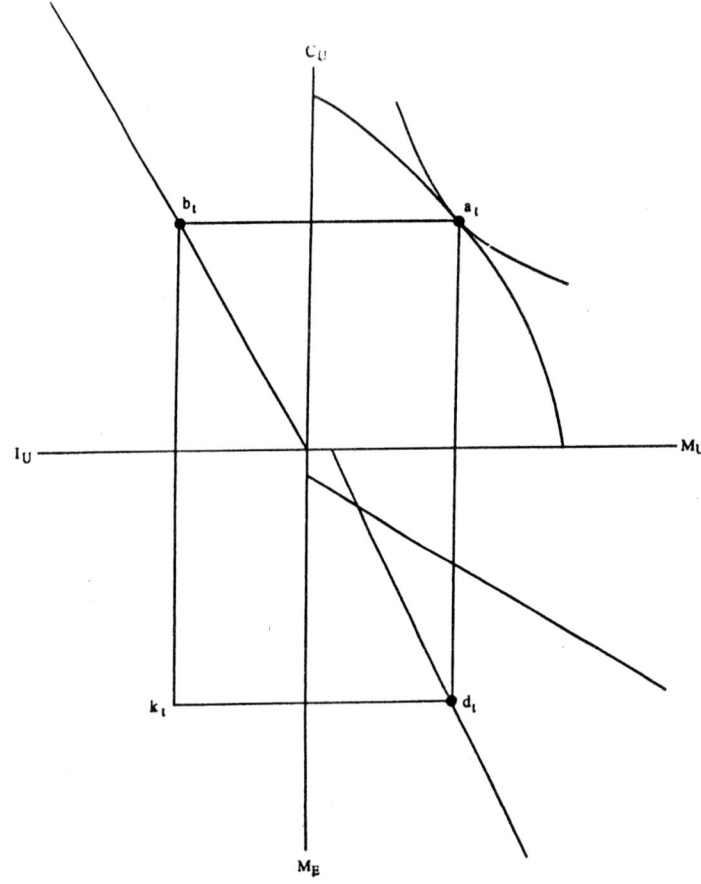

Figure 5. Internal and International Equilibrium

Initially, before the world policeman role is embraced, the U.S. might be internal equilibrium and international deterrent equilibrium at time t with respect to a potential adversary (Figure 5). With production possibility frontier F_t, and indifference curve system H, it would maximize utility along H_0 at in the first quadrant.[7] Its military acquisitions would just suffice to deter the enemy at d_t. The resulting civilian income would join the savings-investment line at b_t and gross investment would be at I_t. For simplicity we describe this level of investment as consistent with static equilibrium, the amount required to replace capital depreciation. Alternatively, it might represent that rate of capital accumulation, required to expand the production possibility frontier in step with the growth of a potential rival. In quadrant three, the U.S. is at k_t.

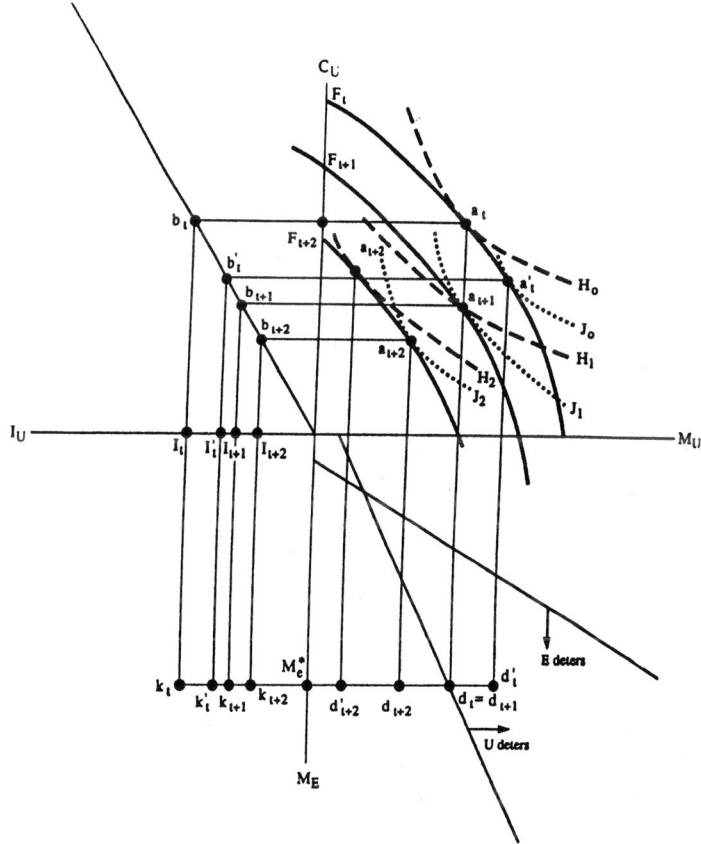

Figure 6. World Policeman

---

7. For convenience we graphically treat utility as a function of C and M. Utility is also a function of effective deterrence, and switches drastically downward when the arms trajectory slips out of the zone of deterrence. Explicit switching functions are discussed in and Shabahang.

Suppose now that the U.S. takes on the role of world policeman with respect to third countries (Figure 6). This means it has a greater taste for military acquisitions. Its utility function will have shifted in favor of M and might be represented by the J series of indifference curves. Its maximum utility now is achieved at a'_t. On the perhaps generous assumption that its weapons are completely flexible and could be used either against its adversary as well as the nations it is policing[8], it would deter E handily at d'_t. However, since its civilian income would have reduced as a result of the switch into M it reaches the savings-investment line at b'_t; its investment falls to I'_t and in the third quadrant conjuncture of investment and M is at k'_t.

Having reduced its investment[9], the policeman's production possibility frontier in period t+1 shifts inward (absolutely or relatively to the rest of the world) to F_{t+1}, so that utility is maximized at a_{t+1}. The amount of M is reduced as a consequence, so deterrence capacity is reduced. Let us take it that the reduction is such that U.S. is now just able to deter E, so that $d_{t+1}=d_t$, the equilibrium level of deterrence before the change of taste. While it was impossible to say whether the U.S. was better or worse off immediately after the change of taste, the reduction is production possibilities unambiguously results in a lower level of utility; the highest attainable indifference curves has retreated in both the J and H systems and the level of deterrence is as it was at the outset.

Moreover, the savings-investment line is met at now b_{t+1}, and investment is reduced to I_{t+1}, so the U.S. production possibilities shrink again relative to its opponent to F_{t+2}. Tangency is along J_2, and militarily the U.S. chooses d_{t+2}. Not only is it worse off with respect to the military and civilian components of utility, but it is now not able to deter its potential enemy E. It has slipped out of the zone of deterrence.

Seeing the danger of economic retreat, the U.S. might attempt to reverse the process. That is not easy. Suppose the U.S. were to change its mind at time t=2, and abandon the world policeman role thereby reverting to the H system of indifference curves. To be sure it would now be able to save and invest proportionately more since there would be an in-

---

8. This might become a clay-putty question if the US were policing less developed countries such as Iraq or Viet Nam with weapons designed to combat the USSR or Japan.
9. We may take investment to include investment the increase the stock of human as well as physical capital whether privately or publicly owned.

crease in its civilian income. But, its civilian income would start from a lower base than before it embarked on the policeman role. Consequently, given a constant average propensity to save of civilian income it would be able to save less in absolute amount than it would at high levels of income. More ominous, if it chooses a'_{t+2}, its military acquisitions would lead it to d'_{t+2}. It is less able to deter its adversary than ever and runs a greater risk of attack and defeat in war. Consequently it might not dare to reverse its choice of military versus civilian goods because it now needs the arms it once planned on aiming against those it was to policy to deter its more dangerous adversary. It is now trapped in a spiral of deteriorating economic growth with progressively lower levels of welfare and greater exposure to attack.

I leave it to the reader to ring the changes on this exercise by shifting the parameters of the model or by considering the possibility of inhomogeneity of the relevant functions. For instance by examining what would happen if the shifts in production possibility were biased in favor of military goods? What would happen as a result of changed savings rates? These questions are discussed in some detail in another context in Wolfson and Shabahang (1987, 1992).

V. Conclusions

War is a very expensive business. There are special circumstances where this truth is obscured by the ability of a nation to shift the burden of war to others, or to conduct it for short periods at low opportunity cost. This was the case in the Gulf War.

Unfortunately, the ease with which the Gulf War was carried out, prompted some thinkers to conclude that the U.S. must always be able to do it again. This analysis suggests that if we are always able to do it again we most likely will. Furthermore, continuing such a role implies that we will be always building up our military at some expense, in the periods prior to its use. The result is that we will be induced to divert more to military purposes than we would if the expenditures and use were coincident in time. It then may be the case that just as in the cases of the pax Romana, the pax Britannica and the erstwhile pax Sovietica, we will overspend. In the long term military overspending produce results which were no part of our original intention. It will harm our level of economic welfare and reduce our military capacity to defend ourselves against aggression.

REFERENCES

Intriligator, M., "Strategic Considerations in the Richardson Model of the Arms Race," *Journal of Political Economy*, 1975, 339-53.

M. Intriligator and Brito, D., "Can Arms Races Lead to the Outbreak of War?," *Journal of Conflict Resolution*, 1984, 28(1), 63-84.

Wolfson, M., "Notes on Economic Warfare," *Conflict Management and Peace Science*, 1985, 8(2), 1-20 (Reprinted in Wolfson 1992).

Wolfson, M., "A Theorem on the Existence of Zones of Initiation and Deterrence in Intriligator-Brito Arms Race Models," *Public Choice*, 1987, 54, 291-297 (Reprinted in Wolfson, 1992).

Wolfson, M., *Essays on the Cold War*, (London: Macmillan, 1992).

Wolfson, M., "Wrap-up On the Cost of the Gulf War," *Defense and Peace Economics*, 1994, 5(4), 339-40.

Wolfson, M. and Farrell, J.P., "A Framework to Study Economic Warfare Between the U.S. and USSR," in *Peace Defense and Economic Analysis*, ed., F. Blackaby and C. Schmidt, (London: Macmillan, 1987) (Reprinted in Wolfson 1992).

Wolfson, M. and Guttierrez, S., Smith, R. and Traynor J., "Competing Optima in the Gulf War," in *The Economics of Arms Reduction and the Peace Process*, eds., Isard, W. and Anderton, C. (Amsterdam: North Holland, 1992).

Wolfson, M. and Shabahang, H., "Economic Causation in the Breakdown of Military Equilibrium," *Journal of Conflict Resolution*, 1991, 35(1), 22-43 (Reprinted in Wolfson 1992).

Wolfson, M. and Smith, R., "How Not to Pay for the War," *Defense Economics*, 1993, 4, 299-314.

THE POLITICAL ECONOMY OF OIL: UNITED STATES AND MIDDLE EAST POST-WORLD WAR II RELATIONS

Behrooz Fattahi
CalResources LLC
Shell Plaza Tower
Bakersfield, CA 93309

Omid Fattahi
School of International
and Public Affairs
Columbia University
New York, NY 10027

Abstract—Since its discovery, the role of oil in influencing global relationships has been undeniably significant. The intricacies of the political economy of oil and its impact on the internal affairs of nations has continued to lead to protracted repercussions on their external interrelationships. The 1973 oil embargo, the downfall of the monarchy in Iran, the Iran-Iraq war, the Iraqi invasion of Kuwait, and the disintegration of the former Soviet Union are vivid examples of this claim in our modern history. This chapter examines the anatomy of the political economy of oil and in particular the impact on the interrelationship between the United States and the Middle Eastern nations from the 1940s through the end of the century.

I. INTRODUCTION

In their essay, "Industrial Competitiveness and National Security", Michael Borrus and John Zysman (Borrus and Zysman, 1992) warned:

"... In the world we are describing [post-Cold War], the continued erosion of America's international economic position is a national security issue."

In a sweeping global change, economic considerations have begun to replace military ones at the top of national political agenda. The United States as the world's most powerful military and economic force has not remained immune to these changes and has had to take steps to deal with this post-cold war phenomenon. America's main concern is no longer its ability to withstand a Soviet first-strike and mount a viable response; but to protect and promote its economy in an increasingly multi-polar and interdependent world.

In the post-World War II era, a key element in the formulation and implementation of U.S. foreign policy, both military and economic, has been the oil factor. Since its discovery, oil has been a highly volatile blend of politics and economics. Time and again, the wheels of this nation's policy-making have in the past influenced the global political economy of oil, while in return, the forces in control of this commodity have played a major role in carving America's economic and military policies. Ramifications of oil on policy making, and policy making on oil are quite complex. The underlying factor has been the post-World War II gradual transformation of the United States from a major oil producer to a major importing nation, with increasing reliance on the producing nations of the Middle East (Figures 1 and 2).

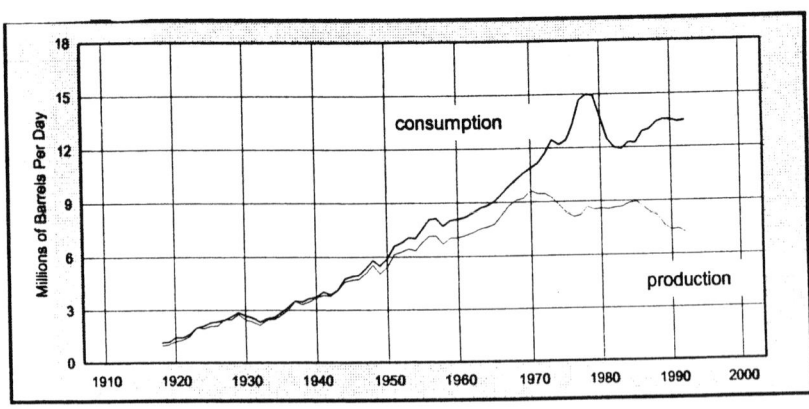

Figure 1. United States Domestic Crude Production and Consumption

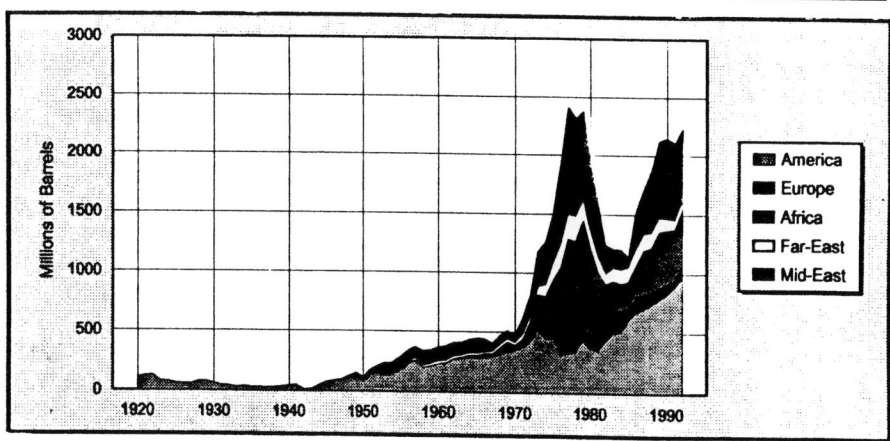

Figure 2. United States Crude Oil Imports from Different World Regions

In the following segments we will explore the role of oil and the producing countries in the dynamics of American political environment. We will study various historical episodes and examine the political and economic factors that have forced oil to remain an integral part of United States' national policy. And finally, we will examine America's energy interests and options for the future.

II. OIL AND GLOBAL GEOPOLITICS

Although the discovery of oil is attributed to the first drilling in 1859 in the town of Titusville, Pennsylvania, the first use of hydrocarbon may be traced back to the days of the Persian Empire in the fifth century B.C. The Empire, stretching from India to Greece and North Africa, was the sight of numerous oil and gas seepage in large areas in the southern stretches of what is today known as Iran. The oozing was used by the locals for waterproofing boats and binding of bricks. Where gas leaked to the surface, it became the sight of temples preserving the constant burning of fire, an element of divine proportion to the ancient Persians. Yet, it was not until mid nineteenth century and the re-discovery of oil in Pennsylvania, that the economic significance of this energy resource became obvious to the modern man. Since then, petroleum has fueled the modern industrial economies and consequently has played a major role in the dynamics of international diplomacy. Early on, as more domestic hydrocarbon accumulations were discovered and developed, the attention of oil companies were directed toward those worldwide discoveries that offered much greater incentives due to their immense size and cheap labor. Thus, the Middle East became the arena for the Western industrial nations' competition to seek and control the flow of oil.

Table 1. Distribution of World Remaining Oil Reserves and Ultimate Recovery (Millions of Barrels)

	Reserves as of 1/94	Percent of World Reserves	1993 Oil Production	Percent of World Production	Life Index, R/P
North America	76,620	7	4,136	19	18.6
South America	77,131	7	1,748	8	43.2
Eastern Europe	183,314	17	3,025	14	60.7
Western Europe	37,940	3	1,720	8	21.0
Africa	73,866	7	2,457	11	30.2
Middle East	595,195	54	6,777	30	87.9
Far East	53,255	5	2,466	11	21.5
World	1,097,320	100	22,329	100	49.0
World without Middle East	502,125	46	15,552	70	32.3
U.S.	22,957	2	2,499	11	9.3

Source: Twentieth Century Petroleum Statistics, 1994, (Dallas, Degolyer and MacNaughton, 1994)

As of January 1994 the world's remaining proved oil reserves amounted to more than one trillion barrels. The cumulative world production up to that date was some 719 billion barrels, resulting in an estimated ultimate recovery of 1.8 trillion barrels of oil worldwide. Table 1 shows the distribution of the remaining reserves and ultimate recovery as well as 1993 production volumes for different regions of the world. Graphical representations of the contents of Table 1 are shown in Figures 3 and 4. Of special interest is the significance of the Middle East's remaining reserves and the production life index (R/P) relative to other world regions. A measure for comparing the producing life of hydrocarbon fields is the production life index or the ratio of remaining reserves to current production. The United States' share of the world remaining reserves at only two percent is dwarfed by Middle East's 54 percent. With a cumulative production of 166 billion barrels, the United States' ultimate recovery is at about 189 billion barrels or 11 percent of the world ultimate. The producing life index for the Middle East is approximately 10 times

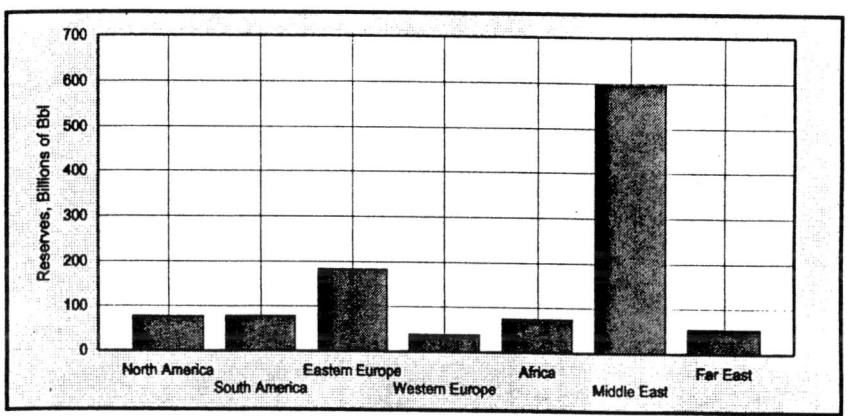

Figure 3. Worldwide Distribution of Remaining Oil Reserves on January 1, 1994

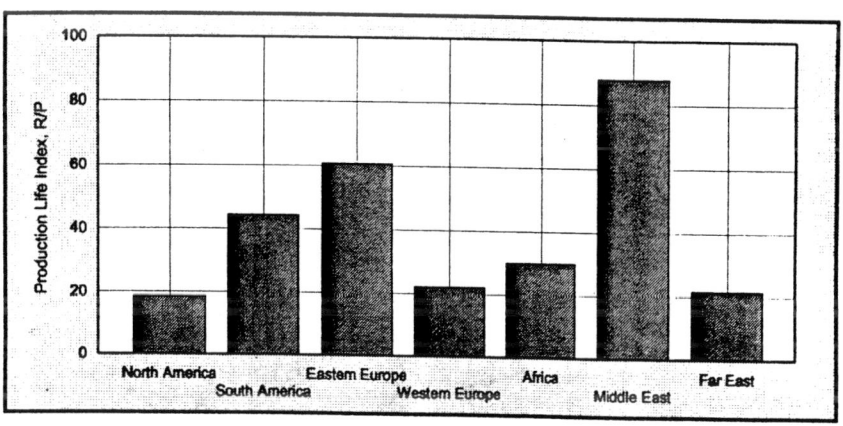

Figure 4. Worldwide Distribution of Production Life Index, R/P on January 1, 1994

greater than that of the United States. Examining the data signifies the importance of the Middle East to the Western industrial nations, and in particular, to the United States.

Prior to World War II, the domestic production of the United States closely followed its demand for this source of energy. However, immediately after the war, it became gradually evident that the production trends would not satisfy the consumption needs of a country emerging from a world conflict and ready to expand. Figure 1 shows the trends of domestic crude production and demand in the United States from early twentieth century to the present. During the period from 1920 to 1993, the U.S. crude oil consumption escalated from 1.5 to more than 13.5 million barrels a day while during the same period, domestic production only rose from 1.5 to only 6.8 million barrels a day. Of particular interest, is the appearance of a shortfall of domestic crude supply in mid to late 1940s.

At the end of the Second World War, this country's infrastructure was in place and entirely untouched by the sort of devastation that Europe and Japan had experienced through the conflict. Being remote from the battle grounds had placed the United States in an advantageous position to escape destruction, permitting it to rapidly grow its industrial economy and seek prosperity through achieving technological leadership. It was then, that the lessons of World War II and the increasing national demand for energy, led the policy makers of this nation to move toward ensuring adequate and uninterrupted supply of petroleum energy.

As the world's leading petroleum consumer, the United States' interest in this valuable commodity has always been focused toward those regions of the world where significant reserves are available. This country found itself relying largely on petroleum and its sources abroad. Yet, for almost half a century, America's involvement was purely economical with no significant political component. American oil companies, having realized the economic significance of the Middle Eastern oil, became involved in the region's affair at the turn of the century (Sampson, 1984). However, this country's attempt to formulate a policy toward the region lagged many years behind Western Europe, mainly Britain, itself heavily dependent on oil. In fact, the rise of the United States as a major actor in Middle East politics did not manifest itself until 1947 when President Harry S. Truman asked the Congress for $400 million in aid for Greece and Turkey sighting support for "..... free peoples who resist outside pressures." (Rustow, 1982). It was in the same year that the United Nations resolution on the partition of Palestine paved the way for British withdrawal and the beginning of America's political involvement in the Middle Eastern affairs.

The inception of the political interest of the United States in the Middle East was merely the result of realization of the country's commitment to contain the Soviet expansionism in light of Britain's imminent departure from the area. In subsequent years, the principle of containment asserted by the Truman Doctrine and the ever increasing reliance of the United States on imported oil enhanced America's interest and involvement in the Middle East.

Armed with little experience in Middle Eastern affairs, political and economic interest in the region led Washington to define a vision of prosperity for the area. Truman's "Point Four" was an attempt to mimic successes of the European "Marshall Plan" in creating democracies in the region and to deprive the Soviets from their expansionist intents. The post-World War II process of decolonization in the Middle East, like in many other regions in Asia and Africa, had resulted in creation of many new nations with arbitrary boundaries that were not respected by the succeeding governments. The ever lasting border conflicts between Saudi Arabia, Kuwait, Iraq, Syria, Jordan, Israel and Egypt are vivid examples of the post-colonial realities of the Middle East. In the ensuing years, the fear of Soviet expansionism, and the constant turmoil in the region led to the derailing of America's vision of institutionalized democracies in the Middle East. Washington's recognition of the significance of the region's oil in driving Western industrial economies enticed policy makers to abandon the originally well intended democratization programs in favor of dealing with the blooming post-colonial authoritarian regimes. Thus, instead of aiding the newly established nations to develop their energy resources, mainly oil, toward their economic prosperity, the policy of Soviet containment led to support of corrupt regimes with great appetite for spending their wealth on military hardware. Even today after the disintegration of the Soviet empire, the repercussions from the almost half century old shift in policy haunts the American policy makers.

America's political debut in the Middle East faced its first crisis in 1953 in Iran. Iran's nationalization of its oil, owned exclusively by British since its first production, was not well received in London. The nationalization campaign was orchestrated by Dr. Mohammad Mossadegh, a popular Premier and the leader of the National Front. In response, the British navy blockaded the export of Iranian oil in an attempt to bankrupt the country. Meanwhile, Mossadegh's confrontation with Shah of Iran led to the Shah's fleeing the country, only to return three days later with the help of "Operation Ajax," a coup staged and financed by the CIA and directed by the well known CIA operative Kermit Roosevelt (Yergin, 1992). In the following year, oil production was resumed with the help of a multinational consortium, 40 percent of which was owned by American companies. The turmoil in Iran offered the United States an opportunity to test its new policy in the Middle East, significantly increase its share of the region's oil concessions, and strengthen its political and economic foothold in the area.

Prior to the 1953 events in Iran, the United States involvement in the region was merely limited to economic interest in the giant hydrocarbon holdings of Saudi Arabia. In defiance of the British, Saudis had granted a concession to the Arabian American Oil Company, ARAMCO, in 1933. Although the first oil was found in 1935, it was not until 1948 when the discovery of the super-giant Ghawar field made Saudi Arabia and the entire Middle East most prominent in the policy making circles of the United States government. It then became evident that the region would play an extremely important role in supplying energy of the future industrial world and consequently the control of the flow of oil through Persian Gulf could not be compromised.

The events in Iran, discovery of super-giant oil fields in the Middle East, and the United States government's realization of the significance of uninterrupted flow of oil in the post-World War II era, strengthened the principles of Truman Doctrine which had initially been presented to contain Soviet expansionism in the Middle East. Whether the main thrust of the United States policy was truly directed to keep communism from spreading, or to ensure flow of oil to the free world, is in itself debatable. Yet the economic significance of oil in transformation of the U.S. policy in the Middle East in the late 1940s and early 1950s can not be denied.

In the ensuing years, with the post-war recovery in Japan and Europe, and America's ever increasing demand for energy, the Middle East remained the center of political attention for American administrations. The 1954 formation of the Iranian oil consortium served to forever displace

British as the sole operators of the Iranian oil and to further strengthen the political and economic foothold of the United States in the Middle East. For the British, already weakened by many years of involvement in the region, this was the beginning of the downfall of the Empire. The United States was now becoming the major power broker in the area replacing European colonialism with governments that would rely almost entirely on their oil income. The lessons learned from the Iranian crisis, led the United States to encourage economic development of these countries. Prosperity would discourage communism and provide flourishing market for the Western goods while the flow of oil to the industrial West could be ensured. This was the political and economic world order that America was seeking to establish. Having sensed Iran's dissatisfaction with the British operation of its oil, Aramco encouraged by Washington, replaced Saudis' royalty interest of 12.5 percent with a 50 percent share of profits in 1950. Similar royalty conversion terms were eventually established in Kuwait, Iraq and Iran in the early to mid 1950s. Since the increased share of interest was cleverly termed as the host country corporate tax, the lost profits to American oil companies were compensated by corporate income tax credits extended to them in the United States (Rustow, 1982).

The new accords were the result of an important step by Washington in enhancing its involvement in the political economy of oil in the Middle East and consequently around the world. The new agreements seemed to benefit all participants. The royalty owner nations would gain due to increased revenues and their pro-American regimes would achieve popularity within their borders for demonstrating nationalism. Their peoples would prosper and consequently would become customers of goods imported from the industrial West. And the oil companies would find the host countries more receptive to their proposals for acquiring new concessions which were needed for long term investments and revenue growth. Yet, the most fascinating aspect of these accords was in how Washington accomplished the goals of Truman Doctrine, playing an intricate political game both at home and abroad. While America's presence in the Middle East was a pre-requisite to ensuring Soviet containment and the free flow of oil, support of the newly formed nation of Israel was an obstacle in providing foreign aid to most of the countries in the area. Strong congressional lobby of the pro-Israeli forces in the United States would make any foreign aid proposal to most of the Middle Eastern countries quite controversial. Yet, tax credits to the oil companies required no legislation. Thus, by replacing the foreign aid program with the "fifty-fifty" oil contract, the entire legislative system was bypassed, avoiding prolonged discussions of politically sensitive issues. Once again, oil had become the vehicle to achieve Washington's political goals in the Middle East.

In the ensuing years, cheaper imported oil in particular from the Middle East displaced the more expensively produced domestic production. Figure 2 shows the rapid growth of America's import from the Middle East with volumes second only to imports from the countries on the American continent. The desire to generate revenues, the prediction of increasing demand, and the inability of the United States domestic production to adequately satisfy consumption, caused other countries especially in Africa to embark on developing their oil resources. As a result, in the late 1950s, the prospect of increasing supply applied a downward pressure on the world oil prices as shown in Figure 5. However, the low pace of exploration and development of new hydrocarbon resources coupled with an global demand prevented a price collapse. In real terms however, the flat oil prices of the 1960s vastly reduced the income of the oil producing nations, who almost entirely relied on oil revenues for their economic growth.

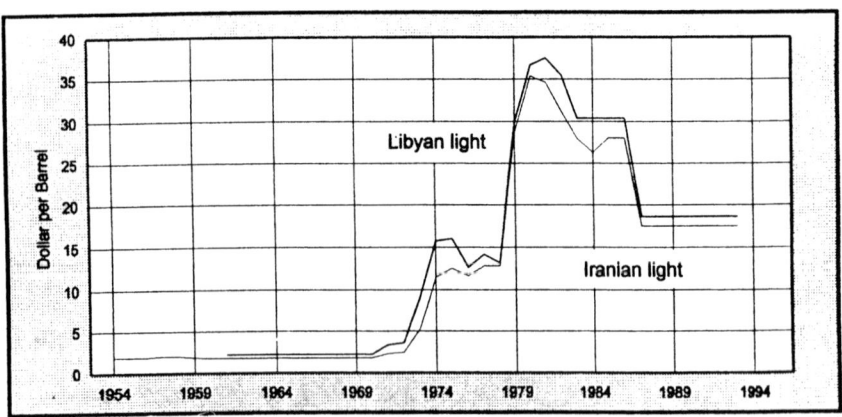

Figure 5. Posted Oil Price Trends for Persian Gulf and North America

As early as 1949, the petroleum producing countries had realized the necessity of an alliance to protect their interests against the wishes of the oil companies. But because of the rapidly changing political environment in the Middle East and the inexperience of the post-world war governments of the region, all attempts to form an alliance failed until 1960 when the steady decline in prices necessitated adoption of a common political and economic front among the petroleum producing countries. The birth of OPEC, the Organization of the Petroleum Exporting Countries, occurred on September 14, 1960. During a meeting in Baghdad, the major exporting countries of Venezuela, Iran, Saudi Arabia, Kuwait and Iraq formally signed an agreement to coordinate and unify their petroleum economic policy. With the oil cartel in place, the days of setting oil prices by the operating companies were over. OPEC's immediate achievement was forcing the oil companies to pay the income share of the producing countries on the basis of a fixed and predetermined "posted price" as long as actual world oil prices were falling. A few years later, the emboldened OPEC also re-established the royalty payment in addition to the fifty percent share of profits, increasing the producing countries' share to more than sixty percent.

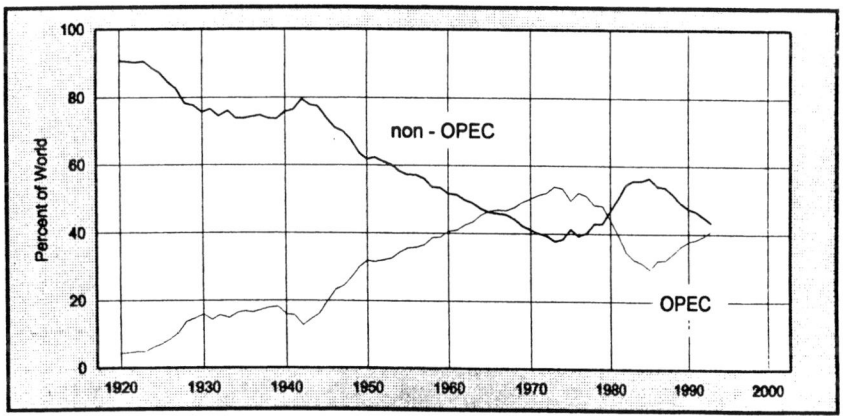

Figure 6. OPEC's Share of World Crude Oil Production

During the 1960s, the low world oil prices and America's preoccupation with the war in Vietnam, reduced Washington's attention to the Middle East. But during these same years, member countries of OPEC were preparing for the 1970s and control of the flow of oil leading to what would be recorded in the history of oil trade as the "first price shock." In the meantime, world oil demand grew rapidly which led to a net increase in income for both oil companies and producing governments. It was during this same decade that major OPEC producers (Figure 6) surpassed the fifty percent mark of total world oil production, thus becoming a formidable factor in the arena of the global political economy of oil.

The events of 1960s represented a determination by the oil producing countries to influence their destiny and gain economic control of their oil. It is an irony that during this very eventful decade for the Middle East, Washington's political reaction to these events was at its lowest. This was a decade that America's resolve was to contain Soviet expansionism in Southeast Asia and next door in Cuba. The decade that started with OPEC revolution saw Arab-Israeli conflict to flare up once more in June of 1967, further straining United States' relations with most of the Arab nations. At home, Washington's protectionist policy of oil import quota, that had resulted in higher but stable domestic oil prices, prevented American consumer to benefit from the lower world prices. The domestic reserves were dwindling and the ever-increasing consumption made America even more dependent on the Middle East oil. It was to no one's surprise that the "subsidy to the domestic oil industry" came to an end in 1973 with the phase out of the quota program. The result was a sharp increase in the import of cheaper oil from abroad, particularly from the Middle East and Africa as shown in Figure 2.

Prior to 1973, the price of a barrel of oil was generally determined on the basis of supply and demand. But with OPEC now in control, in a December 1973 meeting of OPEC oil ministers in Tehran, the Shah of Iran proposed a new pricing system based on the cost of alternative energy source, mainly gas and liquids extracted from coal and shale. This proposal culminated in the first decisive price increase by OPEC that sent shock waves throughout the economies of the industrial nations. The trend, however, was not long lasting. A decade later and after a second major price increase by OPEC, it would become evident that the laws of demand and supply were finally taking over the destiny of this important commodity.

The phase-out of import quota and OPEC's simultaneous new price increase coincided with another flare up of the Arab-Israeli conflict, the war of October 1973. With America's commitment to defend Israel, the already strained relations between the United States and Arabs lead to a six-month embargo of oil exports to the United States by all Arab oil producing nations of OPEC. Caught in the middle, the Shah of Iran decided to continue its oil shipments to the United States. Shah's refusal to go along with his Arab neighbors seems to have been fatal to OPEC's solidarity and to himself, as proved by later events in Iran (Woodward, 1987).

The 1973 oil embargo and the use of oil as a "weapon" signalled the dawn of a new era in the international relations: replacement of military considerations with economic options on a grand scale. Nearly a decade later, the United States would use the oil weapon herself to force the eventual disintegration of the Soviet Union and the eventual fall of communism. It was during this decade, that a combination of mounting demand for oil, relative solidarity of OPEC, and eventually the total halt of oil production in Iran in late 1978 resulted in an spiraling increase in the price of oil (Figures 2 and 5). In the 10 year period between 1970 and 1980, oil prices rose by almost twenty folds. Much of the increase however, occurred in 1979 when the price of a barrel of oil rose from approximately 13 dollars in January to almost 35 dollars in June and nearly 40 dollars in November, sending a second price shock wave throughout the industrial world. Although the use of oil as an economic weapon in 1973 was the first large scale attempt by major oil producing nations to advance their political intents, the British backed economic blockade of Iranian oil some twenty years earlier constituted its first use as a weapon in achieving political goals.

The events of the late 1970s in Iran, and the Iraqi invasion of that country signalled the beginning of the decline of OPEC. Yet, ironically the most damaging blow to OPEC's prominence was the spiralling escalation of oil prices which in turn made the development of global hydrocarbon resources economically feasible. With the accelerated development of oil fields in the North Sea, Alaska, and African Offshore, the consequent over-supply of oil once again brought back the reality of the laws of supply and demand into the trade of this commodity. OPEC's loss of solidarity and the controlling share of the market (Figure 6) resulted in its decline from a powerful political and economic entity that once challenged the major economies of the world to a ceremonial alliance torn apart by differences in political convictions and lack of loyalty of its members to its own charter. The decline in oil prices, thus became inevitable. However, the Iran-Iraq war and the resulting decline in their production levels prevented a price crash.

For the United States and its relations with the Middle East, the 1970s was an uneasy and challenging decade. The oil embargo, the rise of OPEC, the spiralling oil prices and the mounting domestic demand for oil, and finally the fall of a close ally in Iran seriously crippled America's political influence in that part of the world. The 1980s was not going to be any different either. With Iran and Iraq tangled in a seemingly never ending war that drained their wealth and resources, Washington's effort was heavily focused on limiting hostilities from engulfing the entire Middle East. The political instability in the region due to the Iranian revolution, the Soviet's invasion of Afghanistan, the lasting Arab-Israeli conflict and America's losses in Lebanon all contributed to Washington's reassessment of its policies in the region. Yet one principle element remained unchanged: to protect the free flow of oil through Persian Gulf. Later, the United States reaffirmed this policy by allowing Kuwaiti tankers to travel through the Gulf under American flag when the regime in Iran threatened to close the Strait of Hormuz, thus cutting the flow of oil.

As Washington watched the events in the Middle East, the policy makers in the White House were busy mapping an attack against the Soviet Union and the weapon of choice was oil. This aggressive policy was a major strategy change from the Truman Doctrine of Soviet containment. In his May 1981 speech at the University of Notre Dame, President Reagan said "...The West will not contain communism, it will transcend communism. We will not bother to denounce it, we'll dismiss it as a sad, bizarre chapter in human history whose last pages are even now being written." At the heart of this new strategy was " .... a campaign to dramatically reduce Soviet's hard currency earnings by driving down the price of oil with Saudi cooperation and limiting natural gas exports to the West." (Schweizer, 1994). As a result, the Saudi oil production (Figure 7) nearly doubled from 3.4 million barrels a day in 1985 to 6.4 million barrels a day in 1990. Other Middle Eastern countries followed suit to fight the declining revenues. Figure 8 reveals that during the latter half of the 1980s, while the rest of the world increased their crude production only negligibly, the Middle Eastern countries were responsible for about 6 million barrels per day in production increase, nearly half of which was produced by the Saudis. Obviously, the over-supply of crude and infighting among OPEC members resulted in another plunge in the world oil prices (Figure 5). Thus, the sequence of events triggered by Saudis' production increase in 1986, seems to have played an important role in collapse of the Soviet economy and the fall of communism. Once again the economic power of oil had replaced military options in achieving political goals.

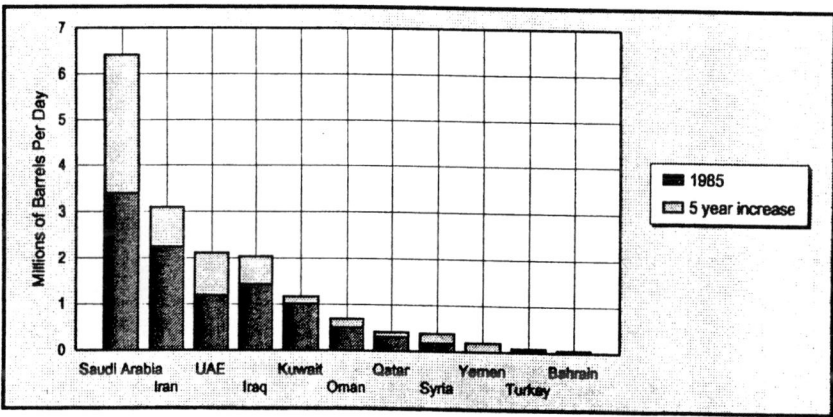

Figure 7. Middle East Crude Oil Production, 1985-1990

The Iraqi invasion of Kuwait in 1990 and Saddam Hussain's ambitions to expand territory and oil reserves was a significant challenge to Washington's long standing political and economic interest in the Persian Gulf region. Rather than acting alone, the United States recruited political and military support from the entire world in condemning the invasion and forcing Iraqis to retreat. America's swift and decisive reaction in the 1990 Gulf crisis once again reaffirmed its resolve to protect the free flow of oil from the Gulf at any cost. In the first half of this decade, Washington's relations with the Middle Eastern countries has been governed by the slowly evolving peace process between Arabs and the Israelis, and America's significant dependence on imported oil. The politically divided OPEC has not been able to shore up the prices and the over-supply of oil and the prospects of Iraq's return to full production has limited its ability to be effective in the arena of political economy of oil.

III. OIL AND U.S. NATIONAL POLICY

Since the early years of nationhood, the United States has sought to establish a national policy based on a national interest. This interest has rested upon a collective set of values and views, put together over a period of time. These principles have come to form the basis of U.S. policy, especially in the foreign arena. An example of this is the concept of "moral pragmatism", which states that the right solution is the American solution. President Woodrow Wilson's "Fourteen Points" was an example of American policy based on national views. Since the onset, American national interest has been influenced by various factors such as politics and economics. The "Monroe Doctrine", Teddy Roosevelt's "Big Stick" diplomacy in the Americas, and U.S. involvement in World War I are examples of this notion. Although isolationism had been a popular stance before and after World War I, the U.S. could not deny the realities surrounding it. The outbreak of World War II and the Allied victory in 1945 signalled the end of American "outcastness" from the rest of the world. A Europe in need of rebuilding and the specter of Soviet expansionism propelled the United States into the international spotlight. This new role made it vital that the U.S. safeguard and strengthen its position in the realm of new challenges. This meant that every effort was to be made in order to economically, politically, and militarily protect the American national interest. As oil became a strategic commodity, the United States began to consider its flow a matter of national security. This notion, along with the security of the resource against ever threatening Soviet expansionism, became a cornerstone of American Cold War policy. Nowhere in the world was this policy more played out than in the Middle East and in the Persian Gulf region. But with the precarious political atmosphere in the region, the nerves of the American economy, has been tested and challenged several times in past decades (Jordan *et al*, 1990).

At the conclusion of World War II, the "Truman Doctrine" defined America's concern for Soviet expansionism in the Middle East and proposed a strategy in the wake of departure of British colonialism from the region. The grand design for the Middle East included a mimic of the

European Marshal plan implemented by the United States with the region's oil wealth maintaining growth and development. The later events however, proved quite challenging for the inexperienced policy makers in Washington. Eventually the Middle East development plan was dropped in favor of containing the Soviets by supporting post-colonial dictatorships that would harshly confront leftist ideology, and in many cases any opposition.

For the next twenty five years, the containment of Soviet expansionism and maintaining the flow of oil remained as the backbone of America's post-World War II strategy in the Middle East. Yet, the Soviet influence gradually grew in the area in countries such as Egypt and Iraq, threatening the very fundamental element of the United States political and economic interest. With the formation of OPEC and mounting demand for oil in the United States, maintaining the flow of oil became at times a factor beyond control of Washington's policy makers. The use of oil as a weapon by the British against Iran in 1953, and by Arab members of OPEC against the United States in 1973 underscored the significance of the economic power of oil in achieving political ends. It was as a result of this realization and the repercussions on America's national security that on November 7, 1973, in a major Presidential address, Richard Nixon declared (Yergin, 1992):

> "Let us set as our national goal, in the spirit of Apollo, with the determination of the Manhattan Project, that by the end of this decade we will have developed the potential to meet our own energy needs without depending on any foreign energy source".

But in the ensuing years, America's demand for oil rose at a faster pace compared to what domestic production could supply leaving the United States more than ever in need of imported oil. Another significant change was Nixon administration's redefinition of America's role in Asia and particularly in the Middle East (Jordan *et al*, 1990). In 1969, in a policy statement that became known as the "Nixon Doctrine," the President stated:

> "The United States will provide a shield if a nuclear power threatens the freedom of a nation allied with us or of a nation whose survival we consider vital to our security. In cases involving other types of aggression we shall furnish military and economic assistance when requested in accor-

dance with our treaty agreements. But we shall look to the nation directly threatened to assume the primary responsibility of providing the manpower for its defense."

Throughout the next decade, America's Middle Eastern policy continued to be driven by the ideas of the Nixon Doctrine. Under this doctrine, the United States would no longer participate in local conflicts, but would provide the countries involved with military assistance. It was during these same years that while the Soviets were arming Iraqis with the latest military equipment, the Nixon administration as a principle honored all items on Iran's military shopping list without questioning the need. Soviet's invasion of Afghanistan in the late 1970s showed that although the policy had limited success in Oman, it was not deterrent to Soviet aspiration of reaching the warm waters of Persian Gulf. Consequently, in a short number of years, America's Middle Eastern strategy had to be reassessed and redefined.

In a 1980 policy statement, reacting to Soviet's occupation of Afghanistan, President Carter announced (Rustow, 1982 and Han, 1994):

" ... any attempt by any outside force to gain control of the Persian Gulf region will be regarded as an assault on the vital interests of the United States of America, and such an assault will be repelled by any means necessary, including military force."

The so-called "Carter Doctrine," once again, asserted the willingness of this nation to protect the supply of oil from the Middle East at any expense, including military confrontation with the then Soviet Union. This major revision of America's political and economic strategy required a growing U.S. commitment in the Middle East. The first test of the new policy came with the outbreak of the Iran-Iraq war in September of 1980. The United States chose to remain officially neutral as long as the conflict remained limited in extent, but unofficially provided intelligence to Iraq while developing a brief, covert arms supply relationship with Iran, the so-called "Iran-Contra Affair."

Carter Doctrine was vague and was pronounced after the Soviets had made their move in Afghanistan. The friendly countries in the region were uneasy and uncertain as to whether they qualified as "vital interests" to the United States. In 1981, President Reagan expanding on the Carter Doctrine stated: "... there is no way that we could stand by and see Saudi Arabia taken over by anyone that would shut off that oil." The policy statement known as "Reagan Corollary" once again reaffirmed America's conviction to protect the free flow of oil from the Persian Gulf at all costs. As a sign of support for the increasingly active role in the Middle East, the United States formed a Rapid Deployment Force with the responsibility for the Middle East, Southwest Asia, and Eastern Africa.

It was during the Reagan years, that policy planners in the White House with the help of Saudis sought to bankrupt the Soviet economy by reducing the worldwide price of oil. The successfully implemented plan, underscored the significant impact of the political economy of oil and its utility as an economic weapon to bring about the unthinkable fall of the communism. The disintegration of the Soviet Union eliminated one principle element of cold war rivalry from America's long term strategy in the region: the need for Soviet containment. But new challenges demanded America's readiness to respond to threats to its vital interests in the area. In 1990, the Iraqis having recovered from an eight year long border war with Iran, invaded Kuwait in a surprise attack. The occupation of Kuwait and sudden shift in oil reserves picture, prompted the United States to respond swiftly, by massive deployment of U.S. and allied forces to the Saudi Arabia and the Persian Gulf region. America's reaction to Saddam Hussain's ambitious plans of permanent annexation of Kuwait was swift and decisive. Eventually, in early 1991, Iraqis were handed a heavy defeat and forced to pull out of Kuwait. The episode reaffirmed Carter's Doctrine and America's resolve to defend its economic interests in the Middle East at any cost. In a speech to Congress in 1991, President Bush restated America's commitment: "Our vital national interests depend on a stable and secure Gulf."

IV. PROSPECTS FOR THE FUTURE

In attempting to forecast the future, one must remember that in a global system many factors impact relations among nations, and that these factors interact in such complex manners that isolating one may be an impossible task. The foregoing historical review of the anatomy of the political economy of oil identified the driving elements that became the foundation of the post-World War II interrelationship between the United States and the Middle East. These elements were: to contain Soviet expansionism, to ensure security of the state of Israel, and to provide uninterrupted flow of oil from Persian Gulf to the world industrial economies. Today, with the disintegration of the Soviet Union, the containment issue has disappeared, and the concern over the security of Israel is gradually being resolved with the expanding peace between Israel and her Arab neighbors. It is then very likely that the political economy of oil will become the dominant feature of Washington's future foreign policy in the Middle East. Immersed in this foreign policy direction are other elements of political interest namely prevention of arms proliferation, growth of democracy, economic development, and generally stable political environment in the region.

Obviously, America's presence in the region will offer many political and economic benefits and some drawbacks. The growing reliance of the majority of the Middle Eastern nations on the United States for providing regional security, particularly in the aftermath of the 1991 Gulf war, has multiple implications. The prospect of America's commitment to ensure regional security has provided a favorable long term economic environment for American firms to expand trade. On the military side, many Persian Gulf states have provided the United States military staging facilities and bases for prepositioning military equipment. Washington has signed a bilateral defense agreement with Kuwait with cash contribution from Kuwait and Saudi Arabia to defray the costs of military on the ground, in the air and in the waters of Persian Gulf. On the political front, Washington has gained a significant influence in the Middle East mainly for its stance against the Iraqis aggression and for its leadership in bringing long time adversaries to the peace table. As a result, security of the Gulf and the undisrupted flow of oil is presently achieved. But the Gulf war and America's economic, military and political presence in the region have widened the possibility of broader and more direct U.S. military involvement in the Middle East.

To calm the American public and to lower the risk of direct military involvement, the United States will likely provide arms to the friendly countries in the region so they can assume more responsibility for providing regional security (a partial revival of Nixon Doctrine). Perhaps Saudis and Kuwaitis with large oil revenues and with most at stake will be the proper candidates for this role. But the sales of the state-of-the-art equipment to the countries in the region may in itself bear many risks. The fall of the military hardware in the hands of hostile hands may occur through a surprise invasion by an unfriendly neighbor or replacement of friendly governments through a coup, public uprising, or revolution such as that of Iran. To avert this, in the 1990s, America's foreign policy in the Middle East will have to encourage growth of democracy, to foster socio-economic

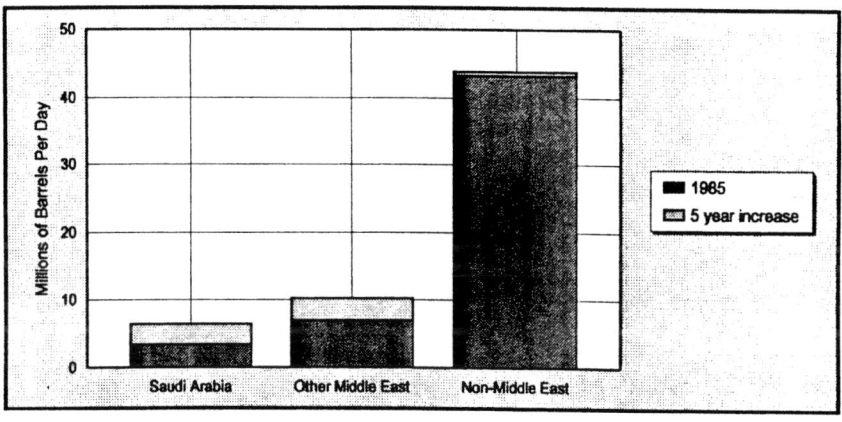

Figure 8. Relative Impact of Saudi Arabia's Increase in Crude Oil Production, 1985-1990

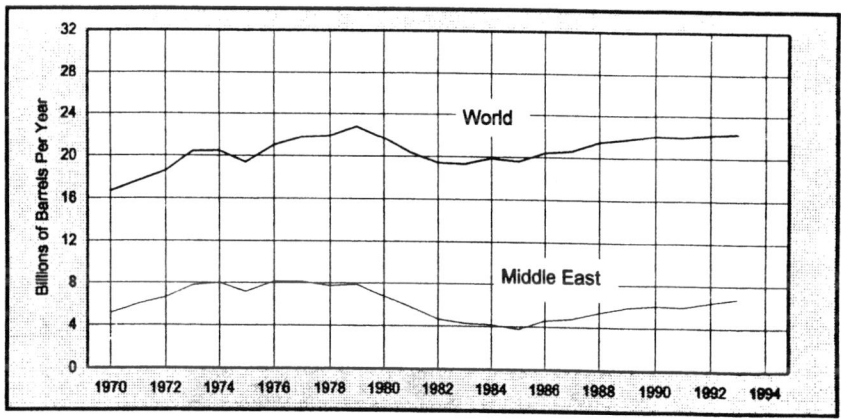

Figure 9. Crude Oil Production Trends After OPEC's First Price Shock

development, and to reduce the deep class contrast between the poor and the wealthy (revival of the Truman Doctrine). America's foreign policy endorsement of democratic changes in the region will be extremely critical as with the expanding peace among the former adversaries, the peoples of the Middle East will turn politically inward in seeking freedom and democracy, peace and prosperity. To finance development and to assure prosperity and political stability, the Middle Eastern nations will need a sustained cash income generated by export of oil to the West.

Ironically, while a threat to national security, the daily import of approximately eight million barrels of oil, places the United States in a strong position to impact the price of oil. Through the threat of imposing import tariff or reduction of import, Washington can impact the global supply and demand structure of the oil trade and thus exert political pressure on oil producing countries, in particular those in the Middle East. To protect its political influence and economic interest in the Middle East, the United States will likely keep its oil import at the current levels. The world crude oil trend in the past twenty years has remained at about 21 billion barrels a year with little fluctuations as shown in Figure 9. Although it is likely that demand will increase in some regions of the world due to the growing energy consumption of the developing economies, it is also expected that energy conservation and more efficient use of petroleum, along with increased use of other sources of energy will keep the global demand for oil flat for the foreseeable future. Undoubtedly, the collapse of the Soviet Union and the resulting significant change in the political map of the world is bound to influence the energy outlook (Sahimi, 1996). However, according to a 1992 Congressional study, the six countries of Azerbaijan, Kazakhstan, Turkmenistan, Uzbekistan, Kyrgyzstan and Tajikistan held an insignificant seven billion barrels of oil reserves in 1991 as compared to more than 726 billion barrels for the OPEC countries. With the declining Russian oil production, the internal political instability and ethnic and territorial conflicts within the Commonwealth of Independent States (CIS), and the rising internal demand for energy, the impact of the Union's breakup on the energy outlook will remain minimal for at least the next two decades. To influence the global energy picture, large cash infusion will be required which is not very likely to materialize as long as internal conflicts exist within the CIS.

It is then expected that although the price of oil will increase in nominal terms, it will remain somewhat constant in real terms. There are other political and economic elements that support the flat price forecast. Those that exert downward pressure on oil price increase are the need of the United States and all the other importing nations for economic growth and reduced outpour of cash. The fall in oil prices may also be discounted as it results in economic and political instability in the Middle East and consequently upward movement in the oil prices.

While it seems that for the foreseeable future the supply and demand for oil will remain at current levels, it should be remembered that oil is a declining asset. The oil production life index, R/P, can be applied to reserves and production from different regions of the world. Since flat production rates are predicted, then R/P becomes an accurate measure to determine the future significance of these regions in the arena of political economy of oil. With 54 percent of the worlds remaining reserves and an R/P of just under ten times of that of the United States and three times of that of the rest of the world, once again it becomes undeniably evident that the Middle East and its affairs will always remain a key element in the formulation of the American foreign policy.

V. CONCLUSION

The current direction of America's foreign policy in the Middle East has evolved from the experience of a half a century of intense political and economic interrelationship between the United States and the Middle East. During the post-World War II era, several elements namely containment of the Soviet Union, assuring the security of the state of Israel, and the need for uninterrupted flow of oil to the technologically driven economies of the West especially to that of the United States have been quite prominent in formulating the relations between the United States and the Middle East. However, the political economy of oil has continuously been the centerpiece of this association.

It is most interesting to note that the inception of America's involvement in the affairs of the Middle East was a politically driven desire to contain Soviet expansionism. But the events in Iran in the early 1950s leading to nationalization of the country's British owned oil industry changed the impetus for America's presence in the region. In the ensuing years, oil remained a controlling element in the Middle Eastern policy of this nation, with either political or economic component of this commodity significantly influencing the other. Both components were repeatedly used by either the United States or the Middle Eastern nations to influence the course and the nature of their affiliation. The formation of OPEC, the oil embargo and the price shocks of 1970s, and the use of oil as a weapon to bring Iran to its knees in the early 1950s, against the West in the 1970s and the former Soviet Union in the 1980s demonstrates the significance of the political economy of oil. Presently in the 1990s, the political economy of oil is being applied to punish Iraq and the threat of banning import of Iranian oil is looming. The policy makers in Washington have repeatedly pressured the economies of Syria, Libya and most recently Iran by banning American oil companies to participate in oil and gas exploration and production in these countries.

Based on the foregoing discussions, it is proposed that the future of American-Middle Eastern relationship is not going to be significantly different from that of the past. The quick U.S. military mobilization in response to re-massing of Iraqi forces near its southern borders in 1994, and to the suspicious Iraqi troop movements in 1995, demonstrates Clinton Administration's resolve to continue with the previous administrations' policy of maintaining the security of the Persian Gulf region at all cost. To promote regional stability in the aftermath of the 1990 Gulf crisis and to further isolate Iraq, the Clinton Administration has been encouraging Jordan to distance herself from her belligerent neighbor. Jordan is also attempting to reformulate its regional role in search of a new political framework that allows co-existence with Israel and continued support for U.S. interests in the region while keeping the radical fundamentalism in check. The combination of oil and national security concerns continues to dominate the relationship between the United States and the six-member Gulf Cooperation Council (GCC) including Saudi Arabia. The "over the horizon" state of U.S. military forces, replaced by a symbolic small number of ground troops and air force units stationed in these countries, emphasizes America's presence and resolve in the region. Meantime, the Clinton Administration is pursuing a strategy of "dual containment" against both Iran and Iraq. The aim of the strategy, first declared by President Bush in April 1993, is to neutralize both nations' efforts to develop offensive military capabilities. The endorsement of the previous administration's Middle East policy, underlines the continued U.S. interest to remain consistent and actively present in the politics of the region.

It is suggested that the inadequacy of energy self-sufficiency of the West, the existence of vast and lasting energy reserves in the Middle East, and the economic and security needs of the countries in the region will keep the Middle East and its affairs the centerpiece of America's foreign policy. In the "New World Order," the political economy of oil will continue to dominate the nature of U.S. relations with the Middle East, and as in the past will dictate America's presence in the region independent of the political affiliation of the administration in Washington.

REFERENCES

Borrus, M. and Zysman, J., "Industrial Competitiveness and National Security," in *Rethinking America's Security: Beyond Cold War to New World Order*, eds., G. Allison and G.F. Treverton, (New York: W.W. Norton and Company, 1992), pp. 168.

Han, V. X., *Oil, the Persian Gulf States and the United States*, (Westport, CT.: Praeger Publishers, 1994), pp. 1.

Jordan, A.A., Taylor, W.J., and Korb, L.J., *American National Security: Policy and Process*, (Baltimore, Md., The Johns Hopkins Press, 1990), pp. 305-307, 388.

Rustow, D.A., *Oil and Turmoil: America Faces OPEC and the Middle East*, (New York, Norton, 1982), pp. 74, 101, 247.

Sahimi, M., "Factors Affecting the Development of Fossil Energy Resources of Developing Countries," in *Third World-United States Relations in the New World Order*, eds., A. Grammy and C. K. Bragg, (New York, Nova Science Publishers, 1996), pp. 361-89.

Sampson, A.: *The Seven Sisters, The Great Oil Companies and the World They Shaped*, (New York, Bantam Book, 1984), p. 72.

Schweizer, P., *Victory*, (New York, The Atlantic Monthly Press, 1994).

Woodward, B., *Veil: The Secret Wars of the CIA, 1981-1987*, (New York, Simon and Schuster, 1987), pp. 108-111.

Yergin, D., *The Prize: The Epic Quest for Oil, Money, and Power*, (New York, Simon and Schuster, 1992), pp. 468, 617.

THE AMERICAN DOCTRINE OF LOW INTENSITY CONFLICT IN THE NEW WORLD ORDER

Beau Grosscup
Department of Political Science
California State University, Chico
Chico, CA 95929-0455

Abstract—An examination of past and current American counter insurgency or Low Intensity Conflict (LIC) doctrine. The focus is on how the end of the Cold War has affected the United States strategic analysis and what changes, if any, have occurred in LIC doctrine in the post Cold War period. The conclusion reached is that the basis of American 1960s counterinsurgency doctrine remains intact even through the identified sources and threat of insurgency have changed.

I. INTRODUCTION

The end of the Cold War nullified the basic premise of American strategic doctrine that Soviet power was the major threat to the post World War II capitalist system. In assessing the post-Cold War climate American strategic analysts quickly identified various regional Third World powers or "rogue states" as the new threat to United States power. A new strategic paradigm calls for the United States to fight mid-intensity conflicts (MIC), particularly in the Middle East and North Asia. The 1990-91 slaughter in the Persian Gulf was the prototype of the successful MIC.[1]

The analysts also warn that, like the Cold War, the United States must prepare to fight wars at the low level of conflict. Thus the doctrine of counterinsurgency or Low Intensity Conflict (LIC) remains central to United States' strategic thinking. This essay will examine why LIC is of major concern and what changes, if any, have occurred in American LIC doctrine in the new global climate.

II. THE AMERICAN DOCTRINE OF COUNTERINSURGENCY: AN OVERVIEW

The American doctrine of Cold War counterinsurgency came of age in the late 1950s and early 1960s to counter the rising tide of nationalist guerrilla wars in the colonial and former colonial areas of the Third World. The doctrine is based on three strategic maxims. First, the state, assumed to be absolute, is defined as an organic, living entity capable of contracting a disease. In the Cold War the disease was diagnosed as the cancer of Soviet-backed communism. Secondly, the state is postured as engaged in a permanent and total war against a determined, dangerous and omnipotent internal enemy bent on subversion. To be successful requires a permanent and total commitment to victory, a wide array of weapons and tactics and a strategy that would completely eradicate the subversive "disease" infecting the organs of the "body politic." Finally, for American counterinsurgency strategists, professional military leadership is imperative to successful "nation building," a process in which the development of a fascist National Security State (NSS) is a welcome outcome. Set in European fascist security maxims, the NSS is considered best suited to protect foreign corporate investment, suppress nationalist-reformist movements

---

1. For a full discussion of this point see Michael Klare, *Rogue States and Nuclear Outlaws: America's Search for a New Foreign Policy* (New York: Hill and Wang 1995) and Noam Chomsky, *World Orders Old and New*,(New York: Columbia U. Press, 1994. It is Chomsky who opines that Persian Gulf slaughter is more appropriate than Gulf War since "the term "war" hardly applies to a confrontation in which one side massacres the other from a safe distance, meanwhile wrecking the civilian society." *World Orders*, p.9.

and remain on high alert against any new outbreak of infectious disease to the "internal organs" of society.[2]

The American counterinsurgency strategy of "nation building" involved the dual tasks of providing security and promoting modernization.[3] In its nation building efforts, the United States concentrated on developing "adequate internal defense forces" which meant providing two lines of defense against insurgency. The first focused on upgrading the instruments of coercion through the development of effective police and military capabilities. The second line of defense concentrated on rooting out and curing the disease through social and economic reform, attempting to eliminate the causes of discontentment or to immunize the populous against the appeals of the insurgents.

Under American counterinsurgency doctrine, the coercive line of defense has been strongly prioritized since coercive security measures can be incorporated immediately and with relative ease. In comparison, social and economic reform is slow, arduous and politically unpopular with national elites. Acting on this priority, early in the 1960s American advisors (Mobile Training Teams or MTT) began "on the spot" training of hundreds of thousands of Third World military forces. Thousands more of foreign military officers attended special United States-run counterinsurgency training schools in the United States (at Ft. Benning, Ft. Bragg and Ft. McNair), Panama (the School of the Americas or "School of Coups"), Okinawa and Germany. Both "on the spot" field and academic training were conducted under the dual assumptions that (1) insurgents knew no moral qualms or limits in their conduct of total war and (2) to win, the United States and its allies must "fight fire with fire" or "anything goes."

To ensure that client governments institutionalized the coercive function, MTT advisors helped establish prototype anti-guerrilla organizations (Third World Special Forces) and trained them in a wide array of tech-

---

2. For further discussion of the parallel between European fascism, in particular Nazi security doctrine and United States counterinsurgency canons see Raymond Aron, *Clausewitz, Philosopher of War*, trans. Christine Booker and Norman Stone (London: Routledge and Kegan Paul, 1983), pp. 308-309, Edward S. Herman, *The Real Terror Network*, (Boston: South End Press, 1982), pp. 119-137; Michael McClintock, *Instruments of Statecraft*,(New York: Pantheon Books, 1992), pp. 59-99; and Noam Chomsky and Edward S. Herman, *The Washington Connection and Third World Fascism*, (Boston: South End Press, 1979), pp. 251-298.
3. On the tasks of nation building see Lucian Pye, *Armies and the Process of Political Modernization*, (Cambridge MA: MIT Press, 1959).

niques including terrorism and torture. They also recommended the organization of secret paramilitary groups to perform "vigilante" violence against domestic opposition or "subversive do-gooders" who most often included peasants, labor and student groups, church and health workers and educators. Thus was born the infamous "death squads" of El Salvador, Guatemala, Honduras, Vietnam and other Third World clients of the United States.

Counterinsurgency coercion also involved "public safety" training of foreign police forces through the Overseas Internal Security Program. Halted in 1975 for "abuses" such as "an ambivalent attitude toward torture" and instruction in terrorism and bomb-making at the Border Patrol Academy in Los Fresnos, Texas (known as the "Bomb School"), it was restarted under the Reagan Administration as an anti-terrorist program. Counterinsurgency training also included lessons in propaganda for national information services, courses for United States' foreign service officers in covert subversive political operations (labeled "overseas internal defense" activity) and CIA covert operations including organizing insurgent movements to overthrow unfriendly governments.

From the beginning, terrorism and "counterterrorism" played a central role in American counterinsurgency "special warfare." Declassified government documents, congressional testimony, military officer writings and Army and intelligence agency training manuals propose that "fighting fire with fire" requires both "defensive" and "offensive" terrorism.[4] All openly advocate that to be successful against the enemy, United States forces and their allies must use terrorism. This advocacy is based on the dual premise that the enemy does it so we must and that terrorism is effective as it will save lives since it is a short term tactic designed to quickly end conflict. For architects of the counterinsurgency doctrine, the use of terrorism is not a moral problem but rather (1) a problem of scale; how to keep those the United States trained in "just a little terror" from escalating their terrorism to genocidal levels, and (2) a public relations problem; handled via a three-pronged strategy of manipulating the media, creation of unofficial terror groups untraceable to the United States

---

4. As an example of this literature see Joanne Omang and Aryeh Neier, *Psychological Operations in Guerrilla Warfare*, (New York; Vintage Books, 1985).

(death squads) and impersonating rebel forces while committing terrorism.[5]

The development side of counterinsurgency doctrine rests on the assumption that "insurgency results at least in part from the articulated dissatisfaction arising out of underdevelopment and unfulfilled expectations."[6] The task of civic action, as it has come to be called, is to win back and/or hold on to the hearts and minds of the indigenous population through education, agriculture, transportation, communication, sanitation, health and public works projects.

The use of American and indigenous military forces in short-term and limited civic action followed on the heels of President John F. Kennedy's premise that "The new generation of military leaders has shown an increasing awareness that armies cannot only defend their countries--they can help to build them."[7] Internal defense and loyalty to the status quo would be greatly enhanced if the populous saw a "softer more benevolent" military involved in non-military tasks of social and economic reform.

The premise that the military is a progressive institution, well-suited as an agent of modernization for "nation-building," is at the heart of American counterinsurgency doctrine. Professor Lucian Pye provides the rationale for this assumption in his *Armies and the Process of Political Modernization*. He justifies United States' support of Third World military regimes on a three-fold basis: (1) military intervention into politics does not threaten democracy; (2) military rule can establish the necessary basis for the development of democratic institutions; and (3) military rule should be welcomed as the least problematic development in the politics of Third World nations and the most effective way to counter the communist threat.

---

5. For extended analysis see Richard Falk, "Western Foundations of US Foreign Policy," in *Western State Terrorism*, ed., Alexander George,(New York: Routledge, Chapman and Hall, 1991) and Ulrich Duchrow, Gert Eisenburger and Jochen Hippler, *Totaler Krieg gegen die Armen*, (Munich: Chr. Kaiser Verlag, 1989).
6. John W. De Pauw and George A. Luz, eds., *Winning the Peace*: The Strategic Implications of Military Civic Action, (New York, Praeger, 1992), p.4.
7. See Major General William B. Rosson, "Understanding Civic Action," *Army*, July, 1963, pp. 46-52.

III. THE COLD WAR COUNTERINSURGENCY EXPERIENCE

Three decades of American Cold War counterinsurgency substantiate that the coercion task of internal security far outweighed the development side of nation building. Indeed, by May 1965, the United States Congress had limited the scope and funding of military civic action, making clear that development should not interfere with the primary defense function of "security through coercion." The failure of MCA to win the "hearts and minds" of the South Vietnamese raised further questions about the development side of counterinsurgency. The atrocities of the Phoenix Program, a classic example of providing security by assassination, terror and torture and the ultimate failure of the United States' military to defeat the Vietnamese Communist "disease" further discredited major aspects of American counterinsurgency.

Contrary to the counterinsurgency failure in Vietnam, emphasis on the coercive side of American "nation building" paid off with the emergence of National Security States in key parts of the Third World. By the mid-1970s the governments of Chile, Brazil, Argentina, Guatemala, El Salvador, Nicaragua, Paraguay, Honduras, Iran, Thailand, Zaire, the Philippines and Indonesia were ruled by fascist elements directly beholden to military elites trained in the art of United States counterinsurgency.

The institutionalized terror of the National Security States provoked the Carter Administration's effort to regain the high moral ground through a high profile "human rights campaign" and pitch the reform side of counterinsurgency. The Reagan Administration, looking to divorce itself from the failures and atrocities of the past and heighten public support for a revitalized Cold War offensive, repackaged 1960s counterinsurgency policy as the doctrine of Low Intensity Conflict (LIC).

As LIC, American counterinsurgency re-emphasized the coercive side of national security and added an offensive posture through the utilization of "presidential wars of liberation" to "roll back" communism. To deflect criticism of its renewed support for Third World fascism, the Reagan Administration encouraged its military clients to exchange their uniforms for pin-stripped business suits and make sure they won the "free elections" in the now reformed NSS or "stable democracies."[8] Finally, for Reagan officials the communist "virus" included an even more insidious "terrorist" strain. Annihilating the Soviet "agents of terrorism" meant a greater commitment to "fighting fire with fire" and utilizing all the instruments of total war within a heightened climate of moral rectitude. For the remainder of the Cold War, as Reagan officials pitched their antiterrorist morality to the court of public opinion, in private, the United States government accentuated its terrorist character, guided primarily by "realist" criteria of effectiveness.[9]

IV. THE POST COLD WAR DOCTRINE OF LOW INTENSITY CONFLICT

Enough time has passed since the end of the Cold War to assess (1) the relevance of counterinsurgency in the new global political climate and (2) what changes, if any, have occurred in the United States doctrine of Low Intensity Conflict. In particular, it will be important to explore whether the threat of insurgency has diminished sufficiently to allow the United States to develop and apply its low level security policy consistent with its often-stated public commitment to freedom, equality and high moral purpose. Or does the assessment of the new threats posed to American interests require that the "realist" maxim of "fighting with fire" in a "total war" still guides American security policy at the low intensity level?

In the Cold War, United States' counterinsurgency efforts were focused on the communist threat in general and Soviet activity in particular. Now that the Soviet Union is gone it would appear that the era of insurgency and low intensity conflict has ended. Yet, for American strategic analysts the opposite is true. The orderly and stable context that characterized the Cold War is gone. Rising from the remote corners of the Third World to dominate a "new world disorder" are the twin catastrophes of uncertainty and instability.

This new analysis contradicts the basic Cold War assumption that the Soviet Union was responsible for every challenge to the status quo and

---

8. For an in-depth analysis of the Reagan Administration's effort to democratize the National Security State see Michael McClintock, *Instruments of Statecraft*, pp. 417-420.
9. Falk, "Terrorist Foundations of US Foreign Policy," in George, *Western Terrorism*, p.113.

thus undermines the very premise upon which American counterinsurgency doctrine was constructed. But for American strategists, it documents the heightened relevance of Low Intensity Conflict Doctrine in the emerging global climate. Bruce Hoffman of RAND Corporation captures this central point when he writes:

"Nor is there much hope of these so-called "low-intensity" conflicts abating. On the contrary, as the once rigid, bipolar international order loosens and superpower influence declines, regional nationalist and ethnic tensions--often combined with intercommunal religious antagonism--long held in check or kept dormant by the cold war, are likely to erupt and produce even greater levels of non state violence than occurred during the 1980s."[10]

The continued, indeed increased instability in the regions and nations of the Third World from a variety of sources and for a variety of reasons generates new threats to the would-be architects of the new world order. The multiplicity of mid and low-level threats coming from a decentralized and disparate global context raises the stakes for the "winners of the Cold War," in particular the United States, which sees it as its right to devise and enforce the ground rules for proper and responsible behavior in the post Cold War climate.

The vision of a "world in disorder" has produced the new American commitment to addressing mid-level and low-level conflicts. Mid-level conflict doctrine requires quickly confronting and smashing the conventional armies and weapons of mass destruction of the "regional rogue states" such as Iraq, Iran, Cuba, Syria, North Korea and Libya.[11] As "international bomb-throwers, countries which are on the periphery of the international system, countries which have little stake in international order and seeking through various reprehensible means to disrupt that order," the rogue state threat comes from their sponsorship of international terrorism, control over the global drug traffic and efforts to acquire nuclear weapons.[12]

---

10. Bruce Hoffman, "Current Research on Terrorism and Low-Intensity Conflict," *Studies in Conflict and Terrorism* Vol. 15, p.27.
11. Michael T. Klare, "Rogue States," *The Nation*, May 8, 1995, Vol. 260, No. 18.
12. "U.S. Security Policy Toward Rogue Regimes," *Hearings Before the Subcommittee on International Security, International Organizations and Human Rights of the Committee on Foreign Affairs,*

To American analysts, the low-level threat is more diverse and insidious than ever. While its agents do include foreign national forces, in the main low-intensity conflicts involve sub-national groups and individuals or "irregular forces--guerrilla armies, national liberation movements, terrorist groups, private militias, and narcotics traffickers."[13] These diverse forces utilize a variety of weapons, foremost among which is a new form of revolution, terrorism and drug trafficking.

To Jeffrey Simon, the fall of the governments in Iran, Burma, Haiti and the Philippines revealed a new strategy to foment rapid political and social change via a combination of urban mass actions initiated by coalitions of political, social and ethnic-religious forces.[14] V. K. Sood extends Simon's point through his analysis of the catalytic role corrupt civil administration plays in fomenting instability and terrorism in India.[15]

The growing popularity of the instrument of terrorism among "fanatical" sub-national religious groups such as Lebanon's Hezbollah and more recently individuals like Ramzi Ahmed Yousef make the low intensity conflicts of the 1990s even more threatening than those of the Cold War. For Richard Shultz: "The lessons derived from the activities of Hezbollah and several other international terrorist groups will provide guidelines for those conducting this form of LIC in the 1990s."[16] Indeed, the terrorism of the post Cold War climate "fueled by nationalism, irredentism and religion" as opposed to ideology is predicted to be more bloody and dangerous than ever.[17] Increasingly, terrorism "experts" are warning that weapons of mass destruction, including nuclear weapons, are likely to become the "weapons of choice" among terrorist groups and are, with the loosening of Cold War controls, more readily available to anyone who wants them.

Finally, the international narcotics trade, especially as it is connected with guerrilla and terrorists groups, raises the threat of low intensity con-

---

House of Representatives, One Hundred Third Congress, First Session, July 28 and September 14, 1993, (Washington D.C., U.S. Government Printing Office), p.1.
13. Hoffman, "Current Research in Terrorism," p.26.
14. Jeffrey Simon, *Revolutions without Guerrillas*, (Santa Monica, CA: RAND, 1989).
15. V.K. Sood, "Low-intensity Conflict: The Source of Third World Instability," *Studies in Conflict and Terrorism*, Vol. 15, pp. 233-250.
16. Richard H. Shultz, "The Low-intensity Conflict Environment of the 1990's," *The Annals of the American Academy of Political and Social Science*, September 1991, Vol. 517, p.130.
17. Hoffman, "Current Research in Terrorism," p.29.

flict to new heights. The insidious nature of the drug culture, its infectious undermining of the moral and psychological health of a nation's people, particularly its youth, is considered more dangerous than the physiological addiction. Focused as they are on the drug habits of North Americans and Europeans, specifically the youth of America, the well-armed, well-financed and politically well-connected international drug lords are "viewed both as an internal threat to the stability of friendly governments in Latin America and as a serious domestic social problem for the United States."[18]

To American analysts, the indigenous roots of low intensity conflicts throughout Third World societies produce an endemic security problem for the United States on local, regional and global levels. As the architect, enforcer and principal beneficiary of the new global order, unfavorable results at the low-level of conflict threaten United States access to strategic resources and undermine the global "suitable business environment" for profitable trade and investment. Timidity at the low level of conflict sets an unwelcome precedent that could extend to the mid-level arena. This in turn raises the possibility that the United States could find itself fighting more regional conventional wars and losing important regional allies. In sum, low intensity conflict is a serious problem for contemporary United States security. The question is: has it been taken seriously enough to impact the doctrine of Low Intensity Conflict?

By all accounts, the new elements of low intensity conflict have produced serious and considerable analysis of how to combat the threatening dimensions of the new world disorder.[19] Indeed, as the Cold War wound down a consensus developed as to the six mission areas of LIC.[20] They include:

1. *Counterinsurgency.* Headlining LIC is the application of standard 1960s principles of security through coercion along with a secondary emphasis on the political, cultural and economic roots of anti-American insurgency. The internal police forces are considered the appropriate agents

---

18. Shultz, "Low-intensity Climate of 1990's," p.132.
19. US Army Command and Staff College (USACGSC), *Low Intensity Conflict*, Field Circular FC 100-20, (Fort Leavenworth, Kansas: Staff College, 1986).
20. These missions are identified in Robert C. Freysinger, "US Military and Economic Intervention in an International Context of Low-intensity Conflict," *Political Studies*, 1991 Vol. XXXIX, pp. 321-334.

of coercion, intelligence and psychological warfare to legitimize the government and undermine the rebels. For combat situations, indigenous military forces, operating from secure enclaves are to utilize "surgical violence" to coerce rebel forces into submission while keeping civilian and property damage to a minimum. Continuing to apply the lessons of Vietnam, United States' forces are to be used in combat only when absolutely required.

2. *Proinsurgency.* There remains a central place in LIC for the "presidential wars of liberation" in which the United States military organizes and trains rebel groups to battle an anti-American regime. On behalf of the rebels, United States Special Forces are to engage in sabotage operations against important components and personnel of the social, political and economic infrastructure. In short, the offensive terrorist side of LIC remains intact following the successful examples set in Nicaragua, Afghanistan, Ethiopia and Angola during the 1980s.

3. *Peacetime Contingency Operations.* These involve United States' forces in abrupt warning, quickly executed "power projections" of short duration. The purpose of these operations is to demonstrate the scope of United States' power, the ability to deliver instruments of violence in the "violence-prone Third World" and the political will to use violence. The USS New Jersey's off-shore bombing of villages in Lebanon's Bekaa Valley (1993), the Grenada invasion (1983), the air strikes on Tripoli, Libya, in the effort to assassinate Muammar Kaddafi (1986), the invasion of Panama (1988) and the air strikes on Baghdad (1993) as retribution for the alleged assassination attempt on former President George Bush exemplify this mission.

4. *Anti-terrorist Operations.* This mission involves the effort to label and locate "terrorist" groups and individuals. This is the crux of LIC as it frees United States policy makers to use whatever means and measures to wipe out the "terrorist enemy" while holding the high moral ground. The "anti-terrorist" posture can be defensive and offensive, involving retaliatory actions and pre-emptive and preventive strikes against individuals, groups and their government sponsors, all undertaken with the American public's blessing.

5. *Anti-drug Operations.* There is a strong consensus that the narco-terrorist is an important "new enemy" in the post-Cold War era. Though questions remain about the proper role of United States military person-

nel in anti-drug efforts, agents from the Drug Enforcement Agency and other civilian agencies are already working closely with many Latin American military and police forces. The growing propensity of United States analysts to define the war on drugs as "guerrilla war" forecasts an even greater military involvement. The United States has had its Special Forces in Peru, Colombia and Bolivia since 1989 ostensibly to fight narcotics traffickers. It has also sent long-range surveillance technology to Colombia, provided intelligence to Haiti and encouraged crop substitution in many countries. Armored helicopters, troop-carrying aircraft for jungle warfare and "narcodiplomats" from the Narcotic Assistance Units of the Foreign Service are also being utilized in many Latin American nations. Not surprisingly, the "rogue states" of Iran, Iraq and Libya are identified as the masterminds behind the international drug trade.

6. *Peacekeeping Operations*. Under this mission the United States' military is sent into the middle of conflicts to act as a buffer between combatants and hopefully bring the conflict to an end. In these efforts, the United States military puts on a humanitarian and diplomatic face in areas where the continuation of fighting will harm American strategic interests. The 1992 Somalia operation and the 1994 invasion of Haiti are examples of this LIC mission.

The multi-dimensional mission called for under current LIC doctrine requires "a shift in the understanding of organization, required equipment and training.[21] As of 1991, important changes in the organization and equipping of Special Operations forces, Light Infantry Divisions and Power Projection forces confirmed that the United States was enhancing its LIC capabilities. By 1990, active duty Special Forces personnel, the participants in the "dirty jobs" of counterinsurgency, numbered 21,000. They were assigned to a variety of units including the US Army Special Forces, Delta Force, US Army Rangers, 160th Army Aviation Battalion, US Navy SEALS and the US Air Force Special Operations Wing. A new unified command to coordinate all training and equipping of the Special Forces accompanied the growth in Special Forces units. A new Assistant Secretary of Defense for special Operations and Low-Intensity, a new Deputy Assistant to the President and a special LIC group in the National Security

---

21. Ibid., p.326.

Council give LIC advocates an important presence in the highest circles of the United States government.

As of 1989, five new Light Infantry Divisions and three other active duty divisions were established with the capacity of being airlifted to any part of the world within a maximum of six days. Utilizing light howitzers, mortars, TOW and DRAGON anti-tank missiles, jeeps, new one-and-a-quarter ton trucks, helicopters, Vulcan and Stinger anti-aircraft systems and small armored vehicles, these forces are trained to fight in both the urban and rural environment of the Third World.

Finally, an array of larger forces with airlift and sealift capabilities have been assigned to accompany large scale naval forces to present an impressive "power projection" capability for specific situations anywhere in the world. The development at Los Alamos Laboratory of a new generation of very small tactical nuclear weapons underscores LIC strategists' intention to breach the ever-shrinking firebreak between conventional and nuclear weapons in future Third World conflicts. Among these weapons are the 10-ton "micronuke" for the destruction of underground bunkers, the "mininuke," a 100-ton antimissile warhead to counter nuclear, biological and chemical missiles, and the 1,000 ton "tinynuke" counter-projection warhead for use against ground troop attack.

In sum, driving recent United States enhancements of low-level bureaucratic organization, force structure and weapons systems is the assumption that LIC will be even more important to the United States' strategic doctrine. As the world shifts from an East-West to a North-South dynamic, the United States has also shifted its strategic posture. It is now prepared to respond in one of two ways to any given situation anywhere in the Third World. It has the option of sending in overwhelming force and going for the quick kill as in Grenada, Panama, Kuwait-Iraq and Haiti. It is also prepared, if necessary, to stay for the long haul fighting at the low intensity level with all the coercive instruments of "nation building" that it has developed and utilized for decades in Africa, Asia and Latin America.

The one question remaining is whether or not there have been significant changes in the principles of LIC doctrine since the end of the Cold War. In his scholarly review of recent LIC literature, Richard D. Downie, an enthusiastic supporter of counterinsurgency and LIC, examines whether or not there are any changes in LIC doctrine and whether or not they focus on the factors responsible for the failure of United States counterinsurgency policy in losing Vietnam.[22] In his survey he investigates whether or not the authors address:

1) the impact of local conditions on an insurgency, or does it continue to recommend the application of a standard-package prescription as an adequate and appropriate response?
2) the prevention of the commitment of U.S. assistance in an unwinnable situation and the requirement for analytical capabilities to assess whether intragovernmental constraints in the threatened state will permit necessary, positive reforms?
3) the availability or acquisition of leverage over the threatened government to ensure the reform of government policies or actions that perpetuate the underlying political, social and economic conditions for the conflict?
4) the requirement to ensure a coherent, unified and integrated effort among the military and civilian agencies involved in the execution of a LIC strategy?[23]

Downie's review confirms that though the old strategic Cold War order now longer exists the conceptual basis of United States Vietnam-era counterinsurgency remains intact. He writes:

> "On balance, the only substantial measure of change reflected in the doctrine is in the area of Question 1. Here the effort to tailor counterinsurgency programs to specific vulnerabilities demonstrates attentiveness to local conditions and selectivity concerning prescriptions for counterinsurgency."[24]

In other words, under the "new doctrine" the United States is more likely to approach the task of counterinsurgency on a case by case analysis of local conditions rather than applying its generic Brand X counterinsurgency package to all locales as it did in pervious decades. However, current LIC, like past counterinsurgency doctrine remains committed to the following:

---

22. Richard D. Downie, "Low-Intensity Conflict Doctrine and Policy: Old Wine in a New Bottle?" *Studies in Conflict and Terrorism*, Vol. 15, pp. 53-67.
23. Ibid., p.58.
24. Ibid., p.64-65.

1) A refusal to establish a formal mechanism to explore whether the United States can win or not before getting involved. Thus current LIC doctrine continues to assume, as in Vietnam, that with enough firepower the United States will always prevail.

2) A reluctance to push the local government to make any necessary social, economic and political reforms. Thus the development side of nation building continues to take a back seat, and the United States ends up supporting repressive regimes or, as in Vietnam, Panama and Haiti, having to instigate a coup against the unwanted leader.

3) The non-unification of the military and civil sides of counterinsurgency. Thus the military remains the primary agent of counterinsurgency and most of its activities classified and unavailable for public scrutiny.

Based on his stated agenda, it is clear Downie is not interested in exploring the extent to which any "new" American LIC doctrine creates or supports repressive NSS or relies heavily on terrorism and torture. Yet, in his conclusion that the essential elements of United States Vietnam-era counterinsurgency doctrine are unchanged and unchallenged, Downie confirms that contemporary LIC remains committed to coercion, to fighting fire with fire in a total war of annihilation against all agents of the designated disease.

It is left to others, notably LIC expert Michael McClintock, to evaluate whether or not United States' counterinsurgency doctrine as presently conceived has resolved the contradiction between its long and heavy dependence on coercion and the often stated commitment to high moral principles, democratic freedoms and human equality.[25] At the very end of his studied assessment, McClintock concludes that with respect to United States' counterinsurgency doctrine and actions, past practices guide the present. McClintock writes:

> "At the local level, the small wars and police actions of counterinsurgency and unconventional warfare continue to be waged. The states that enthusiastically adopted U.S. Cold War precepts and counterinsurgency doctrine have always looked toward the enemy within as their primary challenge.

---

25. Michael McClintock, *Instruments of Statecraft*,

The Soviet presence in the Southern Hemisphere was always largely abstract, and rather less important than the continuing threat of labor unrest, class struggle, subversion, and insurgency. As long as the United States continues to fund the counterinsurgency states, to arm and train their armies and police, and to work with them in the suppression of dissidents and insurgents as before, the auguries for change are poor."[26]

V. CONCLUSION

Though their analyses of current LIC doctrine are very different, McClintock and Downie both conclude that little has changed in LIC doctrine. Highly publicized revelations in late 1994 and early 1995 about United States support for Haitian military thugs and terrorists and C.I.A. links to Guatemalan death squads support their separate analyses that coercion remains the priority.[27] What has changed is that for the first time in fifty years the United States' rationalizations of the goals, mission and tactics of counterinsurgency go unchallenged by any comparable power. In the emerging era, American versions of events, threats and solutions reign supreme. While other states occupy the top ranks of the Department of State's annual list of states sponsoring terrorism, the United States continues to utilize terrorism as a central component of LIC as it enforces its will in the Third World. While American leaders decry the crimes of "rogue states," the United States pursues its own "rogue-like" actions in enforcing a new Pax Americana at the mid and low-intensity levels. As in the decades of Cold War counterinsurgency, the United States engages in "rogue-like" and terrorist pursuits not by accident or inference but by counterinsurgency-LIC strategic design. It does so boldly and purposefully based on careful calculations of what must be done to effectively protect its foreign and domestic interests, regardless of who the designated enemy is or if it is contrary to its publicly stated principles.

---

26. Ibid., p.462.
27. For discussion of these revelations see Allan Nairn, "Occupation Haiti: The Eagle is Landing," *The Nation*, October 3, 1994 Vol. 259, No. 10, Allan Nairn, "Our Man in FRAPH: Behind Haiti's Paramilitaries," *The Nation*, Oct. 24, 1994, Vol. 259, No. 13 and Allan Nairn, "C.I.A. Death Squad," *The Nation*, April 17, 1995, Vol. 260, No. 15.

AIDS IN LATIN AMERICA AND THE CARIBBEAN: NEW CHALLENGES FOR UNITED STATES FOREIGN POLICY

Robert McNamara
Department of Political Science
Sonoma State University
1801 East Cotati Avenue
Rohnert Park, CA 94928

Abstract—This essay explores the link between United States foreign policy in the Latin American/Caribbean region and the socio-economic consequences of the HIV/AIDS epidemic. Relevant issues include: the impact of the HIV/AIDS epidemic on the region; the delayed response by government officials in the early 1980s; and the role of USAID/AIDSCAP in HIV/AIDS prevention. In spite of the fact that the region is headed towards an AIDS epidemic of disastrous proportions, the future looks bleak for sustained funding of prevention programs. The political current in Washington suggests HIV/AIDS will be relegated to the back burner along with most other foreign assistance programs.

I. INTRODUCTION

While AIDS is first and foremost a medical condition, it has increasingly taken on a distinct role in the shaping of nations' social, economic, and political developments. The implications and reactions of these new developments have come to be described by Jonathan Mann, former director of the Global AIDS Program, as the "Third AIDS Pandemic:"

> The third epidemic closely follows the first two, of HIV infection and AIDS. It is the epidemic of economic, social, political and cultural reaction. In the words of Javier Peres de Cuellar, ..."AIDS raises crucial social, humanitarian and legal issues threatening to undermine the fabric of tolerance and understanding upon which our societies function." (Connor)

After 15 years into the global battle against AIDS, the pandemic is only getting worse. Prospects are poor for the development of a vaccine in this century. As of January 1, 1995, it is estimated that more than 18 million adults and 1.5 million children have become infected with HIV, the virus that causes AIDS. By the end of the 1990s, the numbers could reach 40 million. Today, about eighty percent of all infections occur in the developing world. By the end of the decade, that number is estimated to be ninety percent. (World Health Organization, 1995)

Number of Reported AIDS Cases as of March, 1995

Country	Through 1988	1989	1990	1991	1992	1993	1994	Total
Brazil	8,136	5,348	7,315	9,645	11,508	12,128	4,515	58,595
Honduras	309	254	592	505	745	965	742	4,145
Dominican Republic	707	481	257	279	327	311	227	2,589
Haiti	2,002	451	1,216	492	806	---	---	4,967
Jamaica	73	66	62	133	99	237	359	1,029

Source: World Health Organization/Global Program on AIDS, 1995

In spite of the fact that the overwhelming number of new cases of HIV are in the developing world, very few of the world's resources are devoted to AIDS prevention there. The World Health Organization (WHO) estimates that an effective AIDS prevention program for the developing world would cost up to 2.5 billion dollars a year, thus averting some 10 million new infections over the next five years. Yet current global spending on AIDS is 1.5 billion dollars, of which the developing world receives only about ten percent in annual external assistance (U.S. Congress, 1994). Because AIDS affects the "breadwinners," i.e., the work force, it is having an economic impact well out of proportion to the numbers of people infected. According to M.H. Merson, Executive Director WHO's Global Program on AIDS (WHO/GPA), by the year 2000 close to 5 million children worldwide will have lost their mother or both parents to AIDS. The situation will only worsen considering that by the year 2000 and estimated 13 million women will have been infected by HIV. Medical care alone is consuming an inordinate percentage of a family's annual income. Yet, Merson points out, "these enormous health care costs are actually minor compared with the other costs to the economy of adults falling ill...depleting the workforce of invaluable manpower. A single case of AIDS could reduce a family's income by as much as 75 percent" (U.S. Congress, 1994).

II. HIV/AIDS IN LATIN AMERICA AND THE CARIBBEAN

The "third epidemic" has arrived in the countries of the Latin American/Caribbean region (LA/C) and has challenged the international community to view AIDS not solely as a medical problem, but rather one intrinsically linked to poverty, class, and economic development. Medical care is not an option for most in Latin America and the Caribbean. While in the industrialized countries a person with AIDS (and access to health care) may live for years following diagnosis, in the LA/C region the average person lives six months after being diagnosed with AIDS. With access to medical services considered a luxury, many die of AIDS without knowing it (confusing their symptoms with other common diseases of poverty). With Latin America's growing urbanization (approximately 75 percent), slums have become a breeding ground for the HIV virus that causes AIDS. Soaring inflation and one of the worst debt crises in the world have further compounded the situation. In addition, years of authoritarian military governments helped to undermine the legitimacy of both civil and state institutions resulting in neglect and mismanagement of the public health sector. And throughout the region, multilateral lending institutions have had a direct affect by forcing debt-ridden governments to reduce spending. Thus, already inadequate health care budgets in many LA/C countries are the first to be cut. Public health workers are faced with tough choices: do they devote dwindling resources to combat cholera, malaria, diarrhea, or do they aggressively go after AIDS. The result has been a long delay in government action, a lack of direction in public policy, and a lack of adequate preventive information. In most cases, HIV/AIDS has clearly been relegated to the back burner in spite of the fact that there are an estimated two million people with HIV in the LA/C region today.

Finally, the traditional opposition of the Church to family planning and sex education has also contributed to a general lack of AIDS awareness throughout the region by refusing to support government efforts toward an effective HIV/AIDS prevention campaign, including the use of condoms. Needless to say, given the influence of the Church in the LA/C region, any opposition from this sector is bound to have a significant effect on governmental efforts to promote HIV prevention campaigns in the schools and elsewhere.

III. Epidemiological Trends

The geography of the region, the large number of tourists and business travellers, and the increasing numbers of migrant workers (both legal and illegal), have all been cited as factors accommodating the rapid spread of HIV both within and across country borders. (USAID, 1993) The cumulative number of AIDS cases "reported" in the LA/C region has surpassed 113,000 (PAHO, 1995). This is compared to fewer than 8,000 cases just 7 years ago. Brazil has the fourth highest reported number of AIDS cases in the world and in Central America, fully one-half of all reported cases are in Honduras alone. The highest levels of HIV infection in the region are reported Haiti where the epidemic is similar to that seen in the Sub-Saharan, with a seroprevalence among "low-risk" populations between six and eight percent. (AIDSCAP, 1995) Those carrying the HIV virus have well surpassed two million. And while the epidemic is older in the United States where many of the virus carriers have already developed symptoms, in Latin America the epidemic is newer. Given these demographic trends, health officials predict a surge of new cases in the coming years with a pronounced impact on health, socio-economic and political factors.

Since many of those infected are young adults, the expected labor shortages (especially among migrant workers) may have a significant adverse impact upon the region's economy (USAID, 1993).

Seroprevalence is currently highest in the urban areas, yet it is increasingly moving to the rural regions, e.g., in Haiti and Mexico. High rates of STDs throughout the LA/C region contribute to the growth of the epidemic and in several countries infection rates among commercial sex workers are alarmingly high. Surveys indicate that over 40 percent of the commercial sex workers in selected urban areas in Haiti and 40 percent in certain Honduran cities are infected with HIV (USAID, 1993).

AIDS transmission patterns in the LA/C region have changed considerably since the first cases were diagnosed in the mid-1980s. Early in the epidemic, most infections were attributed to homosexual contact between men, IV drug use, and contaminated blood products. By the early 1990s, heterosexual contact became the primary means of transmission. Heterosexual intercourse now accounts for at least 75 percent of all new infections (PAHO, 1994). The result has been increasing rates of infection among women and subsequent transmission from mothers to infants.

There are many societal and cultural factors which render women particularly vulnerable to HIV, including poverty, sexual violence, lack of access to health care and economic dependence (Roitstein and Becker). Added to these cultural and social factors are the biological factors which determine that women become infected more easily than men.

IV. CHALLENGES FOR UNITED STATES FOREIGN POLICY

The challenges associated with these trends for the United States in the post-Cold War are significant. AIDS can no longer be simply considered a medical condition. As noted by Timothy Wirth, Counselor for the Department of State, "now, and increasingly in the future, AIDS is a political, social, economic, health and security issue with profound implications for U.S. foreign policy, American leadership and global cooperation" (U.S. Congress, 1994).

The full economic impact of those countries most severely affected by AIDS, many which are recipients of United States foreign aid, is only beginning to be felt. In fact, the economic losses related to HIV/AIDS can well be expected to exceed the total foreign aid these countries are receiving. The United States Department of State reports:

> AIDS threatens the objective of promoting economic development in developing countries. Although the economic impact of AIDS cannot yet be quantified, it is hard to conceive of a developing country with both a serious AIDS problem and a thriving economy. The badly infected countries will be radically transformed, with greatly reduced chances for economic growth. Economic assistance will become less effective in AIDS-ridden countries. Generating private enterprise activity and foreign investment will be more difficult. Whatever the scale of the future international aid programs, a growing proportion of assistance is likely to be directed at the myriad of problems associated with HIV/AIDS pandemic (State, 1992).

In addition to the domestic economic impact of HIV/AIDS in the most affected countries, as the disease spreads so do other attendant international concerns. At least 50 countries have requirements for HIV testing of foreign visitors. If the trend continues, tougher restrictions on the movement of people would undermine not only the basic human rights of those with HIV, but would also restrict the free flow of labor and investment-- an issue of particular concern for the United States as it moves towards closer economic cooperation and more open markets with the Latin and Caribbean countries.

How the United States will continue to confront this and other attendant issues relative to the HIV/AIDS epidemic with its southern neighbors is still unknown. Yet one thing is certain- HIV/AIDS will increasingly present itself as an issue to contend with as the United States makes foreign policy decisions relative to the LA/C region.

Yet, in spite of the growing humanitarian crisis, the international AIDS crisis is unlikely to get a more favorable response from the United States government any time soon. In this post-Cold War era of the 1990s, the prospects for United States foreign aid have never been more dim, especially in the area of development assistance. During the Cold War, activities in promoting economic growth and social progress in poor countries were directly linked to security issues, i.e., containing the spread of communism. In the 1990s, however, debates over the size of the foreign aid budget, the most efficient means of delivering program assistance, or whether or not to even have a foreign-aid program in the post-Cold War world have intensified. (Rondinelli, 1995) With the continuing budget deficits, leading members of the new Republican-controlled Congress have begun calling for cutbacks in United States contributions to programs overseas.

Thus, the question raised today in the United States during a time of continued deficits and a growing population of underserved people with HIV/AIDS in the United States, is "why spend all that money on something like AIDS in foreign countries?" Again, Timothy notes, "As these individuals die, not only is there enormous cost to the society, but our ability to maintain civil societies in the fabric of a country that works declines very, very rapidly. Coming behind with that decline is a kind of social and economic chaos, and that ...is enormously problematic for us." Dr. Satcher from the CDC adds:

> ...it is really a matter of pay me now or pay me later, so to speak...The United Sates will not be able to sit idly by as societies break to their knees and fall apart and at an increasing pace around the world. We will be drawn into responding at a humanitarian level, as we do with regularity, at a political level, and on occasion even at a military level. And I think the AIDS and HIV epidemic is a major contributing...factor in this equation of the future (US Congress, 1994).

V. USAID RESPONDS TO HIV/AIDS

United States foreign assistance comprises a variety of programs for developing countries, including military and economic assistance. In FY 1995, Congress appropriated 13.7 billion dollars for foreign aid programs. About half of that, 7 billion dollars, is devoted largely to human-development programs related to health, family planning and economic-self help. This non-military foreign aid is administered by the United States Agency for International Development (USAID).

At a time when Federal bureaucracies are fighting for their existence all over Washington, USAID is no exception. Created in 1961, USAID was to focus on the developmental aspects of foreign aid, while the Department of State focused on shorter-term diplomatic concerns. Yet, with its 2,950 employees, USAID has been subject to major criticism by Jesse Helms, Chairman of the Senate Foreign Relations Committee, and others on Capitol Hill who criticize United States foreign aid as nothing more than an international welfare program. As of mid-1995, USAID had already closed 23 offices overseas and cut its staff by 10 percent, with more cuts projected. None of this bodes well for prospective funding for HIV/AIDS prevention programs overseas which are primarily funded through USAID funds. For fiscal year 1995, USAID allocated a total of 115 million dollars for HIV/ AIDS prevention.

Prevention is the cornerstone of USAID's HIV/AIDS program. Given that the most prevalent modes of HIV transmissions in the developing world are through sexual contact and contact with tainted blood, USAID HIV/AIDS programs focus on the following factors:

1. high risk sexual behaviors, including multiple sexual partners, not using a condom or ineffective use of condoms,and frequent use of commercial sex;
2. high rates of sexually transmitted diseases (STDs). The presence of STDs increases the efficiency of sexual transmission of HIV by 5 to 20 times;
3. limited public health interventions.
4. migration from rural areas to urban centers or by migratory, seasonal laborers.
5. women's lack of access to economic resources, inequity in social/religious conventions, and inferior legal status.

Since local community-based organizations are deemed best to deliver services, a significant portion of USAID's prevention efforts are undertaken by these groups.

VI. PROGRAM IMPLEMENTATION

While the United States has contributed significantly to the World Health Organization's Global Program on AIDS (88.5 million dollars between 1986 and 1991) and other international organizations' HIV prevention programs, the bulk of USAID's efforts in HIV/AIDS prevention today goes to bilateral programs. Such bilateral programs are funded both by central USAID funds and Mission funds. Since 1987, over 300 million dollars has been spent in bi-lateral support to assist developing countries in HIV prevention. Such programs are frequently coordinated with other donors and multilateral organizations, including some already supported by USAID, as well as the United States CDC (blood screening) and the Peace Corp (education and HIV prevention counseling).

During 1987-92, USAID executed most of its HIV/AIDS bilateral activities through two independent projects: AIDS Public Health Communications (AIDSCOM) and AIDS Technical Support (AIDSTECH). USAID's strategy for HIV/AIDS prevention during this period focused on five basic goals: changing high-risk sexual behavior; reducing the number of sexual partners; reducing the incidence of STDs; increasing access to and use of condoms; reducing the transmission of HIV through blood (USAID, 1993).

In 1991, USAID redesigned its HIV/AIDS prevention program, acknowledging that project resources were too thinly spread and that there was a need for management changes. The major component of the new HIV/AIDS prevention program is the AIDS Control and Prevention Project (AIDSCAP) which focuses funds, although not exclusively, on priority countries. Approximately 25 percent of USAID's HIV/AIDS prevention budget is devoted to the Latin American/Caribbean region.

VII. AIDSCAP

AIDSCAP is the principal element of USAID's HIV/AIDS global program. Implemented by Family Health International (FHI) in 1992, in collaboration with nine separate subcontractors (approximately 87 percent of AIDSCAP programs are subcontracted out to other non-governmental organizations and private voluntary organizations), this five-year program has been allocated 168 million dollars in USAID funds and is designed to support the local capacity of developing countries to prevent HIV/AIDS.

The AIDSCAP project is designed to provide resources and technical expertise to government and private organizations, universities, and community groups to mobilize HIV/AIDS prevention programs in 15 developing countries. Approximately 68.5 million dollars comes from USAID's Research and Development Bureau while another 99.2 million dollars comes from USAID's regional bureaus and missions. As of 1995, the priority countries in the LA/C region have been listed as: Brazil, Haiti, the Dominican Republic, Jamaica, and Honduras.

VIII. BRAZIL

Brazil currently accounts for the fourth highest reported number of AIDS cases in the world. According to figures from WHO/GPA, 58,595 cases of AIDS had been reported through January 1995 (PAHO, 1995). The epidemic has been showing a significant increase over time in heterosexual transmission. Women are the most vulnerable group with the male to female ration in adults decreasing from 9:1 in 1987 to 4:1 in 1994. The high rates of STDs in high risk populations have contributed heavily to the spread of the HIV/AIDS epidemic in Brazil. For example, in the city of Sao Paulo, the prevalence rates for syphilis are 66 percent among female prostitutes. It is generally understood that the infrastructure for diagnosis and management of STDs in Brazil is not well developed (PAHO, 1994).

The earliest confirmed cases of AIDS were reported in Brazil in 1982. Yet the Brazilian government failed, for a number of reasons, to allocate sufficient funds or define a coordinated national plan to aggressively confront the epidemic. Finally, in May 1985, a government executive order called for the establishment of a national AIDS program (Programa Nacional da AIDS) to be coordinated with a newly developed National Division for the Control of Sexually Transmitted Diseases and SIDA-AIDS within the Ministry of Health. A five-year plan was eventually developed, aimed at directing Brazil's response to the AIDS crisis during 1988-92. Yet, even with this newly formed institution, it wasn't until the end of 1986 that the Ministry of Health signed a further order mandating the compulsory notification of AIDS cases, thus making it possible to track the epidemic nationally. Still, many doctors do not comply with the order, instead following the wishes of their patients who fear having their illness documented (Parker, 1992).

Screening for the virus in the nation's blood supply began in May 1987, yet the lack of legal sanctions made it impossible to enforce adequate screening procedures in Brazil where blood has traditionally come from the poorest sectors of society with the least access to adequate medical care. Consequently, a significant number of the earlier cases of AIDS in Brazil are linked to blood transfusions--9.1 percent in 1990 (PAHO, 1994).

And while important advances have been made to regulate the blood industry, these efforts are often frustrated by a parallel (black) blood market.

In addition, IV drug use (while still lagging behind other modes of transmission) has recently become the most rapidly expanding mode of transmission. When compared to the situation in some other Latin American/Caribbean countries, IV drug use in Brazil is less clearly defined. For instance, IV drug use is high among some groups, such as commercial sex workers in major urban centers. Thus, there exists a complicated overlapping of multiple risk factors.

Given the magnitude of the HIV epidemic, AIDSCAP designated Brazil as one of the earliest priority countries. The program focuses on the states of Sao Paulo and Rio de Janeiro, where 62 percent of Brazil's AIDS cases have been reported (AIDSCAP/ Brazil Monthly Report, December 1994). Four high risk populations have been targeted: male and female commercial sex workers (CSWs), men who work away from home (e.g., migrant workers, long-distance truck drivers), men who have sex with men and people with STDs and their partners. In addition to these focus groups, AIDSCAP has also initiated a project to help street children with STD and HIV prevention programs. AIDSCAP works in collaboration with a number of governmental and nongovernmental organizations as well as the private sector in HIV prevention. Such collaborative projects include:

Interventions with men who have sex with men: In association with the Brazilian Interdisciplinary AIDS Association (ABIA) in Rio de Janeiro, and Grupo Pela Vidda in both Rio de Janeiro and Sao Paulo, this program is designed to reach men who have sex with men through outreach activities, peer education, and group dynamics. Its purpose is also to target the wider community with information "to destigmatize both homosexuality and AIDS."

Intervention for Commercial Sex Workers in Rio de Janeiro: This project is being implemented by the Institute for Religious Studies, an ecumenical organization involved in social and human rights issues. Activities include promotion of safe sex through peer education and outreach programs whereby CSWs act as health promotion advocates in the specific areas where they work.

STD Management in Rio de Janeiro and Sao Paulo: In conjunction with the Rio de Janeiro State Department of Health and the Institute for Religious Studies, AIDSCAP is working to improve STD diagnosis and treatment. AIDSCAP is also working the Brazilian Union Against Sexually Transmitted Diseases to improve STD management in Sao Paulo by training health care providers, strengthening laboratory services, developing educational materials and condom distribution systems, and establishing a management information system at STD clinics.

Condom Marketing: AIDSCAP supports DKT do Brazil, an affiliate of Population Services International to expand the marketing of condoms to outlets near other AIDSCAP sub projects in Rio, Santos, and Sao Paulo.

Support to the Ministry of Health: AIDSCAP provides technical assistance (private sector leveraging, condom programming, and surveillance) to the Ministry of Health in the logistical management of HIV/AIDS prevention in Brasilia, Sao Paulo, and Rio de Janeiro.

Low Income Youth: AIDSCAP collaborates with Childhope, a U.S.-based private voluntary organization in conjunction with the Rio de Janeiro State University Adolescent Clinic to promote educational activities for safer sex practices among youths from low income areas and encourage them to seek STD treatment.

Behavioral Research Cohort Study: AIDSCAP has a subproject with the Center for AIDS Prevention Studies to implement two research activities which began 1993: 1) a controlled intervention trial with lower-class young adults in Sao Paulo, in collaboration with the University of Sao Paulo; and 2) a study of the sexual behavior of male port workers and their interaction with CSWs, in collaboration with the Santo Health Department and the Santos Port Authority.

In addition to the above sub-projects, AIDSCAP has been laying the groundwork for implementation of a wider prevention program with World Bank funding. The Brazilian Ministry of Health has signed a loan from the World Bank for US 160 million, dollars which together with the government of Brazil's matching contribution of 90 million dollars, brings the government's HIV/AIDS/STD Control Project to US 250 million dollars. Part of AIDSCAP's contribution to this project has been to develop model programs which can be replicated throughout the country (AIDSCAP/Brazil, 1994).

IX. Haiti

AIDS was first recognized in Haiti in 1982. Since then, the number of reported cases, based upon 1993 data, has surpassed 5,000 (WHO/GPA, 1995). Epidemiological data for Haiti is considered quite inaccurate, however. Underreporting is estimated at 80 percent. Nevertheless, generally accepted projections estimate that ten percent of Haitians are HIV positive. In the United States, the comparable estimate is about one percent.

The sex ratio of reported AIDS cases is now 1:1 with a high prevalence of HIV in urban sex workers and STD patients, estimated at around 42 percent (AIDSCAP, 1994). Following the 1991 military coup that overthrew President Jean-Bertrand Aristide, the HIV/AIDS epidemic was quickly transformed into a nationwide disease: HIV-infected urban dwellers fled to the countryside in search of tranquility from the violence of the major cities. Infection rates were soon to rise in more remote villages and today urban and rural Haitians in the general population are believed to have an infection rate of eight and five percent respectively (AIDSCAP Annual, 1995). During the embargo, the Haitian Health Ministry virtually ceased combating AIDS, thereby severely restricted the ability of doctors and clinics to treat HIV-positive patients. Money became so tight that few Haitians were willing even to pay the bus fare to visit clinics for testing. Even after the ousting of the military government in 1994 and with the resumption of aid, there continues to be a high level of denial in Haiti surrounding HIV/AIDS. Angry at the rest of the world community that subscribes to the myth that AIDS was created in Haiti, many Haitians view HIV as a blameworthy disease and still refuse to discuss it (Robberson).

The AIDSCAP program for Haiti was redesigned in 1992 to compensate for the absence of a public sector or support from donor agencies (most suspended activities in Haiti following the 1991 military coup). The strategy now focuses on adolescents, sexually active men and women in the general population, and individuals symptomatic for AIDS, STDs and tuberculosis. The general implementation plan includes both public and private/non-governmental organizations.

The primary focus of AIDSCAP in Haiti has been in the urban and suburban areas. Yet, now that the epidemic has reached such a significant level in the countryside, AIDSCAP is giving more attention to these areas, reaching six out of nine health districts. Other agencies, such as CARE,

PAHO, and UNDP are also being encouraged to work in those areas not yet served by AIDSCAP.

In addition to establishing a condom social marketing program (67 percent of the geographical areas in Haiti now have access to condom sales outlets) USAID/AIDSCAP has also launched a program focusing on adolescents and women. With hopes for new opportunities in the public sector under the Aristide government as well as mobilization in the PVO/NGO community, AIDSCAP projects that many more people will at least be aware of the need to take personal action to prevent HIV infection. Yet, given the great periods of political instability in the 1980s in Haiti, the dire economic conditions and the continued high levels of denial, the USAID-funded HIV/AIDS prevention program in this country clearly faces many hurdles before it can be called "successful."

X. THE DOMINICAN REPUBLIC

The first AIDS cases in the Dominican Republic were reported in 1983; by August 1994, the National AIDS Control Program reported 2,536 AIDS cases. As is the case with many developing countries, underreporting is significant--estimated at 50-70 percent. The sex ratio for men to women has decreased from 7:1 to 2:1.

The first cases of AIDS were reported in homosexual and bisexual men. The epidemic quickly spread to commercial sex workers and their clients, and eventually reached the general population. In 1995, it is estimated that the Dominican Republican has more than 100,000 HIV positive individuals, with projections for as many as 300,000 HIV positive adults (about five percent of the population) by the year 2000 (WHO/GPA, 1995).

USAID/AIDSCAP describes a general lack of awareness among policy makers in government, the private tourist and commercial sectors, and among international donors regarding the seriousness of the epidemic, all leading to a confusing AIDS policy. There appears to be a hesitation among some in the private sector, especially those in the tourist industry, toward the full implementation of a comprehensive HIV/AIDS prevention program for fear of scaring away tourists. And while interest may be increasing for the development and implementation of a policy, the fact remains that the government lacks a comprehensive HIV/AIDS prevention program.

In light of this lack of planning on the part of government officials and the private sector and the obvious seriousness of the epidemic, AIDSCAP designated the Dominican Republic as one of its priority countries. Funding is under the broader USAID/ Dominican Republic Family Planning and Health Project. Strategic objectives, thus far, include: 1) raise awareness of HIV/AIDS/STDs to generate and sustain prevention interventions; 2) expand access of the general population to HIV/AIDS/STD prevention, and 3) build the capacity of local institutions to carry out HIV/AIDS/STD prevention. Target groups include people in workplaces, adolescents and young adults, family planning acceptors, sex workers and men who have sex with men (AIDSCAP, 1995).

AIDSCAP's goal is to strengthen the capacity of local organizations to integrate HIV/AIDS prevention activities into existing programs and services. Separately, USAID began the implementation of a seven-year Family Planning and Health Project in 1993. It is expected that AIDSCAP will work closely with this family planning project as well as with other national and international efforts, including a more efficient system of condom distribution, improvement in the quality of STD services and support for HIV surveillance data collection.

XI. JAMAICA

In Jamaica, the first reported cases of AIDS were in 1982, with the mode of transmission being primarily heterosexual. As of December 1994, there were 1,029 reported cases of AIDS in Jamaica, rather low in comparison with other Caribbean countries (PAHO, 1995). Nevertheless, the STD rates are significantly higher with one out of every 30 STD patients infected with HIV (AIDSCAP, 1994). Given the large tourism and commercial sex industry high levels of drug and alcohol use, substantial numbers of migrant workers, and high levels of STDs, USAID/AIDSCAP has designated Jamaica as a "priority country," suggesting that HIV could rapidly spread among the general population.

USAID began in 1988 with activities to address the growth of STDs in Jamaica and expected rise in HIV/AIDS. In 1992 the project was extended to include AIDSCAP. Stronger emphasis was placed on increasing access to condoms, with a particular focus on STD patients, commercial sex workers, men who have sex with men, adolescents, people with multiple sex partners, and those who are HIV positive. This program is integrated with Jamaica's National HIV/STD Control Program. Activities are implemented by both public and private sector agencies (e.g., public STD clinics, the Medical Association of Jamaica, the Jamaica Red Cross). Specific projects have included: The Jamaica AIDS Support project--targeting young men who have sex with men; The ACOSTRAD project--intervention for sex workers in Kingston and Montego Bay; and a media campaign (AIDSCAP, 1995).

XII. HONDURAS

Honduras has more recently been designated as a "priority country," given its high incidence of HIV/AIDS. By January 1, 1995, there were 4,145 reported cases of AIDS in Honduras (PAHO, 1995). The rate of HIV infection in Honduras is one of the highest in the region. The Honduran Ministry of Health estimates an HIV seroprevalence for people 15-49 years old at 4 percent in San Pedro Sula. Employed people comprise more than 50 percent of the cases. Again, women represent the group most at risk. It is estimated that women account for 70-80 percent of the workforce in the industrial park communities, which include many garment factories known as "maquiladoras" (Calderon, 1994).

In 1994, USAID/AIDSCAP, in conjunction with the Honduran Ministry of Health, developed a STD/AIDS prevention plan which forms the basis of HIV/AIDS prevention through 1996. Interventions target high risk groups: people in the work place, core groups (commercial sex workers and their clients and men who have sex with men), and the Garifuna population. The principle activities include supporting STD programs, providing technical services, developing subprojects for people in the workplace, developing seminars with the commercial industrial and religious sectors, and working with the Ministry of Health, donor agencies, and international organizations to assure the availability of a consistent supply of condoms.

XIII. ASSOCIATE COUNTRIES

In addition to the "priority countries," USAID, in conjunction with AIDSCAP, has a number of other smaller projects supporting HIV/AIDS prevention in the Latin American/Caribbean region. Such "subprojects" are meant to respond to requests for technical support (e.g., blood screening, STD case management) from already existing programs or to support pilot projects (e.g., condom promotion, education programs, public awareness campaigns, etc.). Targeted countries include Mexico, Ecuador, Bolivia, Colombia, Costa Rica, Nicaragua, and Guatemala.

XIII. CONCLUSIONS

The goal of USAID's HIV/AIDS prevention programs--stopping the spread of HIV--is realistically unattainable in the five-year project lifespan of AIDSCAP. Nevertheless, that does not mean that evaluation should not play a critical role within a wider strategic approach. AIDSCAP does have an Evaluation Unit to "define, measure, document, and disseminate findings related to effective interventions" (AIDSCAP, 1994). The difficulties in measurement of behaviors related to HIV prevention, however, are significant, especially when considering incomplete reporting, inaccurate diagnoses, uneven access to medical care and other variables.

Success stories are to be found. A review of STD/HIV prevention programs worldwide reveal large observed changes in sexual behavior and marked increases in condom use in a number of programs. Condom social marketing programs, for one, illustrate the successful use of marketing skills by the private sector in conjunction with HIV/AIDS/STD prevention programs.

Yet, if prevention programs do work, why does AIDS continue to spread so rapidly throughout the LA/C region and the rest of the developing world? Thus far, prevention programs supported by the USAID have not been sufficiently comprehensive, large or sustained to have a measurable impact on the epidemic. The most successful interventions have been small-scale and limited to selected communities. If AIDS prevention programs are to have a global affect, they will need to cover much larger portions of those populations at risk, for much longer periods of time. Unless health services are improved and educational programs more fully developed, it is unlikely that these programs, however well-meaning, will have much impact on the HIV/AIDS epidemic in the developing world.

It is even more unlikely that the funds will be forthcoming for the development of the necessary HIV/AIDS prevention programs. And without these additional resources, eventually both prevention and care will cost far more than is currently being allocated. WHO/GPA estimates that well-designed prevention programs in all developing countries would cost about 2.5 billion dollars a year. By the year 2000, this would save some 10 million lives and 90 billion dollars in prevention and care (WHO/GPA, 1995).

Unfortunately, the future looks bleak, especially for the LA/C and the rest of the developing world. Few of the funds now spent on the global AIDS programs are devoted to the developing world, where 90 percent of the AIDS cases will be by the year 2000. This situation is unlikely to change in the near future until the industrialized world can be convinced that it is in their interest otherwise to significantly change spending priorities. And although the United States' 120 million dollar annual program accounts for roughly 50 percent of all AIDS prevention assistance to developing nations, this too may change with the political tide on Capitol Hill. Speaking before House Appropriations Committee, Rep. Jim McDermott expressed the concern of many who make spending decisions in Washington during these times of close fiscal scrutiny:

> ...I am convinced we need to rethink our strategy. We need to reevaluate the effectiveness of our delivery system, and I think we need to redefine what we think our dollars can really accomplish, because, in my opinion... our efforts have failed to deliver down to the community level the tools and the programs to fight this epidemic. There are a limited number of success stories, but they are becoming less and less relevant as the epidemic continues its rather relentless march from country to country (U.S. Congress, 1994).

While it is true that USAID has not had a long history of dealing with medical epidemics, nor trying to change people's personal behavior when it comes to sexual contact, the fact remains that the HIV/AIDS epidemic in the Latin American/Caribbean region and elsewhere in the developing world is going to have an increasing impact on United States foreign policy. Thus, whether funds should continue to be primarily directed for HIV/AIDS prevention programs through USAID or whether other programs would be more appropriate (United Nations programs, WHO/GPA, NGOs, etc.), the fact remains that only through financial resources will this epidemic be stemmed. Playing ostrich will not protect the United States from this global reality. Without increased resources, development efforts thus far financed by the United States in the LA/C region and elsewhere will soon experience dramatic reversals. This is not in the United States best foreign policy interest.

As Congress moves to cut foreign aid and overhaul the Agency for International Development, evidence points to the fact that Americans are not nearly as generous as some would think. It is a myth that the United States is a very generous nation; the percentage that the United States spends on foreign aid is the lowest for the industrialized countries. In fact, the number has been declining for years. The United States devotes 0.15 percent of its GDP to foreign aid, approximately 44 dollars of the taxes paid annually by an average American family. In Denmark, the equivalent is 900 dollars (Crossette). Whether or not the foreign aid that the United States does give is "going down a rat hole," (referring to a comment by Senator Jesse Helms, Chair of the Senate Foreign Relations Committee) is certainly a worthwhile debate. It was perhaps much easier to measure this in terms of foreign policy goals during the Cold War when aid was given to the Latin American/Caribbean region to contain communism and its success was measured accordingly. This included development aid. In the post-Cold War era, however, the same countries that were once deemed vital for United States national security may now be deemed "rat holes." Thus, measuring the success of development aid, including HIV/AIDS prevention, is going to require an entirely new set of rationales and values in this post-Cold War world where epidemics like HIV/AIDS know no borders.

REFERENCES

AIDSCAP, *Quarterly Country Update*, (Mimeographed document, December 1993).

AIDSCAP, *Latin America and the Caribbean: 1994* (Mimeographed document, 1995).

AIDSCAP, *1994 Annual Report,* (Mimeographed document, 1995).

Calderon, M. Ricardo, et al., "Detailed Implementation Plan of Assistance for the National STD/AIDS Prevention and Control Program in Honduras: A Report to the U.S. Agency for International Development, Tegucigalpa," (Mimeographed document, May 1994).

Cardenas-Elizalde, M.R., "Migration and AIDS in Mexico," *Salud Publica de Mexico,* 1988, 30(4), 613-18.

Crossette, Barbara, "U.S. Foreign Aid Budget: Quick, How Much? Wrong," *New York Times,* February 27, 1994.

Golden, Tim, "AIDS is Following Mexican Migrant Workers Back Across the U.S. Border," *The New York Times,* March 8, 1992.

Greenhouse, Steven, "Despite Pressure, Christopher Brings No Ax to Foreign Aid," *The New York Times,* February 7, 1995.

Hamilton, Kimberly, "The HIV and AIDS Pandemic as a Foreign Policy Concern," *The Washington Quarterly,* Winter 1994, 17(1).

Mann, Jonathan et al., *AIDS in the World: A Global Report,* (Cambridge: Harvard University Press, 1992).

Mathews, Jessica, "The Assault on AID," (editorial) *The Washington Post,* February 28, 1995.

Pan American Health Organization, *AIDS: Profile of an Epidemic,* (Washington, D.C.: Pan American Health Organization, 1989).

Pan American Health Organization (PAHO), "AIDS Surveillance in the Americas: Quarterly Report," (Washington, 1995).

Panos Institute, *AIDS and the Third World,* (Philadelphia: New Society Publishers, 1989).

Parker, Richard G., et al., *A AIDS No Brazil,* (Rio de Janeiro: ABIA, 1994).

Parker, Richard G., "AIDS Education and Health Promotion in Brazil: Lessons from the Past and Prospects for the Future," in *AIDS Prevention Through Education: A World View,* Jaime Sepulveda et al., eds., (New York: Oxford University Press, 1992).

Robberson, Tod, "Battling AIDS in Haiti," *The Washington Post,* November 6, 1994.

Roitstein, Florencia and Julie Becker, "Reaching Women in Latin America and the Caribbean: An Integrated Approach to Safer Sex," (Paper presented at the Tenth International Conference on AIDS, Yokohoma, Japan, 1994).

Rondinelli, Dennis A., "American Foreign Aid Policy in the Post-Cold War Era," in *Post-Cold War Policy: The International Context*, William Crotty, ed., (Chicago: Nelson-Hall, 1995).

United States Agency for International Development, *A Report to Congress on the Program for Prevention and Control of HIV Infection*, (Washington, D.C., 1993).

United States Agency for International Development, *U.S. Agency for International Development Responds to AIDS*, (Mimeographed document, Washington, D.C., 1993).

United States Agency for International Development, *HIV/AIDS : The Evolution of the Pandemic, the Evolution of the Response*, (Washington, D.C., 1993).

United States Congress, House Committee on Appropriations, *Foreign operations, Export Financing, and Related Programs: Appropriations for 1995* 103rd. Congress, 2d. session, April 28, 1994.

United States Department of State, *The Global AIDS Disaster: Implications for the 1990s*, (Washington, D.C., 1992).

United States General Accounting Office, *Foreign Assistance Combatting HIV/AIDS in Developing Countries: Report to Congressional Requesters*, (GAO/NSIAD-92-244, 1992).

World Health Organization, Global Program on AIDS, "The Current Global Situation of the HIV/AIDS Pandemic," (Washington, D.C., 1995).

CULTURAL BARRIERS TO EFFECTIVE TRADE BETWEEN THE UNITED STATES AND LATIN AMERICA

Joanne Schmidt
Department of Foreign Languages
California State University, Bakersfield
9001 Stockdale Highway
Bakersfield, CA 93311

Janis Ruiz
Department of Finance and Accounting
California State University, Bakersfield
9001 Stockdale Highway
Bakersfield, CA 93311

Abstract—This chapter will address how trade has been inhibited by cultural differences between the United States and Latin America. While there are cultural differences between the Latin American nations themselves, no effort is made to discuss these country-specific characteristics. Instead, this paper focuses on the differences which pertain to all of Latin America vis-á-vis the United States. The chapter concludes with a discussion of how American businessmen have much less foreign language training and fewer experiences with other cultures than their Latin American counterparts. This lack of cultural awareness by American businessmen may be the biggest barrier to trade of all.

I. INTRODUCTION

With the end of the Cold War, ideological orientations which tended to inhibit commercial activity in Latin America have greatly diminished and trade of all kinds is being actively promoted. After nearly 30 years of aggressively pursuing import substitution through tariff protection, Latin American nations are beginning to lower their protective tariffs and other barriers to effective trade with the United States. Latin American nations such as Chile, Mexico, Peru, and Argentina have now decided that the growth of foreign trade is beneficial to their nations and is to be encouraged. The United States has affirmatively responded to this desire for an increase in international trade with the passage of the North American Free Trade Agreement (NAFTA) with Canada and Mexico and the passage of various other free trade agreements with nations such as Chile.

Many see this process as part of the evolution of a New World Order in which the world will no longer be aligned along Communist and non-Communist lines. Ideological barriers to trade are falling. With the end of the Cold War, the United States no longer views Latin American nations as either pro-Communist ("foes") or anti-Communist ("friends"). Business opportunities are increasingly being evaluated by all parties involved on their economic merits rather than on a project's ability to fit into a certain ideological agenda. Even Cuba is beginning to loosen trade and currency restrictions. As a result, investors from nations such as Canada, Spain, France and Japan are beginning to make substantial investments in the island's economy.[1]

Even if all economic and ideological barriers to trade between the United States and Latin America were abolished, significant cultural barriers to effective commercial intercourse would continue to exist. It is a fact that the "rules of business communication shift with each country" and that in "any international business exchange, it is advisable to learn as much about the other culture as possible."[2] The purpose of this chapter is to discuss how these cultural differences impede the growth and further development of trade between the United States and Latin America.

II. Language

The first and most obvious cultural barrier to trade is language. The predominant language of the United States is English, while the Latin Americans speak primarily Spanish or Portuguese.

---

1. See Lee-Faulkner (1995) for an excellent discussion of recent developments in the Cuban economy.
2. Victor, (1992) pp. 2 and 3.

This language barrier is partially overcome by the fact that many Latin American businessmen[3] speak at least some English -- they have to. English is currently the *lingua franca* of the business and technical world. According to *The Story of English* (McCrum, et al. 1992):

> Today, English is currently used by at least 750 million people, and barely half of those speak it as a mother tongue. Some estimates have put that figure closer to 1 billion. Whatever the total, English at the end of the twentieth century is more widely scattered, more widely spoken and written, than any other language has ever been. It has become *the* language of the planet, the first truly global language (p. 1).[4]

English is the world's most studied second language. Three-fourths of the world's mail, telexes and cables are in English. To be able to participate effectively in the international business arena, one must be able to communicate in English.

In contrast, most American businessmen are not fluent in any foreign language. In general, public schools in the United States do not begin teaching their students a foreign language until high school - a time which many language acquisition experts feel is too late for the optimal assimilation of a new language.[5] In 1993, only 17 percent of public elementary schools offered any form of language instruction, and barely one-third of all high school students take any foreign language. Only 8 percent of U.S. colleges and universities require a foreign language for admission while only 9 percent require one for graduation. Those students who do study a foreign language usually do so for only one or two years and rarely attain any realistic level of proficiency.[6] In 1983, over a decade before the passage of NAFTA, U.S. Department of Education wrote a report on the role of foreign language training and international trade which stated:

> Because of our lack of competence in foreign languages, American business stands to loose markets to foreign competition (U.S. Department of Education, 1983).

---

3. For the sake of editorial simplicity, a *businessman* could be either male *or* female.
4. McCrum, Cran, and MacNeil (1992) p. 2.
5. See Snow and Hoefnagel-Hohle (1982) and Lenneberg (1967) for studies that indicate that foreign language acquisition is best completed by the onset of puberty.
6. Johnson (1994) p. 2.

Few business schools accredited by the American Association of Collegiate Schools of Business require that their graduates be fluent in a foreign language.[7] Most do not require any foreign language training at all.[8] In contrast, most Latin Americans begin to learn English as a second language in elementary school.[9] While it is true that English as a second language is universally the second language studied in Latin American schools, Americans should not discount the importance of second language learning in the U.S.:

> Americans .... who speak only English, find the world-wide diffusion of English a great convenience--which it is--but it is also a snare and delusion, leading most Americans to believe that second language mastery is unnecessary. Indeed, language is a perfect metaphor for culture. (Doyle, 1994)

Through language study, cultural literacy is acquired and should be an important priority for American businessmen doing business in Latin America.

Even if the Latin American trading partner of a monolingual American is fluent in English, this unilateral knowledge impedes effective trade in many subtle ways. First and foremost, the necessity of having all documents and discussions translated into English causes the monolingual American to be totally dependent upon whoever is translating to properly portray and interpret many of the subtler nuances of any business deal. Many linguistic misunderstanding may result from American overreliance on translators who may lack technical expertise pertinent to business.

---

7. One of the few schools that does require its graduates to study a foreign language is the American Graduate School of International Management in Arizona. However, this program is only available at the MBA level and is dedicated to training competent internationally oriented businessmen.

8. See Schmidt and Ruiz (1992) for a list of the American Association of Collegiate Schools of Business that do require foreign language training of their graduates.

9. According to the last Joint National Committee for Languages Fact Sheet on Languages in the U.S. some significant change is occurring at the elementary school level between the years 1992 and 1993 "elementary school foreign language programs are the fastest growing area of language instruction. This is fortunate, since very early exposure to foreign languages will likely prove to be a decisive factor in future competitiveness." See American Association of Teachers of French, *National Bulletin*, p. 5.

General Motors Corporation had to learn the importance of foreign language proficiency the hard way. During the 1960s General Motors encountered difficulty marketing its Chevrolet Nova model in Mexico. Chevrolet executives were unaware that "no va" means "it doesn't go", in Spanish, until the Nova's marketing campaign was well under way. None of the translators involved in the project knew enough about the overall business goals of Chevrolet to pick up on the problem and warn company officials about the inappropriateness of using the name Nova in a Spanish speaking nation. Only when "No Va" was renamed the "Caribe" (the Carribean) was General Motors able to salvage its marketing campaign. Similar problems were also encountered by General Motors when the phrase "Body by Fisher" was mistranslated as "Corpse by Fisher." These examples clearly demonstrate the importance of being proficient in the language of your trading partner. As Paul Simon once stated, "...you can buy in any language, but sell only in the language of your customers," Simon (1987).

III. CULTURAL HERITAGE AND COMMUNICATION STYLE

Even if both trading partners are fluent in each others' language, there can still be problems with communication. Many of these problems center around a lack of awareness of many American businessmen of the cultural differences between nations. According to Douglas Doyle in *The Innocents at Home*:

> As a general rule, Americans know little and care less about foreign languages and cultures. Superpower and world cultural arbiter, America remains relentlessly provincial, Doyle (1994).

While few U.S. students study a foreign language, even fewer of these students obtain an in-depth awareness of a foreign culture by studying abroad. Less than .5 percent of all U.S. students enrolled at the baccalaureate level in any given year are studying abroad, and business majors account for only about 11 percent of this very small .5 percent figure. Nearly 80 percent of all students studying abroad do so in Europe, while only 9 percent study in Latin America (Johnson, 1994, p. 1).

In contrast, the last two Presidents of Mexico received their baccalaureate degrees from U.S. universities as well as their graduate degrees. The current President of Ecuador was born and spent part of his life in Boston, Massachusetts. Historically, Texas summer camp programs for children find that approximately 10 percent of their campers are from wealthy families in Mexico who wish their children to improve their English and become familiar with American ways.[10]

Study abroad patterns, both coming and going, reveal an asymmetry that is startling: big trade imbalances inversely correlate with study abroad. Americans are less likely to study in the country with a trade surplus, and that country's nationals are more likely to be studying in the U.S (Doyle, 1994).

There are many ways a lack of knowledge about the interrelationships between a trading partner's language and culture can impede successful business relationships. Patterns of conversation will vary from culture to culture. This is not just a function of differences in grammar and syntax between the foreign languages. The Latin Americans use formal titles such as "ingeniero" (engineer) and "economista" (economist) in all correspondence and formal business situations. Not to use the title "ingeniero" in business correspondence to an engineer would be considered an insult in Latin America. Furthermore, gestures, in and of themselves, are culture-specific and may create great misunderstandings or even block otherwise destined-to-be-successful business deals with Latin America.

Latin American gestures across 18 different countries are quite different from those in the United States. Central and South Americans initiate all business greetings and introductions with a warm handshake sometimes "accompanied by a light touch on the forearm or elbow" (Axtell, 1991). These gestures are especially appropriate in Argentina, Brazil, Ecuador, Colombia and El Salvador. Other Latin American countries such as Bolivia, Chile, Mexico, Venezuela, and Peru add pats on the back to the traditional handshake as business associates become closer friends. Casual physical contact among men is considered an accepted social interaction for men in Latin America; however, this type of physical contact with

---

10. This information is based upon a survey of 10 summer camp programs in the Hill Country of Texas for the summers of 1993-1995.

women business associates is considered taboo, "men should be careful about public physical contact with women" (Axtell, 1991).

In addition, letters and business conversations in Spanish usually begin with extensive pleasantries and inquiries about the health and welfare of the business associate. This type of opening paragraph would seem inappropriate in an American business environment. Due to their lack of understanding of the importance of opening pleasantries and respect for titles in the Latin American business environment, the American businessman is often stereotyped by Latin Americans as being cold and tactless. Even if every aspect of a standard American style business letter had been correctly translated into Spanish, the letter may be ineffective in Latin America if a "cultural translation" had not been performed as well.

IV. CULTURAL HERITAGE AND ADMINISTRATIVE STRUCTURES

Latin American and U.S. businessmen work in very different legal and socio-economic environments. The Latin American business environment is, in general, more bureaucratic and legalistic than the American business environment. Foreign currency controls and restrictions on foreign ownership are all constraints that many Latin American businessmen must deal with that American businessmen have never encountered.

Almost all of Latin America inherited the Iberian colonial legacy of large bureaucratic governments involved in essentially all aspects of human activity. Local colonial governments of royal representatives, town officials, and priests were centers of political power with almost limitless authority. The intimate, complex and continuous control by Spanish and Portuguese governmental authorities is well documented throughout Latin America.[11] This is very different from the American experience of a somewhat looser and less complex control by colonial Britain.

Unlike the United States, Latin America also has a long tradition of large, very centralized bureacratic structures empowered and carefully regulated by one individual such as the King or in the post-colonial period, a charismatic political leader. From the time of King Ferdinand and

---

11. Stein and Stein (1970) present an excellent summary of the role of government in the economic development of colonial Latin America.

Queen Isabella of Spain, political appointments in Latin American governments were seen as economic rewards for political favorites. Unlike the American experience, almost all land ownership in Latin America was established through very large land grants by the crown to favored individuals. These grants usually included both economic control of the land and absolute political control of the indigenous populations living in the area.

With the Latin American history of extensive bureacracy, centralization of power, and political patronage comes what many individuals only familiar with American administrative traditions would call "corruption." In Latin America, bureacracies still tend to be built on the basis of patronage and not as a result of merit. Similar to the old colonial land grants, it is expected that a given department or ministry will be run as the personal fiefdom of the director or minister. Informal "contacts" and "middlemen" are an integral part of this system.

While "contacts" and "middlemen" are not unknown among Washington lobbyists, there is not such a longstanding tradition which institutionalizes the use of personal influence in the United States. For example, the Foreign Corrupt Practices Act of the United States is often poorly understood in Latin America. There is a long tradition of "contacts" and "middle-men" in Latin America who help businesses to negotiate various hurdles imposed by government bureaucracies. What may be considered an agent's "fee" in Latin America could be considered a "bribe" in the United States.

Even fairly large and sophisticated U.S. based multinational corporations do not always completely understand the differences in Latin American and United States administative structures and traditions. In December of 1994, J.C. Penney had to delay the opening of its first two stores in Mexico until May of 1995 because the corporation did not adequately anticipate the complexity of the paperwork required to open the stores. Mr. Hand Rusman of J.C. Penney was quoted as stating,

> There is cumbersome paperwork and there are official negotiations taking place in order to alleviate that paperwork. (J.C. Penney, 1994)

The negotiations described by Rusman centered around the development of a less cumbersome process of certifying merchandise under a complex system of Mexican rules for the certification of a good's country of origin--a problem which Penney had not anticipated as such complex rules simply do not exist in the United States.

This tradition of large, centralized bureacracies based upon personal contacts extends through all aspects of Latin American life. Latin American corporations rely on family ties and personal contacts just as much as the governmental bureacracies. In all aspects of Latin American business, *who* you know is absolutely essential in order to be able to perform *what* you know in a particular business context. If an American businessmen is to succeed in Latin America he must understand these differences in administrative traditions.

V. CULTURAL HERITAGE AND BUSINESS NEGOTIATIONS

No type of business procedure is more critical than the negotiation of a business deal. It involves a subtle give and take in which excellent communication skills and the promotion of mutual understanding are paramount. It involves an understanding by both sides of where each party is coming from and the constraints and limitations each party is working under.

Business negotiations always involve a complex interplay between the negotiating parties. Numerous stories exist of potential deals "gone sour" due to the cultural differences of the people involved. A Latin American negotiator brings his or her own unique heritage to the negotiating table. An American negotiator will most likely approach the same issues from a completely different perspective.

For example, Americans tend to take pride in being "straight talkers" and are often very blunt. In general, Latin Americans place a great value on courtesy an do not normally like to use blunt language. A good example of these differences is a comparison of a typical political speech in the United States versus one in Latin America. The Latin American speech will be longer, more complex in its overall structure and be more elaborate and "flowery" in the presentation. These different communication styles must be understood by all parties if negotiations between them are to succeed.

American and Latin American businessmen will also be negotiating various issues from a very different historical perspective. All of Latin

America is very sensitive to the fact the U.S. is by far the dominant economic and military power in the Western Hemisphere. As a result of a long history of "gunboat diplomacy" by the U.S., there is substantial fear and resentment by Latin America of the power and wealth of their neighbor to the north.

Numerous examples exist of this resentment and/or fear. Venezuelans are quick to point out to Americans that U.S. oil companies were both the midwives for the birth of several of Venezuela's more controversial governments and the authors of the first Venezuelan laws on hydrocarbon production. In this context, it is not surprising that the Organization of Petroleum Exporting Countries (O.P.E.C.) was first proposed by a Harvard-educated Venezuelan, Juan Pablo Perez Alfonso, as a result of his anger over interference by American oil companies in the Venezuelan economy.

Mexican school children are taught with great pride about the nationalization of American oil fields by President Cardenas in the 1938. The feeling of nationalistic pride and the resentment of the hegemony of the U.S. are difficult for Americans to comprehend. And yet, they impact every business deal between the U.S. and its Latin American neighbors.

VI. OVERALL CULTURAL DIFFERENCES

Finally, there are overall cultural differences in the cultures of the U.S. and the L.A. trading partners which impede trade. American housewives prefer larger package sizes in consumer products. They tend to shop fewer times a week and bring their purchases home in automobiles. In contrast, many Latin American housewives tend to shop for food and consumer products daily. They tend to buy in smaller quantities as they usually carry their purchases home by foot or on public transportation.

WalMart has had substantial difficulty in adjusting its product lines in Mexico away from jumbo "economy size" packaging so popular in the U.S. to smaller quantities. Similarly, Mexican exporters have had to adjust to the larger sizes and fancier packages demanded by the American consumer.

VII. CONCLUSION

With the end of the Cold War and a diminished emphasis on trade sanctions and subsidies as ideological weapons, significant new trade opportunities exist for commerce between the United States and Latin America. With improvements in telecommunications and transportation, more and more linkages are forming between what were once separate and distinct economic systems. This very increase in global economic integration is promoting what Buell (1994) refers to as the "circulation of differences" among cultures. There are more types of barriers to trade than just sanctions and tariffs. In order for international trade to grow and develop in the New World Order, cross-cultural barriers as well as ideological and economic barriers to trade have to be overcome.

How can these cross-cultural barriers be lowered more easily in the future? The answer probably lies in improved education. Unfortunately, this type of cross-cultural education is sadly lacking in the average American businessman. Within business education itself, foreign language training is often disregarded and professional translators are remunerated at low fee levels. Part of this egregious disregard for professionals in the linguistic fields and the uninformed manner in which their expertise is treated is the fault of business authors. For example, "the issue of the language barrier... is given only the briefest of treatments in the broad spectrum of English-language literature on international business and management." (Holden, 1987)

The major roadblocks to sensitizing American businessmen to the cultures of Latin America are found in the "old corporate culture," which still determines and dominates the direction and practices of U.S. and international business. This "old corporate culture" (Lambert, 1990) has created an environment that places little value on foreign language training for business graduates. It also has led to downsizing in overseas assignments over the last ten years for U.S. businessmen. Few rewards are given towards promotion and extra pay for U.S. businessmen who have sought international business training:

Foreign language competence in the business world seems like good teaching in research universities: everyone is in favor of it, but detecting its influence on promotion, pay, or other dividends of the reward structure is difficult" (Lambert, 1990).

The currently evolving New World Order has the ability to create an increased demand for business school graduates in the United States who do have international business training. The "old corporate culture" can be changed by promoting and fully utilizing those graduates who have acquired advanced levels of proficiency in foreign languages and are trained to operate in multicultural business environments. These graduates may be the beginning of a new corporate culture that recognizes the ideological and structural changes currently taking place in the global economy and places a value upon a businessman's ability to effectively operate in a multicultural business environment.

In addition, the population of the United States includes approximately 13 million Mexican-Americans and several million immigrants from other Latin American countries. By definition, these people are well-versed in cross-cultural issues and often possess excellent language skills appropriate for international business between the United States and Latin America. Historically the "old corporate culture" has not recognized the value of these cross-cultural and foreign language skills. These people represent a valuable untapped national resource for American businesses.

Will a new corporate culture evolve in United States businesses which fully utilitizes the language and cross-cultural skills of the millions of people currently residing in the United States? Most likely the answer is "yes." With the impact of the New World Order and the related reduction of economic barriers to international trade, only businesses capable of adapting to these new operating conditions will survive. The "old corporate culture" will have to pluralize and new types of entrepreneurs will have to develop in a very pragmatic reaction to the new economic environment.

United States citizens capable of speaking Spanish and/or with international business training are currently being sought out by some United States businesses in an effort to take advantage of the business opportunities offered by the North American Free Trade Agreement. These businesses are seeking employees which will help them fully take advantage of the economic opportunities which await them in Latin America.

In conclusion, cultural barriers to effective trade with Latin America will have to crumble as businesses that are incapable of adapting to the New World Order simply will not survive. Unless United States corporations employ businessmen with appropriate skills in foreign languages and cross-cultural issues, Americans are jeopardizing their ability to effectively compete in the integrated global economy which is evolving with the end of the Cold War and the rise of a New World Order.

REFERENCES

American Association of Teachers of French, *National Bulletin*, November 1994, 20(2), p. 5.

Axtell, Roger E., *The Do's and Taboos of International Trade*, (New York: John Wiley & Sons, Inc., 1994).

Axtell, Roger E., *Gestures: The Do's and Taboos of Body Language Around the World*, (New York: John Wiley & Sons, Inc., 1991).

Buell, Frederick, *National Culture and the New Global System*, (Baltimore: John Hopkins Press, 1994).

Doyle, Denis P., *Innocents at Home: American Students and Overseas Study*, (Washington, D.C.: American Institute for Foreign Study Foundation, July 1994), pp. 1-8.

Holden, Nigel, "The Treatment of Language and Linguistic Issues in the Current English-Language International Management Literature," *Multilingua: Journal of Interlanguage Communication*, 1987, 6(3), 233-246.

"J. C. Penney Delays Mexico Openings," *The Bakersfield Californian*, December 31, 1994, p. a14.

Johnson, Joseph, Jr., "Internationalizing U.S. Higher Education," *The Key Reporter*, Summer, 1994, pp. 2-4.

Kras, Eva S., *Management in Two Cultures: Bridging the gap between U.S. and Mexican managers*, (Maine: Intercultural Press, 1989).

Lambert, Richard, "Foreign Language Use Among International Business Graduates," *The Annals: American Academy of Political and Social Science*, 1990, 511, 47-59.

Lee-Faulkner, Roy, "Cuba-Trick or Treat? Crisis or Opportunity before the Millennium," *Proceedings: International Business Association Meeting*, (Acapulco, Mexico, 1995).

McCrum, Robert, William Cran, and Robert MacNeil, *The Story of English*, (New York: Penguin Books, 1992).

Simon, Paul, *Tongue-Tied American*, (New York: Continuum Publishing Corporation, 1987).

Stein, S. and B. Stein, *The Colonial Heritage of Latin America*, (New York: Oxford University Press, 1970).

Storti, Craig, *The Art of Crossing Cultures*, (Yarmouth, Main: Intercultural Press, 1990).

Victor, David, *International Business Communication*, (New York: Harper Collins Publishers, Inc., 1992).

RELATIONS AMONG NEIGHBORING NATIONS IN SOUTH AMERICA

Freeman J. Wright
Department of Political Science
California, State University, Fresno
Fresno, CA 93740

Abstract—Bordering South American nations have become more important to one another than at any time in history. Although there are variations by nation and type of interaction, and the United States remains powerful in international economics, neighborly influence in South America merits description, analysis, and perspective. This is determined through study of interactions in border disputes, migration, trade, and the non-trade economic areas of drug-trafficking, joint development projects, and cross-national investment. By way of perspective, the conclusion considers the role of the United States in each area.

South America's bordering nations are more important to each other than at any time in history. Three long-standing disputes over territory remain unresolved and one has been recently settled. Migration from bordering nations grew substantially from the 1960s until the 1980s, especially to Argentina and Venezuela. More recently, these flows have ebbed, but others have increased. Lowered tariffs have greatly increased trade and economic integration among some neighbors. Narcotics have caused problems between several bordering nations, but drugs also have led to joint control efforts. Finally, an array of new non-trade economic activities have brought South American neighbors closer together.

Discussion of these topics will reveal that, by 1990, key external influences on South American nations clearly included those from neighbors, not just those from the United States. By 1995, this point had become even more obvious.

I. TERRITORIAL DISPUTES

The four main modern territorial disputes in South America have involved Ecuador and Peru; Chile, Bolivia and Peru; Venezuela and Colombia, and Argentina and Chile -- the only one to be resolved. Unsettled disputes adversely affect binational relations, while the settled conflict has improved them.

Ecuador-Peru. As measured by public passions, impact on other national policies, and recurring violence, the most serious territorial dispute in South America is between Ecuador and Peru. Through the 1942 protocol of Río de Janeiro, Ecuador lost over half its territory after Peru used force to acquire land that, although wild and sparsely populated, has abundant resources.

Both nations trace legal claims through the colonial, early republican, and modern eras.[1] In 1951, Ecuador renounced any boundary in the area until Peru recognized its right to an Amazonic outlet; and, in 1960, it declared the 1942 protocol null and void.

While Peru regards the case as closed, Ecuador has developed a "formal iconography" of the lost territory to keep national passions intense and will not let the matter rest. National maps show pre-1942 Ecuador, official slogans refer to Ecuador as an Amazonic nation, and school curricula include large sections which present Ecuador's side of the dispute (Elbow, 1995). Ecuador unsuccessfully tried to tie Amazonic demands to the first Andean Pact and to the multinational Amazon Basin Treaty of 1978. Subsequent tensions led to fighting in 1981 and again in January 1995.

---

1. The Ecuadorean position on the dispute is argued in scores of treatises, including Valencia Rodriguez (1988); for a presentation of the Peruvian side in English, see Gorman (1982).

The 1995 conflict centered around three military bases established by Ecuador in an area claimed by both countries, but, of course, officially part of Peru. In March, Ecuadorean forces held on to one of the three bases; both nations were claiming control of the other two with Peru showing the most evidence, including a film of President Alberto Fujimoro raising the Peruvian flag at them. Fujimoro ordered fighting restricted to the border region, while Ecuadorean president Sixto Durán spoke of the skirmishes as the first stage of the war. Most analysts agreed that if diplomacy failed, more fighting would be likely (Lara, 1995).

Chile-Bolivia-Peru. Resentment over territory lost through war also explains persistent Bolivian efforts to regain an outlet to the sea lost to Chile in the War of the Pacific (1879-1883). A 1929 treaty between Chile and Peru reduced tensions by returning to Peru some land lost to Chile in the same war but complicated matters by giving Peru a veto over future Chilean-Bolivian accords.

In 1976, Chilean president Augusto Pinochet offered Bolivia an exchange of roughly 2,000 square kilometers across Chile's extreme north for a similarly-sized piece of inland Bolivia. Bolivian president Hugo Banzer first accepted the plan but reconsidered. Peru vetoed it and made a counterproposal unacceptable to Pinochet. Banzer severed relations with Chile (Whelan, 1989: 677-78).

In 1994, Bolivia continued to pursue Pacific access, while Peru was more conciliatory. The Bolivian military petitioned President Gonzalo Sanchez de Lozada to make approval of a Bolivia-to-Chile gas pipeline dependent on the outlet (*La Epoca* [Santiago], November 9, 1994: 12). After noting that he had withdrawn "entire battalions" from the border in part to reverse the arms race "which has caused so much damage to our two nations," Peruvian president Alberto Fujimori agreed with his Chilean counterpart, Eduardo Frei, to pursue an economic cooperation pact (BBC, 1994).

Colombia-Venezuela. Colombia seeks a larger share of the Gulf of Venezuela and the Monjes Archipelago, a group of Caribbean islets close to the gulf's mouth. The gulf links the Caribbean Sea with Venezuela's Lake Maracaibo. Oil formations below the lake are thought to extend to the gulf.

This dispute also has a lengthy, complex history of competing claims and international accords (Area and Nieschulz de Stockhausen, 1984). A 1941 treaty gave the gulf's western shore to Venezuela, which has claimed and controlled most of the gulf. Colombia seeks about two-thirds of the gulf.

Sporadic negotiations since the early 1960s have led to nothing concrete. Venezuelans "view the conflict as being between Colombian avarice and Venezuelan historical rights" (George, 1988-89: 155), and they are well-served by the status quo. Colombia's commitment to non-violent conflict resolution is reinforced by such pragmatic factors as coping with *narcoguerrillas*. Presidents Ernesto Samper of Colombia and Rafael Caldera of Venezuela met in 1994 to discuss binational questions, but the gulf issue was overshadowed by commitments to closer economic relations and to coping with a spreading "undeclared war" between the drug-financed Colombian *Frente de Liberacion Nacional* and official Venezuelan forces (*La Epoca* [Santiago] November 7, 1994: A2).

Argentina-Chile. The major event in modern Argentine-Chilean relations was the 1984 settlement of the Beagle Channel Island dispute, which also initiated successful efforts to resolve dozens of less volatile border questions.

The Beagle Channel Island dispute followed Argentina's rejection of a 1977 International Court of Justice ruling which awarded Chile three islands.[2] When a binational commission could not reach an accord, tensions increased. Argentine president Raul Alfonsín finally secured plebiscital and Congressional support for a Papal arrangement which also gave the three islands to Chile but reduced the surrounding maritime limit.

In 1991, presidents Carlos Menem of Argentina and Patricio Alywin of Chile signed twenty-two supplementary accords. By 1994, all but two matters were settled. In October, President Eduardo Frei of Chile endorsed a Latin American Arbitration Tribunal award giving Argentina sovereignty over the Laguna del Desierto. An accord on the last question, continental ice fields, was before both national legislatures (*La Epoca* [Santiago] October 25, 1994: 11).

Territorial Disputes in Perspective. Social Science research helps explain the durability of territorial disputes. A geographer compared two in Africa and Asia with the one dividing Ecuador and Peru and concluded that territory is so often a source of conflict because "the state is fundamentally

---

2. For the Beagle Channel Island negotiations and their impact on Argentine politics, see Fraga (1985: 135-37) and Garrett (1985). For the background in international law, see F. V. (1977).

a place; its very existence and autonomy are rooted in territory," which lies "at the heart of national identity and cohesion" (Murphy, 1990: 531). A political scientist listed nine questions linking South American domestic politics and foreign policy. The issue of "sovereignty and territorial integrity" ranked second behind "regime surviveability" (Wiarda, 1990: 46).

The peacefully resolved Beagle Channel Island dispute has points in common with the Gulf of Venezuela issue. Both involve maritime territory as well as land; neither has an emotionally charged history of armed conquest; the rough military balance between Argentina and Chile was closer to the one between Colombia and Venezuela than to the imbalances which help permit Peru to disdain negotiations with Ecuador and Chile to do the same with Bolivia;[3] and economic interactions between both Chile and Argentina and Colombia and Venezuela are more important than those among the republics in the other two disputes.

The 1990s have offered scattered signs of improving relations between long-time South American rivals not in current territorial disputes. In Argentina, Brazil, and Chile, military expenditures dropped from $4.9 billion in 1985 to $3.7 billion in 1992. In 1993, Paraguayan president Juan Carlos Wasserman visited Bolivian Chaco War veterans in Santa Cruz. In 1994, Bolivian President Gonzalo Sanchez de Lozada came to Asunción to sign an agreement to repave the Trans-Chaco highway and to build a gas pipeline from Bolivia to Paraguay (Brooke 1994).

II. MIGRATION

Bordering-state migration to South America's two main receptor nations peaked about 1980, when over 1.2 million such migrants were in Argentina and Venezuela to make up about three percent of the population in each country. In the 1980s, movement from neighbors to these republics declined, but remained high. In recent years, Chile has replaced Paraguay as Argentina's main source of migrants; return migration from Venezuela to Colombia and from Argentina to Paraguay has grown; and many Colombians have moved to Ecuador. Cross-border migration affects the economies of both expulsing and receiving nations and influences public

---

3. For the numbers of armed forces, military aircraft, and naval vessels in the South American nations involved in territorial disputes, see Wilkie, Contreras, and Weber (1993: 373).

opinion in host nations. Economics causes most migration, but some is due to politics.

Migration from Neighboring Nations to Argentina. Migrants to Argentina from Paraguay, Bolivia, Chile, Uruguay, and Brazil grew from 314,000 in 1947 to 467,000 in 1960, 533,000 in 1970, and 734,000 in 1980. From 1960 to 1980, migrants in urban areas rose from 26 to 45 percent (Pellegrino, 1988: 57).

In 1980, 263,000 Paraguayan migrants made up the largest single national grouping; 62 percent lived in the city and province of Buenos Aires, and 32 percent in northeastern provinces. Roughly half of the 216,000 Chileans were located in Patagonia, with about one-fifth in Buenos Aires and its province. Of the 118,000 Bolivians, 46 percent resided in the Buenos Aires region, with most of the rest in the west and northwest. Four-fifths of the 114,000 Uruguayans lived in and around Buenos Aires. Well over half of the 49,050 Brazilians resided in the northeast, with nearly one-quarter in the city and province of Buenos Aires (Pellegrino, 1988: 59).

From 1980 through 1991, Argentina recorded 430,220 migrants, over 80 percent from bordering nations, including 139,772 Chileans, 79,300 Uruguayans, 65,210 Paraguayans, 59,295 Bolivians, and 7,483 Brazilians. The average annual number of these migrants for the first six years was 14,475; for the last six it was 19,602, though it fell to 8,720 in 1990 and 12,376 in 1991, reflecting a marked drop in Paraguayans. A 1984 decree gave legal status to 135,902 *indocumentados* (Instituto de Estadística y Censo [INDEC], 1993: 54-55). In 1990, 817,144 natives of bordering nations constituted most foreign-born Argentines and made up 2.6 percent of the national population (Instituto de Estadística y Censo [INDEC], 1991: 103). A 1992 decree gave legal status to over 200,000 *indocumentados*. Presidents from all six neighboring nations attended the signing ceremony in Mendoza (*El Mercurio* [Santiago], June 26, 1992: 1).

Migration from Colombia to Venezuela. Colombian-born residents of Venezuela rose from 102,312 in 1960 to 180,144 in 1970 and soared to 508,166 in 1980 when they replaced Europeans as the largest immigrant grouping (Bidegrain Griesing and López, 1987: 35). In 1980, nearly three of four Colombian migrants lived in (1) two border states, (2) the Federal District, which includes Caracas, or (3) the state immediately east of Caracas (Oficina Central de Estadística 1980: 76, 88-90). The highest density was in the border states of Táchira and Zulia, with most migrants in agricultural work and urban jobs in San Cristóbal and Maracaibo (Bidegrain Griesing and López, 1987: 78-80).

Venezuelan reaction to Colombian migration became adverse. A 1980 decree awarded amnesty to 266,795 *indocumentados* (92 percent of whom were Colombians) and recognized their manpower value, especially in agriculture (Bidegain Griesing and López, 1987: 17), but, in 1987, 2,156 Venezuelan pollees called for restrictive immigration policies. In response to the question, "which of the following would you prefer concerning illegal immigration into Venezuela," 63 percent opted for closing the border and ousting illegals, 31 percent chose deportation without border closure, and a mere 6 percent preferred an open border policy (Martz 1992: 132-33).

Of Venezuela's 1987 foreign-born population fifteen years and over, 377,655 were Colombian-born, a drop to 42.0 percent from the 47.7 percent of 1980 (Oficina Central de Estadística, 1987: 4). During the late 1980s, more Colombians still entered Venezuela than left it, but reverse flows of 1,987 and 46,200 marked 1990 and 1991 (Central Office of Statistics and Information, 1993: 2).

Migration from Colombia to Ecuador. In 1991, Colombian president César Gaviria and Ecuadorean president Rodrigo Borja discussed the fate of about 1,200 undocumented Colombians living just inside Ecuador in violation of a law restricting aliens from residing within fifty miles of the border. In keeping with the neighbors' good relations, the matter was resolved (*El Comercio*, [Quito] April 8, 1991: A-3).

These farmers formed a small portion of recent Colombian migrants. From 1982 to 1990, the Ecuadorean provinces nearest the border, Carchi and Imbabura, outgrew all other rural provinces, and Colombians moved to Quito in large numbers (Instituto de Estadística y Censo, [INEC] 1991: 44). Santo Domingo de los Colorados, a city between Quito and Guayaquil, holds so many Colombian migrants that many Ecuadoreans wryly call it Santo Domingo de los Colombianos.

In 1987, over 100,000 Colombians appear to have stayed in Ecuador through visa abuse. Only 15,634 official immigrants entered Ecuador and 16,638 departed, with Colombians constituting only 1,879 of the entrants and 1,779 of the departees. In contrast, of the 331,984 foreigners who entered Ecuador on non-immigrant visas, 151,394 were Colombians, while only 23,866 Colombian visa-holders departed (Instituto de Estadística y

Censo, [INEC] 1988: iv, 33). The 127,428 Colombians staying in Ecuador compared to 7,024 of the 180,590 visa entrants from other nations.

No research explaining the influx of Colombians was found. Conventional wisdom has it that some came to launder and invest drug money and others to escape prosecution, or live in a nation less polluted by drugs. Searching for low-level rural and urban jobs would also be a likely cause.

Political Migration. The migratory flow from Chile to Argentina suggests that expulsor-nation politics can influence emigration. In the 1960s, a democratic period in Chile, 36,800 Chileans were recorded as migrating to Argentina. The average annual flow rose by almost 75 percent to 6,333 between 1969 and 1974, a politically volatile period that included Salvador Allende's 1970-73 presidency and the first fifteen months of General Augusto Pinochet's dictatorship. From 1975 through 1979, Pinochet's repression continued, and the average annual number of migrants to Argentina climbed to over 10,000 (Centro Latinoamericano de Demografía, 1989: 35). A 1984 Argentine amnesty decree for *indocumentados* covered 75,566 Chileans, more than triple the next highest national grouping, and, from 1984 through 1988, as the dictatorship neared its end, a yearly average of 9,372 Chileans entered Argentina. During the democratization years of 1989 through 1992, it fell by over half to 4,175 (Instituto de Estadística y Censo, [INDEC] 1993: 54-55). Chile's vibrant economy worked against emigration during these four years, but it was also strong during most of the Pinochet period, when migration to Argentina was higher.

Return Migration. Return migrants have become a significant dimension of cross-border movement. They have met differing fates in several Colombian cities, grown sharply in number in Paraguay, and found largely unrewarding jobs in Uruguay.

Ungar (1988: 84-95) compares the fate of Colombians returned from Venezuela to four urban centers. In the major expulsor cities of Cúcuta and Cali, most could not find jobs. Employment was made difficult in Medellín by the decline of Venezuelan markets for its industrial machinery. More jobs were available in Cartagena which produced more goods for domestic markets.

There has been a long-run change in Paraguay's migration rate (the difference between gross immigration and emigration per thousand) with Argentina. From 1950 to 1955, during severe repression by General Alfredo Stroessner, this rate was a negative 10.2. From 1970 to 1975, it was minus 3.2. The construction of two huge dams and increased production of cotton and soy beans created jobs, and the rate responded, reaching plus 1.0 in 1990 (Centro Paraguayo de Estudio de Población, 1990: 4-5). Immigrants in Paraguay grew from 160,000 in 1982 to 280,000 in 1992. This grouping included Brazilians, Peruvians, and Koreans, but it also counted about 90,000 migrants from Argentina of two types: (1) native Paraguayans returning from Argentina, some with children, and (2) Argentines drawn by jobs (Maletta, 1992: 32-33).

Most of a sample of 200 returned migrants in Uruguay found jobs, but only about half did so within four months, while roughly one of three took longer, 17 percent had not worked at all, and, at the time of the study, 34 percent were unemployed. Among those with jobs, about one-third felt that their work, most of which was in the service sector, did not permit personal growth. Almost 20 percent received less than the minimum wage, and 44 percent earned under twice this amount (Longhi, 1987: 3, 14, 16).

Migration in Perspective. Migration affects expulsor nations as well as receptors. In 1980, natives living in neighboring countries compared to the following percentages of their homeland's population: Paraguay 9.9 percent; Uruguay, 8.9 percent; Bolivia, 2.4 percent; Colombia, 2.1 percent; and Chile, 2.0 percent (Pellegrino, 1988: 77-81, 99). A study of Colombian migration noted that Venezuelan employment had been "a short-term benefit to Colombia, providing a safety valve for unemployed persons and contributing positively to the balance of payments through money the Colombians take or send home," but the authors warned that this had encouraged Colombian policy-makers "to avoid dealing with unemployment and the balance of payments" (Johnson and Williams, 1981: 94).

Recent surges of returned migrants have diminished or eliminated this "safety valve" factor in Paraguay and Colombia, while citizens of Argentina and, particularly, Venezuela, where economic problems have intensified, still compete with many job-seekers from bordering nations. Because return migration can be driven both by economic hard times in the original receptor-state and better times in the original expulsor-state, it offers an adjustment mechanism for neighboring economies.

III. Trade

In 1991, two regional trading associations formed to include all of the continent except Chile. Countries in the Southern Common Market (Mercosur) are Argentina, Brazil, Paraguay, and Uruguay. The Andean Free Trade Association (ANTA) includes Bolivia, Colombia, Ecuador, Peru, and Venezuela. Among the future members of these associations, both 1985 and 1990 trade was at a higher level in the southeast than in the Andes (Wilkie, Contreras, and Weber, 1993: 862, 864, 866-68, 870, 873-76, 891, 918-19, 921-22).

The 1990 ranking by percentages of world trade with bordering republics was led by Bolivia (38.2 percent), Uruguay (36.8 percent), Paraguay (33.7 percent), and Argentina (21.6 percent). A middle grouping included Colombia (13.7 percent), Brazil (12.3 percent), and Peru (9.5 percent). The lowest three were Ecuador (5.3 percent), Chile (5.1 percent), and Venezuela (4.2 percent).

From 1985 to 1990, trade among South American neighbors grew from $7.7 billion to $17.0 billion, while world trade increased from $92.4 billion to $140 billion. The share of total trade conducted with bordering nations rose from 8.3 percent to 12.1 percent. About 85 percent of the $9.3 billion rise in trade with neighbors was accounted for by Brazil ($3.9 billion), Argentina ($2.9 billion), and Colombia ($1.1 billion). The largest proportional increases were posted by Uruguay (20.6 percent) and Argentina (9.8 percent). On the other side of the ledger, Peru and Bolivia experienced drops both in trade with bordering nations and its percentage of the world total. In Chile and Paraguay, trade with neighbors about doubled, but their share of world trade decreased.

Mercosur. Formed in 1991 through the treaty of Asunción, Mercosur formally became a duty-free association on January 1, 1995.[4] This was achieved despite inadequate transportation, the members' past economic instability, and the complexities of harmonizing tax, customs and trade accords. Of special concern was "whether Brazil could establish enough open-market policies, reduce government deficits, control inflation, and privatize state-owned companies in time to meet the deadline" (Nash, 1992).

---

4. Garre Capello (1991: 279-85) contains Mercosur's constitution.

Despite talks, neither Bolivia, whose leading trading partners include Argentina and Brazil, nor Chile, a key partner of Argentina, were included. However, Mercosur nations and Chile had made some progress in an October 1994 meeting, and, in December, President Carlos Menem of Argentina cited both Bolivia and Ecuador as likely future members (*La Epoca* [Santiago], December 8, 1994: 5).

Mercosur trade levels have soared since 1990, reaching almost $3 billion in the first six months of 1992 and $4.3 billion for the same period in 1993. At this rate, the 1993 yearly total would have been $8.6 billion, almost double the 1990 total. In 1993, Argentina and Brazil traded $6.3 billion in goods, with Brazil becoming Argentina's second trading partner (Inter Press Service, 1993). Higher levels should follow tariff elimination and ambitious projects to improve land and water trading routes (Brooke, 1994).

The Andean Free Trade Area. For a number of reasons, 1988 trade levels among Andean nations were below those of the future Mercosur members. Andean commercial centers are distant from one another. Bolivia borders three Mercosur nations, but Peru is its only Andean neighbor. The Andean countries trade more with the United States than do the Mercosur nations. Political relations among Andean nations suffer from border disputes and narcotics trafficking, neither of which afflicts Mercosur members. Finally, low-level trading within the original Andean Pact provided a weak base for growth.[5] From 1984 to 1988, it rose from $765 million to just over $1 billion. In 1988, Colombia, Peru, and Venezuela experienced an increase over 1987 trade with fellow pact members, but Bolivia and Ecuador sustained decreases (Wilkie and Contreras, 1992: 928).

The promise of increased Andean trade began with a December 1991 agreement signed by the five presidents in Cartagena, Colombia which pledged more trade liberalization reforms than in the history of the Pact. The Andean Free Trade Area (AFTA) began almost at once for Venezuela, Colombia, and Bolivia, with Peru and Ecuador to join six months later. Duties on hundreds of products were to phased out in a few years (MacNamara, 1992: 5). Peru, however, suspended its membership due to

---

5. The original Andean Pact erected high tariff walls against non-members, promoted subsidies for national industries, and otherwise discouraged the free-trade element of economic integration (Puyana de Palacios, 1982: 179).

internal political factors, while Bolivia and Ecuador have made only moderate commitments to the AFTA.

Trade among AFTA members nonetheless has risen. After a 1992 pact slashing tariffs and commercial red tape between Colombia and Venezuela, their trade soared to $1.3 billion in 1993. Much of this increase was in goods that once had been contraband. Colombia's top trade official called this development the "most successful trade integration between any two developing countries." He explained it by asking "would you rather smuggle something and risk losing it or wait a half-hour and pay a small tax?" (Stott, 1994). In 1994, the AFTA members shared trade of $3.4 billion, about half of it between Colombia and Venezuela, who had become each other's second trading partners (Inter Press Service, 1995).

Trade and Economic Integration in Perspective. The expansion of trade in Latin America has its critics. An International Labor Organization study cautioned that Mercosur becoming a common market could "lead to less job security since some firms might close down or switch to other industrial sectors" and warned that "intensified international competitiveness would reduce workers's salaries in order to lower production costs." An Ecuadorean told a 1993 international meeting which claimed to represent 10 million Indians that "while trade is improving ... the situation of the marginal sectors is not changing" (Inter Press Service, 1993).

Nonetheless, trade among South American nations has grown, and more economic integration is planned. The volume of commerce within South America rose to $24 billion in 1993, with the great preponderance exchanged among neighboring nations (*El Mercurio*, [Santiago], October 23, 1994: B8). Trade between Argentina and Chile rose from $811 billion in 1991 to over $1.4 billion in 1994 (Martinez, 1994: 45). In 1995, Mercosur and AFTA leaders spoke of a continent-wide South American Free Trade Association, and Brazil saw itself as a natural centerpiece (Inter Press Service, 1995).

IV. OTHER AREAS OF BORDERING-STATE RELATIONS

Also important to South American neighbors are narcotics, joint power projects, border commissions, and bilateral economic activity other than trade. All of these but drugs have improved bilateral relations.

Narcotics. The coca-cocaine industry is of major importance in Bolivia, Peru, and Colombia. In 1990, Bolivia produced an estimated 116,000 metric tons of coca, Peru 138,000, and Colombia 32,000. The drug industry added as much as $695 to $911 million to Bolivia's economy, $498 to $1,219 to Peru's, and $1,127 to Colombia's, with from $179 to $216 million remaining in Bolivia, $382 to $942 million in Peru, and $645 million in Colombia. Narcotics employment was placed at 207,000 Bolivians, 165,000 to 279,000 Peruvians, and 40,000 Colombians (Painter, 1994: 5). Estimates made in 1992 by Interpol had 300,000 Bolivian families earning money by growing the coca leaf and "millions" of Peruvians and Colombians deriving income from the coca-cocaine business (Notimex, 1992).

Colombian drug traffickers have caused ill will in Venezuela, where, in the 1980s, large caches of coca powder were found, government officials were corrupted, and use of *bazuka*, a cheap coca-based paste increased. Venezuela responded with anti-drug laws, raids on Colombian growers and processing plants within its borders, and initiation of bilateral control negotiations. Over two-thirds of the respondents in a 1987 opinion poll cited Colombian narcotics trafficking and the accompanying violence as the major international problems facing Venezuela (Martz, 1992: 197-98). The two neighbors continue to deplore the problem and to seek more effective controls, but armed clashes between Venezuelan troops and Colombian *narcoguerrillas* still occur.

Multilateral control efforts have not included the use of force. A 1986 pact signed by Bolivia, Colombia, Ecuador, Peru, and Venezuela called for information exchange on traffickers, joint anti-drug campaigns, and common criteria for the seizure of *narcotraficante* assets (Reuters, 1986). In 1989, the Andean Pact parliament stressed the need to increase judicial power to punish drug criminals (Xinhua, 1989). By 1990, the Inter-American Drug Control Abuse Commission (CICAD) of the Organization of American States had programs in "five priority areas: legal development, education prevention, community mobilization, data-gathering, and public information" (Lowenthal, 1992: 310-11).

Cross-national Hydroelectric Power Projects: Argentina, Brazil, and Paraguay. In one of the world's largest water systems, the Paraná River Basin, hydroelectric power has been generated by the Itaipú Dam, erected by Brazil in Paraguayan territory, and the Yacyretá Dam, constructed by Argentina not far downstream. Treaties signed in 1973 recognized Paraná water as a common pool resource for interdependent use through jointly owned public corporations to be commonly administered by the three nations. Power was to be sold back to Brazil's ELECTROBRAS, Argentina's Agua y Energías, and Paraguay's ANDE (DaRosa, 1983).

Itaipú's construction brought employment to Paraguay, and its completion meant cheap power in the mid-1980s. Still not finished, Yacyretá began generating power in 1994. At full capacity, estimated for 1998, the dam would could meet 40 percent of Argentina's hydroelectric power needs with 2,700 megawatts, about one-fifth of the capacity of Itaipú, the world's largest hydroelectric project (Reuters, 1994). In order to complete the financing, Argentina is considering privatization schemes, though Paraguay is opposed to them (Reuters, 1995).

Other Cross-national Economic Activity. A broadly charged border commisssion formed by Ecuador and Colombia is one of many in South America. Often called *comités de la frontera*, no fewer than twenty-seven joint South American groups plan border projects of various kinds (Herzog, 1992: 16). Another noteworthy recent economic development is cross-national investment.

A joint presidential order charged the Ecuadorean-Colombian commission with developing plans for regional cooperation; migratory regulation; intraregional land transport of passengers and cargo; smuggling and customs-house problems; binational enterprises; and the promotion of tourism (República del Ecuador - República de Colombia, 1989).

The commission has made important proposals. Public health recommendations ranged from a general three-year plan to specific immunization campaigns against tropical diseases. Commercial projects would promote goods made near the border and exonerate them from tariffs. Reported also was progress on or the need for cross-border superstructural development through roads, bridges, electricity, and telephone service (Ministerio de Relaciones Exteriores, 1991).

Argentine and Chilean oil companies extract gas from a common field under the Magellan Straits (Bolin, 1992: 177-78). In 1992, Argentina and Chile planned joint exploitation of Patagonian coal, timber, and maritime resources (*El Mercurio* [Santiago], May 30, 1992: C7). In 1994, a pipeline from Argentina's Nequén basin to Chile's central zone opened with expectations of adding $500 million yearly to Argentine exports and saving Chile $20 million annually in import costs (Noticias Argentinas, 1994), and bilateral planning was underway for ports along a 300-mile bioceanic corridor in the far south, (*El Mercurio* [Santiago], October 13, 1994: B2).

Cross-national investment has grown in significance. Between 1974 and 1980, 27 percent of all investment in Paraguay was from Brazil and 13 percent from Argentina, compared to 16 percent from the United States (Birch, 1992: 223). Brazilians have opened companies in Argentina and bought enough land to make a prediction that they "will own one-quarter of Uruguay's interior by the end of the decade" (Brooke, 1994). By 1992, Chileans had purchased key segments of Argentina's privatized electrical and transport industries (República de Chile, 1992: 65). By 1994, one Chilean conglomerate had created or purchased stakes in five companies in Argentina; in Peru, Chileans are "building supermarkets, distributing pharmaceuticals, and helping run the telephone system" (Moffett, 1994).

In northern South America, Colombians have invested in Venezuelan commerce and industry, while Venezuelans have put money into the Colombian banking sector. Under bilateral planning are a transmission line; development of the port of Buenaventura, Colombia (which would give Venezuela a Pacific outlet); and improvements in the land transportation infrastructure (Martinez, 1993).

V. Conclusion

Perspective on the importance of South American nations to one another can be gained from comparisons with the roles of the United States in the categories discussed in this study. In territorial disputes, the United States has been of virtually no significance, and its importance in migration has been less than that of bordering nations. In international economics, the United States has had more overall influence, though its extent varies greatly by nation. Moreover, neighbors increasingly influence each other through a wide variety of economic means, including cross-border projects. The United States has tried to exercise control over the South American drug business, but neighboring nations also have undertaken joint efforts.

The United States has not been directly involved in South American territorial disputes since it promoted and co-guaranteed the Rio de Janeiro pact in 1942. As a member of the Organization of American States (OAS), the United States has endorsed Bolivian access to the Pacific, but the OAS has never resolved a South American territorial dispute (Scheman, 1988: 15-16). Prospective oil sales to the United States may have intensified the Gulf of Colombia dispute, but it clearly would exist without them. Argentina and Chile chose the Vatican to arbitrate the Beagle Channel Island dispute and accepted the verdict on their own volition.

A 1988 study reported that circa 1980 about 400,000 natives of South America lived in the United States, but over three times as many resided in nations bordering their native land (Pellegrino, 1988: 136-42, 144-45, 150). Almost 150,000 Colombian migrants were in the United States, over 50,000 more than from any other South American nation, but several times more Colombian natives were living in Venezuela, and, by 1988, well over 150,000 Colombians were residing in Ecuador. Peru and Ecuador were the only nations which sent more migrants to the United States than to all of their neighbors combined. Argentina was the only other country with fewer migrants in any single bordering republic than in the United States, but Argentine natives living in its five neighbors were almost double those residing in the United States. Return migration has brought an increasing number of South Americans back across borders, but the significance of migration to neighbors still exceeds that of emigration to the United States due to volume and also because neighbors are affected both as expulsing nations and receptors.

Compilations from trade figures for 1990 show that South American nations traded $39.1 with the United States and $17 billion with their neighbors (Wilkie, Contreras and Weber, 1993: 862, 864, 866-68, 970, 873-76, 891, 912-14, 916, 918-19, 921-22). The United States thus accounted for 27.9 percent of South America's world commerce as opposed to 12.1 percent for bordering countries. Ratios between trade with the United States and bordering republics varied greatly by South American nation. Venezuela's ratio of 12 to 1 was highest, followed by those for Ecuador (8.0 to 1), (Chile 3.6 to 1), Colombia (3.0 to 1), Peru (2.7 to 1), and Brazil (1.9 to 1). The ratios favoring neighbors were Paraguay, 4.0 to 1, Uruguay 3.7 to 1, Bolivia 1.8 to 1, and Argentina 1.4 to 1.

Since 1990, the United States has increased trade with South America, but trade among neighbors also has risen. The Andean Free Trade Association and Mercosur were not formed until 1991, the sharp growth in trade between Colombia and Venezuela began in 1992, and Argentine-Chilean trade almost doubled between 1991 and 1994.

The United States is the largest consumer of South American drugs, and recent administrations have pressured Bolivia, Colombia, and Peru to suppress the coca-cocaine industry. Although the United States provides virtually all of the enforcement assistance wanted by these countries (and perhaps more), the coca eradication efforts it has endorsed have been largely circumvented (Sanabria, 1993). Nonetheless, United States drug policies constitute its most direct form of intervention in recent South American affairs.

Joint projects in South America have been principally undertaken by neighboring countries, though national programs funded by the United States Agency for International Development might be considered binational efforts. Moreover, when bordering-nation projects use funding from first-world governments, banks, or international lending agencies, United States money may be involved. Of special interest to this study, would be for the United States to support regional development in South America through the Organization of American States. With this approach, the bilateral impact of the United States economic influence would be mitigated.

The role of the United States in joint South American projects is limited, but in other economic areas it is highly influential. Despite the growth of neighboring-nation trade, investments, and the movement of more companies across borders, these economic activities pale in comparative significance to United States trade, investment, and the role of its transnational corporations.

The point remains, however, that neighboring South American nations are of major, immediate, and continuous importance to one another even though the literature largely ignores the point. Many political analyses of South America are restricted to domestic topics, while those which assess external influence typically do so only for the United States, whether in the context of development or dependency theory. Even with the importance of international economics duly recognized, it would be wrong to omit consideration of neighbors in any balanced and comprehensive study of international influences on South American national politics.

REFERENCES

Almond, Gabriel A., "The Development of Development," in *Understanding Political Development*, ed., Myron Weiner and Samuel P. Huntington, (Boston: Little Brown, 1987).

Area, Leandro and Elke Nieschulz de Stockhausen, *El Golfo de Venezuela*, (Caracas: Universidad Central de Venezuela, 1984).

BBC, "Interview with Eduardo Frei," March 17, 1994, LEXIS/NEXIS.

Bidegain Griesing, Gabriel and Diego López, *Las migraciones laborales Colombo-Venezolanos*, (Caracas: Instituto Latinoamericano de Investigaciones Sociales, 1987).

Birch, Melissa H., "Pendulum Politics: Paraguay's National Borders, 1940-75," in *Changing Boundaries in the Americas*, ed., Lawrence A. Herzog, (San Diego: Center for U.S.-Mexican Studies, University of California, San Diego, 1992), pp. 203-28.

Bolin, William H., "The Transformation of South America's Borderlands," in *Changing Boundaries in the Americas*, ed., Lawrence A. Herzog, (San Diego: Center for U.S.-Mexican Studies, University of California, San Diego, 1992), pp. 169-83.

Brooke, James, "The New South Americans: Friends and Partners," *The New York Times*, April 8, 1994, A3.

Central Office of Statistics and Information, *Venezuela*, (Caracas: Office of the Presidency, 1993).

Centro Latinoamericano de Demografía, "Investigación de la migración international en Latinoamerica," *Boletin Demográfico*, 1989, 23 (Enero), 19-169.

Centro Paraguayo de Estudios de Población, *Encuesta Nacional de Demografía y Salud*, (Asunción: República del Paraguay, 1990).

Child, Jack, *Geopolitics and Conflict in South America*, (New York: Praeger, 1985).

Child, Jack and Phillip Kelly, eds, *Geopolitics and Conflict of the Southern Cone and South America*, (Boulder, Colo.: Westview, 1988).

Da Rosa, J. Eliseo, "Economics, Politics, and Hydroelectric Power: the Paraná River Basin," *Latin American Research Review*, 1983, 18(3), 77-107.

Elbow, Gary S., "The Border Conflict with Peru: Shaping Images of National Territory in Ecuador," Paper presented at the Association of Borderland Studies meeting, Oakland, Calif., April, 1995.

F. V., "The Beagle Channel Island Affair, "*American Journal of International Law*, 1977, 71(4), 733-40.

Fraga, J. A., *Ensayos de geopolítica*, (Buenos Aires: Instituto de Publicaciones Navales, 1985).

Garre Capella, Belter, *El Tratado de Asuncion y Mercado del Sur*, (Montevideo: Editorial Universitaria, 1991).

Garrett, James L., "Beagle Channel: Confrontation and Negotiation in the Southern Cone," *Journal of Interamerican Studies*, 1985, 27(3), 93-104.

George, Larry N., "Realism and Internationalism in the Gulf of Venezuela," *Journal of Interamerican Studies and World Affairs*, 1989, 30(1), 149-157.

Gorman, Stephen M., "Geopolitics and Peruvian Foreign Policy," *Inter-American Economic Affairs*, 1982, 36(4) 66-88.

Haggard, Stephen, "The Political Economy of Direct Foreign Investment in Latin America," *The Latin American Research Review*, 1989, 24(1), 184-208.

Herzog, Lawrence A., ed., *Changing Boundaries in the Americas*, (San Diego: Center for U.S.-Mexican Studies, University of California, San Diego, 1992).

Herzog, Lawrence A., "Changing Boundaries in the Americas: an Overview," in *Changing Boundaries in the Americas*, ed., Herzog, (San Diego: Center for U.S.-Mexican Studies, University of California, San Diego, 1992), pp. 3-24.

Instituto de Estadística y Censo (INDEC), *Censo Nacional de Población y Viviendas: Resultados Definitivos -- Características Selecionadas*, (Buenos Aires: Ministerio de Economía y Obras Servicios Publicos, 1991).

------------------, *Anuario Estadístico de la República Argentina*, (Buenos Aires: Ministerio de Economía y Obras y Servicios Publicos, 1993).

Instituto Nacional de Estadística y Censo (INEC), *Anuario de Estadísticas de Migración Internacional*, (Quito: República del Ecuador, 1988).

------------------, *Censo de Población y de Vivienda: Población del Ecuador por area y sexo*, (Quito: República del Ecuador, 1991).

Inter Press Service, "Latin American Integration Moves Ahead, But For Whom?," October 26, 1993, LEXIS/NEXIS.

------------------, "Mercosur Offers the Lure of Brazil," February 21, 1995, LEXIS/NEXIS.

Johnson, Kenneth F. and Miles W. Williams, *Illegal Aliens in the Western Hemisphere*, (New York: Praeger, 1981).

Lara, Abraham, "Ecuador-Peru: Did Anyone Win the Border War," *Inter Press Service*, March 10, 1995, LEXIS/NEXIS.

Lowenthal, Abraham, "The Organization of American States and the Control of Dangerous Drugs," in *Drug Policy in the Americas*, ed., Peter H. Smith, (Boulder, Colo.: Westview Press, 1992), pp. 305-13.

Longhi, Augusto, *Reinserción laboral de retornantes: primeras approximacciones*, (Montevideo: Impreso General, 1987).

MacNamara, Laurie, "Andean Region Makes Integration Effort," *Business America*, March 22, 1992, 5-6.

Maletta, Hector, "International Migration in Paraguay and the Southern Cone: a Research Programme," *Latin American Migration Journal*, 1992, 10(2/3), 29-59.

Martinez, Roberto, "Colombia and Venezuela: Partners in Economic Success," *Corporate Finance in Latin America*, December 1993, LEXIS/NEXIS.

Martinez, Rodolfo, "El poder del dinero," *Hoy* [Santiago], November 13, 1994, 903, 43-45.

Martz, John D., "National Security and Politics: the Colombian-Venezuelan Border," in *Changing Boundaries in the Americas*, ed., Lawrence A. Herzog, (San Diego: Center for U.S.-Mexican Relations, University of California, San Diego, 1992), pp. 185-201.

Ministerio de Relaciones Exteriores, *Actas Oficiales de las Comisiones Limitrofes*, (Quito: República del Ecuador, 1991).

Moffett, Matt, "Chilean Firms Cross Border Trails," *The Wall Street Journal*, November 7, 1994, A11.

Murphy, Alexander B., "Historical Justifications for Territorial Claims," *Annals of the Association of American Geographers*, 1990, 80(4), 531-48.

Nash, Nathaniel, "Free Trade Talks in South America, *New York Times*, June 28, 1992, LEXIS/NEXIS.

Notícias Argentinas, "Argentine-Chilean Pipeline Opens," February 16, 1994, LEXIS/NEXIS.

Notimex, "Drug Production, Trafficking and Consumption on Rise in Latin America," September 29, 1992, LEXIS/NEXIS.

Oficina Central de Estadística, *XI Censo de Población*, (Caracas: Presidencia de la República, 1980).

----------------, *Encuesta Nacional de Población*, (Caracas: Ministerio del Trabajo, 1987).
Painter, James, *Bolivia and Coca: a Study in Dependency*, (Boulder Colo: Lynne Reiner Publishers, 1994).
Pellegrino, Adela, *Migración internacional de Lationamericanos en las Americas*, (Caracas: Universidad Catolica Andrés Bello, Instituto de Investigaciones Económicas y Sociales, 1988).
Puyana de Palacios, Alicia, *Economic Integration Among Unequal Partners: the Case of the Andean Group*, (New York: Pergammon Press, 1982).
República de Chile, *Chile*, (Santiago: Secretaria de Communicacion y Cultura, 1992).
República del Ecuador - República de Colombia, *Comisión de Vecinidad: Documento Referencial*, (Ibarra, Colombia: Impresa General, 1989).
Reuters, "Five Andean Countries Sign Anti-Narcotics Cooperation Pact," May 1, 1986, LEXIS/NEXIS.
----------------, "Argentina and Paraguay Switch on a $10 Billion Dam," September, 2, 1994, LEXIS/NEXIS.
----------------, "Argentina: Paraguay Against Privatizing Yacyreta Dam", January 30, 1995, LEXIS/NEXIS.
Richards, Donald G., "Booming-sector Economic activity in Paraguay 1973-86: A Case of Dutch Disease," *Journal of Development Studies*, 1994, 30(2), December, 310-33.
Sanabria, Harry, *The Coca Boom and Social Change in Bolivia*, (Ann Arbor: University of Michigan Press, 1993).
Scheman, Ronald, *The Inter-American Dilemma: the Search for Inter-American Cooperation at the Centennial of the Inter-American System*, (Boulder, Colo.: Westview Press, 1988)
Stott, Michael, "Simon Bolivar International Bridge," *Reuters*, March 14, 1994, LEXIS/NEXIS.
Ungar, Elizabeth, "Impact of the Venezuelan Recession on Return Migration to Colombia," in *When Borders Don't Divide: Labor Migration and Refugee Movements in the Americas*, ed., Patricia Pessar, (New York: Center for Migration Studies, 1988), pp. 73-95.
Valencia Rodriguez, Luis, *El conflicto territorial Ecuatoriano-Peruano*, (Quito: Casa de la Cultura, 1987).
Whelan, James R., *Out of the Ashes: Life, Death and Transfiguration of Democracy in Chile*, (Washington, D.C.: Regnery Gateway, 1992).

Wiarda, Howard J., "South American Domestic Politics and Foreign Policy," in *South America into the 1990s: Evolving International Relations in a New Era*, ed., G. Pope Atkins, (Boulder, Colo: Westview Press, 1990), pp. 27-52.

Wilkie, James W. and Carlos Contreras, eds., *Statistical Abstract of Latin America*, vol. 29, (Los Angeles: UCLA, Latin American Center Publications, University of California, 1992).

Wilkie, James W., Carlos Alberto Contreras, and Christof Anders Weber, eds., *Statistical Abstract of Latin America*, vol. 30, (Los Angeles: UCLA, Latin American Center Publications, University of California, 1993).

Wright, Freeman J., "National Boundaries and Foreign Policy: the Case of Argentina," in *Changing Boundaries in the Americas*, ed., Lawrence A. Herzog, (San Diego: Center for U.S.-Mexican Studies, University of California, San Diego, 1992), pp. 229-45.

Xinhua News Service, "Andean Parliament Agrees to United Front on Drugs," August 26, 1989, LEXIS/NEXIS.

POST-DEVALUATION MEXICO AND THE NEW WORLD ORDER

Mark A. Martinez
Department of Political Science
California State University, Bakersfield
Bakersfield, CA 93311

Abstract—During the administration of former President Carlos Salinas de Gortari (1988-1994), two of the most significant events of the post-war era occurred: the fall of communism in the former Soviet Union and Eastern Europe and global collective military action against Saddam Hussein. These events established the conditions for leaders to proclaim a New World Order had arrived - one where free markets and collective security would prevail over the anarchy of the past. While the promise of collective security remain elusive, the promise of free-markets remains as the cornerstone for attracting developing states into the growing economic network of the New World Order (NWO). Mexico, like all reformist authoritarian states who have embraced the market over the past ten years has attempted to enter this growing network. Driven by the need to compete in the new interdependent global economic order, Mexico's on-going transition to free market status, in many respects, is a microcosm of what is occurring in the NWO's "emerging markets." In this chapter, I will look at the challenges Mexico faces in the NWO and the impact the December 1994 devaluation has had on Mexico's development prospects as it attempts to make the transition to market economy status. In particular, I will look at Mexico's experience as an emerging market in the NWO.

I. Introduction

During former President Carlos Salinas de Gortari's time in office (1988-94), Mexico -- like the world -- witnessed two of the most significant events of the post-war era: the fall of communism in the former Soviet Union and Eastern Europe and global collective military action against Saddam Hussein in Kuwait. These events established the conditions for leaders and analysts alike to proclaim that a New World Order (NWO) had arrived - one where free markets and collective security would prevail over the anarchy of the past. While the political and military promise of collective security remain dubious at best, the transition to market economies in Latin America and in the former Soviet bloc remains as one of the cornerstones of contemporary NWO proponents.

As such, today NWO proponents are largely identified by their commitment to the market and reliance on economic interdependence. Mexico, like all reformist authoritarian states who have embraced the market, is no different in this respect. Driven by the need to compete in the new interdependent global economic order, Mexico's transition to a market system, in many respects, is a microcosm of what is occurring in much of what we call "emerging markets." Mexico's experience as an emerging market in the NWO is the focus of this paper. In particular, I will look at the challenges Mexico faces in the NWO, the impact of the December 1994 peso devaluation, the impact of the NWO and the devaluation on internal politics, and Mexico's future prospects as it attempts to make the transition to a market economy in the NWO. To understand Mexico's transition to a market economy, we need to look a little more closely at what has occurred in Mexico since Carlos Salinas de Gortari began his neo-liberal revolution. This is the focus of the following section.

II. The Setting

To understand the significance of the transition from a closed and command economic system to an open market economy, we need to recognize that making this transition requires that old ways of doing business be disrupted, if not entirely discarded. In Mexico changing the way things were done was deemed necessary by President Carlos Salinas de Gortari to convince international investors that he was serious about Mexico's embrace of the market. For example, selling off public corporations, privatizing small parcels formerly held in usufruct by peasants, negotiating the North American Free Trade Agreement (NAFTA), reducing tariffs unilaterally, and other changes during his administration were distinct departures from past practices. These and other changes have had a tremendous impact on internal developments since 1988.

In particular, as the avenues for commerce have opened up, so too have the avenues for political ideas widened. Not surprisingly, as the Mexican government's control over the flow of information has been reduced (whether it is tied to business or politics), demands for political and professional accountability have also risen. Responses to these changes have varied but there is no doubt that many entrenched powerful groups believe that their interests are undermined by a more open and democratic system. This is one of the primary reasons that Mexico's political scene was marked by political assassinations and other political intrigue toward the end of the Salinas administration (1988-94).

In some corners the political violence and peasant uprisings that occurred in Mexico from 1993-95 are seen as the primary causes of Mexico's December 1994 devaluation and subsequent economic problems. Political violence and peasant uprisings, in turn, have compelled casual observers and experts alike to offer a wide range of advice, analysis, and cures. Given the range of topics that one can start from when looking for the roots of Mexico's current economic problems -- the January 1994 Indian peasant rebellion in the state of Chiapas, political assassinations, NAFTA, privatization, the rise of the drug economy, etc. -- it should come as no surprise then that explanations abound and, to date, have generated no consensus among analysts in Mexico or the United States. While there is no real consensus on the source of Mexico's political and economic problems during this period, in this chapter I will argue that Mexico's problems can be tied to the demands of, and Mexico's responses to, the new international financial system. This point is important to understand because, as we will see below, Mexico has little control over the post-Cold War international financial system that will govern its future prospects for growth and has a big hand in determining the tone of its internal political debates.

III. THE NEW WORLD ORDER AND ITS IMPACT ON MEXICO

For some, Mexico's internal problems are directly attributed to the political uncertainty brought on by the political "cannibalism" that has gone on at the highest levels within the Institutional Revolutionary Party (*Partido Revolucionario Institucional*, PRI) and, allegedly, between Mexico's new political heavyweights, the *narco politicos*. (Gonzalez, 1995; Resillas, 1995; Rotella, 1995; Trejo and Perez, 1995). For others, the primary reasons behind Mexico's political and economic problems are tied to the historically weak export position of Mexico's economy. Mexico's dependence has created the condition where it is essentially at the mercy of external sources to finance consistent current account deficits and to service past debt obligations. Because loans and other financial instruments are negotiated from a position of weakness (i.e., dependence), Mexico has had to generally accept terms imposed by external sources like the International Monetary Fund (IMF) when seeking the credit necessary to remain solvent (Bonilla Sanchez, 1995).

While blaming Mexico's contemporary problems on politics and the growing *narco politico* threat is compelling, in this chapter I will argue that Mexico's contemporary problems are structural and tied to the demands of the emerging international financial system. I do so primarily because, while both arguments have merit, there can be no denying that the impetus behind Mexico's desire to generate balance of trade surpluses, to privatize, and to change its constitution are a product of the need to be competitive in international markets. Much like Mikhail Gorbachev in the former Soviet Union, Carlos Salinas de Gortari recognized early in his administration that Mexico could no longer sustain wasteful government bureaucracies and populist policies which were draining the public treasury, and doing little to make the Mexican economy competitive. In sum, Salinas recognized that the only way Mexico would be able to compete with the West was if Mexico did away with past practices like providing massive consumer subsidies[1], subsidizing state companies and maintaining protective tariffs and quotas.

As the Salinas administration began to unilaterally remove barriers to foreign competition, and introduced new programs to open up the system, it should come as no surprise that -- much as was the case during Gorbachev's reign -- former standards and norms were also undermined. In the economic sphere, this meant that markets would be disrupted as new competitors challenged inefficient industries for a market share. In the political sphere, formerly repressed groups took advantage of President Salinas' need to promote the idea that a new Mexico had developed under his administration. Because of the governments desire to promote the impression that Mexico was ready to enter the First World, over time these and other groups were able to marshal resources and accomplish things that were almost unthinkable in the past (e.g., the church speaking out on political issues, opposition parties winning gubernatorial races, a more vigorous press corps, etc.). However, this process backfired as numerous groups took advantage of the opportunities presented by becoming bolder in both their goals and efforts.

For example, peasant groups in the southern state of Chiapas were able to build up a large cache of arms throughout 1992 and 1993 because the government was fearful of cracking down and exposing rebel strongholds before Salinas' much coveted free trade agreement was passed in the U.S. Congress (it should be noted that, for a variety of reasons, Salinas staked the success of his six year presidency to the successful passage of NAFTA). This point is interesting because it demonstrates that image was so important - to maintain international investment and to keep the NAFTA dialogue going - that the Mexican government deemed it necessary to downplay or ignore the threat of rebel insurrection and rampant poverty in the state of Chiapas. As a result, in spite of numerous warnings from local ranchers, Chiapas rebels were able to build arms stockpiles that were crucial to the military successes of the January 1, 1994 rebellion.[2]

---

1. The two major exceptions to this have been the *Pronasol* (National Solidarity Program) and *Procampo* programs. For a review of the Solidarity program see Dresser, (1991). For a review of *Procampo* see Cruz Gomez, et al., (1993).
2. For an explicit account of how the Chiapas guerrilla movement was a able to grow with the knowledge of government officials in Mexico see Corro, et al. (1994).

The primary reason for these and other developments that sabotaged the authority of the state and challenged the status quo is that change - whether it is evolutionary or revolutionary - undermines old structures, both political and economic. The Soviets, with their rigid inability to adapt to the demands of the global economic system, became the first to fall to the forces of change that characterize and define the NWO: free markets, access to information, open competition, increased productivity, market responsiveness, and access to credit. In Mexico, we are finding that adapting to these changes - as is the case for all states that are emerging from an authoritarian past - is very disruptive to interests that were accustomed to operating according to rules that required very little accountability.

Given neo-liberal developments that demanded more accountability in the NWO, it should come as no surprise that ex-PRI presidential candidate Luis Donaldo Colosio would be seen as a threat. Viewed as a legitimate democrat who spoke openly about dealing with the more corrupt elements of the Mexican political system, Colosio's presence was a destabilizing force for the darker elements of the Mexican political system. In this manner, Colosio's assassination - and Gorbachev's fall from power - demonstrates how the forces of change can destroy leaders with honorable intentions (Silk, 1992/93: 173). Just as well, it shows how forces driven by power and violence, rather than governed by the rule of law, can come to dominate the political scene of any state.

IV. INTERNATIONAL MARKETS AND THE DECEMBER 1994 PESO DEVALUATION

While the NWO has had a significant impact on Mexico's political system, its potential to destroy even the best laid economic plans became quite apparent with the December 1994 peso devaluation. Demonstrating that today's market will punish the uncompetitive and those who borrow recklessly, Mexico's December 1994 devaluation illustrated what could happen to an economy that attempts to attract foreign exchange by borrowing rather than by increasing direct investment or savings. Nonetheless, just four months after the December 1994 devaluation, it was actually being discussed whether the structural conditions for a new "Mexican Miracle" had been created (Rebello Pinal, 1995).

Based on a scenario that simply tracks trade and current account surpluses, it is my view that this type of analysis is both misleading and wrong. There are primarily three reasons why any economic recovery that Mexico experiences in the short-term should be seen as largely illusory and transitory. The first is tied to Mexico's current dependence on the 1994 devaluation to improve its trade balance. The second reason is tied to the fact that President Zedillo's *National Development Plan, 1995-2000* (or *Plan Nacional de Desarrollo, 1995-2000,* PND) is flawed and filled with many contradictions. The final reason is tied to Mexico's continued dependence on speculative and costly short-term portfolio investments to create current account surpluses (dependence on portfolio investment will be addressed in another section below).

The first reason why Mexico's initial recovery should be seen as short-term and illusory is that simply tracking current account surpluses can be misleading. For example, following the July 1995 announcement that Mexico had run a US$6.9 billion trade surplus with the United States from January to July, 1995, Mexico's Secretary of Commerce Herminio Blanco boasted that Mexico's export policy and austerity program was a "success". However, he failed to mention that the announced US$6.9 billion trade surplus was only with the United States (total U.S.-Mexican trade during this period reached US$42.9 billion); nor did he mention that Mexico's *total trade surplus* during this period was only US$2.2 billion (total Mexican foreign trade during this period reached US$60.6 billion) (*The News*, 1995).

Moreover, we have to remember that if you devalue your currency, other currencies are worth more than yours, which means that foreigners can buy more of your goods (at least until internal inflation catches up with the devalued currency). Because a devaluation means your money is worth less in international trading circles, it follows that it will cost more for the devaluing country to buy imported goods. This means, in very general terms, that any economy that devalues its currency should experience an increase in exports and a decrease in imports immediately after it devalues its currency.³ This expected short-run effect is essentially what occurred during the first six months of post-devaluation Mexico's "recovery." In this sense, Mexico's forced devaluation (because it could not pay interest on loans) and its subsequent inability to buy foreign goods in 1995, cannot be seen as a sign of economic strength - even if trade surpluses are the result.

In the case of the PND we find that the goals of the plan - a stable economy, increasing the amount of resources available for productive investment, and economic modernization - are almost impossible to reach given that the strategy virtually guarantees that consumption and investment will be reduced internally (Calva, 1995). In an excellent analysis which breaks down the PND into six areas, UNAM economics professor, Jose Luis Calva, explains how and why President Zedillo's economic program is really designed to attract and maintain foreign investment, and will do little for the average Mexican in the immediate term. For example, after reviewing the plans overemphasis on inflation, Calva points out that the strategy of "reduced real wages", "lower public spending", a sudden "rise in prices and tariffs" (*Mexico & NAFTA Report*, 1995iii: 7), "a severely restrictive monetary policy"[4], unprincipled privatization[5], and the fact that external financial commitments are given a higher priority than national development programs that promote small and medium sized industries[6],

---

3. It should be noted that improvements in a nations balance of trade are also tied to price and income elasticities for import and export demands. However, it has been argued that as the peso stabilizes in international markets, the generous trade surpluses Mexico experienced in the first six months of 1995 will eventually decline and could become trade deficits. This is especially the case if the U.S. economy slows down (Martinez, 1995).

4. According to standard economic principles, restricting a nations money supply is crucial to keeping inflation down. Nonetheless, the standard assumption that inflation at any level is detrimental to an economy has come into question. For example, Paul Krugman argues that "it is very difficult to pin down any large gains from a reduction in the inflation rate from, say, 20 percent to 2 percent" (Krugman, 1995: 33).

5. While many state firms were sold to close political associates of President Salinas de Gortari, many monopolistic structures were also maintained (Baker, 1991; Rodriguez Castaneda 1995 & 1993). On another level, it has been argued that rather than being part of the solution, Mexico's newly privatized banks are actually part of Mexico's recovery problems (Soto, 1995iii; Acosta Cordova, 1995). Finally, the FBI has reported that privatization under the Salinas administration may have been tainted by money-launderers who needed fronts for drug business (El Financiero: International Edition, 1995iii: 8).

6. For an excellent review on the limits of promoting large-scale industries and focusing on the export sector alone see Jorge Basave Kunhardt (1995).

virtually guarantees that Mexico's economic growth will be sacrificed to external interests. Here, Calva argues that President Zedillos' economic program is not designed to benefit the average Mexican, but is "a program designed to save Wall Street" (Calva, 1995: 34).

Because contradictions are built into President Zedillo's recovery-austerity program, while Mexico has had to depend on the December 1994 devaluation and U.S.-backed credits to improve its current accounts position[7], we should not expect the structure or output of the Mexican economy to improve over the immediate term. On another level, because the political situation remains uncertain, the natural question is, "What does this all mean for Mexico in the NWO? " To answer this question, we need to know more about Mexico's political system and how it is tied to the NWO. After discussing the politics behind the political assassinations that occurred in Mexico from 1993 to 1995, I will address the issue of Mexico's increased dependence on portfolio investments in the NWO.

V. MEXICO'S POLITICAL FUTURE: *LA COSA NOSTRA* OR DEMOCRATIC OPENING?

The Indian peasant rebellion in the southern state of Chiapas on January 1, 1994 was a significant event in Mexico because it demonstrated that Mexican governments - past and present - are nowhere near solving the developmental problems that plague the marginalized areas of rural Mexico. While Chiapas raises many domestic issues for Mexico's political leaders, other events that followed pointed to larger political problems. For example, the 1994 political assassinations of the PRI's presidential candidate, Luis Donaldo Colosio, and the PRI's Secretary General, Jose Francisco Ruiz Massieu, raised many questions because they were political murders that Mexico had not experienced since the 1920s following the Mexican Revolution.

---

7. Using U.S.-backed credits to produce international reserve surpluses occurred several times during 1995. One of the more blatant examples was when the United States and Mexico announced that Mexico would prepay $700 million dollars right before President Zedillo visited the United States in October of 1995. However, both countries failed to announce that the $700 million was not Mexico's, and did not come from Mexico's reserves. The funds were created by a German mark-denominated bond issue. (*El Financiero: International Edition*, 1995: 1, 16).

Because this type of political cannibalism had not been a part of Mexico's political scene for over 60 years, many analysts were tempted to view the Colosio and Ruiz Massieu murders as part of larger political battles over who would control the ideological future of the Institutional Revolutionary Party, or the PRI (which has governed Mexico for over 65 years). Would it be the old-guard party-hacks, otherwise known as *politicos* (often referred to as *dinosaurios)*? Or would it be the Mexico City-bred, foreign-educated, market-oriented technocrats, or *tecnócratas?*. When ex-president Carlos Salinas de Gortari's brother, Raul, was arrested on charges of being the "intellectual author" of the Ruiz Massieu murder, the issue of ideological dominance became even more pronounced.

The significance of these events is that they destroyed many of the "rules of the game" that helped maintain political stability in Mexico for over 65 years. At the core of these rules was a code of silence and respect surrounding the money and power of PRI elites. According to Mexican historian Lorenzo Meyer these codes operated to maintain a structure and mentality that is comparable to that of Sicily's *La Cosa Nostra*. While this analogy may - or may not - be overstated, Meyer's comparison helps us understand that, at the very least, the PRI operated much like the political machines of Richard Daly in Chicago in the 1950's and New York's Tamany Hall at the turn of the century.

Crucial to maintaining the discipline of machine politics in post-revolutionary Mexico were "rules of the game" (Smith, 1979) that centered around two cardinal principles. First, infighting within the party was to be kept political. Second, no matter how much may have been taken from the public treasury, once out of office former presidents, their families, and close associates were generally above investigation or prosecution. The murders of high ranking officials in 1994 and 1995 and the incarceration of Raul Salinas de Gortari broke all of these rules (Chavez, 1995; Mexico & NAFTA Report, 1995: 2). When we consider ex-president Salinas' government imposed exile to the United States and Canada, it becomes apparent that - for better or worse - politics as usual is not in Mexico's political future.

To understand the battles that pitted one group of PRIista's (followers of the PRI) against another requires an understanding of Mexico's version of *La Cosa Nostra* and Tamany Hall. At the core of Mexico's political system are political cliques, or *camarillas*. Operating on the principle of reciprocity and patronage, Mexico's political *camarillas* generally evolves around one key individual who controls resources - like jobs and access to political posts - and people (Cornelius & Craig, 1988). For years, a one party system of patronage developed and prospered in Mexico because of two conditions.

First, Mexico's constitution provides that no individual can serve more than one successive term in office (a product of Mexico's effort to prevent the rise of dictators and rogue *caudillos*). As a result, there was a constant turnover of political posts which enabled the PRI to reward party faithful by nominating them to run for public office under the PRI banner. Party discipline was maintained because the PRI rewarded those who disciplined themselves and worked their way up through the PRI party system. Not only did this process help establish and maintain the rules of the game in Mexico, but as Peruvian novelist Mario Varga Llosa argued, because the PRI won the parade of regularly scheduled elections, the PRI had achieved the "perfect dictatorship" - a self-perpetuating system that allowed the same group, or class, of people to dominate the political system.

Second, the one party system of patronage worked because the economy was dominated by the government which, not surprisingly, was controlled by the PRI. Because the government controlled over 1,150 public companies (Camp, 1993: 168) the PRI could dangle politically attractive - and financially rewarding posts - to *politicos* who adhered to and promoted the rules of the game. Over time, however, as more and more Mexicans secured advanced degrees at home, or went abroad and returned with degrees from the United States and England, a new class of political elites began to develop in Mexico's extremely class conscious society. Because their advanced degrees enabled them to claim specialized knowledge *políticos* could not offer, these technocrats, or *tecnócratas*, were able to bypass grass-roots politics and jump over party faithful during the Luis Echeverria (1970-76) and Jose Lopez Portillo (1976-82) administrations. This process culminated in the selection of Harvard educated Miguel de la Madrid as the PRI's presidential candidate for 1982.

VI. THE DYNAMICS OF DEMOCRATIC OPENING IN MEXICO

During the same time pressures from grass-roots organizations and opposition political parties began to demand more accountability and representation in the system. As pressures for democracy and accountability grew, opposition groups slowly began to gain concessions like proportional representation in congress in the 1970s. This helped make opposition parties viable alternatives to the PRI and created additional pressures for accountability. In an attempt to address these concerns, De la Madrid broke from tradition in 1988 and, rather than simply selecting one individual to run as the presidential candidate from the PRI, he nominated six pre-presidential candidates to present their presidential programs and platforms - ostensibly - to the people.

Because the competition for the nomination was fierce, not only did this process open up all the political sores of the PRI machine, but it also demonstrated something that many had suspected all along: the PRI was no singular monolith. What this showed was that, presented with the proper conditions, PRIistas would turn on each other. When De la Madrid finally selected fellow *tecnócrata* (and Harvard educated) Carlos Salinas de Gortari as the PRI's candidate in 1988, De la Madrid's pseudo primary run-off not only showed everyone in Mexico that Carlos Salinas de Gortari was the least popular candidate among the party faithful, but it also demonstrated that the reign of the *tecnócratas* would continue. To consolidate and enhance his position - after fraud-filled elections - Salinas moved quickly to jail corrupt officials (who, not surprisingly, were also his political enemies).

However, Salinas commanded worldwide attention for Mexico when he announced that Mexico would fully embrace the market, and then moved quickly to promote Mexico's economic integration into the North American economy. Making promises to his countrymen that these changes would bring Mexico into the First World, the Salinas administration embraced the privatization of publicly held agencies for three reasons. First, he felt that government agencies were a financial burden on the state. Second, Salinas needed to generate operating funds for the national budget. The sale of state run agencies would help in this process. Third, because the federal government subsidized money-losing state businesses, not only did the state discriminate against private industry, but it skewed the natural workings of the market by keeping uncompetitive and inefficient firms in business. To become competitive in international markets, Salinas recognized that this situation would have to change

While reducing the number of state run businesses helped trim national budget outlays for money losing enterprises, and increased general operating funds, there were political costs to Salinas's privatization program. For example, as the number of state run agencies were cut, the PRI's pool of political resources began to evaporate. Because opposition parties were increasingly winning more seats at the state and local level, not only had the PRI's capacity to deliver political seats been undermined by the increased legitimacy of opposition political parties, but the PRI could no longer guarantee government jobs to the party faithful because the number of state run agencies controlled by the government (i.e., the PRI) had been reduced substantially. In sum, pressures for change from without helped reduce the PRI's pool of political and economic resources by establishing the need for increased efficiency in government and in the private sector.

Given the pressures for democratic opening, it is no wonder that as the PRI's political and economic resources eroded, the more entrenched elements of Mexico's political system began to fear for their future. Simply stated, they believed their days would be numbered under a more accountable and democratic Mexico. The issue of accountability becomes even more important as the connection between drugs, corruption, the political assassinations, and suspected *narco-políticos* continues to grow. It is for this reason that casting Mexico's post-devaluation political problems as a battle for ideological dominance of the PRI is, largely, a failure of analysis. The battle isn't ideological. It is a struggle over power, and how Mexico will be ruled in the future.

With this in mind, it should come as no surprise that the forces of the NWO should be seen as a double edged sword. On the one hand they help promote and sustain the pressures for democratic opening that the West believes will be Mexico's salvation. However, with an economic base that can not generate genuine balance of trade surpluses, these forces may create the conditions for financial anarchy as investors and money houses alike will be sure to cry foul over Mexico's need to borrow, and its subsequent inability to pay their external debt obligations. This no doubt could lead to instability if investing institutions shy away from Mexico's money markets in the future. To attract the investments they need to remain solvent in the future, Mexico has privatized and restructured its economy in an effort to generate confidence among international investors.

VII. THE LIE OF PRIVATIZATION AND POST-DEVALUATION RESTRUCTURING

In the euphoria that followed the Salinas administration's embrace of free market principles, many political and financial analysts conveniently, and naively, ignored the fact that the vast majority of Mexico's newly privatized companies were not ready to compete in global markets. Their need to retool and upgrade equipment, coupled with high credit costs, meant that many companies found themselves at a comparative disadvantage vis-avis foreign competitors who were invited to compete in Mexico's economy. However, caught up in the free market enthusiasm that enveloped the Salinas administration, many of the newly privatized firms were, prematurely, marketed as competitive companies by financial houses like Goldman Sachs and Bear Stearns (the Bush administration had a hand in this as well by encouraging U.S. investors to support Mexico's privatization efforts). The end result? A perception in the U.S. that all was well in Mexico.

Indeed, up until the December 1995 devaluation, market guides like *U.S./Latin Trade* and *Banamex: Review of the Economic Situation in Mexico* (the monthly review of the Mexican economy put out by Mexico's largest bank, *Banco Nacional de México*) were waxing over the strength of the Mexican economy and extolling the virtues of investing in Mexico. Basing their analysis on the assumption that privatization, portfolio investment, and development are somehow synonymous, these and other investment guides somehow forgot to mention that unemployment, export earnings concentrated in the hands of a few industrial firms, mounting external debt obligations, peasant economies, general poverty, corruption, and black markets were not disappearing. Indeed, with the exception of a handful of firms that made new buyers extremely wealthy overnight - the classic example is *Teléfonos de Mexico* - the reality was that most of these firms were inefficient, uncompetitive, and underfinanced (which is the primary reason the state decided to unload them in the first place). In sum, they were largely incapable of generating and sustaining economic growth to produce the surpluses necessary to pay off Mexico's growing debt obligations. This is a condition that continues to exist today.

On another level, we must keep in mind that while the U.S. led $50 billion bail-out and President Zedillo's emergency economic plan worked wonders to soothe the immediate fears of international investors in the first three months of 1995, they did little to address the needs of the average Mexican consumer. For example, holding down wages, increasing taxes and raising the price of government controlled goods - like gasoline, cooking oil, toll road tariffs, etc. - put all of the responsibility for Mexico's economic recovery on the backs of the middle class and the working poor; i.e. the economic classes who gained the least from Salinas' economic miracle. Indeed, by June 1995 it was reported that inflation and steady drops in wages and consumer power over the past two decades have made real wage levels in Mexico "one of the lowest in the world" (*Financiero: International Edition,* 1995ii: 5).

One of the biggest problem with placing the burden of Zedillo's austerity program on the backs of the average Mexican is that the two government approved programs that were designed to cushion the impact of inflation and declining wages have been poorly received and, more to the point, are considered failures. For example, the Unit of Investment (*Unidad de Inversión, UDI*) program was designed to index saving and investment accounts to national inflation levels. In very general terms, the idea was that if investors placed their money in UDI notes (which were managed by banks), these notes would mature, and the investor would be paid their original investment, plus inflation (as indexed by Mexico's central bank). In the case of the Debtor Aid Plan (*Acuerdo de Apoyo Inmediato a los Deudores de la Banca,* ADE), simple debt restructuring was the goal, with both the government and the bank absorbing some of the losses incurred by the banks planned reduction in interest rates (Taranto, 1995; Banamex, 1995; Soto, l995i, 1995ii).

Because these programs were very confusing, poorly implemented, had unattainable standards (for the ADE program), suffered from poor public relations, and generated confusion among both bankers and the public alike, both the UDI and ADE program have been widely ignored by the general public. When we add to this the contradictions inherent in

President Zedillo's PND program, the economy's continued high credit costs and falling real wages, it becomes obvious why little hope exists for the average homeowner, individual and small and medium sized industrialist. Knowing that the Bank of Mexico is committed to a stringent monetary policy (and has President Zedillo's support), we should not be surprised in the future to see social pressures and movements increase as investment and growth continues to be choked off in post-devaluation Mexico.

The issue of future growth is significant because the number of Mexicans entering the workforce has climbed exponentially while the number of jobs created continues to grow arithmetically in Mexico. According to several studies, in the 15 years between 1985 and 1999, the Mexican economy will have created only 881,000 jobs in the formal sector. In the same period, demand for new jobs will reach 17.1 million (half of Mexico's population is 16 years old or younger). This means that between 1985 and 1999, 16.2 million Mexican's who look - or who have looked for work - find nothing but frustration (Ramirez, 1995). As one commentator put it,

> The cold facts are that a country that does not generate employment will not become viable. [President] Zedillo's economic program is therefore mistaken. The program seeks to make Mexico a viable debtor nation rather than support the viability of Mexico based on stable employment (Ramirez, 1995).

What this means is that if Mexico is to have any hope of creating a viable economy that generates jobs, new programs that focus on small and medium sized industries need to be developed. At this point Zedillo's PND program and the government-private sector supported UDI/ADE programs appear ill-equipped to remedy the immediate investment needs of Mexico. This suggests that Mexico's only real option is, once again, investment from without. What this means is that Mexico will have to turn to the new miracle makers of international development - the portfolio managers of international money houses.

VIII. PORTFOLIO MANAGERS AS THE NEW MIRACLE MAKERS

Because of collective ignorance and because Mexico's economic situation continues to be rather precarious, many people in the United States had little idea what the Clinton adminstration's February 1994 bail-out was all about. However, as I will outline below, one thing will become clear: the bail-out should be seen as a stop-gap measure because it did absolutely nothing to increase Mexico's productive capacity, nor did it address Mexico's capacity to pay growing debt obligations in the long-term. The reason for this is that the bail-out simply provided Mexico with funds to pay debt obligations to ill-advised investing money houses. Because these investors - or portfolio managers - bought over US$50 billion in Mexican government securities, they provided enormous financial resources which helped create the illusion that an economic miracle was occurring in Mexico.

However, it is my view that the bail-out was irresponsible because it rewarded rather than punished - investors and securities analysts who have short-term time horizons and, quite frankly, did not do their homework on Mexico. The primary reason for this is that as long as fund and portfolio managers can secure quick and high rates of returns, they don't really question what "emerging markets" experts are saying in financial centers like New York or London. Instead, with their commissions guaranteed (coming and going), they tend to overlook underlying problems in places like Mexico and, quite frankly, could really care less about the consequences of short-term portfolio investment in the developing world. To be sure, fund managers want their investments to do well, but their cavalier attitudes come either from incompetence or from knowing that losses can be glossed over, or made up relatively quickly because additional opportunities lie elsewhere in the emerging market bonanza that we see in the NWO[8].

---

8. Part of the reason for professional incompetence lay not so much with untalented brokers as it does with the difficulty of consistently trying to beat the market. Numerous studies have shown that, over the long haul, the odds of beating the market are astronomical and that someone who buys a representative cross-section of the market and holds onto it, comes out better statistically than someone who trades in and out of markets. For an excellent review of

In this sense, international investors who promote portfolio-type investments in developing countries may actually make the problem worse by dangling badly needed short-term investment funds in front of desperate government officials who know all too well that they will not be held responsible for paying loans back once they've left office. This is interesting because it demonstrates that a new force has entered the picture of international development - the managers of portfolio investments. Indeed,

> . . . [b]etween 1977 and 1981, 67 percent of Latin America's external financing came from commercial banks. Between 1989 to 1992, this share plummeted to 14 percent Meanwhile, money from mutual funds and other stock and bond investors grew to 40 per cent of foreign investment in the region, up from a paltry 15 per cent in the late 1970's. Between 1990 and 1994, the World Bank disbursed $84 billion to all developing countries. In the same period, private investors poured a net $660 billion into these countries (Naim, 1995: 122).

As these trends continue, the biggest problem for the future is that fund managers from international money houses - whose primary interest logically lies in protecting investor interests first - have become more involved in "advising" countries like Mexico. There are many problems with this arrangement; the most significant being the obvious conflict of interest. On this we have to remember that portfolio investment is generally short-term, speculative and directly tied to their clients financial future. For this reason fund managers are less concerned with investing and maintaining funds in a strategic country like Mexico for the long-term then they are with getting their money into areas that offer higher rates and, ostensibly, more security in the immediate term. What makes the conflict of interest thesis even more compelling is that in addition to protecting their clients interests, it must be remembered that fund managers must also protect their institutions position and prestige.

For example, after Mexico's financial insolvency and subsequent devaluation, fund managers realized that the lawsuits they saw after Orange

---

the difficulties - and costs - in trying to beat the market, see chapter 7 of Millman (1995). For an interesting review on simple incompetence in brokerage houses see Leah Nathans Spiro and Michael Schroeder (1995).

County's bankruptcy were going to come their way as well if they could not secure their clients investments in Mexico. It was at this time that a U.S. government bail-out for Mexico began to be discussed. Soon after, fund managers realized that securing a U.S. bail-out would require convincing Mexico to accept austerity measures that the Clinton administration would no doubt mandate for any type of aid package. The result was that the prescriptions of these instant Mexican economic advisers not only reduced Mexican sovereignty because of what they prescribed, but their advice had as much to do with "reducing the huge losses they and their gullible clients were facing" as it did with the plight of the Mexicans (Naim, 1995: 122).

In the immediate term, the argument that much of Mexico's debt will be rolled over provides some hope in that it buys Mexico more time, but does not address, let alone solve, the underlying structural and competitive problems that continue to plague Mexico's industrial sector. Moreover, rolling over loans may make the situation worse because the process simply brings in more money to temporarily stabilize the situation (thus making the original loan larger) and capitalizes interest due which, unfortunately, lets everyone pretend that original loans are performing. In the end, the recent devaluation was, and continues to be, a product of structural problems in the economy that inhibit Mexico's ability to compete and generate trade surpluses. In the absence of a concerted long-term plan to generate jobs (e.g. helping deserving small and medium sized industries obtain credit) this problem will continue to exist and will dominate the Mexican economy for years to come.

In this manner, as the patient capital of foreign direct investment begins to take a back seat to the demands and realities of portfolio investment, long-term stabilizing projects and industrial development programs will become even more scarce in developing countries like Mexico. The lesson of Mexico's devaluation and its dependence on portfolio investment, then, is not one of interdependence as unimaginative proponents of the NWO claim. Instead, the real lesson of Mexico's December 1994 devaluation is that it provides us with a glimpse of the new international financial system and Mexico's future in the real NWO - and, for better or worse, that glimpse is one of impatient capital and reduced state sovereignty for developing nations like Mexico (Millman, 1995; Kurtzman, 1993).

IX. Analysis

It should come as no surprise that the forces of the NWO should be seen as a double edged sword. On the one hand they help promote and sustain the pressures for democratic opening that the West believes will be Mexico's salvation. However, with an economic base that can not generate genuine balance of trade surpluses, the same forces that help create the NWO may also generate the conditions for financial chaos as international money houses and those who like to bet on the "hot tip of the month" will be sure to cry foul over Mexico's borrowing, and its subsequent inability to pay growing external debt obligations. In spite of the considerable forces that make up the world of international finance in the NWO, it is my view that President Zedillo can still help Mexico control its fate, but he needs to act decisively if this fate is to be a favorable one.

Among the things that President Zedillo can do to enhance Mexico's political future are tied, but not limited to: (1) arresting and convicting several high profile *narco-politicos*, (2) getting to the bottom and solving the political assassination cases (probably tied to number 1), (3) making deals with credible and legitimate *politicos*,[9] (4) developing a comprehensive economic plan that gains the confidence of business, government, and labor leaders, (5) settling the Chiapas affair; (6) designing a viable program for dealing with rural poverty, (7) finding a way to increase industrial capacity so that Mexico's export base is enhanced (the last two are, admittedly, long-term projects), and (8) finding a way to deal with the demands and fickleness of the NWO's financial markets (perhaps the most difficult of all).

Obviously these goals are not mutually exclusive. Indeed, the development of at least four of these events would go a long way in helping Mexico sustain itself against the forces of the NWO. To promote these developments, President Ernesto Zedillo initiated a comprehensive economic plan designed to revitalize the Mexican economy, the National Development Plan. However, while President Zedillo's economic plan may be sane and logical in developed Western economies (and in introductory

---

9. There is little doubt that President Zedillo initiated this process by replacing the head of the Secretaria de Gobernacion (Secretary of Internal Security, the most powerful post in Mexico outside of the presidency), Esteban Moctezuma, who was known as a democrat, with hardliner Emilio Chuayffett in July of 1995 (Caballero, 1995).

economic textbooks), his plan falls on its face when we consider the following economic realities in Mexico: the country is still dependent on a handful of firms for its export earnings; Mexico's external debt has surpassed US$152 billion and continues to grow; it must generate between US$12-15 billion in current account surpluses per year to keep up with interest payments alone (*Mexico & NAFTA Report*, 1995i: 1); the newly privatized banking system is on the verge of collapse; black markets (including drugs) continue to dominate many parts of Mexico's economy, and; peasant economies are still an integral part of Mexico's economic scene. The last may be the most troubling characteristic because it underscores the fact that there are structural divisions in the Mexican economy which many politicians and economists tend to ignore: (1) a concentrated group of exporters tied to the First World; (2) a much bigger group that remains tied to the shrinking internal economy; and (3) the subsistence economy dominated by peasants.[10]

With the exception of the newly privatized banking industry, all of these point to sectors of the economy that have little to do with (nor are they responsive to) economic programs like Zedillo's in the immediate term. When we consider that there are only two ways to obtain dollars to pay off external obligations - increasing exports, or paying attractive interest rates to those willing to lend - Mexico's continued dependence on outside support for short-term capital suggests that it lacks the capacity to determine its own fate in the NWO. As noted above, this problem is made worse by false prophets who point to post-devaluation trade surpluses as a sign of economic strength and national recovery.

Moreover, we need to consider the real value of a devalued currency if inflation can wipe out the gains tied of a cheap peso. For example, if inflation runs at a rate of 50 percent, then it follows that the peso must fall against the dollar by a similar magnitude just to maintain the real, inflation-adjusted value, or parity, against the dollar. If this does not occur then the peso is overvalued. UNAM economics professor, Jose Luis argues that the rising real value of the peso is a genuine threat to the Zedillo administration's exchange rate policies. This is especially so because the

---

10. In my view, these divisions are what allow politicians and the press to suggest that recovery is occurring in the Mexican economy. They are able to point to one sector of the economy (in particular, the export sector) and claim success while ignoring the realities that exist in the larger real economy where the vast majority of Mexican's work and live.

policy of a fixed peso is mandated by Mexico's agreement with the IMF and the Clinton administration. As such, if the peso continues to appreciate against the dollar, while current accounts surpluses continue to be generated by forces other than genuine growth, financial insolvency can only be a matter of time.

X. Conclusion

While developing countries have always depended on foreign capital, technology, and markets, the biggest difference between today and 25 years ago (as Moises Naim points out) is that the immediate macroeconomic balance of a host country - for financing trade deficits and other financial obligations - has never been as dependent on the decisions of a few nongovernmental money managers as is the case today. Just as significant, the continued and long-term failure of the neo-liberal economic model in Mexico suggests that Mexico needs to reevaluate how it will apply the remedies of neo-liberal doctors in the future. This point is not to suggest that we devalue the role of capitalism and the market in Mexico. For it certainly has a place in generating efficiency and production, and is by far the best tool for maintaining market discipline.

However, if the past 20 years are any indication of what Mexico - and Latin America - can expect from neo-liberalism, perhaps Mexico needs to start developing a market model that reflect internal realities and is more realistic about the prospects for Mexico's middle and subsistence classes in the immediate term. As the president of the Mexican Association of Employers *(Confederacion Patronal de la Republica Mexicana,* or Coparmex) put it, while Mexico cannot ignore the basic tenets of the market, it needs to "humanize" its economic program for the benefit of all involved. He added that,

> What should be clear to our creditors around the world is that it is better for everyone involved, beginning with us Mexicans, to have a living Mexican economy, not a clean cadaver; [it is better to have] a viable and live economy, although it has a few diseases, [rather than] one that is in constant recovery *(Reforma,* 1995).

This statement certainly suggests that Mexico should develop a market model whose terms are not dictated from without.

What all of this means for Mexico's political scene is difficult to say. However, it does suggest that things may destabilize even further if current accounts don't begin to show genuine surpluses; i.e., surpluses not induced by devaluations, borrowing, or drawing on credits. As noted above, moderate balance of trade surpluses in the first half of 1995, while encouraging, are largely illusory because they are surpluses generated by the 1994 devaluation (rather than by increased competitiveness). When we consider that Mexico will have to service at least $13.5 billion in external debt obligations in 1995 (*Mexico & NAFTA Report*, 1995ii: 1), it appears that Mexico has three options. The first is to simply declare a moratorium and not pay. The second option involves a rescheduling of the debt until the macroeconomic program brings stability and real growth to the economy. The third is tied to promoting additional portfolio investment in Mexico.

Obviously the first option is (at this point) viewed as a non-option by the Zedillo administration because of the ideological and policy symmetry that exists between his administration, the developed Western economic states and supra-national lending agencies like the IMF. The problem with the next two options (rescheduling and portfolio investment) is that, if history is any indication, domestic recovery will end up taking a back seat to the demands of international financial markets. Unfortunately, this may be the only option because there is little doubt that the Mexican government has proven itself incapable of designing an economic model that supports growth and employment in the formal sectors of the Mexican economy.

What Mexico needs to remember is that trade surpluses generated by a devalued peso and borrowing to pay debts and to generate international reserves does not equal sustainable economic growth and political stability. More than paying debts on time with borrowed funds, or how many dollars show up as international reserves as a result of these borrowed funds, what really matters for an economy is its ability to generate stable jobs in the formal economy. Failing this, we shouldn't be surprised to see many of political events that we saw occur in Mexico from 1993 to 1995 repeated sometime during President Zedillo's administration. In the end, there is no doubt that the stakes are high for Mexico, and those who see their interests threatened are willing to resort to violence to maintain or guard their interests in the future. What this means is that Mexico and the PRI may have entered into an era of political cannibalism that will end with either a more open democratic society, or degenerate into an authoritarian regime dominated by drug thugs like those of the *La Cosa Nostra*. Given the alternative, we can only hope that the pressures created for democracy and reform by the New World Order prevails.

REFERENCES

Acosta Cordova, Carlos, "La banca comercial se desploma en los numeros rojos: recibe del gobierno mas de lo que presta y mas de lo que costo," in *Proceso*, 1995, July 31, 978, pp. 12-17.

Baker, Stephen, "The Friends of Salinas," in *Business Week*, 1991, July 22, pp. 14-16.

Banamex, "Acuerdo de Apoyo Inmediato para Deudores de la Banca," in *Banamex: Examen de la Situacion Economica*, 1995, September, LXXI (838), pp. 343-349.

Basave Kunhardt, Jorge, "El capital financiero nacional e internacional: sustento del modelo neoliberal mexicano," in *Problemas del Desarrollo-Revista Latinoamericana de Economia*, 1995, Julio-Septiembre, 26 (102), pp. 57-69.

Bonilla Sanchez, Arturo, "Mexico: la primera gran crisis en la globalizacion financiera," in *Problemas del Desarrollo: Revista Latinoamericana de Economia*, 1995, Julio-Septiembre, 100 (102), pp. 85-108.

Caballero, Alejandro, "El talentoso, pero inexperto Esteban Moctezuma, abre paso, con su renuncia, a un politico ligado con Carlos Hank," in *Proceso*, July 3, pp. 6-13.

Calva, Jose Luis, "Plan Nacional de Desarrollo, 1995-2000: Los fines, los medios y las alternativas," in *Problemas del Desarrollo: Revista Latinoamericana de Economia*, 1995, Julio-Septiembre, 26 (100), pp. 29-55.

Camp, Roderic A., *Politics in Mexico*, (New York: Oxford, 1993).

Chavez, Elias, "Literal: sangrienta lucha por el poder entre los grupos del PRI," in *Proceso*, 1994, November 21, pp. 24-27.

Cornelius, Wayne A. and Ann L. Craig, *Politics in Mexico: An Introduction and Overview*, (La Jolla, California: Center for U.S.-Mexican Studies, 1988).

Corro, Salvador, et al., "Denme 400 hombres armados, y les controlo dos municipios en un ratito!: Constantino Kanter," in *Proceso,* 1994, April 18, pp. 32-35.

Cruz Gomez, Manuel, et al., "Procampo o Anticipo?", in *El Financiero* (Enfoques), 1993, October 20, p. 30A.

Dresser, Denise, "Neopopulist Solutions to Neoliberal Problems: Mexico's National Solidarity Program," *Current Issue Brief,* no. 3, 1991, Center for U.S.-Mexican Studies, University of California, San Diego.

El Financiero: International Edition, "Mexico Short $1.3 Billion," 1995i, October 9-15, pp. 1, 16.

"Mexican Wages Fall to Worldwide Lows," 1995ii, June 19-25, p. 5.

_____. "Privatizations Under Salinas Scrutinized", 1995iii, May 15-21, p. 8.

Gasca, Armando, "Propone IP humanizar programa economico," in *Reforma,* 1995, July 31.

Gonzalez, Hector A., "La PGR, sin capacidad para administrar los bienes decomisados al narco," in *El Financiero,* 1995, June 28, p. 31.

Krugman, Paul, "Dutch Tulips and Emerging Markets", in *Foreign Affairs,* 1995, July/August, pp. 28-44.

Kurtzman, Joel, *The Death of Money: How The Electronic Economy Has Destabilized the World's Markets and Created Financial Chaos.* (New York, NY: Little, Brown, 1993).

Martinez, Oscar, "Podria retornar el deficit de la balanza comercial en 1996," in *El Economista,* 1995, September 14, p. 41.

Mexico & NAFTA Report, "New Evidence Implicates Carlos Salinas: Raul, his brother, is already up to his eyeballs," in *Latin American Regional Reports,* 1995i, October 12, p. 2.

_____. "Will Mexico have to reschedule its debts again in 1995? Yes, Probably," in *Latin American Regional Reports,* 1995ii, September 25, p. 1.

_____. "VAT: Misguided, Unfair, and Piddling," in *Latin American Regional Reports,* 1995iii, April 20, p. 7.

Millman, Gregory J., *The Vandals' Crown: How Rebel Currency Traders Overthrew the World's Central Bankers.* (New York, NY: Free Press, 1995).

Naim, Moises, "Mexico's Larger Story," in *Foreign Policy,* 1995, Summer, pp. 112-130.

Nathans Spiro, Leah and Michael Schroeder, "Can You Trust Your Broker?," in *Business Week*, 1995, February 20, pp. 70-76.

Ramirez, Carlos, "The Fourth World," in *El Financiero: International Edition*, 1995, April 17-23, p. 6.

Rebollo Pinal, Herminio, in *El Financiero: International Edition*, "New Mexican Miracle on the Way?", 1995, May 8-14, p. 8.

Resillas, Andres, "Senalan a RSG como narco," in *Reforma*, 1995, July 4, p. 6A.

Rodriguez Castaneda, Rafael, "Entre Salinas and Zedillo golpearon a quince de los supermillonarios, hijos consentidos del regimen tecnocrata," in *Proceso*, 1995, July 10, p. 6.

_____. "El reparto de la riqueza en tiempo de Salinas de Gortari: En 1991 habia dos mexicanos con mas de 1,000 de dolares; En 1992 habia siete; ahora ya hay trece," in *Proceso*, 1993, July 12, pp. 6-9.

Rotella, Sebastian, "Mexico's Cartels Sow Seeds of Corruption, Destruction," in the *Los Angeles Times*, 1995, June 16, pp. A20-21.

Silk, Leonard, "Dangers of Slow Growth," in *Foreign Affairs*, 1992/93, 72 (1), pp. 167-182.

Smith, Peter H., *Labyrinths of Power: Political Recruitment in Twentieth-Century Mexico*. (Princeton, NJ: Princeton University Press, 1979).

Soto, Luis, "Confused Bankers," in *El Financiero: International Edition*, 1995i, September 25-October 1, p. 13.

_____. "The Errors of Advertising," in *El Financiero: International Edition*, 1995ii, September 18-24, p. 13.

_____. "Skeptical 'Gringos'," in *El Financiero: International Edition*, 1995iii, September 4-10, p. 3.

Tankersley, Robyn, "Banking Commission Seizes Four Institutions," in *The News*, 1995, July 1, pp. 1, 39.

Taranto, Al, "UDI's - and Now for the Details," in *El Financiero: International Edition*, 1995, April 10-16, p. 5.

The News, "Do More Exports Automatically Spell Recovery?," 1995, July 24, p. 33.

Trejo, Amparo and Santiago Perez, "El Senor: Se Va al Cielo," in *Reforma*, 1995, July 1, p. 5A.

UNITED STATES-EAST ASIAN TRADE IN THE NEW WORLD ORDER

Margaret M. Malixi
Department of Economics
California State University
Bakersfield, CA 93311

Mohsen Bahmani-Oskooee[*]
Department of Economics
The University of Wisconsin-Milwaukee
Milwaukee, WI 53201

Abstract—In this chapter an analysis of U.S.-East Asian trade is presented within the context of the new world order. Cointegration analysis is applied to a reduced form bilateral trade balance model. Our results indicate one cointegrating vector each for Indonesia and Korea and none for either Singapore and Malaysia. Depreciation appears to be an effective policy tool for improving the U.S. trade balance, while U.S. output growth is irrelevant in explaining bilateral trade flows. Sustained East Asian output growth is expected to further improve East Asian trade balances and worsen U.S. bilateral deficits. The implications of these results for U.S.-East Asian trade relations and East Asia's place in the New World Order are discussed.

I. INTRODUCTION

The phenomenal growth rates of the export-oriented economies of East Asia have produced a profound shift in the world's economic geography. Despite the new economic landscape, the United States remains a major player in the success of the rapidly industrializing countries of East Asia.

---

[*] We would like to thank Andrew J. Caffrey for efficient research assistance.

The U.S. is still about the most significant export market for most of the emerging economies of the Asian Pacific Rim, where astounding growth in per capita income and productivity have made the region an attractive market for U.S. goods and investment. The U.S. is also a vital source of imports for these countries, which have aggregate import values rivaling those of Japan.

The magnitude of the trade interdependence between the U.S. and its East Asian trading partners makes it clearly beneficial to learn more about the important factors that drive trade flows between them. This is the primary motivation of the present study. Our task becomes even more consequential when we consider that the U.S. maintains persistent trade deficits with a majority of these countries.

The Newly Industrializing Economies (NIEs) of the region have experienced some of the highest real growth rates of recent times. Hong Kong, Korea, Singapore and Taiwan have had real gross domestic product annual growth rates of between 7 and 10 percent sustained over more than thirty years (Naya and Imada, 1990). Indonesia, Malaysia, the Philippines and Thailand; collectively known as the Association of Southeast Asian Nations Four (or ASEAN-4), are widely considered to be the next tier of NIEs, with sustained annual real growth rates of between 3 to 5 percent.[1]

Export growth has been undeniably important to the development of the East Asian economies. Primarily due to the performance of the developing economies and the NIEs, East Asia's share of world exports more than doubled from 10 percent in 1970 to 21 percent in 1990.[2] Barring a serious adverse turn of events, it is anticipated that the export dynamism of the region will continue with the same vigor and will be more likely accelerated by industrial growth in China and the Southeast Asian nations. In fact, the Japan Center for Economic Research (1992) forecasts that East Asia's share of world exports will increase from 21 percent in 1990 to 27 percent in 2000 and to 31 percent in 2010 (Young, p.119).

In anticipation of the accuracy of these forecasts, it is expected that the rest of the world, and especially the European Community (EC) and the

---

1. Philippine growth rates have been weaker on the average due to prolonged political instability and infrastructural bottlenecks. There are, however, signs of an economic revival that foreshaddow a more optimistic future for the Philippines, more in line with the other ASEAN countries.
2. Source: IMF, *Direction of Trade Yearbook*, 1970 and 1990.

U.S., will continue to intensify regional trade relations and use discriminatory protection to ensure the competitiveness of their own industries, as well as defend against the tremendous import competition from East Asian industries. According to Young (1993), the increase in East Asia's share of world exports will have to come at the expense of the U.S. and the EC, as well as their regional partners, and will inevitably pose serious threats to their industries.

The emergence of the European Economic Community (EEC) and the North American Free Trade Agreement (NAFTA) in the 1990s as regional trading blocs, has led to predominantly discriminatory trade expansion in these areas and serious speculation of a regional discriminatory bloc within East Asia itself. East Asian trade expansion has, however, been associated with reductions in barriers to international, including intraregional trade. Intra-East Asian trade increased from around 30 percent of the East Asian total in 1970 to around 40 percent in 1990 (Drysdale and Garnaut, p.183).[3] The character of trade liberalization in East Asia has been overwhelmingly nondiscriminatory and unilateral. Drysdale and Garnaut (1993) make the observation that in the case of East Asia, it appears that western Pacific economies have realized the highly beneficial effect of liberalization on their own trade expansion and that whatever policies others follow, they will benefit more from keeping their own borders open to trade than from protection. Gains have also been realized in the reduction of nonofficial barriers to trade of various kinds, as part of the regions efforts towards deeper integration into the international economy.[4]

Although recent economic trends have been toward regional trading blocs and discriminatory protectionism, East Asian countries are very much aware that their economic interests are global. Unlike much of the rest of the world, there has been a clear trend toward trade liberalization and greater openness throughout the western Pacific. Nevertheless, the increasing dominance of the Asian economies increases the possibility that external barriers in the rest of the world are likely to be raised, especially

---

3. East Asia includes China, Japan, Hong Kong, South Korea, Taiwan, Brunei, Indonesia, Malaysia, Philippines, Singapore, and Thailand.
4. The process has been driven by independent enterprises' search for more profitable patterns of trade sometimes assisted by provisions by governments of public goods that affect the operation of private markets (Drysdale and Garnaut, p.193).

in sectors experiencing acute adjustment difficulties. Young (1993) asserts that this "new regionalism", which is characterized by the absence of a dominant economy thus making economic conflict much more likely, is a threat to the world as a whole and the dynamic exporters of East Asia in particular. This chapter is an empirical investigation into U.S.-East Asian trade within the context of the New World Order. The rest of the chapter is organized as follows: the bilateral trade balance model is presented in section II, section III is an explanation of our methodology, section IV is a presentation and discussion of the empirical results, and in section V we summarize and conclude the chapter.

II. THE BILATERAL TRADE BALANCE MODEL

At the onset of the regime of floating exchange rates various studies, both theoretical and empirical, have concentrated their efforts on identifying and isolating the effects of changes in the value of a country's currency vis-a-vis other international currencies on its trade balance. Two prominent approaches in the literature are the income absorption and the elasticities approach. These approaches differ markedly in two respects: (1) each identifies a different variable as a source of the disequilibrium and consequently, (2) each approach recommends a different policy measure as a means of correcting an external deficit.

The income absorption approach attributes the imbalance in the external accounts to a more rapid rate of growth in domestic income relative to that of the rest of the world and thus, supports a deceleration in growth as a means of recovering the external balance. In contrast, the elasticities method derives the necessary and sufficient condition for an improvement in the trade balance in terms of demand and supply elasticities of a country's imports and exports. Successful devaluation is characterized by sufficiently large demand elasticities combined with sufficiently small supply elasticities. The Marshall-Lerner condition is the traditional criteria set forth for successful devaluation. It states that, in order for devaluation to improve the trade balance in the long run, the sum of the price elasticities of domestic and foreign import demand must be greater than one.

Our trade balance model draws on both these approaches. Following Rose and Yellen (1989), we specify the bilateral trade balance equation as a function of its most important determinants: the real bilateral exchange rate, domestic and foreign real incomes. The appropriate methodology for our econometric investigation is cointegration analysis, which calls for the specification of a reduced form trade balance model such as equation (1).

$$\text{Log TB} = F[\text{ Log Y, Log YUS, Log REX }] \qquad (1)$$

where TB = bilateral trade balance between the U.S. and trading partner i, Y = real domestic output of country i measured by the real Gross Domestic Product (GDP), YUS = U.S. real domestic output, and REX = real bilateral exchange rate, defined as the number of country i's domestic currency per U.S. dollar. Detailed variable definitions and a list of data sources are contained in the appendix to this chapter. Our sample was limited by the availability of consistent quarterly data for the period 1973I to 1993IV.

The Asian trading partners included in our sample are Indonesia, Korea, Malaysia and Singapore. Following Haynes and Stone (1982), Bahmani-Oskooee (1991) and Bahmani-Oskooee and Malixi (1992), we express the trade balance as the ratio of country i's exports to the U.S. to its imports from the United States.[5] There are a number of advantages to expressing the trade balance in ratio form: (1) the ratio is insensitive to the currency units, whether foreign or domestic, used to measure both exports and imports;[6] (2) it is also insensitive to whether the trade balance is measured in real or nominal terms and therefore it is also not sensitive to the price index used to deflate it (Bahmani-Oskooee, 1991); and (3) the ratio enables us to estimate the trade balance equation in log form.

Increases in domestic income or output (Y) stimulate an increase in imports and therefore lead to a deterioration in the trade balance. Thus, we expect the coefficient of Y to be negative. On the other hand, it may be that at high levels of income or output, the domestic production of importables may rise more rapidly than consumption, resulting in an eventual decline in imports. It is therefore possible to obtain a positive coeffi-

---

5. Haynes and Stone (1982) actually used the ratio of imports to exports in their evaluation of the impact of the terms of trade on the U.S. trade balance.
6. The choice of currency units (whether domestic or foreign) used to measure the trade balance can actually impact the empirical results. For example, Miles (1979) measured the trade balance in terms of domestic currency and found that devaluation did not significantly impact the trade balance. Using the same sample countries, but measuring the trade balance in foreign currency units (U.S. dollars), Himarios (1985) demonstrated that devaluation can significantly impact the trade balance (Bahmani-Oskooee, 1991).

cient for Y as well. Parallel reasoning would lead us to expect either a positive or a negative sign for the coefficient of YUS.

The bilateral exchange rate (REX) is measured as the number of i's domestic currency per U.S. dollar. Hence, an increase in REX is a depreciation of i's currency and the expected result is an improvement in country i's bilateral trade balance as exports rise and imports fall in response to the depreciation. An increasing foreign price index and/or a decreasing domestic price level will yield similar results. A depreciation or devaluation of country i's domestic currency is expected to improve i's bilateral trade balance with the U.S., thus we expect a positive coefficient.

III. THE METHODOLOGY

Our focus in this study is to identify the long-run equilibrium relationship between the bilateral trade balance of the U.S. with each of the four Asian trading partners and the variables most often considered to be its most important determinants: (1) the real output of trading partner i (Y), (2) U.S. real domestic output (YUS) and (3) the real bilateral exchange rate (REX). The appropriate analytical procedure is cointegration analysis. The method of cointegration is based on the idea that certain pairs or sets of economic time series move together over the long-run without straying very far apart. These long-term relationships are often interpreted as equilibrium relationships between pairs or among a set of variables.

In particular we use the cointegration technique of Johansen (1988) and Johansen and Juselius (1990). They employ a maximum likelihood estimation procedure that provides two test statistics, the *trace* and the *λ-max*, for the determination of the number of cointegrating vectors as well as estimates of all cointegrating vectors which may exist among a set of variables.

Johansen (1988) defines a distributed lag model of a vector of variables, X as

$$X_t = \Pi_1 X_{t-1} + \Pi_2 X_{t-2} + \ldots + \Pi_k X_{t-k} + \varepsilon_t \qquad (2)$$

where X is a vector of N *stationary* variables. It is important that the data be stationary otherwise the time series' may drift apart over time. In case the variables in X are non-stationary and achieve stationarity after being differenced once, equation (2) can be rewritten in its first differenced form similar to the Augmented Dickey-Fuller (ADF) test as indicated by equation (3):

$$\Delta X_t = \Gamma_1 \Delta X_{t-1} + \Gamma_2 \Delta X_{t-2} + \ldots + \Gamma_{k-1} \Delta X_{t-k+1} - \Pi X_{t-k} + \varepsilon_t \quad (3)$$
$$\text{where } \Gamma_i = -I + \Pi_1 + \Pi_2 + \ldots + \Pi_i \ (i = 1, \ldots, k)$$
$$\text{and } \Pi = -(I - \Pi_1 - \Pi_2 - \ldots - \Pi_k).$$

The long-run cointegrating matrix is given by Π which is an NxN matrix and includes r cointegrating vectors which is the rank of Π. If we define two matrices α and β (both Nxr) such that $\Pi = \alpha\beta'$, the rows of β form the r cointegrating vectors. Johansen and Juselius (1990) demonstrate that one can test the hypothesis that there are at most r cointegrating vectors by calculating the two likelihood test statistics known as the *trace* and the λ-*max* tests.

IV. THE EMPIRICAL RESULTS

Equation (1) is a reduced form trade balance model to which cointegration analysis is applied. Our sample consists of quarterly data over the period 1973I to 1993IV. The first step in our analysis is to verify whether all the variables in the model are of the same order of integration and therefore stationary. The order of integration, I(d), refers to the number of times a series must be differenced in order to obtain a stationary series. Standard critical values used in the determination of the significance of estimated coefficients are rendered invalid when the data series are nonstationary.

The Augmented Dickey-Fuller (ADF) test with a trend term included, is applied to test for stationarity. In general, for a variable Z_t the ADF test for a unit root is of the form of equation (4):

$$Z_t = \alpha + \beta t + \sigma Z_{t-1} + \sum_{i=1}^{k} \gamma_i \Delta Z_{t-i} + w_t \quad (4)$$

where w is an error term. The ADF test statistic is calculated as the ratio of the estimate of $\sigma-1$ to its standard error, where σ is the coefficient of Z_{t-1} in equation (4). The cumulative distribution of the ADF statistic is provided by MacKinnon (1991). If the calculated ADF statistic is less than its critical value, then Z is said to be stationary or integrated of order zero, denoted by I(0). However, most economic time series are I(1), that is, stationarity of the series is achieved after being differenced once. The results of the ADF test appear in Table 1.

Table 1. The ADF Test Results for the Level and for the First Differenced Variables, 1973I - 1993IV

Country i	A: Level of the Variables			
	Log TB	Log Y	Log YUS	Log REX
Indonesia	-3.01[2][a,b]	-2.46[3]	-2.06[1]	-3.37[1]
Korea	-1.59[4]	-3.15[3]	-2.06[1]	-1.95[4]
Malaysia	-2.52[2]	-2.16[4]	-2.06[1]	-3.24[1]
Singpore	-2.08[4]	-2.41[4]	-2.06[1]	-1.32[1]

Country i	B: First Differenced Variables			
	Log TB	Log Y	Log YUS	Log REX
Indonesia	-6.36[4]	-9.17[2]	-6.04[1]	-6.54[1]
Korea	-9.48[2]	-7.32[4]	-6.04[1]	-5.08[1]
Malaysia	-7.71[2]	-6.49[1]	-6.04[1]	-7.43[1]
Singpore	-8.48[1]	-4.07[3]	-6.04[1]	-7.66[1]

Notes: a. The number enclosed in brackets is the number of lags in the ADF test.
b. The Mackinnon (1991) critical value of the ADF statistic (with a trend term in the procedure) for 84 observations is -3.46 at the 5% level of significance.

The critical value of the ADF statistic is -3.46 for 84 observations at the 5% level of significance. Comparing the calculated ADF statistic to its critical value, we conclude that none of the statistics is less than the critical value for the level of the variables (panel A), indicating that none of the variables are stationary. However, when we consider the first-differenced variables (panel B), all variables achieved stationarity. Therefore all variables are I(1) and we are able to proceed with the Johansen-Juselius cointegration procedure using the first-differenced variables.

Table 2. Johansen's Maximum Likelihood Procedure Results for the Variables of the Trade Balance Model, Four Lags in the Procedure, 1973I - 1993IV.

| \multicolumn{6}{c}{A: Results for Indonesia - U.S. Trade Balance Model} |

Null	Alternative	λ-max Statistic	95% Critical Value	Trace Statistic	95% Critical Value
r = 0	r = 1	33.76	27.14	47.91	48.28
r ≤ 1	r = 2	7.97	21.07	14.15	31.53
r ≤ 2	r = 3	5.05	14.90	6.17	7.95
r ≤ 3	r = 4	1.12	8.18	1.12	8.18

B: Results for the Korea - U.S. Trade Balance Model

Null	Alternative	λ-max Statistic	95% Critical Value	Trace Statistic	95% Critical Value
r = 0	r = 1	29.16	27.14	49.06	48.28
r ≤ 1	r = 2	11.31	21.07	19.91	31.53
r ≤ 2	r = 3	7.37	14.90	8.60	17.95
r ≤ 3	r = 4	1.23	8.18	1.23	8.18

C: Results for the Malaysia - U.S. Trade Balance Model

Null	Alternative	λ-max Statistic	95% Critical Value	Trace Statistic	95% Critical Value
r = 0	r = 1	20.38	27.14	41.63	48.28
r ≤ 1	r = 2	15.80	21.07	21.25	31.53
r ≤ 2	r = 3	5.44	14.90	5.45	17.75
r ≤ 3	r = 4	.0025	8.18	.0025	8.8

D: Results for the Singapore - U.S. Trade Balance Model

Null	Alternative	λ-max Statistic	95% Critical Value	Trace Statistic	95% Critical Value
r = 0	r = 1	22.91	27.14	39.10	48.28
r ≤ 1	r = 2	9.48	21.07	16.19	31.53
r ≤ 2	r = 3	6.13	14.90	6.70	17.95
r ≤ 3	r = 4	.5684	8.18	.5684	8.18

In making a decision concerning the order of the underlying Vector Autoregression (VAR) model, we follow Pesaran and Pesaran (1993), who suggest that given the quarterly nature of the data, selecting four lags is a reasonable choice. Nevertheless, in order to determine whether the results are sensitive to the choice of the number of lags, we perform sensitivity analysis similar to that suggested by Enders (1995) and experimented with five and six lags. The results of the λ-*max* and *trace* tests for each of the four U.S. trading partners are reported in Table 2.

Consider the results for Indonesia (Panel A) where four lags are imposed in the procedure. We reject the null hypothesis of no cointegration, i.e., r=0 is rejected because the calculated λ-max statistic is greater than its critical value. This indicated that there is at least one cointegrating vector among the variables in the trade balance model. The null of r$\leq$1 versus r=2, however, cannot be rejected suggesting again, that there is one cointegrating vector. The same is true for the null of r$\leq$2 versus r=3 and for r$\leq$3 versus r=4. All the results are consistent in indicating one cointegrating vector. Alternatively, sensitivity analysis was conducted for each of the four countries by imposing five lags.[7] The results for all countries were no different from those obtained from the four-lag procedure and we therefore did not find it necessary to report them here.

The results for Korea (Panel B) are similar to those for Indonesia and again, there is evidence of one cointegrating vector using the four-lag procedure for Korea. The test results for both Malaysia (Panel C) and Singapore (Panel D) indicate zero cointegrating vector when four or five lags are imposed. The null of r=0 versus r=1 cannot be rejected because the calculated λ-max statistic is less than its critical value. This indicates the absence of a cointegrating vector. The same is true for the null of r$\leq$2 versus r=3 and the null of r$\leq$3 versus r=4. We therefore report, one cointegrating vector each for Indonesia and Korea and none for Malaysia and Singapore. The finding of no cointegrating vector implies the absence of a stable long-run relationship among the set of variables in the model, i.e., there are no cointegrating relationships among the variables in the model.

As noted earlier, we extended our sensitivity analysis to six lags. The only discernible change was in the results for Malaysia. One cointegrating vector was indicated and the hypothesis of no cointegration is rejected,

---

7. Cointegration analysis involves vector autoregressions, where all equations have the same lag length and all polynomials, $A_{ij}(L)$, are the same degree. This is necessary in order to preserve the symmetry of the system. In this case because of this cross-equation restriction, an equation by equation test such as the FPE criterion, is not an appropriate method of selecting the number of lags. Instead, a likelihood ratio test such as that suggested by Engle and Granger (1987) and Enders (1995), employed in this chapter and called sensitivity analysis, is an appropriate and accepted method of determining whether cointegration results are sensitive to the choice of lags (see Bahmani-Oskooee, 1995).

i.e., r=0 is rejected because the calculated λ-max statistic is greater than its critical value. However, caution must be exercised in assessing the validity of this result since the real bilateral exchange rate variable (REX) carries the wrong sign.

Table 3. Estimates of the Cointegrating Vectors for the Trade Balance Model

A: Indonesia - U.S. Trade Balance Model				
	Variables			
	Log TB	Log Y	Log YUS	Log REX
Vector	-1.0000	-1.3952	-0.5512	2.8835
χ^2 statistic	10.90	17.50	0.42	6.94

B: Korea - U.S. Trade Balance Model				
	Variables			
	Log TB	Log Y	Log YUS	Log REX
Vector	-1.0000	.2951	.1043	1.8419
χ^2 statistic	14.9	7.270	0.29	17.30

Note: There are no cointegrating vectors for Malaysia and Singapore and therefore, none are reported here. The critical value of χ^2 is 3.84 at the 5% level of significance.

Table 3 reports each of the cointegrating vectors and the associated maximum eigenvalues for both Indonesia and Korea. In general, the rejection of the null hypothesis of no cointegration is an indication of convergence toward some long-run equilibrium due to a strong relationship among some but not necessarily all of the variables. For the purpose of determining which variable(s) should be excluded from the cointegrating space, we perform an exclusion test which requires the application of the likelihood ratio (LR) test for the exclusion of each variable in each case as described by Johansen (1988, p.237) and Johansen and Juselius (1990, p.194). Accordingly, the LR test for excluding a variable or for restricting the coefficient of that variable to zero is based on the estimates of eigenvalues of unrestricted and restricted cointegrating space according to the following quantity:

$$-2\text{Ln}(Q) = T \sum_{i=1}^{r} \ln\{(1-\lambda_i^*)/(1-\lambda_i)\} \tag{5}$$

where r is the number of cointegrating vectors, λ^* is the eigenvalue of the ith vector from the restricted space and λ is the eigenvalue of the ith vector from unrestricted cointegrating space. The quantity in (5) has a χ^2 distribution with r(p-s) degrees of freedom where r is the number of cointegrating vectors, p is the dimension of unrestricted cointegrating space. In each case, one of the coefficients is restricted to zero, s=p-1, implying that each χ^2 statistic has r(p-p+1)=r degrees of freedom which is equal to the number of cointegrating vectors in each case. Table 3 reports each of the cointegrating vectors for Indonesia and Korea along with the calculated χ^2 statistics. Normalization of the coefficients by setting one of them to negative one (-1) is a common practice and for this purpose we set the coefficient of Log(TB) to negative one.

In the case of Indonesia, the negative coefficient of the Log Y variable is indicative of a deterioration in the trade balance as domestic output grows. As mentioned earlier, this relationship may well be reversed as Indonesia approaches higher levels of income or output and the production of import substitutes outpaces consumption. A depreciation of the Indonesian Rupiah relative to the U.S. dollar improves Indonesia's bilateral trade balance with the United States. This is significant when one considers that the U.S. is one of Indonesia's major trading partners with which Indonesia maintains a significant trade surplus.[8] Future depreciations of the Indonesian Rupiah vis-a-vis the U.S. dollar are expected to exacerbate the U.S. trade deficit with Indonesia.

Although a negative coefficient on the Log YUS variable was obtained, this result is meaningless because the calculated χ^2 statistic of 0.42 for this coefficient is far less than its critical value of 3.84 at the 5% level of significance. Hence, we are unable to reject the null hypothesis of excluding the variable, Log YUS, from the cointegration space. Our cointegration results for Indonesia indicate that the relevant variables impacting bilateral trade between Indonesia and the U.S., and therefore, the variables included in

---

8. The 1993 annual trade balance estimates between the U.S. and Indonesia indicate that the value of Indonesian exports to the U.S. is in the area of 1.8 billion U.S. dollars, while Indonesian imports from the U.S. amount to approximately half this amount.

the cointegrating space, are the Indonesian domestic output and the bilateral exchange rate.

A similar exclusion result was obtained for Korea with respect to the Log YUS variable in the cointegrating space. It appears that in the long-run, the relevance of U.S. output growth to U.S. bilateral trade with Indonesia and Korea are, at best, questionable.

Domestic output expansion in Korea has a positive impact on its trade with the U.S., as does a depreciation of the Korean Won against the U.S. $. The relative sizes of the Korean and the Indonesian economies may help explain the difference in the sign of the coefficient of the domestic output variable. The Korean output level is approximately three times greater than that of Indonesia and as a result, the production of importables in Korea may have exceeded consumption causing a significant decline in imports in the long-run.

The depreciation of the Won against the U.S. dollar improves the Korean trade balance with the U.S., and further exacerbates the U.S. trade deficit with Korea.[9] U.S. pressure on Korea to revalue its currency, therefore, has significant empirical merit and could effectively lead to a dissipation of the U.S. bilateral trade deficit.

The results of the LR test for excluding a variable from the cointegrating space indicate that except for Log YUS, as in the case of Indonesia, all the other variables cannot be excluded from the cointegrating space. Our guess is that although the U.S. output level may be irrelevant in determining bilateral trade flows, it is most probably important in explaining the U.S. aggregate trade balance as well as the aggregate trade balance of most of the U.S.'s major trading partners.

V. SUMMARY AND CONCLUSIONS

The purpose of the current study is to learn more about the nature of the long-run bilateral trade flows between the U.S. and some of its East Asian trading partners within the context of the new world order. Our sample was limited by the availability of consistent data for the period under consideration, 1973.I to 1993.IV. A bilateral trade balance model was con-

---

9. Korean exports to the U.S. were valued at approximately 5.7 billion U.S. dollars in 1993 and Korea imported about 4.9 billion U.S. dollars from the U.S. in the same year.

structed for the U.S. and each of the East Asian trading partners in the sample. Cointegration analysis was applied to first-differenced stationary data for the U.S., Singapore, South Korea, Indonesia and Malaysia.

Our results indicate one cointegrating vector each for Korea and Indonesia, regardless of whether the vector order is four, five or six lags. We were unable to reject the null hypothesis of no cointegration for Singapore and Malaysia, implying the absence of a long-term equilibrium relationship among our set of variables, which include the bilateral trade balance and its most important determinants: trading partner i's domestic output, U.S. output, and the bilateral exchange rate measured in units of country i's domestic currency per U.S. dollar.

The resulting cointegration vectors for Indonesia and Korea indicate that depreciation or devaluation improves their bilateral trade balance with the U.S., such that pressures from the U.S. on these countries to revalue or to allow their currencies to appreciate relative to the U.S. dollar lead to an improvement in the bilateral trade balance in favor of the United States. Caution must be exercised, however, in generalizing these findings to other East Asian countries. We should recall that in the cases of Malaysia and Singapore, no long-run equilibrium relationships and no cointegrating vectors were found, casting doubt on the existence of any underlying stationary relationship between the trade balance and its most important determinants, including the exchange rate. Until more is known about U.S. trade relations with other East Asian countries, such as Singapore and Malaysia, we can only conclude that they are at best, unstable and unpredictable.

The impact of domestic output levels on the trade balance is less clearcut. In the case of Korea, higher rates of output growth imply further deterioration of the U.S. bilateral trade balance with Korea, i.e., the U.S. trade deficit worsens. On the other hand, Indonesia's trade balance deteriorates as domestic output expands. If, however, this relationship is reversed at higher levels of output and Indonesia's production of importables outpaces consumption, then like Korea, growth will improve the Indonesian trade balance and therefore worsen the U.S. bilateral deficit. Considering the aforementioned projections of sustained export and output growth for East Asia, it seems reasonable to conclude that the U.S. may experience increasingly unflavorable balance sheets with its East Asian trading partners.

The empirical results also indicate that the U.S. domestic output (YUS) should be excluded from the cointegrating regression and at least in the case of the countries in the sample, is irrelevant in explaining bilateral trade with the United States. This is consistent with the observation that East Asian countries have been able to maintain high growth rates despite weaknesses in the U.S. and other developed countries, primarily due to increasing domestic demand and expansion in intraregional trade (Bergsten and Noland, 1993).

If projections of vigorous output and export growth are accurate for the East Asian NIEs and developing economies, their success can only validate the belief that whatever the trends are toward regionalism and discriminatory protection in the rest of the world, East Asia's interests are clearly enhanced by the increased liberalization and the greater openness of their economies. As long as trade diversion is modest in NAFTA and the EEC and there are no new trade barriers, it is hard to imagine that East Asia would gain from the formation of its own defensive bloc. Expansion in intraregional trade within East Asia has occurred in the absence of a formal trading bloc and primarily on the basis of comparative advantage.

Regional trade groupings such as the NAFTA, are part of the reality of the New World Order, along with increased export competition from the republics of the former Soviet Union and the new eastern European capitalists. The U.S., like other industrialized economies, has began to retaliate against what it considers unfair trade practices especially by its East Asian trading partners, by imposing quotas or countervailing duties. In this new world environment, East Asian exporters, especially the emerging economies, are faced with a more competitive challenge, but one in which opportunities still abound. In contrast to earlier export drives by Japan and the NIEs, which depended primarily on increased consumption in industrial economies, the success of the export drives of East Asia's developing economies will depend on consumers in the U.S. and the rest of the industrialized world purchasing goods made in East Asia instead of goods made elsewhere (World Bank, 1993).

We expect U.S.-East Asian trade relations to be strengthened as the growth of export-oriented economies create markets for U.S. exports. Successful exporters must comply with global quality and price standards demanded by U.S. consumers and investors. They will experience greater pressures to open their economies to U.S. goods and investment, and bring their business practices in line with those of the industrialized countries. Those that attempt to use the more interventionist versions of the the export-push model, such as those of Japan and Korea, will risk retaliation from industrial-economy markets or punishment under the General Agreement on Tariffs and Trade (GATT) (World Bank, p.365).

Therefore, even if some of the rules of the game have changed with the emergence of the New World Order, we expect East Asia to rise to the challenge and the U.S. to be an integral partner in their success. After all, one of the essential features of the East Asian export-oriented model has been the ability to adapt to the changing global environment.

REFERENCES

Bahmani-Oskooee, Mohsen, "Is There a Long-run Relation between the Trade Balance and the Real Effective Exchange Rate of LDCs?" *Economics Letters*, 1991, 36, 403-7.

Bahmani-Oskooee, Mohsen, "Source of Inflation in Post Revolutionary Iran," *International Economic Journal*, Summer 1995, 9, 61-72.

Bahmani-Oskooee, Mohsen, "What are the Long-Run Determinants of the U.S. Trade Balance?" *Journal of Post Keynesian Economics*, Fall 1992, 15, 85-97.

Bahmani-Oskooee, Mohsen and J. Alse, "Short-run versus Long-run Effects of Devaluation: Error Correction Modeling and Cointegration," *Eastern Economic Journal*, Fall 1994, 20(4), 453-64.

Bahmani-Oskooee, Mohsen and Margaret Malixi, "More Evidence on the J-Curve from LDCs," *Journal of Policy Modeling*, Oct. 1992, 14(5), 641-53.

Bergsten, C. Fred and Marcus Noland, eds., *Pacific Dynamism and the International Economic System*, (Washington, D.C.: Institute for International Economics, 1993).

Diaz-Alejandro, Carlos F., "A Note on the Impact of Devaluation and the Redistributive Effect," *Journal of Political Economy*, August 1963, 71, 577-80.

Dysdale, Peter and Ross Garnaut, "The Pacific: An Application of a General Theory of Economic Integration," in *Pacific Dynamism and the International Economic System*, eds., C.Fred Bergsten and Marcus Noland, (Washington, D.C.: Institute for International Economics, 1993).

Edwards, Sebastian, "Are Devaluations Contractionary?" *The Review of Economics and Statistics*, August 1986, 68, 501-8.

Enders, Walter, *Applied Econometric Time Series*, (New York: John Wiley & Sons, Inc., 1995).

Engle, R.F. and C.W.J. Granger, "Cointegration and Error Correction: Representation, Estimation and Testing," *Econometrica*, 55, 251-276.

Gangnes, Byron and Seiji Naya, "Why East Asian Economies Have Been Successful: Some Lessons for Other Developing Countries," Working Paper No.92-2, May 1992.

Guitian, Manuel, "The Effects of Changes in the Exchange Rate on Output, Prices and the Balance of Payments," *Journal of International Economics*, February 1976, 6, 65-74.

Gylfason, Thorvaldur and Michael Schmid, "Does Devaluation Cause Stagflation?" *Canadian Journal of Economics*, November 1983, 16, 641-54.

Haynes, Stephen and Joe Stone, "Impact of the Terms of Trade on the U.S. Trade Balance: A Reexamination," *The Review of Economics and Statistics*, Nov. 1982, 702-6.

Himarios, D., "The Effects of Devaluation on the Trade Balance: A Critical View and Reexamination of Miles' New Results," *Journal of International Money and Finance*, December 1985, 4, 553-63.

Johansen, Søren, "Statistical Analysis of Cointegration Vectors," *Journal of Economic Dynamics and Control*, June/September 1988, 12, 231-54.

Johansen, Søren and Katarina Juselius, "Maximum Likelihood Estimation and Inference on Cointegration With Application to the Demand for Money," *Oxford Bulletin of Economics and Statistics*, May 1990, 52, 169-210.

Krugman, Paul and Lance Taylor, "Contractionary Effects of Devaluation," *Journal of International Economics*, August 1978, 8, 445-56.

Lipschitz, Leslie, "Domestic Credit and Exchange Rates in Developing Countries: Some Policy Experiments with Korean Data," *IMF Staff Papers*, December 1984, 595-635.

Lizondo, J. Saul and Peter J. Montiel, "Contractionary Devaluation in Developing Countries: An Analytical Overview," *IMF Staff Papers*, March 1989, 36, 182-227.

Mackinnon, James G., "Critical Values for Cointegration Tests," in *Long Run Economic Relationships: Readings in Cointegration*, eds., R.F. Engle and C.W.J. Granger, (New York: Oxford University Press, 1991).

Mahdavi, Saeid and Ahmad Sohrabian, "The Exchange Value of the Dollar and the U.S. Trade Balance: An Empirical Investigation Based on Cointegration and Granger Causality Tests," *The Quarterly Review of Economics and Finance*, Winter 1993, 33(4), 343-58.

Marquez, J., "Bilateral Trade Elasticities," *The Review of Economics and Statistics*, February 1990, 70-7.

Miles, Marc A., "The Effects of Devaluation on the Trade Balance: Some New Results," *Journal of Political Economy*, June 1979, 87, 600-20.

Naya, Seiji and Pearl Imada, "Development Strategies and Economic Performance of the Dynamic Asian Economies: Some Comparisons with Latin America," *The Pacific Review*, April 1990, 3.

Pesaran, Hashem M. and Bahram Pesaran, *Microfit 3.0, An Interactive Econometric Package*, (Oxford: Oxford University Press, 1991).

Rana, Pradumma B. and J. Malcolm Dowling, Jr., "Inflationary Effects of Small but Continuous Changes in Effective Exchange Rates: Nine Asian LDCs," *The Review of Economics and Statistics*, August 1985, 496-500.

Rose, Andrew K. and Janet L. Yellen, "Is There a J-Curve," *Journal of Monetary Economics*, 1989, 24, 53-68.

Rosensweig, Jeffrey A. and Paul D. Koch, "The U.S. Dollar and the Delayed J-Curve," *Federal Reserve Bank of Atlanta Economic Review*, July/August, 2-15.

Solimano, Andres, "Contractionary Devaluation in the Southern Cone: The Case of Chile," *Journal of Development Economics*, September 1986, 23, 135-51.

Spitaller, E., "Short-run Effects of Exchange Rate Changes on the Terms of Trade and the Trade Balance, *IMF Staff Papers*, 27, 320-48.

Warner, Dennis and Mordechai Kreinin, "Determinants of International Trade Flows," *The Review of Economics and Statistics*, Feb. 1983, 65, 96-104.

Wijnbergen, Sweder Van, "Exchange Rate Management and Stabilization Policies in Developing Countries," *Journal of Development Economics*, October 1986, 23, 227-47.

World Bank, *The East Asian Miracle*, (New York: Oxford University Press, 1993).

Young, Soogil, "Globalism and Regionalism: Complements or Competitors?" in *Pacific Dynamism and the International Economic System*, eds., C.

Fred Bergsten and Marcus Noland, (Washington, D.C.: Institute for International Economics, 1993).

APPENDIX

DATA DEFINITION AND SOURCES

All data are quarterly over the period of 1973I to 1993IV and were collected from the following sources:

a. International Financial Statistics of the International Monetary Fund (IMF), various issues.
b. Direction of Trade Statistics of the IMF, Yearbook, 1970 and 1990.
c. Foreign Trade Statistics, Series A of the Organization for Economic Cooperation and Development (OECD), various issues.

Variables:

TB = Bilateral trade balance, defined as the ratio of country i's exports to the U.S. to country i's imports from the U.S. The data are from source c.
Y = Real output of country i measured by Gross Domestic Product in index form. The data are from source a.
YUS = Real U.S. domestic output in index form. The data are from source a.
REX = Real bilateral exchange rate defined as the number of country i's currency per U.S. dollar. The data are from source a. REX is calculated as follows:

$$REX_i = (CPI_{US} EX_i / CPI_i)$$

where CPI_{US} is the U.S. price level, CPI_i is the price level in trading partner i, and EX_i is the nominal bilateral exchange rate defined as the units of country i's currency per unit of the U.S. dollar. All the data are from source a.

UNITED STATES-ASEAN ECONOMIC RELATIONS

Robert L. Curry, Jr.
Graduate Program in International Affairs
California State University, Sacramento
Sacramento, CA 95819

Abstract—The United States and the countries making up the membership of the Association of Southeast Asian Nations (ASEAN) share a common strategic, geopolitical and economic agenda. The common economic agenda has permitted the two partners to maintain open and accessible markets in which their private sectors participate. The main features of co-operation include the Asian Dialogue Partnership Program (ADPS) and the ASEAN -U.S. Initiative. These mechanisms have proven to be successful both because of the shared economic agenda and the fact that the private and public sectors have cooperated to develop and impliment the cooperative mechanisms.

I. INTRODUCTION

The Association of Southeast Asian Nations (ASEAN) currently includes Brunei, Indonesia, Malaysia, the Philippines, Singapore and Thailand. Vietnam and Laos are observer states because each has signed the amity agreement that binds ASEAN members to certain principles. Vietnam has made formal application to join ASEAN when its Ministerial Meeting is held in Brunei during 1995. This study of U.S.-ASEAN economic relations is based upon three propositions: (1) U.S. and Southeast Asian firms -- particularly those in ASEAN countries -- enjoy largely open access to Southeast Asian and North American markets because of the economic, strategic and geopolitical agendas shared by the U.S. and ASEAN; (2) the Association operates in ways that contribute to global and regional amity with the U.S., and vice-versa; and (3) most importantly, both the private and public sectors in ASEAN and the U.S. have recognized and built upon the economic symbiosis that binds their shared economic and business interests in ways that yield amity. The study herein focuses on proposition (3), and in particular on the factors responsible for the validity of the proposition (Chng 1990, and Wood and Wheeler, 1990).

II. BACKGROUND TO ASEAN

ASEAN was founded in 1967 with the signing of the Bangkok Declaration by the leaders of Indonesia, Malaysia, the Philippines, Singapore and Thailand (later to be joined by Brunei). The Declaration articulated a number of broad aims and principles for regional cooperation and established basic machinery to carry these out, most notably an annual ASEAN Ministerial Meeting. A feature of this machinery was the absence of a centralized administrative body. Decision-making powers and policy formulation were deliberately left in the hands of foreign ministers, reflecting the importance members attached to consensus-seeking (Kintanar and Tan, 1987).

Despite the Bangkok Declaration's emphasis on economic, technical and social cooperation, ASEAN was slow to make progress in these areas, as it initially focused on political and security matters. This reflected regional concerns not only about the war in Vietnam, but also about bilateral disputes and political instability within ASEAN itself. In its early years, the Association helped to build regional confidence and trust by establishing a pattern of regular and periodic contacts between member countries' foreign ministers and other senior officials. During ASEAN's formative years, these contacts fostered an emerging sense of common economic purpose and mutual interest (Tan and Akrasanee, 1988).

ASEAN Ministerial Meetings (AMMs) through the late 1960s and early 1970s modestly advanced the agenda of economic cooperation but continued their essentially geopolitical-strategic focus. For example, the second

AMM (held in Jakarta in 1968) identified priority areas for regional cooperation: that is, food production, communications, shipping, civil aviation and tourism -- and approved a work program and permanent committee in each area. By the time of the fourth AMM, in Manila in 1971 these permanent committees had recommended 121 projects, of which 48 had been approved for implementation. Importantly, however, this meeting discussed ultimate goals for ASEAN, including a limited free trade area and customs union. But the lack of direct involvement of ASEAN economic ministers in regional cooperation schemes in these early years limited the impact of ASEAN efforts in this area (Chua, 1990; De Rosa, 1988; and Doraisamy, 1988).

All of this changed in 1975 when, at the Bali Summit, new agreements were signed. Of these, the *Treaty of Amity and Cooperation in South East Asia* was the most broad-ranging, providing an update of the 1967 Bangkok Declaration. The second major agreement was the ASEAN Concord, which specified an action plan for ASEAN cooperation in the areas of politics, economics, society, culture and society. Priority areas identified for economic cooperation included: the supply and production of basic commodities; large-scale industrial plants; trade (including preferential trading arrangements); and external economic relations. The Concord directed that detailed proposals would be developed by ASEAN Economic Ministers who would henceforth meet on a regular basis. ASEAN countries also agreed at the Bali Summit to establish a secretariat in Jakarta (Nemetz, 1990).

The course of change toward a more integrated regional economy took place in 1990 when ASEAN Economic Ministers agreed to apply a Common Effective Preferential Tariff (CEPT) on selected industrial products within the context of an ASEAN Free Trade Area (AFTA). The finishing touches were put on the idea of AFTA in 1991 by Thai Prime Minister Anand Panyarachun who was supported by Prime Minister Goh Chok Tong of Singapore. At an ASEAN Foreign Ministers' Meeting held in Kuala Lumpur in July 1991 their proposal received enthusiastic support, with only Indonesia and the Philippines expressing reservations. ASEAN Economic Ministers reached agreement on the creation of a free trade area in October 1991. AFTA was formally launched by ASEAN leaders at their Summit in Singapore in January 1992 (ASEAN Secretariat, 1993).

III. THE EVOLUTION OF COLLABORATION: ASEAN AND THE U.S.

Despite the potential for conflict between AFTA and the North American Free Trade Area (NAFTA), the relationship between the United States and ASEAN continued to be far more harmonious than confrontational. The United States is ASEAN's largest export market, especially for manufacturers, and its second largest source of imports after Japan, and it has in general supported the rise of ASEAN as an institution. The constant growth in trade and investment between ASEAN and the United States has been due to changes in the international trade situation. Following the period of turmoil and transition for the world economy in the 1970s, the international trading environment became more stable and yielded the opportunity for some developing countries to resume the momentum of trade expansion, especially in manufacturing. The growth and trade policies in industrial countries have had a direct bearing on export opportunities for developing countries. Steady growth and more liberal trade policies in developed countries have generated enormous opportunities and benefits for the wider world economy throughout the post-war period. Prudent domestic macroeconomic policies and outward-looking strategies have also given developing countries greater resilience and flexibility (Naya, et. al., 1989).

The United States remains an important catalyst of growth in ASEAN. In the context of the world economic environment, the policies of the United States helped to promote a rapid rise in both trade and investment, and these led to expansion and diversification in ASEAN's economic relationship with the United States. The increased investment by the United States in the region, due in part to the fact that ASEAN exhibits one of the highest rates of return on investment in the world, contributed to the increasing interdependence of the United States and ASEAN.

IV. THE COMMON AGENDA AND COOPERATIVE RELATIONS

There are several key indicators that define the nature of the U.S.-ASEAN relationship, and the consequences arising from their association. Political indicators include their shared voting record at the United Nations, and their common participation in organizations such as the Asia Pacific Economic Council (APEC) and the Pacific Economic Cooperation Council (PECC). Economic indicators are reflected in their joint support of the aims of the Uruguay Round, the creation of the World Trade Organization, and a continued commitment to the principles of multilateral economic openness that are central to the GATT-framework.

There is also an emerging geo-political, strategic agenda having to do with resolving extra-regional issues. A major issue has to do with the territorial dispute over the Spratley Islands where two of the main antagonist are Viet Nam and the People's Republic of China (P.R.C.). On this score, Viet Nam's imminent entry into ASEAN will offer the U.S. and ASEAN (including Viet Nam) a conflict-resolving framework. Indeed, a meeting has already been held on the issue, and it took place with ASEAN's assistance. Held in Jakarta, Indonesia, it involved the ASEAN group, the U.S., Viet Nam and the P.R.C.

These political, economic and strategic indicators reflect clearly that the ASEAN group and the United States share a symbiosis based upon complimentary economies, geo-political and strategic harmony and a joint commitment to conflict management and dispute resolution. The symbiosis began to take shape during the post World War II era and, as a consequence, it is not surprising that the United States welcomed the creation of an association among these friendly nations of Southeast Asia. It hoped that this association would help prevent conflicts of the type that troubled Indonesian, Malaysian, and Philippine relations in the first part of the 1950s and encourage development-oriented economic policies. The United States regarded ASEAN as a force for regional stability, and one favorable to a U.S. presence and role in the region. Despite their differing histories and issues in their individual bilateral relationships with the U.S., ASEAN members agreed on one thing: they want the United States to continue to make a positive contribution to regional stability.

However, in retrospect, it is important to note that despite the emerging symbiosis and the extensive political and economic ties that have come to exist between the ASEAN countries and the United States, both sides avoided formal links until the first ASEAN-U.S. dialogue in 1978. This reflected concern within both ASEAN and the United States that the association needed to establish its legitimacy as an economic, social, and cultural organization before engaging informal relations with a superpower (Naya, et. al., 1988).

Indeed, U.S. policy towards ASEAN, from its founding, was one of strong, but low-key endorsement. But by 1977 a new Southeast Asian environment had emerged in which a closer and more formal dialogue process seemed important. After the end of the Vietnam War, there was some concern in Southeast Asia that the United States was disengaging from the region, especially from the countries on the Southeast Asian mainland. The ASEAN group hoped to encourage the United States to remain involved, especially economically. It also believed it could play a role in influencing U.S. economic policy towards the Third World in general through the dialogue process. On the U.S. side, it hoped that the dialogue process would demonstrate a continuing U.S. interest in the region, encourage mutually beneficial economic relations, and provide a venue for the discussion of potentially divisive issues.

By the late 1970s, new political issues had emerged as important in the ASEAN-U.S. relationship. There was a strong coincidence of U.S. and ASEAN interests regarding the Vietnamese invasion of Cambodia. The United States decided to defer to ASEAN for international leadership on this question and ASEAN's positions strongly influenced U.S. policies towards Cambodia. ASEAN looked to the United States and other dialogue partners for support on this and other issues relating to Indochina, including the huge flow of Indochinese refugees into the ASEAN countries.

Leaders in both Japan and the United States sought to improve their co-operation in helping the ASEAN group. The bilateral U.S.-Japan Advisory Commission reflected these sentiments, calling on Japan and the United States to work together in accelerating ASEAN development, maintaining access to developed country markets, and supporting ASEAN efforts towards Cambodia and Vietnam (East Asia Analytic Unit, 1993). In effect, the Commission built upon the ASEAN's instruments of collaboration that were in effect when the U.S. and Japan began to work together on maintaining an open economic region through Southeast Asia.

V. INSTRUMENTS OF COLLABORATION

The central instrument of collaboration with Southeast Asia began to take shape when ASEAN launched a formal dialogue program at its Second

Summit in 1977. Called the ASEAN Dialogue Partnership System (ADPS), it enabled ASEAN and Foreign Ministers from key countries such as Japan and the U.S. to meet on a regular basis. The first dialogue meeting with the United States took place very shortly afterwards. ASEAN now conducts dialogues with the European Communities and the five developed countries of the Asia-Pacific region -- Australia, Canada, Japan, New Zealand, and the United States -- as well as the United Nations Development Program. In addition to these bilateral dialogues, ASEAN initiated in 1979 a series of post-ministerial conferences (PMCs) in which the ASEAN foreign ministers meet with their colleagues from the dialogue partner countries following their own annual meetings. The PMCs have, in fact, become the main instrumentality of dialogue between ASEAN and the major developed countries although the bilateral meetings also continue. This reflects two features of the environment: the interdependence of economic, political, and strategic issues; *and* the growing interdependence of the Pacific Basin. The PMC's permit a free-flowing discussion of major issues on a multilateral basis with ASEAN's major economic partners.

In effect, via the ADPS and the MPC initiatives the U.S. and ASEAN leadership have taken two key steps. The first is that they recognize their shared agenda, and the second is that they have taken concrete steps to see to it that the greatest mutual benefits are derived from the situation (Naya, et. al., 1988 and Curry, 1991 and 1993).

VI. THE ROLE OF THE PRIVATE SECTOR

Another key step was taken when ASEAN and the U.S. began to forge their official, public sector linkages. It was to integrate the private sector into the process because, after all, it was the business sectors in ASEAN and the U.S. that undertake trade and investment activities. The process started with the first ASEAN-U.S. Business Conference which took place on July 22-24, 1979, in Manila. The Conference was attended by approximately 250 senior level executives representing the private sectors of ASEAN and the United States. It was co-hosted by the ASEAN Chambers of Commerce and Industry (ASEAN CCI) and the Chamber of Commerce of the United States. The most significant action of the Conference was the establishment of the joint ASEAN-U.S. Business Council. The Council institutionalizes an ongoing dialogue on bilateral economic relations between the business communities of ASEAN and the United States. It would provide a mechanism for recommending policies to the governments to strengthen and stimulate trade, investment and technology transfer. In other words, business would be *directly* linked to ADPS and PMC processes.

The establishment of the Council was supported by the governments at the Second ASEAN-U.S. Ministerial Dialogue held in Washington, D.C. in August 1978. The Council, to be composed of senior level business executives from both sides, would be cochaired by the chairman of the ASEAN section which is an organization of the ASEAN CCI and the chairman of the U.S. section, operated by the Chamber of Commerce of the United States.

It was recommended that the ASEAN and U.S. governments examine the desirability of establishing an ASEAN-U.S. Economic and Commercial Cooperation Commission as part of the ASEAN-U.S. Ministerial Dialogue. In addition, the ASEAN governments were asked to explore the possibility of establishing Trade and Investment Promotion offices in the United States, and the U.S. government was asked to consider sponsorship of a foreign investment orientation seminar for ASEAN government officials. As a direct result of the Manila meeting, in 1979 private sector representatives in the United States and ASEAN countries created the ASEAN-U.S. Business Council to serve as a forum to discuss critical trade issues, to connect the governments on specific policies and to facilitate contacts among United States and ASEAN companies. In 1984, the Council broadened its scope by creating the U.S.-ASEAN Center for Technology Exchange whose mission was to conduct industry and country-specific programs designed to expand trade and investment ties between the United States and the ASEAN region (ASEAN-U.S. Business Council, 1988).

By 1986, the Council's participants had come to agree on a broad range of principles. Each principle would provide for market access and lead to economic efficiency and generate legitimate business gains. At its Fifth Plenary Meeting, held in Jakarta, Indonesia in May 1986, the Council issued a substantive Joint Communique, and its general contents follows.

A. Protectionism in any form impedes trade and threatens ASEAN-U.S. relations,

B. Trade restrictive bills pending in the U.S. Congress, if enacted, will weaken U.S. political and economic ties with ASEAN.

C. The Council endorses the negotiation of bilateral investment treaties between the U.S. and ASEAN governments. National treatment of foreign firms should be included in the negotiations of these treaties.

D. The Council encourages efforts made by the ASEAN governments to improve the investment climate for both domestic and foreign investors.

E. Adequate protection of intellectual property (e.g., patents, trademarks, copyright) is a vital precondition to the transfer of technology needed for continued ASEAN development.

F. The Council encourages the U.S. and ASEAN governments to conclude and expedite ratification of bilateral tax treaties as appropriate (ASEAN-U.S. Business Council, 1986).

The pragmatic but fundamental principles were similar to those being fostered by academics who, during the late 1980s, began to take an interest in the matter of ASEAN-U.S. economic relations. While more general in scope than the specifics endorsed by the Council, the essence of the points raised by the academicians were that trade liberalization initiatives could bring greater gains from trade between the ASEAN countries and the U.S. and lead to improved global resource allocations and economic efficiencies. From the ASEAN perspective, they could include chiefly initiatives to remove (or reduce) restrictions on U.S. textile and apparel imports, *safeguard measures protecting* the U.S. sugar industry, and U.S. tariff protection favoring basic labor-intensive industries. From the U.S. perspective, it was argued, trade liberalization initiatives could include removing (or reducing) ASEAN tariff and other import controls restricting U.S. exports of capital-intensive goods. Recognizing these points, academicians joined business leaders and political decision-makers in noting that the essential question remained: "How to promote changes in ASEAN and U.S. trade and other policies to the benefit of all parties?" The answer turned out to be in the form of broader Pacific Basin initiatives, and in a strengthened ASEAN-U.S. Dialogue Partnership (Naya and Plummer, 1991; Curry, 1991; and Langhammer, 1991).

VII. THE ASEAN-U.S. DIALOGUE PARTNERSHIP

The dialogue partnership between ASEAN and the United States was enhanced recently by the contents of a Memorandum of Understanding (MOU) recently signed by the partners. The MOU, signed in late 1990, became effective in late 1991. The MOU, based on the contents of a final report titled *The ASEAN-U.S. Initiative (AUI)*, put into place a trade and investment co-operation committee aimed at monitoring and reviewing trade and investment relations. The committee identifies opportunities for expanding trade and investment and related transfer of technology and human resource development, and holds consultations regularly on trade and development matters. The U.S. and ASEAN agreed that the committee would be comprised of senior officials of both parties with the ASEAN side chaired by the chairman of its Economic Ministers' group, and the U.S. side by a Deputy U.S. Trade Representative. The committee would be convened at least once a year and, when necessary, at times agreed to by both parties. Importantly, either party may invite representatives in meetings provided that both parties agree that it is appropriate (Curry, 1991).

The ideas and inherent spirit in the AUI served as the basis for bilateral Trade and Investment Framework Agreement between the United States and an ASEAN member, Singapore. The countries created a Trade and Investment Council (TIC) based upon open regionalism and GATT principles, and designed as another feature of conflict resolving institutions among Pacific Basin partners. The TIC focuses on issues more amenable to bilateral rather than regional discussion. It is taken so seriously by Singapore that it upgraded its representation at the July 1993 TIC meeting to involve its Minister of Trade and Industry rather than its Trade and Development Board director as previously had been the case. The TIC, then, provides yet another element of a system designed to provide dialogue and collaboration as a means of conflict resolution and dispute management (Curry, 1993).

While the above instrumentalities involve middle-level policy strata and the private sector, Ministerial Ministers bring together upper echelons of policy-makers. Indeed, the Ministerial Meetings among ASEAN and its global partners were so useful that in 1979 they were extended to include Post Ministerial Conferences (PMCs). The PMC forum provides an ideal instrument via which to raise the issue of further collaboration with ASEAN based appropriately upon the TICC and TIC as ways of assuring "level regional playing fields" for Southeast Asians *and* the U.S. in each other's market area. (Naya, et. al., 1989, p. 4).

VIII. THE ASEAN-U.S. DIALOGUE AND THE AUI

The complementary nature of U.S. and ASEAN economies and the extensive economic interchange suggested to some policy-makers that bilateral agreements under the umbrella designed to resolve any disagreements or seize important opportunities would enhance welfare without contradicting multilateralist ideals. As they develop over time, all actions would be consistent with GATT and, most importantly, they would be aimed at providing market access which would tend to permit economies of scale to be taken advantage of in ways that would promote economic efficiency and business profitability.

It was argued that the initial umbrella should consist of these components. *First*, it should establish a set of basic guiding principles for the conduct of trade and other economic relations between the United States and ASEAN, based on GATT compatibility and affirming the primacy of multilateral liberalization. It should be grounded on the presumption that trade and investment flows are determined by market forces as much as possible; the nature of government intervention should be strictly defined and temporary. Most basically, the United States and ASEAN should commit themselves to the principle of "stand-still and roll-back" of trade barriers. Moreover, measures harming other trading partners should be avoided.

Second, it should establish the administrative and implementing guidelines for the United States and ASEAN negotiating a series of subsidiary agreements on subject such as subsidies, double taxation, intellectual property rights, investment, services, non-tariff barriers, and safeguards (discussed below), supplemented by more detailed accords where needed. *Third*, it should delineate effective procedures to administer the agreement and resolve disputes in a timely and efficient manner. *Fourth*, it should create a Consultative Committee, composed of government representatives at the level of trade minister and advised by experts and private-sector representatives, which should meet at least on an annual basis. The Consultative Committee should have several important tasks: (a) responsibility for considering trade and investment disputes in a manner defined by the umbrella agreement; oversee the negotiations of the subsidiary agreements; serve as a forum for molding joint ASEAN-U.S. positions on these issues at the current and subsequent GATT rounds; authorize the preparation of studies, formation of working groups, and other vehicles for improving understanding of and co-operation in bilateral economic relations.

Fifth, and very importantly, the umbrella agreement should lay the foundation for further bilateral and multilateral co-operation. For example, after establishing the umbrella agreement, the United States and ASEAN could negotiate a series of bilateral pacts, from a formal FTA to sector-specific agreements. Any bilateral ASEAN-U.S. trade and investment agreements should complement the GATT talks and, perhaps, provide an exemplary framework in certain areas (Naya, et. al., 1989; also see Snow, 1989).

The AUI noted that an ASEAN-U.S. FTA should be the ultimate goal of the Framework Agreement. An ASEAN-U.S. FTA would be very complex and is likely to take a long time to negotiate. However, there is great potential for improved trade and investment relations in such a pact. Commissioning a comprehensive study should be among the first inquiries the Consultative Committee should launch. And because of the complicated nature of negotiating something as complex as an FTA, the AUI recommend that the technical details of such an arrangement be studied in depth by a bilateral commission under the supervision of the Consultative Committee. Questions such as the net effect on global efficiency were addressed.

The complementary nature of the U.S. and ASEAN economies suggests that such a trading bloc would significantly expand bilateral trade. In addition, increased DFI flows, trade in services, technology transfer, economies of scale in production and other dynamic benefits would serve to promote the goals of both parties. An effective formal dispute-settlement process is more easily established in the context of a comprehensive accord because there is a larger and more detailed base of jointly agreed disciplines. Based upon this point, the AUI considered several important issues, not necessarily listed in order of priority, that the Consultative Committee should investigate: subsidies, double taxation and tax-sparing provision, intellectual property rights, investment, services, tariff and non-tariff barriers, and safeguard provisions.

Subsidies: The United States and ASEAN should pursue the subsidies issues within the current Uruguay Round, and should seek to set out codes of conduct on subsidies, negotiated by a committee under the auspices of the Consultative Committee, that would govern their bilateral relations in this area. Such an agreement would reduce frictions resulting from the subsidies issue.

The subsidies question may be separated into problems of principle and of implementation. The principle is that subsidies should not discriminate nor should they distort the allocation of resources. Implementation is complicated by difficulties in determining the type and magnitude of the distortions to be overcome. Acceptable standards need to be developed and transparency enforced. Also needed are dispute-settlement procedures to deal effectively with complaints.

Double Taxation and Tax-Sparing Provision: Another area of significance to ASEAN-U.S. economic relations that should be addressed at both the multilateral and bilateral levels is the interaction of tax systems of capital-exporting (source) countries with the tax concessions provided by the recipient (host) countries.

Most countries tax citizens and corporations incorporated within their borders on the basis of a global income concept. Some -- for example, the United States, the United Kingdom, and West Germany -- credit foreign taxes paid on foreign-source income against domestic taxes, while others treat foreign taxes as a business deduction in computing net income for domestic tax purposes. A number of capital-exporting countries have negotiated bilateral tax treaties with various host countries, essentially for the purpose of eliminating double taxation and defining how tax revenues should be shared by the respective governments. Of particular significant is the absence of a tax-sparing provision in these treaties in connection with income-tax holidays granted by the host countries -- an important part of their investment-promotion efforts.

This issue is important and complicated: On the one hand, income-tax holidays often merely transfer revenues from the developing (host) country to the developed (source) country treasury. On the other, double-taxation treaty and tax-sparing provisions would entail changes in domestic U.S. law. Such a change in law to accommodate the outflow of U.S. investment would be met with opposition from those who believe that U.S. jobs would be lost. The issue therefore should be studied at both the bilateral and multilateral level as it is an important concern of developing countries.

Intellectual Property Rights: Bilateral negotiations can serve as a model for multilateral negotiations, where the United States and the ASEAN countries are all supportive of a framework for a GATT intellectual property agreement. But because the laws and implementation of protection of intellectual property are so diverse in ASEAN, these negotiations should continue to take place at the country level. Nevertheless, individual-country negotiations could be undertaken under guidelines established by the United States and ASEAN as a group. This concept could also be applied at the GATT level: developing countries and developed countries could work together to strengthen current international intellectual property organizations, while leaving room for bilateral negotiations between individual developed and developing countries.

Mutually satisfactory agreements on this issue will benefit ASEAN through increased technology transfer, new products, and domestically generated innovations. The United States will benefit through increased incentives promoting research and development, in which it has comparative advantage. Hence, agreements in this area should be welfare-generating and should reduce frictions.

Investment: The Consultative Committee should consider the negotiation of a comprehensive investment pact, perhaps along the lines of a Bilateral Investment Treaty (BIT), which would liberalize bilateral investment by reducing or eliminating existing impediments. The United States already has attempted to negotiate a BIT with two ASEAN countries but to no avail. However, if a U.S.-ASEAN comprehensive agreement were tied in with other bilateral negotiations under the umbrella, as well as allowing flexibility for individual ASEAN members, such a treaty should be beneficial in stimulating welfare-generating investment flows.

Foreign investment is an important part of the ASEAN-U.S. economic relationship. Yet, there exist few standards governing foreign bilateral investment. Since investment affects the location of production and comparative advantage generally, barriers to foreign investment as well as unwarranted or unproductive incentives distort the allocation of resources.

At the national level, it is important that the ASEAN countries and the United States assess domestic policies that might inhibit foreign investment. On the ASEAN side, these include lack of national treatment, equity restrictions, performance requirements, trade-related investment measures, and stifling red tape. On the U.S. side, it may include further revisions in the Foreign Corrupt Practices Act.

The United States and ASEAN should work together to disseminate information about investment opportunities in ASEAN. Small- and medium-sized U.S. firms could benefit from participating in the ASEAN market through trade and investment, but they are often ignorant of the opportunities, because information is either unavailable in the U.S. or is poorly distributed.

Services: The Study recommends that there be rules to reduce barriers to international service transactions. The U.S. has put forth a proposal for a Framework Agreement on services in GATT, and there have been encouraging results in this area at the Midterm Review, where GATT ministers agreed on a number of key concepts for a Framework Agreement on services.

The relevant issues include proper definition of services, establishment of non-discriminatory treatment, transparency, dispute-settlement mechanisms, and enforcement procedures. Because all these issues are important to the U.S.-ASEAN economic relationship, these parties should seek to improve their dialogue in this area.

Tariffs: The U.S. and ASEAN should continue to work together to reduce tariffs at the Uruguay Round. In this context, the question of special and differential treatment should be recognized. However, the issue is complex, as special and differential treatment is not easily accepted by the United States, which is experiencing large trade deficits. For lesser developed ASEAN countries special and differential treatment should be considered.

Although preceding GATT rounds have reduced tariffs substantially, more work remains to be done. Before further tariff reductions can be achieved, an agreement on negotiating procedures is needed. Differences between those advocating the offer/request approach and those who prefer formula cuts need to be resolved. At the Uruguay Round, participants established a goal for general tariff reductions at least as ambitious as that achieved in the Tokyo Round.

The participation of developing countries in tariff reductions needs also to be clarified, although some developing countries have recently undertaken unilateral tariff liberalization which is motivated mainly by domestic considerations.

Non-Tariff Barriers: Non-tariff barriers are a major element of the New Protectionism. Although some such barriers may be implicitly covered by existing GATT rules and codes, others are not. Procedures need to be developed for determining the GATT-legality of existing discriminatory trade practices, and new codes need to be formulated for non-tariff barriers that are not now covered by GATT.

Safeguards: The Consultative Committee should seek to make progress towards an agreement that would codify standards and establish disciplinary measures. One issue that may be addressed jointly is that of selectivity versus Most Favored Nation (MFN) applications of safeguard measures. Other issues include definitions and measurement of inquiry; the duration of safeguard measures and the type of decay provisions that would ensure timely liberalization; and the conditions under which compensation would be required as well as the type of compensation. (United States Trade Representative, 1993).

IX. CONCLUDING OBSERVATIONS

The key matter of safeguard is to keep the Pacific Basin region, including Southeast Asia, open to trade, investment, capital and technology flows. A potential challenge to open regionalism occurred with the implementation of both AFTA and NAFTA. ASEAN decision-makers, to some degree, viewed NAFTA with some concern. The question was whether economic cooperation in North America would lead to open or closed regionalism. U.S. and other North American observers were equally concerned about what an AFTA would mean to their interests. A useful set of economic principles offer insights into the benefits of open regionalism will result. The three economic principles require broad and non-technical understanding, particularly by non-economists who will be in charge of the formulation and implementation of regional agreements among governments where the remainder of the world's economic interests are involved. These principles are trade diversion, trade creation, and trade expansion (Curry, 1993).

ASEAN producers have an interest in open regionalism throughout the broader Pacific Basin, including the NAFTA subregion. From this perspective, their interests would be negatively affected by trade diversion. This economic principle holds that a tariff reduction within NAFTA could divert sources of supply from an external ASEAN supplier to an internal North American one. This could lead to another problem scenario. Direct foreign investment (DFI), which previously went from North America to an ASEAN country whose producers once exported to the NAFTA region could be diverted to a NAFTA country. The NAFTA country would be the one towards which trade was diverted. The export-led growth efforts of the ASEAN country would be impaired by the loss of the DFI.

In response to this type of closed subregionalism, the entire ASEAN group could put their version of closed subregionalism into place. Their AFTA could similarly impair the NAFTA countries' interests in exporting to Southeast Asia. The conceptual result of rampant trade diversion is impaired economic interests in each subregion.

Closed subregionalism could be prevented by mutual commitments to open regionalism. This would call for co-operative and conflict-resolving policy instruments within each subregion, and among members of each subregional agreement. The goal would be to reduce trade diversion effects. ASEAN producers also have an interest in their Pacific subregion becoming more open to free trade. The principles of trade creation and trade expansion serve to explain the phenomenon.

Trade creation within a subregion such as ASEAN occurs when (a) tariffs are reduced or eliminated among AFTA members, (b) the tariff reductions or eliminations change the price structures in particular lines-of-commerce, and (c) the changes in price permits lower-cost ASEAN supplies to gain access to broader subregional markets because protective tariffs no long exist. The favored countries' producers gain broader market access and, because of this, they can reduce costs via rational and effective expansions in the levels of their economic activity. As a consequence, trade creation and trade expansion takes place. To the extent that these phenomena occur, they serve to induce DFI from outside the region. This enhances ASEAN capacities to produce items and thereby generate income and employment within the context of outward-looking, export-led growth and development strategies.

The ASEAN countries have a tremendous stake in DFI if the region's dramatic economic successes are to be maintained. Investment flows from abroad (and from local sources) must continue to be robust. There are two broad reasons prompting the flow of direct foreign investment from the NAFTA region -- mainly from the United States -- to the ASEAN economies. The first is that some DFI is directed towards combining with local resources to supply goods and services that are produced in, and exported from, Southeast Asia. The primary market to which such exports are directed is the United States. Other North American markets, as well as markets in Europe and throughout Asia are also involved.

"Export platform" investment from the United States is important to the ASEAN countries in their efforts to promote export-led growth which generates employment and income-earning opportunities for Southeast Asians. However, if trade diversion as a result of NAFTA diverts the source of U.S. imports of a range of products from ASEAN to Mexican supplies, DFI from the United States would also be diverted from Southeast Asia to Mexico. Investment production, exportation and employment and income generation would move from the ASEAN region to Mexico. In this way, diversion of DFI would accompany trade diversion, thereby posing a constraint to maximizing export-led growth throughout the ASEAN economies.

The second reason prompting the flow of DFI from the United States into ASEAN is to combine the investments with local resources in order to produce products and services destined for ASEAN and other East Asian markets. If trade is created because of AFTA, DFI flows from the United States and other sources would tend to increase because U.S. investors would seek to take advantage of increasingly profitable opportunities to produce with the ASEAN region. Clearly, this phenomenon would enhance the ASEAN countries' export-oriented growth (Curry, 1993 and Elek, 1991)

In conclusion, it is important to understand that with so much at stake, neither the U.S. nor ASEAN stands to gain from closed regionalism. It would therefore be irrational for either partner to stray from the course of collaboration that they have mutually constructed.

REFERENCES

APEC, *Report of the Eminent Persons Group*, (Singapore: APEC Secretariat, 1993), pp. 1-26.
Ariff, M., *The Pacific Economy: Growth and External Stability*, (North Sydney: Allen and Unwin, 1993), pp. 1-388.
Ariff, M. and E. C. Tan, "ASEAN-Pacific Trade Relations," *ASEAN Economic Bulletin*, 1992, 8(3), 258-283.
ASEAN Secretariat, *Doing Business in ASEAN*, (Jakarta: ASEAN, 1993), pp. 1-29.
ASEAN-U.S. Business Council, *Joint Communique: 5th Plenary Meeting*, (Jakarta: May 1986), pp. 1-6.
ASEAN-U.S. Business Council, "The ASEAN-U.S. Economic Relationship: Overcoming Barriers to Business Cooperation," (Washington D.C.: mimeographed, 1987 and 1988), pp. 1-4.
Bergsten, C. F. and M. Noland, *Pacific Dynamism and the International Economic System*, (Washington and Canberra: Institute of International Economics and Pacific Trade and Development Secretariat, 1993), pp. 1-355.
Blomqvist, H. C., "ASEAN as a Model for Third World Regional Cooperation," *ASEAN Economic Bulletin*, 1994, 10(1), 52-67.
Chng, M. K., "ASEAN's Institutional Structure and Economic Growth," *ASEAN Economic Bulletin*, 1990, 6(3), 268-282.
Cowhey, P. and J. Aronson, "A New Trade Order," *Foreign Affairs*, 1993, 72(1), 183-195.
Curry, R. L., "A Policy Analysis of the ASEAN-U.S. Initiative," *ASEAN Economic Bulletin*, 1991, 8(2), 151-159.
Curry, R. L., "AFTA and NAFTA and the Need for Open Regionalism," in *Southeast Asian Affairs*, (Singapore: Institute of Southeast Asian Studies, 1993), pp. 54-70.
DeRosa, D. A., "Global Economic Balance, Protectionism and U.S.-ASEAN Trade Relations," (Paper presented at the Malaysian Association for American Studies Regional Seminar, 23-25 June 1988, Kuala Lumpur, Panel Discussion on U.S.-ASEAN Trade: Current Issues and Future Strategies), various pages.
DeRosa, D. A. "ASEAN-U.S. Trade Relations: An Overview," *ASEAN Economic Bulletin*, (November 1986), 6(2), 169-88.

Doraisamy, J. "Intellectual Property Legislation," (Paper presented at the Malaysian Association for American Studies Regional Seminar, 23-25 June 1988, Kuala Lumpur, Panel Discussion on U.S.-ASEAN Trade: Current Issues and Future Strategies), pp. 1-

East Asia Analytical Unit, *ASEAN Free Trade Area: Trading Bloc or Building Block*, (Canberra: Department of Foreign Affairs and Trade, 1993), pp. 1-155.

Elek, A, "Asia Pacific Economic Cooperation," in *Southeast Asian Affairs*, (Singapore: Institute of Southeast Asian Studies, 1991), pp. 33-48.

Guisinger, S., "A Pacific Basin Investment Agreement," ASEAN Economic Bulletin, 1994, 10(2), 176-183.

Heng, H. and L. Low. *Withdrawal of The General System of Preference*, (Singapore: Institute of Southeast Asian Studies, 1990), pp. 1-19.

Institute of Southeast Asian Studies, *Workshop on OECD and ASEAN: Search for Coherent Policies*, (Singapore: ISEAS [mimeographed set of papers delivered 22-24 June 1994), various pages.

Kim, H. and A. Weston, "A North American Free Trade Agreement and East Asian Developing Countries," *ASEAN Economic Bulletin*, 1993, 9(3), 287-300.

Kintanar, and Tan L. H., *ASEAN-U.S. Economic Relations: An Overview*, (Singapore: Institute of Southeast Asian Studies, 1987), pp. 1-202.

Koh, T.B. "America's role in the Asia Pacific," *Trends*, June 30, 1991, no. 10, p. 1.

Langhammer, R, "ASEAN Economic Co-operation: A Stock-Taking from the Political Economy Point of View," *ASEAN Economic Bulletin*, 1991, 8(2), 137-150.

Lee, K. Y., "NAFTA may be expanded to include parts of East Asia," *Straits Times*, (Singapore: 1 June 1993), p. 5.

Naya, S. and M. G. Plummer, "ASEAN Economic Co-operation in the New International Economic Environment," *ASEAN Economic Bulletin*, 1991, 7(3), 261-276.

Naya, S., et. al., *Asian-U.S. Initiative*, (Honolulu and Singapore: East-West Center and Institute of Southeast Asian Studies, 1989), pp. 1-195.

Nemetz, P., "Primary Commodities and Strategies for Developments in ASEAN," *ASEAN Economic Bulletin*, 1990, 6(3), 237-267.

Petri, P., "One Bloc, Two Blocs, or None?: Political-Economic Factors in Pacific Trade Policy," in *The U.S. Japan Economic Relationship in East and*

Southeast Asia, ed., K. Okuzuma, et. al. (Tokyo and Washington: Asia Pacific Association of Japan and The Center for Strategic and International Studies, 1992), pp. 39-70.

Snow, M.S., "Facilitating ASEAN-U.S. Trade and Direct Foreign Investment in Information Services," *ASEAN Economic Bulletin*, 1989, 6(1), 31-45.

Tan, J. L. H. and N. Akrasanee (ed.), *ASEAN-U.S. Economic Relations: Changes, in the Economic Environment and Opportunities*, (San Francisco and Singapore: The Asia Foundation and the Institute of Southeast Asian Studies, 1988), pp. 1-199.

Tan, J. L. H. and N. Akrasanee (ed.), *ASEAN-U.S. Economic Relations: Private Enterprise as a Means for Economic Development and Cooperation*, (San Francisco and Singapore: The Asia Foundation and the Institute of Southeast Asian Studies, 1990), pp. 1-159.

United States Trade Representative, *Alliance for Mutual Growth: Draft Document*, (Washington and Jakarta, 1993), pp. 1-6.

Wood, P. L. and J. M. Wheeler, *ASEAN in the 1990s: New Challenges and Directions*, (Indianapolis: Hudson Institute, 1990), pp. 1-68.

STRATEGIC ECONOMIC DEVELOPMENT: SINGAPORE STYLE

Robert G. Fletcher
Department of Finance and Accounting
California State University,
Bakersfield
9001 Stockdale Highway
Bakersfield, CA 93311

Brenda J. Moscove
Department of Marketing
California State University,
Bakersfield
9001 Stockdale Highway
Bakersfield, CA 93311

Abstract—Singapore's economy changed from entrepot and import substitution economic activities to skill intensive manufacturing of high technology equipment, to provision of financial services, and to emergence as a regional economic center for Southeast Asia in a short period of time (1960-95). This rapid transformation of the Singaporean economy resulted from active solicitation of foreign direct investment by multinational corporations through various incentive programs and large scale investments in infrastructure by the Singapore government through government ministries, statutory boards and State-Owned Enterprises. This chapter looks at key factors responsible for Singapore's economic development and explores recent alterations in the country's economic and political strategies to compete in the 1990s. These recent changes are the aftermath of the transformation of the Cold War into the New World Order. The direction and ultimate country and regional inter-relationships are the major challenges facing Singapore and its regional neighbors in determining the direction for participating in the New World Order.

I. INTRODUCTION

Singapore actively sought investments by multinational corporations (MNCs) in the late 1960s and 1970s at the same time other developing nations were discouraging similar investments. This city-state country developed a variety of public policies and programs that encouraged and shaped desired economic development patterns by MNCs: direct and indirect subsidies and tax incentives, suitable financing arrangements, attractive land use controls and property rights, immigration policies, and prerequisite infrastructure to attract foreign direct investment (FDI).

To analyze Singapore's economic development and current position in the New World Order, this chapter is organized in the following manner. The first section delineates the various economic development strategies employed by Singapore through its development stages and explores the contribution of FDI by MNCs in stimulating economic growth of Singapore. The second section focuses upon the role of government in constructing infrastructure to attract FDI and facilitate the overall economic growth of the country. Included in this discussion is a look at some of the important government, and quasi-government institutions used in the development process. The next section explores the recent transformation of Singapore and its regional neighbors into a set of nations searching for economic, social, political and military security in a world of changing alliances. The final section considers possible lessons from Singapore's economic development experience in light of the changing New World Order.

II. DEVELOPMENT STRATEGIES AND FOREIGN DIRECT INVESTMENT

Prior to 1959, Singapore's principal economic activity centered around entrepot activities such as trading, processing, storing, reexporting, etc. In the early 1960s, the People's Action Party (PAP), the controlling political party, employed an import substitution strategy because of the possibility of a Malaysia-Singapore common market and the potential problems of developing an export-oriented economy during the initial phase of the country's industrialization. After 1965, the import substitution strategy was no longer practical with the collapse of the common market negotiations with Malaysia, the meager success of Singapore's import substitution strategy, and the impending British withdrawal in 1971 of its military operations[1] in Singapore.

Singapore's small population and geographical size along with minimal natural resources limited the economic strategies open to the PAP. FDI from MNCs was sought by the party because of growing nationalism and protectionism of many countries in their region, and the global rather than local orientation of MNCs. Important factors that led to the success of this change in strategies were the skepticism of many developing country governments about the economic benefits derived from investments by MNCs, the reduction in tariffs and legislative changes that improved the industrial relations' climate and controlled industrial disputes, the introduction of investment incentives to government determined desired types of manufacturing operations, and the development of governmental and quasi-government organizations to support foreign industrial investments (see Role of Government section).

The thrust of this strategy in the late 1960s was to attract labor intensive industries to create local jobs. This approach was modified in the early 1970s, when full employment was reached, to attract FDI that would generate higher skilled jobs and produce quality products. New financial assistance schemes, changes in tax incentives, and manpower training were key elements of this development strategy designed to attract foreign investments that generated skill-intensive employment opportunities.

To further foster the flow of FDI to Singapore, governmental institutions were introduced or modified to support industrial investments. For example, the Development Bank of Singapore (DBS)[2], the Jurong Town Corporation (JTC), and the Singapore Institute for Standards and Industrial Research (SISIR) were established in 1968 to provide industrial financing, industrial estate development and management, and technical services, respectfully.

In the late 1970s, the economic development strategy changed again when the PAP leadership realized that Singapore was likely to face long term competition from other low cost labor countries. A new develop-

---

1. Accounted for approximately 14 percent of Singapore's Gross Domestic Product and 16 percent of its work force.
2. Now known as the DBS bank.

ment strategy emphasizing capital and skill intensive industries such as petrochemicals, electronics, optical instruments and lenses, etc., was designed to provide a "break through" opportunity for the country -- one that would be hard to copy or imitate for a few years. Additionally, the government set a goal for Singapore to become an "information society" through upgrading its technology and services.

The focus of this new strategy shifted in the 1980s to emphasize sophisticated services: telecommunications, computer software, banking and finance, transportation and tourism. The banking and finance sector had been a high priority since the late 1960s when Singapore began to develop its offshore banking activities (Tan Chwee Huat, 1989). To meet the needs of this new strategy numerous manpower development schemes were supported by the government's Development Fund, including the establishment of state subsidized institutes. This emphasis upon the development of human capital also involved changes in the formal education system with a new technical, vocational, and industrial focus.

In 1986, MNCs were encouraged to establish their Asia Pacific regional headquarters in Singapore by the establishment of the Services Promotion Division by the Singapore's Economic Development Board. The division also promoted FDI in a wide range of services. Additional SOEs and statutory boards were established to foster this new change in strategy.

The public sector's role in the economic development of Singapore, however, was not always successful. During the 1984-86 economic downturn in Singapore, the public sector's role in property development and ownership came under scrutiny. One recommendation that arose from an evaluation of the downturn in the real property market was that the public sector curtail its development activities in the retail and office sector and refrain from "leading" the local real estate market in setting prices and rental rates (Report of the Property Market Consultative Committee, 1986).

In the 1990s the country's new economic development plan focused upon five key strategies: (1) revitalizing the manufacturing sector by highlighting design, production, engineering, systems integration and R&D; (2) helping Singaporean businesses develop by sponsoring governmental technical programs designed to push firms through the various stages of growth; (3) encouraging overseas investments, especially regional investments; (4) developing public and private partnerships to attract new investments in Singapore; and (5) promoting vertical and horizontal linkages of public and private sectors to enhance world-class capabilities. For example, the Ministry of Trade and Industry in December 1991 identified targets for its Strategic Economic Plan (Publicity Division, Ministry of Information and the Arts). A part of the plan was to establish

Table I. Net Investment Commitments in Manufacturing (1972-93)

Year	Annual Commitments (S$million)			Percentage Share	
	Total	Foreign	Local	Foreign	Local
1972	194.5	156.3	38.2	80.4	19.6
1973	295.9	224.1	71.8	75.7	24.3
1974	291.9	168.8	123.1	57.8	42.2
1975	306.3	246.8	59.5	80.8	19.4
1976	303.3	260.5	42.8	85.9	14.1
1977	396.4	362.6	33.8	91.5	8.5
1978	812.4	765.7	46.7	94.3	5.7
1979	943.6	823.4	120.2	87.3	12.7
1980	1,417.9	1,199.0	218.9	84.6	15.4
1981	1,877.4	1,234.6	642.8	65.8	34.2
1982	1,704.5	1,162.5	542.0	68.2	31.8
1983	1,775.8	1,269.8	506.0	71.5	28.5
1984	1,828.4	1,334.7	493.7	73.0	27.0
1985	1,120.4	888.0	232.4	79.3	20.7
1986	1,450.0	1,190.6	259.4	82.1	17.9
1987	1,743.0	1,448.0	295.0	83.1	16.9
1988	2,007.4	1,657.8	349.6	82.6	17.4
1989	1,958.7	1,625.4	333.3	83.0	17.0
1990	2,487.4	2,217.9	269.5	89.2	10.8
1991	2,934.0	2,461.1	472.9	83.9	16.1
1992	3,481.0	2,733.0	748.0	78.5	21.5
1993	3,893.3	3,152.3	741.0	81.0	19.0

Source: Department of Statistics, *Economic & Social Statistics Singapore 1960-1982*; and various issues of *Yearbook of Statistics*.

clusters of strategic industries[3] that are linked horizontally and/or vertically. The 14 industry clusters identified in the plan were part of an effort by the Singaporean Government to improve productivity, automation, training and intra-ASEAN[4] trade growth. Components of these strategies also included promoting Singapore migration overseas to develop investment opportunities, introduction of a three percent Goods and Services Tax (GST) to provide revenue to further increase FDI (principally by MNCs) and introduce information technology to all facets of Singaporean life, and promotion of Singapore as a center of excellence in selected fields of science and technology. The success of the various development

Table II. Gross Domestic Product by Industrial Origin

Gross Domestic Product at Current Market Prices In Percent					
Sector	1960	1970	1980	1990	1993
Agriculture & Fishing	3.5	2.3	1.3	0.3	0.2
Quarrying	0.3	0.3	0.3	0.1	0.1
Manufacturing	11.6	20.4	29.8	29.6	27.5
Utilities	2.3	2.6	2.2	1.9	1.7
Construction	3.4	6.8	6.5	5.5	7.4
Commerce	33.5	28.2	22.8	18.6	17.8
Transport & Communications	13.6	10.8	14.3	13.0	12.1
Financial & Business Services	11.5	14.1	17.1	26.1	28.8
Other Services	17.6	13.2	9.6	10.1	9.6
Other Net	2.7	1.3	-3.9	-5.2	-5.2
TOTAL	100.0	100.0	100.0	100.0	100.0

Source: Department of Statistics, *Economic & Social Statistics Singapore 1960-1982*; and various issues of *Yearbook of Statistics*.

---

3. The clusters included petroleum, petrochemical, shipping, information technology, electronics, precision engineering, commodity trading, construction, heavy engineering, finance, insurance, general supporting industries, tourism, and international hubbing.
4. The Association of Southeast Asian Nations includes Singapore, Malaysia, Indonesia, Thailand, Brunei Darussalam, and the Philippines.

strategies to attract FDI is illustrated in Table I, which presents net foreign and local investment commitments in manufacturing for the period 1972-93. The data indicate clearly the major contribution of foreign investment (72 to 89 percent of net investment commitments in manufacturing) in comparison to local commitments. These figures understate the importance of FDI since the data do not include investments in financial and other services, especially in recent years.

In the 1970s, American companies were large foreign investors. European and Japanese foreign investment increased dramatically in the 1980s, especially Japanese investment between 1987-91. By 1991, Japanese equity investment (approximately 20 percent) exceeded all other countries, and the United States investment was second (approximately 18 percent).

Table III. Real Gross Domestic Product Growth by Industrial Origin

Percentage Share of Real Gross Domestic Product Growth				
Sector	1960-70	1970-80	1980-90	1990-93
Agriculture & Fishing	1.3	0.4	-0.5	-0.1
Quarrying	0.1	0.3	0.1	-0.2
Manufacturing	25.9	26.6	28.3	22.2
Utilities	2.8	3.0	2.2	1.8
Construction	8.4	3.6	3.5	12.3
Commerce	25.9	21.7	17.0	17.6
Transport & Communications	9.8	23.3	16.4	16.6
Financial & Business Services	15.4	21.0	31.8	30.1
Other Services	10.6	9.1	9.0	7.7
Other Net	-0.2	-9.0	-7.8	-8.0
TOTAL	100.0	100.0	100.0	100.0

Source: Department of Statistics, *Economic & Social Statistics Singapore 1960-1982*; and various issues of *Yearbook of Statistics*.

A further indication of the success of the Singaporean strategies is shown in Table II and III, which present industrial origins of Gross Domestic Product (GDP) and sectoral origins of real growth in GDP for the period 1960-93. Table II clearly shows the various phases of economic expansion from the development of manufacturing in the 1960s and 1970s, and the more recent growth of financial and business services in the 1980s. Additionally, the table shows the declining role of entrepot trade (commerce) from a high (34 percent) in 1960 to a more modest role (18 percent) in 1993. The decline in agriculture and fishing during the 1960-93 period reflects the modernization and build out of Singapore as well as the governmental policy to downplay these low value added industrial sectors.

Table III further supports the conclusions about the importance of the manufacturing sector in the economic development of Singapore in the early years, and the more recent prominence of the financial and business services sectors in the 1980s and 1990s. Also, commerce's declining role as a percentage share of real GDP is evident. The challenge to Singapore is to continue to attract FDI in manufacturing and to maintain the recent investments in financial and business services.

III. ROLE OF GOVERNMENT

FDI was an important source of capital for Singapore's economic development, but local sources of capital also played a strategic role in the development process. The local financial sources consisted mainly of government owned or controlled organizations in nearly every major industry and private savings through the Central Provident Fund (CPF). The two principal government organizations were statutory boards and State-Owned Enterprises (SOEs). The contributions of the Central Provident Fund, selected statutory boards, and SOEs are reviewed below.

Central Provident Fund

The original goal of the Central Provident Fund was to provide old age security for workers. In 1968, this goal was modified to allow fund members to withdraw funds for public residential housing and health insurance. Further liberalizations were introduced in 1981 with the lifting of restrictions on purchasing private residential properties and in 1984 when payments for health care (Medisave) were approved. Recent program changes allow members to fund education, purchase approved securities, and top up parents' retirement accounts.

The Central Provident Fund was an important financing mechanism for Singapore's economic development because contributions by employers and employees[5] were the major sources of funds for government issued securities, including statutory boards and SOEs. While other financial institutions attracted private savings, the major savings institution in Singapore was the Central Provident Fund (Fletcher and Moscove, forthcoming).

Statutory Boards

Statutory boards, a carryover from British colonial rule, are autonomous organizations created by Acts of Parliament that specify their functions and relationships to specific government ministries. Statutory boards had monopoly powers to generate social and infrastructural development to facilitate economic growth. The funding of these operations generally involved charging fees, issuing of securities and, in some instances, borrowing from the government Development Fund. The chief advantage of statutory boards was the ability to circumvent bureaucratic procedures that would arise if the entities were government agencies.

Three of seven major statutory boards played leading roles in the historical economic development of public housing, manufacturing and commercial sectors of the economy. The three boards included the Housing and Development Board (HDB), Jurong Town Corporation (JTC), and Urban Redevelopment Authority (URA). Another statutory board, the Economic Development Board, acted as the main marketing mechanism (one-stop shopping to obtain land, factory space, long-term financing, skilled labor, etc.) to attract FDI to Singapore.

The Housing and Development Board contributed to Singapore's economic development by providing low cost, high rise flats in housing estates for low income families. In 1960, approximately 9 percent of the population lived in low cost housing while almost 87 percent lived in Housing Development Board flats in 1987. Numerous subsidies were

---

5. Contribution levels of employers and employees have varied through time depending upon prevailing economic conditions in Singapore. In 1991, for example, the contribution was 22.5 percent from the employer and 17.5 percent from the employee up to a maximum monthly contribution of S$1,050 for the employer and S$1,350 for the employee, based on a salary ceiling of S$6,000 a month.

utilized to foster the construction and maintenance of the housing estates although the magnitude of the subsidies is subject to debate (Pugh, 1985).

The Jurong Town Corporation developed and managed industrial property in Singapore. The Corporation provided prepared industrial sites and completed factory buildings while the Singaporean government offered monetary incentives in the form of tax concessions to attract select industries. The Jurong Town Corporation introduced a new strategy for the 1990s when it repositioned itself to encourage and retain high technology oriented businesses through the development of business parks. This new orientation also fit into the government's emphasis on the growth triangle between Indonesia, Malaysia, and Singapore which promotes shared industrial growth within Southeast Asia.

The Urban Redevelopment Agency, established in 1974, is the national planning and conservation organization for Singapore. In the early years, the Urban Redevelopment Agency was responsible for the redevelopment of commercial property in the Central Business District (Central Area) and Orchard Road (the primary shopping and tourist strip). In the 1990s the agency has responsibility for planning and controlling building and land develop throughout Singapore.

State-Owned Enterprises (SOEs)

The purpose of the SOEs was also to facilitate economic development. In many instances, SOEs were created to encourage private investors to enter industries given high priority by the Singapore government. SOEs were also established by the government when the investment requirements were too large in scale or too risky for the indigenous investors (Krause, 1988). The financing for the SOEs came from a variety of sources including government revenues, the national compulsory retirement program (Central Provident Fund or CPF), statutory board's surpluses, and once established and operating efficiently the SOEs' earnings.

Three wholly owned government holding companies (Temasek Holdings, Singapore Technology Holdings, and Health Corporation Holdings) are at the top of a set of tiers that make up the SOE structure in Singapore. These three holding companies then control a set of first tier companies which in turn own second and lower tier subsidiaries. These tiers of companies are spread across the economic sectors of the economy. Data indicate that the SOEs have outperformed MNCs and local private sector firms in average sales and profitability in recent years (*The Straits Times Weekly Overseas Edition*, August 29, 1992).

One SOE that contributed heavily to the development of Singapore was the DBS Bank established in 1968 to finance Singapore's industrial growth (Schulze, 1990). DBS Bank's major role was to provide medium and long-term financing and equity capital to the manufacturing sector. DBS also participated in commercial and residential property markets through a subsidiary called DBS Land. Examples of DBS financial activities include its participation in the development of the Asian Dollar Bond Market, SIMEX (Singapore International Monetary Exchange), and the Asian Dollar Market (ACUs).

IV. IMPACT OF THE NEW WORLD ORDER

While Singapore continues to strive on its own to develop economically, socially and politically, the political leadership of the country recognized in the early 1990s that the alliances and relationships that existed during its economic development are changing at a rapid pace in the aftermath of the demise of the cold war. Singapore's political leadership felt that one of the key facets of the New World Order was the movement toward regional blocs. For example, former Prime Minister Lee Kuan Yew in his last New Year's message before being succeeded by Goh Chok Tong described the "world at the threshold of a new era, witnessing the end of the epoch of Soviet containment and Cold War diplomacy, and at the genesis of a new era of multi-polar geopolitics. (Soong, *Singapore Business Times*, January 1, 1990). According to another article (*Singapore Business Times*, January 16, 1992) describing the world situation for Singapore's new prime minister, Mr. Goh Chok Tong, "The challenge for Asean in a world without the Cold War, for Mr. Goh, is to remain relevant to the big players who now no longer need to woo the Asian States."

Singapore's reaction to the New World Order is illustrated by its participation and support for the proposals of the 1992 ASEAN summit in Singapore. Summit participants agreed to the formation of a Common Effective Preferential Tariff (CEPT) scheme that would lead to the establishment of the ASEAN Free Trade Area (AFTA) with zero to 5 percent tariffs on capital goods, manufactured products and processed agricultural goods by the year 2008. CEPT was to begin the liberalization of trade barriers in January 1993, starting with 15 product groups, as the 15 year transition was made to a free trade area. Summit participants supported the creation of AFTA as a response to the development of the Single European Market (SEM) and the North American Free Trade Zone (NAFTA). ASEAN political leaders felt that without AFTA, Southeast Asian countries would lose investment and trade opportunities to SEM and NAFTA.

The long 15-year period to establish AFTA and the numerous exclusions from tariff reductions by the participating countries make the achievement of a free trade area problematic. The growth triangles mentioned earlier have been progressing since the summit, especially the growth triangle between Indonesia, Singapore, and Malaysia. Growth triangles may be the intermediate step toward more regional cooperation among the ASEAN countries.

At the same meeting, the heads of government also agreed to step up discussion of regional security, a subject previously treated as taboo, and to cooperate in the development of a number of industries (from tourism to communications and finance). The expected reduction in the United States military presence were cited as the principal reason for the shaping of a new regional security order.

Additionally, government leaders at the two-day summit meeting invited all Southeast Asian countries to sign a friendship treaty as a "common framework for wider regional cooperation." The invitation indicated a willingness to eventually accept Cambodia, Vietnam, Laos and Myanmar (formerly Burma) into the ASEAN.

The changing role of the ASEAN nations in the New World Order also received attention (The Xinhua News Agency, September 14, 1994). Singapore's foreign minister S. Jayakumar described a new phase of development that consists of four features. First, the ASEAN economics are expanding as members of the Asia Pacific Economic Cooperation (APEC) that represents 18 economies in the Asia-Pacific. Second, the ASEAN Regional Forum (ARF) is a unique organization for the promotion of peace and security that is under the control of the ASEAN membership. Third, the ASEAN was expanding its membership with the admission of Vietnam in 1995. Finally, the Treaty of Amity and Cooperation in Southeast Asia by the ARF member countries provides the guidelines for the relations of countries with each other. The foreign minister identified these four features as the new directions and challenges for ASEAN. In a recent speech (Ong and Chuang, *Singapore Business Times*, March 10, 1995), Prime Minister Goh cited maintaining social cohesion within national borders and keeping regional trading groups open as key challenges in the New World Order. Social cohesion could not be maintained, according to Prime Minister Goh, unless efforts were made to eliminate the growing disparity between the haves and have nots that was developing because of the globalization of markets. In his opinion, regional trading alliances also are a direct threat to multilateral free trade. He mentioned strategic trading blocs such as the European Union (EC), the North America Free Trade Area (NAFTA), and the Asian Free Trade Association (AFTA) or Asian Pacific Economic Cooperation (APEC) as regional blocs that can either strengthen or weaken multinational free trade. Goh called for many East Asian nations to change their attitudes about open markets[6] so that regional blocs do not stifle the new international environment.

V. CONCLUSION

One implication of Singapore's experience is that an aggressive and well planned set of development strategies is important to the growth of a country's economy. The strategies need to focus upon infrastructure improvements, FDI, and political stability. A further implication of the Singapore development experience is that countries or regions need to act expeditiously in response to changing economic environments and design policies to adapt to sharp fluctuations in external conditions. For example, the switch to skill intensive manufacturing in the early 1970s allowed Singapore to remain competitive in the world market place. The more recent emphasis upon becoming a regional center exemplifies the importance of adopting proactive development strategies. Additionally, Singapore's recognition of the New World Order and the important of establishing regional political, economic and military ties demonstrates the importance of being proactive to changes in world conditions.

Related to the above is the active but not necessarily efficient role that government assumed in developing strategies and schemes to encourage rapid economic growth for the economy. For example, the involvement of

---

6. Wanting open western markets for their goods and services but restrict their own markets.

government enterprises in real estate ventures generally provided by the private sector exposed the government to all the risks associated with entrepreneurial activities as demonstrated by the slump in the demand for both publicly and privately constructed office and retail space.

Finally, replication of the Singapore growth experience may be extremely difficult for other countries or regions since the city-state's small size, political climate, and culture provided a potentially unique environment for planning economic growth. Additionally, the delicate balance between private/public sector policies and programs on foreign and domestic investments and development of infrastructure may be difficult to replicate in other countries.

A further deterrent to pursuing Singapore's economic growth experience is the emerging New World Order that puts a premium on regional economic, political and social alliances. If free trade, a key factor in Singapore's economic growth, is limited or modified, developing countries may experience difficulties in attaining the indigenous environment required to transform their economies. The real challenge of the future, according to Singapore's Prime Minister Goh is for "Asian nations to recognise their 'increasing responsibility in determining whether a liberal world order is sustained'" (Ong and Chuang, *Singapore Business Times*, March 10, 1995). Singapore's advanced economy compared to other nations in the region and stable political environment seem to project the country into a leadership role in the Pacific Rim as the New World Order emerges.

REFERENCES

Department of Statistics, *Economic & Social Statistics Singapore 1960-1982*, (Singapore: Singapore National Printers, 1983).

Department of Statistics, *Yearbook of Statistics Singapore*, (Singapore: Singapore National Printers Ltd., various annual issues).

Fletcher, Robert G. and Brenda J. Moscove, "Singapore's Economic Development: A Financial Perspective," in *Government and Business Finance: Global Perspectives on Economic Development*, eds. Richard D. Bingham and Edward W. Hill, eds., (New Jersey: CUPR Press, forthcoming).

Krause, L.B., Koh Al Tee and Lee (Tsao) Yuan, *The Singapore Economy Reconsidered*, (Singapore: Institute of Southeast Asian Studies, 1988).

Ong, Catherine and Chuang Peck Ming, "PM Goh - Social Cohesion, Open Trade Key Challenges in New World Order,"(Singapore: *Singapore Business Times*, March 10, 1995).

Publicity Division, *Strategic Economic Plan (SEP)*, (Singapore: Ministry of Information and the Arts, 1993), p 7.

Pugh, C., "Housing and Development in Singapore," *Contemporary Southeast Asia*, 1985, 6, 293-294.

Report of the Property Market Consultative Committee, *Action Plan for the Property Sector*, (Singapore: Ministry of Finance, 1986).

Singapore Business Times, "Prime Ministers Goh and Anand on Braving A New World Order,: (Singapore: January 16, 1992).

Soong, Martin, "Real Growth For '89 Hit 9.3PC - PM Lee,"(Singapore: *Singapore Business Times*, January 1, 1990).

Tan Chwee Huat, *Financial Markets and Institutions in Singapore*, Sixth Edition, (Singapore: Singapore University Press, 1989).

The Straits Times Weekly Overseas Edition, "Role of State-Owned Enterprises," (Singapore: The Straits Times, August 29, 1992), p 20.

The Xinhua News Agency, "Asean Entering New Phase of Development, Singapore FM," (China: September 14, 1994).

THE VIETNAM CRUCIBLE: THE POLITICAL ECONOMY OF NORMALIZATION IN THE POST-COLD WAR WORLD

M. Kent Bolton
Department of Political Science
California State University, San Marcos
San Marcos, CA 92096

Abstract—In this chapter I examine U.S. foreign policy with respect to Vietnam. It has been some twenty years since America left Vietnam; relations have been uncomfortable at best ever since. In today's post-Cold War world, a *prima facie* case could be made for more normal relations based on U.S. economic interests in the region and the putative potential Vietnam represents. Nevertheless, relations between the two former combatants improves only incrementally. In this chapter I consider why that is the case focusing primarily on 1991-95. In short, the answer is a classic case of interest-group pluralism shaping U.S. foreign policy.

In light of the thirty-year anniversary (March 1995) of America's official combat-troop deployment to Vietnam and the twenty-year anniversary of America's withdrawal from Vietnam (April 1995) it seems appropriate to look again at U.S.-Vietnamese relations. I do so here focusing on the political-economy of America's foreign policy with respect to Vietnam--in particular on the issue of normalization of relations.

The forces shaping America's foreign policy are manifold and varied. Here, I consider two competing forces, among multiple ones, shaping U.S. foreign policy toward Vietnam. I argue that these two competing forces are demonstrably causal, affecting America's normalization with Vietnam. It is timely inasmuch as America is inevitably--if incrementally--moving toward ultimate normalization. Now is a particularly propitious time to review U.S. foreign policy in light of the anniversaries noted above. It is illustrative of somewhat generalizable trends--continuity and incrementalism--in U.S. foreign policy. And it is indicative of the intersection between economics and politics that is becoming so crucial as the U.S. considers its role in the increasingly interdependent world system.

In this chapter, I define foreign policy conceptually. Foreign policy is: *the set of goals officials seek to attain abroad; the underlying values guiding said goals; and the instruments used to fulfill the goals.*[1] Certain implications follow. First, not every action that takes place between any two countries is foreign policy, since I have specified "officials" in the definition. Further, "seeking to attain objectives" implies purposive behavior. Only if it is intended to produce a response abroad is an official action considered foreign policy.

If political economy is the intersection of economic and political relationships, then U.S. policy toward Vietnam vis-a-vis normalization is a prime example of this intersection. With respect to Vietnam, political interests have clashed with economic interests producing what I call *cautious incrementalism* in America's approach to the normalization issue. In fact this trend appears relatively generalizable, irrespective of which party is in the executive branch or who controls Congress.

What historically have been America's objectives with respect to Vietnam? The answer turns on two sometimes contradictory trends. The first is a fundamentally post-World War Two phenomena: the containment of Communism--whether directly Vietnam's or Soviet influence in Vietnam. Images of falling dominoes were commonly associated with Vietnam and its security relevance to the United States. The second is America's his-

---

1. Charles W. Kegley, Jr. and Eugene R. Wittkopf, *American foreign Policy: Patterns and Process* (New York: St Martin's Press, 1991).

toric goal of expanding commercial ties, primarily free trade, globally. Clearly these two goals are not mutually exclusive: perceived Communist expansion and threat to America's security interests often combined with a view of Marxism-Leninism as antithetical to America's version of export capitalism.

America's Asia goals following World War Two, therefore, included maintaining a military presence in what it viewed as the strategically important Southeast Asia region. Further, the United States sought to secure a place for America's industries throughout the region. Following the Cold War's conclusion, the latter goal has played an increasingly central influence in America's posture toward the region. Put differently, with precious-few dominoes about which to be concerned, containing communism diminished as America's historical commercial tendencies increased. Indeed the Clinton administration has, arguably, placed even greater emphasis on "commercial realism"[2] than its predecessors. And Vietnam is seen as a potentially lucrative market waiting to be tapped; its needs are many ranging from the most basic to the most advanced infrastructure.[3] Additionally, with respect to Indochina generally and Vietnam specifically, the U.S. has held the goal of fullest possible accounting of prisoners of war and those declared missing in action (POWs-MIAs).

Accordingly, one can envision normalization--i.e., the granting of full diplomatic status--as an instrument used to achieve U.S. goals. I do not consider normalization the policy *per se*. Rather, maintaining a strategic presence and fostering market economies in an already quickly developing Southeast Asia represent America's primary goals in the area. Accounting for POWs-MIAs is a goal that arose proximate to the Vietnam war; it is then in some sense a result of the former two goals. The possi-

---

2. See Daniel Williams, "Clinton's National Security Adviser Outlines U.S. 'Strategy of Enlargement,'" *Washington Post*, 22 September 1993, p. A 16. Also, see Jim Mann, "Clinton's Foreign Policy 'Realism' Keeps Eye on U.S. Firms' Bottom Line," *Los Angeles Times*, 3 April 1995, p. A 5.
3. The ongoing normalization process was characterized as reflecting "the reality that without rapid normalization, US business will be closed out of one of the most promising markets in East Asia." And "American businesses have been forced to stand by as foreign companies . . . have cashed in on Vietnam's opening market. With a population of 70 million, Vietnam is an attractive market for low-priced consumer goods ranging from soft drinks to motorcycles . . . ." See George Moffett, "Lured by Promising Vietnam Markets, US tightens Ties with Its Former Foe," *Christian Science Monitor*, 3 February 1995, p. 1.

bility of normalization--"Dangling rewards," as one assessment indelicately put it--is the instrument used for achieving U.S. goals. Conversely, when dangling rewards fails to achieve desired outcomes, the U.S. has been quite prepared to forestall normalization and to block international loans and investment. I concentrate on the use of normalization as the instrument and the crucible in which interest-group pressures shape the process.

It has been argued that the forces shaping U.S. foreign policy in the post-World War Two period have produced considerable continuity in output. Further, it has been argued that U.S. foreign policy, in terms of general trends, changes only incrementally over time (Kegley and Wittkopf, 1991). A similar case may be made for specific policies. With respect to Vietnam, the forces determining the pace of normalization yield *cautious incrementalism*.

Since America's final departure from Vietnam there has lingered an understandably emotional concern regarding the full accounting of America's POWs-MIAs. Both the Bush and Clinton administrations publicly have held the position that the U.S. could never normalize with Vietnam until resolution of this issue. To be sure, there were other issues preventing normalization--notably Vietnam's interference in Cambodia. But as the Cold War receded, so too did this and other issues preventing normalization. Eventually, the only remaining issue was whether or not--and then to what extent--Vietnam's government had complied on the POW-MIA matter.

Concomitantly, Asia increasingly became an area of economic development and "economic miracles." Frequently American companies were involved. New buyers of America's products were created and returns on investments were profitable. Hence the Cold War's demise was generally good for American business interests in Asia. Yet, all the while Vietnam languished behind, as far as American companies were concerned. The embargo preventing Americans from doing business in Vietnam began in 1964; at the time it was directed at North Vietnam. Following America's departure in 1975, the embargo was applied to Vietnam in its entirety.

While American companies were prevented from doing business there, companies from other capitalist countries took advantage of the American absence to penetrate Vietnam. According to one account, prior to Clinton lifting the embargo in February 1994, "Vietnam had licensed more than

800 foreign investment projects for mostly European and rich Asian nations with a total approved capital of $7 billion," noting that America "watched helplessly" its competitors "from France, Japan, Taiwan and South Korea.'"[4] Thus, as the Cold War ended and with it the fear of falling dominoes, previously important ideological obstacles to normalization diminished. Consequently, America's historical commercialism grew in significance. This context forms the crucible in which increasingly important and conflictual interests came to bear on Vietnam and the normalization process. American businesses agitated for an end to the economic embargo with the eventual goal of full normalization. And POW-MIA interest groups opposed normalization on the grounds that it remained the only "leverage" to influence Vietnam's cooperation in accounting for POW-MIAs.

On 13 January 1993, the U.S. Senate Select Committee on POW-MIA Affairs issued an "Executive Summary." What it demonstrates, albeit unintentionally, is the ongoing clash of the aforementioned forces. The Select Committee had a deadline of December 1992. And at the outset the Summary expresses complete fidelity to POW-MIA families. In describing the Committee's purpose the following rational is given: "The most basic principle of personal honor in America's armed forces is never willingly to leave a fellow serviceman behind." It continues:

> The Senate Select Committee on POW-MIA Affairs was created to ensure that our nation meets its obligation to the missing and to the families of those still listed as unaccounted for from the war in Southeast Asia . . . . It is an obligation--a solemn duty--that can be met only with the best and most complete answers that are within our power to provide.[5]

The Committee--led by two senators supportive of normalization-- paid close attention to the special-interest groups that were arrayed against normalization: the POW-MIA lobby. Nor was there anything subtle about the Committee's keen interest in the lobby; as seen, the Committee nomi-

---

4. See the *Los Angeles Times*, 11 April 1995, section H, "A World Report Special Edition on the Pacific Rim, and Patrick Lee, "Asia Looks within to Prosper, *Los Angeles Times*, 26 September 1994, p. D 1& D 4. For direct quote see, *The San Francisco Examiner*, 4 February 1994, p. A 1.
5. U.S. Senate Select Committee on POW-MIA Affairs, Executive Summary, 13 January 1993 , p. 4. Hereafter referenced to as the Report.

nally expressed its deference to the families' concerns. Moreover, the process did not simply materialize out of thin air in the 1990s. The history of the American government's concern with POW-MIA issues dates back to the war. However, a brief review of the Committee's recent struggle to resolve two contradictory demands--focusing on the Bush and Clinton administrations--is illustrative of a process whose origins date to the end of the Vietnam war.

In 1991 the Bush administration fashioned a "roadmap" that would grant Vietnam an end to some eighteen years of American diplomatic, economic, and trade isolation. In fall 1991, in a New York speech, President Bush said:

> We envision normal relations with Vietnam as the logical conclusion to a step-by-step process that begins by resolving the problems in Cambodia and by addressing thoroughly, openly, and conclusively the status of American POW-MIAs.[6]

The effect of the statement was to put each lobby on guard.

One day earlier, the State Department made clear the same position, releasing a dispatch of testimony given on 5 November 1991 before the Senate Select Committee on POW-MIA Affairs. In the dispatch, Kenneth M. Quinn, Deputy Assistant Secretary, characterized the roadmap this way:

> We now have a clear, carefully spelled-out and written-down policy approach on normalization of relations with Vietnam--called the roadmap--which blends two important US foreign policy goals--a comprehensive political settlement on Cambodia and POW-MIA accounting.

Quinn pointed out, for example, that Secretary Baker had met with his Vietnamese counterpart in New York during September 1990. Further he noted General Vessey's two trips to Hanoi in 1991 culminating in the "establishment of our first POW-MIA office. . . ." General Vessey had been appointed by the Reagan administration as a sign of the importance it attached to the POW-MIA issue. Indeed, each subsequent administration

---

6. Jonathon Burton, "US, Vietnam Inch Toward Renewing Ties," *Christian Science Monitor*, 27 November 1991, p. 6.

has gone to great lengths to feature General Vessey's presence as a sort of political cover for its actions. In a terse overview Quinn says: "In sum, the past 15 months have seen diplomatic efforts of an unprecedented breadth and scope on behalf of our POW-MIA effort."[7] Vessey's *imprimatur* is apparently required for such bold declarations.

And in fact, the process of "comprehensive political settlement" continued during the remainder of Bush's tenure--albeit in fits and starts. On 14 December 1992, after Clinton's narrow victory, Bush took the action that his administration had outlined earlier--viz., he allowed U.S. companies to set up offices and sign contracts in Vietnam. By the time the Clintons were ready to occupy the White House, the outgoing administration made a final attempt to claim the victory of opening the Indochina markets. Reuters reported on 6 January 1993, that "The Bush administration is holding out the prospects of lifting the trade embargo against Vietnam before leaving office, . . ."[8] Nevertheless, the prospect continued to languish.

It was not until more than one year later that the Clinton administration completed what Bush had been unable to accomplish. It was reported with flair:

> President Clinton announced Thursday [3 February 1994] he is lifting the U.S. trade embargo against Vietnam, marking a dramatic shift in relations chilled for decades by war and post-war hostility. . . . He said this was not normalization of diplomatic relations, . . . Clinton said he had taken the moves *not for economic reasons* but because he thought it was the best way to get the 'fullest possible accounting' of the 2,238 U.S. serviceman still listed as missing in Southeast Asia.[9]

Note the requirement that when announcing some movement toward normalization that could be interpreted as advancing the cause of business--no matter how nominal the action--the administration couches it in terms of its POW-MIA efforts. The "dramatic shifts" notwithstanding, this

---

7. Department of State, Department of State Dispatch, "Recent Progress on POW-MIA Issues," Kenneth M. Quinn, 11 November 1991 [Online] Nexis: Allnews.
8. Jim Wolf, "Bush Dangles Rewards for Vietnam, But the Clock is Ticking" *Reuter* 6 January 1993 [Online] Nexis: Allnews.
9. Susan Cornwell, *The Reuter Asia-Pacific Business Report*, "Clinton Lifts U.S. Trade Embargo against Vietnam, 3 February 1994 [Online] Nexis: Allnews. (My emphasis.)

step had been slow in coming and was quite measured. It reflected cautious incrementalism.

The Select Committee's Report was intended to be the culmination of a review resulting in an institutional process for the comprehensive accounting of POW-MIAs leading to eventual normalization. Instead, as of this writing, it stands as a testament to the forces at work producing cautious incrementalism by America's decisionmakers and forestalling normalization. The events that followed the Committee's work belie the facile focus the Committee presents as its *raison d'etre* in the Executive Summary. Though only mentioned in rather circumspect and indirect ways in the Report, the quickening pace toward normalization demonstrates that business and its associated interests were not dormant. Indeed, there is a robust record of both influences on U.S. policy coming into conflict in the Committee's deliberations.

Before the Bush administration crafted the roadmap for normalization of relations, the United States was in a peculiarly awkward position. On the one hand, America's businesses were held hostage to the Cold War politics of the Vietnam War. As noted above, there had been an embargo of one fashion or the other since 1964. American business could not "do business" in Vietnam. On the other hand, international organizations were attempting to aid Vietnam, helping to prepare Vietnam for industrialization and modernization. France in particular had spearheaded efforts in the World Bank-International Monetary Fund (IMF) conference in 1991. Thus the Bush administration found itself in the unenviable position of not wanting to see multilateral aid--and resultant business opportunities--going to a country, Vietnam, where U.S. companies could not legally compete.[10]

The Cambodia peace settlement was signed in Paris on 23 October 1991 thus effectively removing an earlier obstacle to normalization. Finding itself in so opportune a spot, the Bush administration announced that talks would start between the U.S. and Vietnam. It deftly announced, however, that the final disposition of relations was to be linked to eventual elections, called for in the Paris accord, scheduled for 1993. Thus it gave itself some room to maneuver. What the Bush administration may

---

10. Tereas Poole, "Why Vietnam Needs America," *The Independent*, 30 December 1991, [Online] Nexis: Allnews, p.19ff.

have misjudged was the resolve of groups for and against normalization. Between fall of 1991 and spring 1995, competing interests mobilized to influence the process.

The general intent behind the administration's efforts became clear immediately. Bush announced a forthcoming trip to Asia and background briefings commenced. In one United States Information Agency (USIA) background briefing--given by unnamed "U.S. officials"--the strategy was revealed.

> As you know, we're facing a new post-Cold War world and in Asia, as in the rest of the world, the post-Cold War situation is one where we still have security concerns, political and diplomatic concerns of longstanding, but the security element and sense of threat are not quite what they were previously.

The briefing goes on to elaborate the administration's "East Asian Strategy Initiative." It notes that the administration is seeking to let friend and foe alike know that the U.S. "is and will remain a Pacific power" and that Bush's trip to the region will so demonstrate. In what was a prescient preview of the emerging new emphasis on economics in U.S. foreign policy, it notes that "[f]or the first time ever, the President will be taking along a business delegation" to the region. "This is an unprecedented development and we think it's a very welcome indication of the higher priority assigned to economics and trade issues in the post-Cold War era."[11]

Business coordinated its own efforts with the administration's announcement. It was reported on 14 December 1991, that the first U.S. commercial delegation since the war was presently visiting Vietnam. The president of the American Chamber of Commerce of Hong Kong (AmCham) is quoted as saying 'We took advantage of changes in U.S. policy' in restrictions on travel to arrange the trip. He further noted that AmCham hoped the trade embargo would soon be lifted allowing Americans to invest in Vietnam.[12]

---

11. Federal Information Systems Corporation, Federal News Service, 18 December 1991, transcript of USIA Foreign Press Center Briefing [Online] Nexis: Allnews.

12. See *Agence France Presse*, "First U.S. commercial delegation since war visits Vietnam," 14 December 1991, [Online] Nexis: Allnews.

With the momentum favoring improved relations, Assistant Secretary of State for East Asia and Pacific Affairs, Richard Solomon announced that "If the Vietnamese keep these promises [on accounting for POW-MIAs and with regard to Cambodia], . . . then partial diplomatic and trade relations between Washington and Hanoi could be achieved by June [1992]."[13] In the above cited dispatch, Kenneth Quinn, enumerated the administration's strategy, vision, and roadmap. He claimed to "have a clear, carefully spelled-out and written-down policy approach on normalization of relations with Vietnam--called the roadmap--which blends . . . foreign policy goals. . . ." It included "an established process to communicate with the Vietnamese Government at the policy level."[14] But, the array of anti-normalization interest groups effectively put the brakes on the process.

What the record shows is that both the Bush and Clinton administrations, while seeking to move the U.S. along the normalization road, have been pushed in that direction by the business lobby, and prevented from going that direction by, or at least made to explain every move in that direction, to the POW-MIA lobby. And each side had become fairly sophisticated in its lobbying efforts.

On the pro-normalization side of the issue is the business lobby. This includes the U.S.-ASEAN Council, the American Chamber of Commerce, area specialists in the State Department, and key Senate sponsors, primarily, Senators John Kerry (D-MA) and John McCain (R-AZ), as well as one key Veteran's group--Vietnam Veterans of America Foundation. On the other side of the issue is the ubiquitous and powerful National League of Families of American Prisoners and Missing in Southeast Asia (known as the League of Families or simply the League), whose very capable and tenacious director is Ann Mills Griffiths. Also there is the less powerful National Alliance of Families, a newer and somewhat less well known group that has nonetheless become important. Additionally, there are key veterans groups, the Veterans of Foreign Wars and a Vietnam veterans group known as NAMPOWS. This side also has its important Senate sponsors, notably Senator Bob Smith (R-NH), and occasionally supported by Senators Grassley (R-IA) and Bob Dole (R-KS).

---

13. He is quoted in Jonathan Burton, "US, Vietnam Inch toward Renewing Ties," *Christian Science Monitor*, 27 November 1991, p. 6.
14. Department of State Dispatch, *loc. cit.*

It is apparently important to each side that their main Senate sponsors be veterans of the Vietnam conflict. Thus on the pro-normalization side are former POW Senator McCain and decorated veteran Senator John Kerry; occasionally Bob Kerrey (D-NE), a "highly" decorated Vietnam veteran comes into play. McCain's status as former POW in Vietnam makes him a lodestar of sorts, and having him on the pro-normalization side is formidable. As for the opposing POW-MIA lobby, Senator Smith is also a Vietnam veteran. And though Senator Dole is not, he is a World War Two veteran--wounded in that war--which has considerable carry-over importance.[15]

The business lobby's influence vis-a-vis Vietnam has not been very dramatic or high-profile. Rather, it has followed the pattern of business influence in China (on recent Most Favored Nation status) or in Indonesia, where it has helped to prevent trade sanctions over Indonesia's annexation of East Timor. Its influence is important and, as noted above, has increasingly ascended since the Cold War's demise. But its lobbying efforts are typically characterized by steady, lower-profile actions. As is well known, however, money has the potential of being a powerful force around political campaigns. And the business lobby has deep pockets. Its results are seen across a spectrum of U.S. foreign-policy issues in promoting commercial ties that foster new investment opportunities and markets for American products. Its effect is evident in each administration's announcements and actions. And it has its own Congressional allies. For example, Senator Frank Murkowski (R-AK) noted in fall of 1991 that "re-establishing ties with Hanoi would be a boon to both the United States and Vietnam.

> "Clearly, an American economic presence in Vietnam would be beneficial to our international trade competitiveness. More importantly, a U.S. presence based on free enterprise would also help foster a more stable economy

---

15. Also there is a cottage industry--conceded by most everyone as tawdry--whose very livelihood is linked to the normalization-POW-MIA issue. This includes the small entrepreneurs selling "Caged POW T-shirts and posters," and the truly despicable POW-MIA trade based primarily in Bangkok, that sells stories, photographs, bones, etc. and in so doing purports to prove that POWs are still alive and being held in Indochina, see Philip Smucker,"MIA Hoax Victimizes Soldiers' Families," *St. Louis Dispatch*, 14 August 1991, p. 3 C [Online] Nexis: All-news.

that would in turn reduce human suffering and promote economic and political reform."

Senator Hank Brown (R-CO) also noted, albeit it with less directness, the potential benefits as the administration was publicly considering exceptions to the economic embargo.[16]

More spectacular has been the lobbying effort preventing what it sees as hasty normalization with Vietnam. It is spectacular in the following way: a small group of individuals concerned about the accounting of missing service persons after the 1973 accords and prisoner exchanges, has developed into a monumental force with which each administration has had to reckon, if not make direct concessions, to assuage its leaders and the families they represent.

The League of Families, for instance, holds an annual meeting for its members and has for some time invited administration officials to speak. This has effectively become *de rigueur*. Around the time that the Bush administration was moving toward normalization via its roadmap, Under Secretary of State for Political Affairs, Robert Kimmitt addressed the annual affair. In his remarks he thanked the group for having him back again. He then referenced his "deep personal commitment to the effort of resolving the fate of Americans who served in Vietnam." Speaking on behalf of Secretary Baker, he explained "what has happened since [he and the League] last met." He goes on to plead that Vietnam had met earlier specified criteria for normalization, but reminding the League, lest it be unhappy with the Bush administration, that "the process of normalization, the pace and scope of that process will be directly affected by the seriousness of Vietnam's cooperation" on the POW-MIA issue.[17]

Not long after this reunion and clarification of the administration's position, the anti-normalization forces expressed their concerns. In response to the administration's October 1991 announcement that the U.S. was ready to discuss normalization with Vietnam, an article noted the an-

---

16. See respectively, Carleton R. Bryant, "POW-MIA Groups Mixed on New Vietnam Relations," *Washington Times*, 24 October 1991, p. A 8, and Kelly Richmond, "Sen. Brown Predicts Partial Normalization with Vietnam," States New Service, 17 November 1992 [Online] Nexis: Allnews.

17. Department of State, *Department of State Dispatch*, "Diplomatic Efforts to Resolve the POW-MIA Issue in the Past Year," 5 August 1991 [Online] Nexis: Allnews.

nouncement "drew warm, tepid and cool responses from groups involved in the prisoner-of-war issue." One group is quoted as: 'We're opposed to any normalization with Vietnam. If we normalize relations, we lose all the leverage we have with them.' The League and the Vietnam Veterans of America were somewhat supportive initially. As for the former, Ann Mills Griffiths allowed that 'The potential for dramatic results exists but only if implemented with integrity by both governments.' And James Brazee of the latter expressed 'cautious optimism.' Senator Smith was less tepid: 'This roadmap is dangerously flawed' and that it was 'vague and neglects to tell the Vietnamese exactly what cooperation is expected."[18]

The League, then, initially conceded possible movement toward normalization in the fall of 1991. It evidently believed that the Vietnamese government would be attentive to the League's concerns and requests. But by the following summer, the League's deference to the administration had ended. As President Bush himself campaigned for re-election, the following incident happened:

> President Bush, ordering them to 'shut up and sit down,' joined in a shouting match yesterday with families of missing soldiers and prisoners of war who interrupted his speech at their convention.

The report goes on to quote Bush "emotionally defending" his record:

> "To suggest that the commander-in-chief that led this country into its most successful recent effort [presumably the Gulf War] would condone for one single day the personal knowledge of a person held against his will--whether it's here or any place else--is simply totally unfair."[19]

Campaign rigors notwithstanding, the deep-running emotions of the POW-MIA issue were clearly wearing on the President.

Similarly, as the Vietnamese themselves made certain concessions, media associated with the two sides of the normalization issue would put their peculiar spin on Vietnam's efforts. For example, in fall 1992, the

---

18. For Bryant quote, see Carleton R. Bryant, loc cit. For Senator Smith see Paul Houston, "Reaction Mixed on Normalizing Vietnam Ties," *Los Angeles Times*, 24 October 1991, p. A 16.
19. Frank J. Murray, "Hecklers Spark President's Temper," *The Washington Times*, 25 July 1992, p. A 1.

Vietnamese opened their "archives" to American POW-MIA investigators, to General Vessey, and to representatives of the United States Senate. In reporting the event the *Washington Times* opined that opening of the archives might have some political link to the Bush administration's campaign. Not long after this announcement, *Business Week* published a pro-business view on Vietnam's potential, entitled rather irreverently, "Ho, Ho, Ho Chi Minh." The article noted that diverse business interests, including petroleum companies, the travel industry, purveyors of consumer items, and heavy equipment companies were all "agitating to get President Bush to lift the 17-year old trade and investment embargo against Vietnam before he leaves office" in January 1993.[20]

Even Governor Clinton involved himself in the controversy--apparently for simple political expediency. In the throes of a presidential bid he entered the fray. During a "town meeting," Clinton was queried by Sue Scott (of the League). Her question was simple: "What would your policy be if elected president regarding the resolution of the fate of the 2,266 Americans who remain missing in Southeast Asia?" Clinton's tortured response was:

> I think what we need to do is make it clear to Vietnam and to the other countries in Southeast Asia that full normalization of relationships depends upon an accounting for every single one of those people. And then I think we need to have a government that basically says--and I would have to say I don't know how many are still living. I don't know what the truth is. But I want to know what happened to them. I want to know who's dead, where they are buried, how many there are, and whether anybody else is still living.[21]

Normally circumspect in questions involving Vietnam and fluent in biblical injunctions as President, it appears that candidate Clinton forgot the biblical warning that "Those who trouble their own house will inherit the wind."

---

20. Joyce Price, "Vietnam to Give All POW Data: Kerry, Vessey Deny 'Politics,'" *Washington Times*, 24 October 1992, p. A 1 1. See Brian Bremmer, Joyce Barnathan, and Larry Holyoke, "Ho, Ho, Ho Chi Minh: Corporate America Rushes In," *Business Week*, 11 January 1993, p. 33ff [Online] Nexis: Allnews.
21. Federal Information Systems Corporation, Federal News Service, "Town Meeting with Governor Bill Clinton," Detroit, Michigan, 22 September 1992 [Online] Nexis: Allnews.

As President, Clinton has indeed inherited the swirling winds as business continues to push for normalization and the League and some Veterans groups continue to push against it. As the administration undertook to review America's policy vis-a-vis Vietnam the winds increased. The *Chicago Tribune* fired off an early salvo. The paper noted that:

> Unfortunately for Motorola--and IBM, Caterpillar, Honeywell, Rockwell, Boeing and dozens of troubled U.S. multinational firms with excellent reputations in long-isolated Vietnam--they cannot parlay their advantage into sales for their firms and jobs for their U.S. workers.[22]

As is frequently the case, the somewhat veiled advocacy was made in terms of tangible things Americans might understand: good-paying American jobs.

The significance was not lost on the POW-MIA lobby. They counterattacked with a campaign in which they claimed proof of Vietnam's duplicity in previous discussions. About that same time, and somewhat fortuitously, a document surfaced in a Soviet military archive as Harvard's Stephen Morris was conducting research in Moscow. Apparently, it quoted a high-level North Vietnamese official, in a 1972 memorandum, telling his Soviet counterparts that the former actually held some 837 more POWs than admitted to the Americans. The headlines splashed across the news stands were dramatic. *USA Today* startled Americans with "POW-MIA Groups say Document Proves Vietnam Lied to U.S." The League's Ann Mills Griffiths, is quoted as saying: 'This document reinforces the view that Vietnam has not been telling us the truth for . . . years about the prisoner list.'[23] Senator Smith found it most disturbing; he raised his concerns in a Senate hearing noting--somewhat out of character for the conservative Republican--that the Soviets took great political risk in providing it and implying that the Clinton administration now sought to suppress it by classifying it.[24] Many of the country's newspapers subsequently rumi-

---

22. Merrill Goozner, "U.S. Firms Losing out in Emerging Vietnam," *Chicago Tribune*, 7 March 1993, p. C 1 [Online] Nexis: Allnews.
23. John Omicinski, "POW-MIA Groups Say Document Proves Vietnam Lied to U.S.," Gannett News Service, 13 April 1993 [Online] Nexis: Allnews. See also, R.W. Apple Jr., "U.S. to Press Hanoi to Explain '72 P.O.W. Report," *New York Times*, 13 April 1993, p. A 1.
24. Federal News Service, News conference held by Senator Smith, Russell Senate Office building, Room 418, Washington D.C., 13 April 1993 [Online] Nexis: Allnews.

nated as to whether Clinton might not be better served by "halting" the process.

Just days later, business struck back. The Boeing Company sought to protect the potential sale of its products to Vietnam and to urge the Clinton administration to continue its efforts. Its vice president, John Hayden, let the press know that his company had a contract worth $110 million dollars pending. It would be jeopardized if the process were to be halted. Moreover, he warned future business with Vietnam worth some $3 billion dollars was at stake. Airbus Industrie, Boeing's European Consortium competition, would surely step in to fill the void.[25]

This round accrued to the pro-normalization forces. Nearly three month's after the Soviet-document scrimmage, the Clinton administration announced it would stop opposing international loans to Hanoi; recall loans were under consideration at the World Bank/IMF. Senators John Kerry and John McCain both made floor speeches defending the administration's move. Ann Mills Griffiths criticized the decision. And the administration plaintively noted only that Clinton "shares the families' belief that our policy toward Vietnam must be driven not by commercial interests but by the overriding purpose of achieving further progress toward the fullest possible accounting of our POW-MIAs."[26]

Though apparently losing that round, the POW-MIA interests effectively fired a warning shot across the administration's bow. It was public information, in July 1993, that the Clinton White House was preparing to consider lifting the embargo completely in September. That was when the embargo would come up for its annual review. The paper reported "rising pressure" to "scrap the 18-year old U.S. embargo of Vietnam." It further noted that Senator Smith (R-NH) was keenly attuned to this fact. Indeed Smith complained that:

> President Clinton, by dropping U.S. opposition to international loans for Vietnam this month, has started down a path that will lead to ending the embargo and normalizing diplomatic ties.

---

25. Byron Acohido, "Veterans, Boeing Spar on Vietnam Relations," *The Seattle Times*, 17 April 1993, p. B 6 [Online] Nexis: Allnews.
26. Michael Ross, "U.S. Will Stop Opposing International Loans to Hanoi--The Decision Draws Mixed Reaction from the Vietnamese-American Community in O.C.," *Los Angeles Times*, Orange County Edition, 3 July 1993, p. A 1.

It appears that the Senator was hoping to forestall that eventuality since he presented Robert Garwood, a former Marine who had remained in Vietnam until 1979, as evidence for POWs being held at least through the late 1970s. Because Garwood told of seeing Americans, Smith felt that the investigation "should be reopened."[27]

By the time of the review, in September 1993, the administration found itself vulnerable. It had pleased the business lobby back in July, but it had angered the POW-MIA lobby in so doing. The latter had reacted strongly to the administration's actions despite Clinton's claim that he was interested in the fullest possible accounting of POW-MIAs. So the administration took a more cautious approach to the review and split the difference. The *Business Times* reported that "the kind of half-pregnancy, split-in-the-middle decision that Mr. Clinton made" had aroused the ire of both sides. Mixed metaphors aside, the opening paragraph of the piece noted that Clinton had managed to disappoint the business community while angering veterans.[28] Evidently the administration's position was to placate, at least partially, the POW-MIAs lobby after its mid-summer defeat by holding the business lobby's influence in check for a few more months.

Further action was in fact put on hold. It was not until some three month's later that the issue resurfaced publicly. In one paper President Clinton is reported to have cited "progress" in accounting for POW-MIAs as a pretext for "further easing or even lifting the U.S. trade embargo against Vietnam." However, the League called Vietnam's efforts a "charade." The article cites Ann Mills Griffiths as saying: 'I could paper my walls with (broken) agreements with the Vietnamese,' and criticizing the administration for praising Vietnam's efforts while getting so little in return.[29] Another paper characterized the president's dilemma this way:

> But pressure to lift the embargo is building within the Clinton administration and the U.S. business community, which is eager to tap the developing potential of Vietnam. The decision Mr. Clinton faces is mostly political and

---

27. Warren Strobel, "Senator Cites Signs of MIAs; Says Trip Supports reported Sightings," *Washington Times*, 14 July 1993, p. A 1.
28. Leon Hadar, "On the Horns of a Vietnamese Dilemma," *Business Times*, 28 September 1993, p. 24ff [Online] Nexis: Allnews.
29. Robert J. Caldwell, "Will Clinton Buy Hanoi's POW Charade?" *San Diego Union-Tribune*, 9 January 1994, p. G 1.

revolves around a single question: Can a president who avoided serving in Vietnam be the one to renew America's ties there?

In an apparent effort to stiffen the president's resolve, the paper provides some ammunition in a thinly veiled rebuke to Ann Mills Griffiths, noting that the League's momentum was dwindling, causing Mrs. Griffiths to cut her staff while still drawing a personal salary of 65,000 dollars.[30]

Ultimately the administration was given cover in the Senate. Senators Kerry and McCain came through again in early February 1994, orchestrating a non-binding sense-of-the-Senate resolution urging an end to the sanctions. The article noted:

> That is the difficult political balance Clinton officials are facing: the opportunities in a growing East Asian economy vs. a powerful symbol of past American involvement in Vietnam.
>
> . . . .
>
> Senate backers of the resolution on sanctions did intend it to provide political cover for a reluctant administration. Its main sponsors were decorated combat veterans--Sen. John Kerry (D) of Massachusetts and former POW Sen, John McCain (R) of Arizona. Medal of Honor winner Sen. Bob Kerrey (D) of Nebraska also signed on.[31]

Unwilling to cave in, the POW-MIA lobby predictably deployed. "From VFW posts to Little Saigon restaurants, from suburban homes to spare storefront offices, the opposition scrambled this week to mobilize a last-ditch campaign to dissuade President Clinton from lifting the trade embargo with Vietnam on Friday."[32]

Nonetheless, with cover provided the president lifted the embargo on 4 February 1994. "The United States and Vietnam restored economic ties Friday [4 February 1994], U.S. business lost no time plunging into the new multibillion-dollar marketplace." PepsiCo had its products out on the

---

30. Mark Mathews, "Families of MIAs Gird for Final Battle of Vietnam," *Baltimore Sun*, 24 January 1994, p. A 1 [Online] Nexis: Allnews.
31. Peter Grier, "Clinton in a Hard Spot on Vietnam Recognition," *Christian Science Monitor*, 2 February 1994, p. 9.
32. Doreen Carvajal and Michael Ross, "O.C. Backers Mobilize to State Hanoi Embargo--Vietnam: Opponents of Normal Ties Work to Change Clinton's Mind But Concede It's Probably too Late," *Los Angeles Times*, Orange County Edition, 3 February 1994.

streets that very day under a giant inflated Pepsi can. In Atlanta, Coca-Cola was gearing up for a 'cola war.' American Express declared, just ten hours after Clinton's announcement, "that its credit cards will be used in Vietnam . . . under an agreement signed with a Vietnamese bank." United Airline announced its intentions to seek "immediate approval of flights from Los Angeles to the former South Vietnamese capital, known until 1975 as Saigon." And both General Motors and Chrysler acknowledged they were already investigating possibilities in Vietnam.[33]

Though the ultimate outcome--normalization--is seen as inevitable, the battle over Vietnam policy continues as of this writing. The most recent demonstration of the Clinton administration's cautious incrementalism was the opening of a liaison office in February 1995.

> Twenty years after withdrawing in confusion and haste, the United States is quietly returning to Vietnam.
>
> . . . . But it reflects a cautious US judgment that Vietnam has become more cooperative in the search for information about US soldiers still missing from the Vietnam War.
>
> It also reflects the reality that without rapid normalization, US business will be closed out of one of the most promising markets in East Asia.[34]

It is clear that the business lobby's recent efforts have been increasingly successful. However the POW-MIA lobby has yet to concede defeat. In the same article, Ann Mills Griffiths rebukes the administration for its actions suggesting that Clinton 'should have used the opportunity of last Friday's signing ceremony to urge Vietnam to implement pledges to increase their unilateral accounting efforts.' The League and its allies continue to urge holding normalization out as leverage.

Full diplomatic recognition--including opening embassies--continues to elude Vietnam. The administration's tepid response, reflective of the passions still clashing in the Vietnam crucible, is simply a restatement of the cautious incrementalism that has become Vietnam policy. A "State Department spokesman reaffirmed last week" that "The administration be-

---

33. The *San Francisco Examiner*, 4 February 1994, p. A 1 [Online] Nexis: Allnews.
34. George Moffett, "Lured by Promising Vietnam Markets, US Tightens Ties with Its Former Foe," *Christian Science Monitor*, 3 February 1995, p.1.

lieves that by opening the liaison offices, we will enhance our ability to make progress toward that goal [accounting for the missing]."

The process could take years, US officials acknowledge.

[And that] US business leaders seek to speed up the process of normalization, while veterans groups and organizations representing the families of soldiers still officially "missing in action" seek to slow it down.

Meanwhile Vietnamese officials and the pro-normalization lobby remain hopeful of quick and complete normalization. The POW-MIA lobby continues to cling to the hope of word of its loved ones. And the intense interaction of each side's passionate and opposing views continues to stoke the Vietnam crucible which yields the predictably measured, half-steps that are cautious incrementalism.

REFERENCES

Acohido, Bryon, "Veterans, Boeing Spar on Vietnam Relations," *The Seattle Times*, 17 April 1993, [Online] (Nexis: Allnews), p. B-6.

Agence France Presse, "First U.S. Commercial Delegation Since War Visits Vietnam," *Economic News*, 14 December 1991, [Online] (Nexis: Allnews).

Apple Jr., R. W., "U.S. to Press Hanoi to Explain '72 P.O.W. Report," *The New York Times*, 13 April 1993, p. A-1.

Bremmer, Brian, Joyce Barnathan, and Larry Holyoke, "Ho, Ho, Ho Chi Minh: Corporate America Rushes In," *Business Week*, 11 January 1993, [Online] (Nexis: Allnews).

Bryant, Carleton R., "POW-MIA Groups Mixed on New Vietnam Relations," *The Washington Times*, 24 October 1991, p. A-8.

Burton, Jonathon, "US, Vietnam Inch Toward Renewing Ties," *The Christian Science Monitor*, 27 November 1991, 6.

Caldwell, Robert J., "Will Clinton Buy Hanoi's POW Charade?" *The San Diego Union-Tribune*, 9 January 1994, p. G-1.

Carvajal, Doreen and Michael Ross, "O.C. Backers Mobilize to State's Hanoi Embargo--Vietnam: Opponents of Normal Ties Work to Change

Clinton's Mind But Concede It's Probably Too Late," *The Los Angeles Times* (Orange County Edition), 3 February 1994.

The Christian Science Monitor, 1995.

Cornwell, Susan, "Clinton Lifts U.S. Trade Embargo Against Vietnam," *The Reuter Asia-Pacific Business Report*, 3 February 1994, [Online] (Nexis: Allnews).

Federal Information Systems Corporation, Federal News Service, "News Conference Held by Senator Smith," Washington, D.C., The Russel Senate Office Building, Room 418, 13 April 1993, [Online] (Nexis: Allnews).

Federal Information Systems Corporation, Federal News Service, "Town Meeting with Governor Bill Clinton," Detroit, Michigan, 22 September 1992, [Online] (Nexis: Allnews).

Federal Information Systems Corporation, Federal News Service, "Transcript of United States Information Service," USIA Foreign Press Center, 18 December 1991, [Online] (Nexis: Allnews).

Goldsborough, James O., "An Honest Book Adds to the Vietnam Saga," *The San Diego Union-Tribune*, 24 April 1995.

Goozner, Merrill, "U.S. Firms Losing out in Emerging Vietnam," *The Chicago Tribune*, 7 March 1993, [Online] (Nexis: Allnews), p. C-1.

Grier, Peter, "Clinton in A Hard Spot on Vietnam Recognition," *The Christian Science Monitor*, 2 February 1994, p. 9.

Hadar, Leon, "On The Horns of A Vietnamese Dilemma," *Business Times*, 28 September 1993 [Online] (Nexis: Allnews).

Houston, Paul, "Reaction Mixed on Normalizing Vietnam Ties," *The Los Angeles Times*, 24 October 1991, p. A-16.

Kegley, Charles W. Jr. and Eugene R. Wittkopf, *American Foreign Policy: Patterns and Process*, (New York: St. Martin's Press, 1991).

Lee, Patrick, "Asia Looks Within to Prosper," *The Los Angeles Times*, 26 September 1992, pp. D-1 and D-4.

The Los Angeles Times, "A World Report Special Edition on the Pacific Rim," 11 April 1995, Section H.

Mann, Jim, "Clinton's Foreign Policy 'Realism' Keeps Eye on U.S. Firms' Bottom Line, *The Los Angeles Times*, 3 April 1995, p. A-5.

Mathews, Mark, "Families of MIAs Gird for Final Battle of Vietnam," *The Baltimore Sun*, 24 January 1994, [Online] (Nexis: Allnews), p. 1-A.

McNamara, Robert S., *In Retrospect: The Tragedy and Lessons of Vietnam*, (New York: Times Books/Random House, 1995).

Moffett, George, "Lured by Promising Vietnam Markets, US Tightens Ties with Its Former Foe," *The Christian Science Monitor*, 3 February 1995.

Murray, Frank J., "Hecklers Spark President's Temper," *The Washington Times*, 25 July 1992, p. A-1.

Newsweek, 17 April 1995.

Omicinski, John, "POW-MIA Groups Say Document Proves Vietnam Lied to U.S," *USA Today*, 13 April 1993, [Online] (Nexis: Allnews).

Poole, Tereas, "Why Vietnam Needs Ameirca," *The Independent*, 30 December 1991, [Online] (Nexis: Allnews).

Price, Joyce, "Vietnam to Give All POW Data: Kerry, Vessey Deny Politics," *The Washington Times*, 24 October 1992, p. 1-A.

Quinn, Kenneth M., "Recent Progress on POW/MIA Issues," Department of State, *Department of State Dispatch*, 11 November 1991 [Online] (Nexis: Allnews).

Richmond, Kelly, "Sen. Brown Predicts Partial Normalization with Vietnam," *States News Service*, 17 November 1992 [Online] (Nexis: Allnews).

Ross, Michael, "U.S. Will Stop Opposing International Loans to Hanoi--The Decision Draws Mixed Reaction from the Vietnamese-Amreican Community in O.C," *The Los Angeles Times* (Orange County Editions), 3 July 1993, p. A-1.

San Francisco Examiner, Examiner News Service, 4 February 1994, [Online] (Nexis: Allnews), p. A-1.

Scheer, Robert, "Sorry Mac--You're Not Forgiven," *The Los Angeles Times*, 16 April 1995.

Smucker, Philip, "MIA Hoax Victimizes Soldiers' Families," *The St. Louis Dispatch*, 14 August 1991, [Online] (Nexis: Allnews), p. 3-C.

Strobel, Warren, "Senator Cites Signs of MIAs; Says Trip Supports Reported Sightings," *The Washington Times*, 14 July 1991, p. A-1.

United States, Department of State, "Diplomatic Efforts to Resolve the POW/MIA Issue in the Past Year," *Department of State Dispatch*, 5 August 1991, [Online] (Nexis: Allnews).

United States Senate, U.S. Senate Select Committee on POW/MIA Affairs, "Executive Summary," 13 January 1993.

Williams, Daniel, "Clinton's National Security Adviser Outlines U.S. 'Strategey of Enlargement,'" *The Washington Post*, 22 September 1993, p. A-16.

Wolf, Jim, "Bush Dangles Rewards for Vietnam, But the Clock is Ticking," *The Reuter Library Report*, 6 January 1993, [Online] (Nexis: Allnews).

INDIAN-UNITED STATES RELATIONS IN THE NEW WORLD ORDER: RESTRUCTURING OF INDIAN FOREIGN POLICY

C. *Kaye Bragg**
Department of Political Science
California State University, Bakersfield
9001 Stockdale Highway
Bakersfield, CA 93311

Abstract—A nation's foreign policy represents a tool used by each nation-state for adaptation to domestic and international change. This paper discusses Indo-U.S. (Indian-United States) relations in the new environment of the post-Cold War period, through analysis of changes in Indian foreign policy. The Rao administration marks a fundamental "restructuring" of Indian foreign policy both in the direction of policy objectives and national participation in international politics. This case highlights the degree to which Indian foreign policy restructuring was influenced by domestic political changes with a new leadership group, a new regime orientation for development and political pluralism with social fragmentation. Understanding the constraints on foreign policy restructuring permits identification of opportunities that could break down the legacy of mutual suspicions characterizing Indo-U.S. relations since the 1950s.

---

* I would like to thank Vickie Carlye for efficient research assistance.

I. INTRODUCTION

The events since the collapse of the Berlin Wall on November 9, 1989 resulting in the unification of Germany promoted recognition of radical changes in structures and relations of the international system. Across Europe, nations began planning for a single market with a common union. This radical change in the map of Europe complemented the "new thinking" in Soviet-U.S. relations. Mikhail Gorbachev discarded old rules of the Cold War promoting the superpowers to initiate actual reductions and a partial destruction of nuclear weapons. Following this thinking, the demise of the Soviet Union and the emergence of liberalism in Eastern Europe established new nation-states with a resurgence of ethnic nationalism. While the ideological battles of the Cold War ended, a world order now emerged characterized by greater global insecurity and interdependency.

This global insecurity reflects an anxiety about the efficacy of nation state policies and their ability to improve the quality of life except at high social and ecological costs. Interdependency means transnationalization of world politics, not just events but also ideas, institutions and decisions. The complexity of the global system produces a sense of "mutual dependence" with a world economy viewed as a single integrated unit and transnational issues beyond a nation's capacity to resolve, such as famine, ecological disaster or nuclear proliferation. In this context of insecurity and interdependency, traditional nation-state behavior must alter producing new patterns of relations identified through each nation's foreign policy.

This chapter discusses Indo-U.S. (Indian-United States) relations in this new environment, through analysis of changes in Indian foreign policy. In the post-Cold War period, Indian foreign policy becomes a window that reflects growing pluralism in domestic politics and security threats of both a military and an economic nature. This chapter examines the sources of change, both domestic and international, and then the impact of these changes on Indo-U.S. relations. Through discussion of changes in foreign policy, we gain insights to understand the opportunities and constraints of international relations between India and United States as the New World Order evolves.

II. CHANGE IN INDIAN FOREIGN POLICY: EXTERNAL

In the post-Cold War period, India initiated a review of its foreign policy framework inherited from the legacy of Jawaharlal Nehru. Foreign policy changes initiated by Indira Gandhi and Rajiv Gandhi with the two superpowers began this review but the administration of Narasimha Rao marked a fundamental "restructuring" of Indian foreign policy. Policy restructuring was a basic comprehensive change in foreign policy orientation over a relatively short period of time. (Volgy and Schwartz,1994, p. 26). In the Indian context, this restructuring was a multidimensional change affecting both the direction of policy and the nation's participation in international politics. During the Rao administration, the restructuring occurred because Indian leaders were able to overcome both global and domestic constraints.

The Cold War blocked affinities, both economic and political, with the U.S. and Western Europe and similarly distorted affinities of the Indo-Soviet relation. The shared ideals of democracy and colonial cultural values of the U.S. and India were not sufficient to negate Indo-Soviet common goals of social and economic development. In that international environment, the U.S. displeasure over the Indo-Soviet relation produced a vicious circle promoting greater closeness to the Soviet Union which directly affected the pace and the quality of Indian economic development. The U.S.-Soviet rivalry also colored Sino-Indian (Chinese-Indian) relations because the Chinese and the Soviets struggled over leadership of the Communist camp which promoted an intra-regional competition between China and India.

With the collapse of the Soviet Union and the subsequent United Nation's victory in the Persian Gulf War of 1991, the global system was no longer bipolar in design or differentiated by ideological and military divisions. Indian foreign policy was no longer constrained by a fear of the reactions from each superpower. This new international environment weakened the restraining effects of the previous bipolar system so that India could now risk a realignment to the sole superpower, U.S., and an expansion of regional relations with Pakistan and China. As Holti notes, nation-states will seek greater advantage by shifting partners in order to gain access to global economic and military resources (1982, p.197-99). In the new global system, India identified security threats that were primarily nonmilitary. By the 1990s, the central foreign policy objective dealt with issues of economic vulnerability given the loss of Soviet assistance and the stagnation of the Indian economy. The Rao administration marked a new orientation of Indian foreign policy based on pragmatism, or problem solving, given the most cost-effective solution to social, economic and political problems confronting India.

III. Regional Relations

Since independence, Indian foreign policy evolved out of a stable constellation of circumstances from which various policy objectives were advocated. As previously noted, the dominant constellations were the Cold War relations of the U.S. to the U.S.S.R. and India to the U.S.S.R. These constellations also shaped the dominate regional relation of India- Pakistan. The end of the Cold War meant the military aspects of America's special relation with Pakistan diminished. Pakistan was no longer a frontline state in Asia that blocked Soviet advancement. Following an end to the Soviet-Afghan crisis, the U.S. grew more critical of Pakistan's nuclear program as evidence of its offensive nuclear capacity emerged. This program challenged the U.S. position on limiting nuclear proliferation. India can use this change in the U.S.-Pakistan, bilateral relation to strengthen the Indo-U.S. relation. In the New World Order, the U.S. has a critical role to play as a hegemon interacting in this regional balance-of-power between India and Pakistan. Specifically, the conventional arms race characterizing this bilateral relation could escalate into a competition of strategic and tactical nuclear weapons. For both nations, this escalation poses a substantial finance burden; a burden neither nation's economic development could support. As both nations redefined their national security interests an opportunity for diplomacy regarding economic issues has replaced military confrontations.

The Rao administration advocated a "non-discriminatory" international nuclear regime under the authority of the United Nations General Assembly. The Rao administration position illustrates a shift in the direction of Indian foreign policy by redefining security threats as management issues and economic concerns among nations. This nuclear diplomacy refined the Nehruian ideas of non alignment into the post-Cold War period emphasizing protection of the nonaligned nations' authority against a major power encroachment. The reorientation of India's nuclear policy permitted a greater emphasis on common issues of regional security between India and Pakistan. In January 1994, the Rao administration proposed to Pakistan an extension of agreements not to attack each other's nuclear facilities in a "no first use" pledge of "nuclear capability." The Rao administration position also complemented the U.S. non-proliferation objectives voiced by the Bush and the Clinton administrations. Similarly statements by Clinton administration officials, such as Deputy Secretary of State Strobe Talbot, illustrated the U.S. recognition that India is a missile power given the Polar Satellite Launch Program of 1993-94 and 1994 Prithvi test launches (Jha, 1994, p.1039). Given the fact that these Indian programs enjoyed overwhelming domestic support, the U.S. began to focus on persuading India not to transfer its missile technology to any third country instead of demanding compliance with the Non-Proliferation Treaty. The question of nuclear weapons remains a constraint on Indo-U.S. relations but India's shift in nuclear diplomacy marked an opportunity for building common interests through regulation and monitoring programs.

A second constraint on Indo-U.S. relations in the New World Order is the problem of Kashmir. The Kashmiri problem was aggravated as Indian politics relinquished two of its founding principles, nationalism and secularism. The efficacy of Kashmiris declined as they no longer perceived a means of participation in Indian state or national politics. Many Kashmiris resented Delhi's authority and questioned the state's legitimacy. Also, Hindu-Muslim confrontations in other Indian states during the 1990s further alienated the Muslim majority. As political parties mobilized support through religious interests, Pakistan asserted religious claims for defending Kashmirs Muslims. In response, the Rao administration moved in a new direction in this dispute by its support of Kashmir's right of self determination. Prime Minister Rao supported an updated version of the Delhi Agreement of 1952. Rao's proposal complemented the 1994 U.S. initiative — presented by U.S. Assistant Secretary of State Robin Raphel's statement — supporting the 1972 Shimla Agreement (Jha, 1994, p 1040). This U.S. position departed from the Pakistani position that advocated support of the United Nations resolutions requiring a plebiscite in Kashmir. The Clinton endorsement of this position marked a tilt toward India and a new direction in American security policy in South Asia.

In addition, by sending Foreign Secretary J.N. Dikshit to Islamabad in January 1994 India initiated a dialogue and offered a six-point formula to normalize Indo-Pakistani relations. This normalization signaled India's willingness to recognize the autonomy of Kashmir based on equal ties to India and Pakistan. Finally, a related issue was the question of human rights violations by Indian security troops in Kashmir and the Punjab. This issue was a constraint on strengthening Indo-U.S. relations because Congressmen, Representatives Waly Herger and Dan Burton, introduced a bill banning development assistance to India unless it allowed Amnesty International to investigate cases of these violations (Thornton,1992, p.1069). The Rao administration established a National Commission on Human Rights with authority to investigate and to address every act of human rights abuse in India. In 1994, the Indian government also permitted several envoys to visit the Kashmir Valley and report on human rights abuses in this dispute. Clearly, the Rao administration proposals for self-determination of Kashmir, for normalization of Indo-Pakistani relations and for investigations of human rights abuses illustrated a willingness for greater involvement in global politics and engagement in reshaping regional relations. Indian foreign policy shifts of accommodation toward Pakistan and the U.S. constituted examples of options available to these states as the bipolar norms collapsed.

In summary, the restructuring of Indian foreign policy in the Rao administration marked a realignment with the U.S. after the Soviet Union fragmentation. This change was not simply a realignment with the sole superpower but a basic shift in policy objectives promoting India's integration and interdependency in the global system. Changes in the structure of the global system permitted new directions for Indian foreign policy that refined the Nehru's legacy of "self-reliance and non-alignment". The replacement of ideological and military interests with common economic concerns prompted a greater involvement of India in international politics. Reduction in international constraints, as the bipolar and ideological relations collapsed, permitted a shift in the direction of policy and India's participation in the evolving global system. As global relations changed India responded by a reduction of ideological dogma in its foreign policy. Policy makers of the Rao administration realized that India could not shape these global changes to its needs; instead, India must restructure its foreign policy objectives giving prominence to economic development issues in order to take advantage of global changes. In the post-Cold War system, the reinforcing issues of bipolar ideology and their security structure are no longer primary in setting the Third World foreign policy agenda.

IV. DOMESTIC CONSTRAINTS OF LEADERSHIP GROUPS

A weakening of the international constraints on Indian foreign policy paralleled shifts in the domestic environment. Domestic factors encouraging a policy change included the type of regime change, the orientation of the regime and the extent of its fragmentation. Drawing from Hagan's framework for comparing foreign policy restructuring, this case study highlighted the degree to which Indian foreign policy restructuring was influenced by domestic political changes with a new leadership group, a new regime orientation for development and a supportive social and economic context for market reform given economic crises.

Rajiv Gandhi's assassination in May 1991 and the unprecedented balance of payments with budget-deficit problems illustrated the political and economic crises that weakened the domestic political constraints on the Rao administration for restructuring foreign policy. These crises represented a "window of opportunity" for redefining national goals. As a minority government the Rao administration needed to re-establish a national consensus merging a commitment to liberal-democratic ideas with a mass popular appeal across caste, ethnic and communal groups. By the late 1980s, the political leadership of Indira Gandhi and Rajiv Gandhi represented a personalized rule that negated the efficient function of the Congress Party and the government as political institutions. These problems of governance were compounded by increased corruption and bribery across all levels of the government. Corruption was the key issue generating the 1989 Congress Party defeat in the parliamentary elections and the appointment of Prata Singh, the "clean minister" in Rajiv Gandhi's cabinet, as the Prime Minister. By the end of the Cold War, the Congress Party's inability to mediate pressures within society permitted a hardening of regional, class and religious interests into opposition political parties, like the Bharatiya Janata Party (BJP) or succession movements, as in the Punjab and Kashmir.

As a minority government, Rao's political survival required an acquisition of power both within the party and the Lok Sabha (Indian legislature). This consolidation of Rao's political power was essential to restore government legitimacy and its successful implementation of economic reforms. A critical change of leadership was Rao's restoration of organizational election in the Congress Party (Tirupati Ten) to democratize the party. The Tirupati Ten was a distinct departure from the elite, consensus decision-making in party selection of members of the Congress Working Committee. Debates over the party platform also signaled a departure from the Nehruian model of socialism with a centralized, planned economy to an advocacy of an open economy supporting Rao's reforms. As commentator Ramoashray Roy noted Rao utilized "the carrot-and-stick strategy to neutralize challenges from within the Congress, and ..... prevent influential leaders like Sharad Pawar and Arjun Singh from joining forces against him" (Economist, 25 December 1993, p124).

This change in Congress Party leadership occurred because of the growing fragmentation of the polity into opposition political parties. For example, the demolition of the Babri Masjid (mosque) in Ayodhya at the end of 1992 prompted communal riots that sharpened political divisions bringing "secularists" and "non-secularists" into direct confrontation. In this political turmoil, Rao dismissed the BJP governments in Himachal Pradesh, Rajasthan, Madhya Pradesh, and Uttar Pradesh, imposed President's Rule, and called for new assembly election in these states. These 1993 elections highlighted the disarray among the political parties: the leadership struggles in the Congress Party, the collapse of the National Front, the division of the Janata Dal into competing segments and the struggle to establish Hindu nationalism as a national political force through the BJP (Roy, 1994, p124-25). These state elections showed a vicious circle of factional politics that mobilized various socio-economic groups into politics.

The moblization of new socio-economic groups integrated traditional ethnic, religious and communal divisions into political platforms. Political participation became more pluralistic with groups competing for access to the state and its resources. In this political climate, effective political leader required coalition building and bargaining among these groups. Finally by the end of 1993, the Congress Party lead by Prime Minister Rao reestablished its presence in the northern states, by defeating the BJP, and in the Parliament by gaining a majority, with the support of opposition MPs. This majority permitted the Rao administration the domestic support for its expansion of the economic reforms through the restructuring of foreign relations.

V. REGIME ORIENTATION OF FOREIGN POLICY

In Hagan's framework a significant regime change refers to a political group or coalition of groups functioning as decision makers who represent a different orientation of foreign policy. Regime change produces foreign policy restructuring if the change meets two criteria: the involvement of political actors with a different orientation of foreign affairs and the regime is politically cohesive enough to implement the change. As presented in the previous section, the Rao leadership of the Congress Party provided a pragmatic response to the competing social and economic interests. His leadership style promoted cross cutting cleavages in the polity among issues that checkmated opposition parties from forging a united front to challenge the Congress Party's dominance. A critical factor in this political control was Rao's ability to initiate economic reforms given new opportunities in the global context.

Prime Minister Rao initiated a basic change in the course of the economic development with the abandonment of the old Nehruian model. His primary development objective was the transition of the Indian socialist pattern of society into a capitalistic economy offering self-sustaining growth and resources for India's masses. In July 1991, the government described the economy as suffering from stagflation: the growth of Gross Domestic Product (GDP) was down to 5 from 10 percent in 1988-89; industrial production remained at 8 percent; and the wholesale price index rose from 5.7 percent in 1989 to 13.6 percent in 1991 (World Bank, 1991, GDP text, Price Index text). In addition, the annual population growth rate of 2.2 percent with a decline of the real GDP per capita of 10 percent in 1960 to 8 percent by 1990 perpetuated the "circle of poverty" with nearly 350 million Indians living in absolute poverty (*Human Development Report* 1994, pp. 130, 135, 175). A persistent resource gap in public sector finances resulted in an overall deficit increase from 5 percent of the GDP in the 1970s to an average of 10 percent in 1985-86 (Government of India, 1988-89, GDP Index). Finance Minister Manmohan Singh confronted the

Lok Sabha, "we have not experienced anything similar in the history of independent India" and his warning that there was no time to lose illustrated the gravity of this economic crisis (McDonald, 1992,p.14).

The Rao administration announced new economic policies to improve economic management , to achieve a credible fiscal adjustment and macroeconomic stabilization during 1991-92, and to increase efficiency and international competitiveness of industrial production. These policies required the replacement of a mixed economic system dominated by the public sector with a "market-friendly" economy. Previous domestic constraints of bureaucratic management collapsed as the Rao administration implemented programs that attracted international aid, trade and investment, revised licensing procedures, and foreign investment restrictions. In the post-Cold War environment, India's search for security concentrated on economic issues that produced a shift in Indo-U.S. relations as the U.S. encouraged the World Bank and the International Monetary Fund (IMF) to provide loans and assistance to India given these economic reforms.

The orientation of Indian foreign policy shifted with this redefining of security problems and this linkage of foreign threats to processes of economic development, international trade and foreign aid and investment. The Rao administration charaterized the moderate regime proposed in Hagan's typology. The moderate regime does not see the international environment as inherently hostile. Foreign threats are issue-specific or situation bond with leaders exercising restraint and flexibility. The Rao administration marked the establishment of a moderate regime replacing the anti-American ones under the Gandhian (1966-84 Indira and 1985-91 Rajiv) leadership. This moderate regime advocated reestablishing a network of economic ties with the United States. Complementing this shift of the Indian regime, there was a subtle shift between the Bush and the Clinton administrations. This shift in American foreign policy denoted a change from pragmatic leadership with military tendencies to pragmatism with a more moderate view of international affairs (Hagan, 1994, p. 151).

By early 1994, Prime Minister Rao had consolidated political power through an electoral majority and his cabinet appointments. This consolidation permitted an acceleration of the economic reforms that required greater participation in regional and international politics. Prime Minister Rao addressed the Lok Sabha: "unless a country's economic sinews are strong, its rhetoric on internationalism will not be taken seriously"

(Hindu, May 4, 1994). The Indo-U.S. relation was pivotal for this strengthening of the Indian economy. Economic statistics underscore the importance of capital transfer from the United States to India, increasing exports and acquiring high technology. For example, in 1993-94 , $1.1 billion or 40 percent of foreign direct investment was from American sources. In addition, the U.S. engaged in over $8 billion of bilateral trade in this period; this amount distinguished the U.S. as the major Indian trading partner. Finally, Prime Minister Rao's visit to the U.S. in May of 1994 reiterated the Indian commitment to economic reforms, to technology imports and to foreign investment while downplaying strategic disagreements regarding Kashmir, missile and arms trade, and nuclear nonproliferation. During 1994, the Prime Minister used his foreign visits to Europe, specifically Britain, Germany and Russia and several East Asian countries, such as Singapore and Vietnam, to reaffirm the "centrality of economic diplomacy" in Indian foreign policy (Hindu, May 19,1994).

In summary, an understanding of the regime change and its orientation focused attention on the leadership's basic beliefs about international affairs and their nation's role in those affairs. Hagan's conceptualization of changes in the political makeup and in the definition of "national interest" of a ruling group distinguishes important characteristics which explain why foreign policy restructuring may occur. The Rao administration presented a shift in factions within the Congress Party illustrating Hagan's type two major factional or coalition shift. The change in the political ideology of this national party characterized Hagan's moderate regime category. The Rao administration built a coalition of social, economic and political interest aligned for the proposed liberalization of the economy. Finally, the identification of foreign threats driven by economic security and development issues replaced the traditional military risks.

VI. REGIME FRAGMENTATION

While new ideas and beliefs of leadership are sufficient for a policy change, the restructuring of foreign policy also requires that leadership have the capacity for initiating a change or for building a consensus regarding new policies. While regime orientation defines the broad outlines of foreign policy it is regime fragmentation that acts as the primary domestic constraint on the restructuring of foreign policy. Regime fragmentation checks the leadership's initiative for shifts in foreign policy objectives (Salmore, 1978, p. 103; Hagan, 1987, pp. 339-45). Volgy and Schwarz's discussion of the "webs of restraint" identify the impact of a complex bureaucracy and a pluralistic regime on policy makers abilities to initiate fundamental changes in the direction of their foreign policies. By 1995, the decentralization of foreign policy decision-making and the fragmentation of the India polity restricted the foreign policy options available to the Rao administration.

Similar to other nations, the bureaucracy was a key element in foreign policy making. The foreign policy bureaucracy gathers and assesses information, identifies problems, analyzes conflicts and proposes solution and finally coordinates implementation of policies. Governing with this bureaucracy representes a process of balancing competing sources of information and interests which produce incremental policy changes. In India, the Ministry of External Affairs is the central foreign policy making institution reviewing and proposing regional and global decisions. The Ministry furishes information used by the Prime Minister to define a policy and the Ministry is responsible for the implementation of the policy. However, the Ministry's influence in foreign policy making has declined as other institutions emerged in the decision making process, such as the Policy Planning and Review Committee, the Prime Minister's Secretariat, and National Security Agency. In addition, whenever foreign policy matters concern other ministries of the government, the Secretaries of those ministries participate in discussions of the Policy Planning and Review Committee. The image of Prime Minister Rao as a "weak prime minister with a minority government" strengthened the independence of these institutions in policy making. Also, Rao's promotion of greater economic ties in the global market meant the economic experts within the Ministry of External Affairs and other economic ministries gained political influence in foreign policy making. Finally, foreign and defense decisions have shifted from the formal, collective body of the Cabinet to a more informal group, the Political Affairs Committee. This institutional configuration provided powerful channels to criticize and positions to challenge Rao's policies that were used by the Employment Minister Arjun Singh, Defense Minister Sharad Pawar, Chief Economic Advisor Ashok Desai and Industries Minister Ajit Singh.

Apart from the presence of this bureaucratic web, there are other considerations within the domestic environment which clearly impeded the prospects for foreign policy restructuring. Not the least important was the social upheaval that fragmented the Indian polity along religious, ethnic and caste lines. This fragmentation promoted a decline in the state's legitimacy that exacerbated the problems of governance. For a democratic regime, cooperative behavior sustains the linkage between the state and society (Volgy and Schwarz, 1994, p. 29). The traditional ideals of "secularism and loyalty to the state" that encouraged a cooperative behavior collapsed as "sub-national, religious and ethnic sectarian organizations" competed for representation in the regime web (Ayoob, 1991-92, pp. 174-78).

Among political parties of the 1990s, numerous caste-communal and regional parties challenged Congress Party leadership in national politics. Three years of economic liberalization have escalated confrontations between social and economic elites against lower castes. These confrontations have been integrated into the political party system through debates about government reservation programs for government jobs and college admission quotas. In a parliamentary system, a minority government requires alliances with other parties in the formation of a coalition government. Prime Minister V.P. Singh's Janata Dal government collapsed in 1990 as upper-caste Hindus joined the BJP party when Singh agreed to lower caste allies demands for reservation quotas. The collapse of Singh's government illustrates the constraint of inter-party fragmentation on Indian policy making.

This political mobilization of lower castes has weakened the traditional national parties such as the Congress. Following the Mandal Report, Prime Minister Rao's proposals for mediation produced numerous withdrawals from the Congress party , such as upper castes supporters fled to the BJP and lower castes and Muslims shifted support to Uttar Pradesh Chief Minister Mulayam Singh Yadav's Samajwadi (Socialist) Party. In addition, lower caste alliances began playing a critical role in state politics, specially in Bihar and Uttar Pradesh. In both national and state politics, leaders played caste politics through rhetoric and patronage with state resources. While the Rao administration has secured a majority in Parliament by 1994, the role of lower castes represented a growing political force.

Paralleling this increase of political participation, there was a decrease in the Rao administration's capacity for additional foreign policy changes. In this web of competing economic forces and social demands, the state's power was dependent on successfully accommodating these demands. Yet, with economic liberalization the market forces decide numerous investment and consumption questions instead of the state. Therefore, the Rao administration's ability to allocate economic resources has declined making accommodation more difficult. So by 1995, the Rao administration confronts a set of security issues, economic and social, which threaten Indian democracy and national sovereignty. Continued economic development requires further involvement of India in the global market. Greater economic interdependency must be complemented by a rejuvenation of the liberal-democratic traditions in India.

VII. Conclusion

Today, the greatest threat to Indian sovereignty is the disintegration of loyalty to the nation and legitimacy of the state. As the New World Order continues evolving, this domestic insecurity constraints foreign policy changes affecting India's territorial integrity and its strategic position in South Asia. The reorientation of India's nuclear policy prompts a greater emphasis on common issues of regional security between India and Pakistan which complements the U.S. non-proliferation objectives voiced by the Bush and Clinton administrations. Given the U.S. position as the sole superpower, India's shift in nuclear diplomacy marks an opportunity for the U.S. to build a practical and cooperative relationship dealing with the growth of military and nuclear technologies. However, the social upheaval and political crisis limit the likelihood that India would accept the status of a camp follower in global relations. India's commitment to rational, secular and democratic principles should be recognized by the U.S. for building leadership and stability in South Asia. The Rao administration proposals for self-determination of Kashmir, normalization of Indo-Pakistan relations and investigations of human rights abuses illustrate a willingness for greater involvement in global politics and engagement in reshaping regional relations.

In the New World Order, national security defines not just military threats but a complex set of social-economic issues. Prime Minister Rao's visit to the U.S. in May of 1994 reiterated India commitments to economic reform, technology imports and foreign investment while downplaying strategic disagreements regarding Kashmir, missile and arms trade, and nuclear nonproliferation. The U.S. may encourage this economic partnership through speedy transfer of dual-use technology, supporting Indian requests for IMF and World Bank assistance, and promoting private business partnerships with Indian entrepreneurs. For both nations, the growth of a middle class in India represents an important asset that could be of mutual benefit for trade relations and market opportunities.

This chapter suggests the importance of understanding the international and domestic constraints on foreign policy changes. A critical characteristic of the New World Order is a dynamic change in the structure and in the norms of global politics. With the growth of interdependence, a set of common international problems confronts all nations. A realistic and productive Indo-U.S. relation in this global system demands examination of these constraints. For example, Rao's leadership style promotes cross cutting cleavages in the polity that checkmate opposition parties but that political control is dependent on Rao's ability to initiate economic reforms given new opportunities in the global context. The building of an economic partnership between India and U.S. could be followed by greater cooperation in strategic issues.

In summary, Indo-U.S. relations play a critical role in restoring the legitimacy of the Indian state through U.S. recognition of India as a significant actor in South Asia, expanding the economic partnership in trade, technology and assistance, and U.S. support of Indian democratic forces building an inclusive nationalism.

REFERENCES

Andersen, Walter K., "India in 1994: Economics to the Fore," *Asian Survey* February 1995, 35, 127-40.

Ayoob, Mohammed, "Dateline India: The Deepening Crisis," *Foreign Policy*, Winter 1991-92, 166-85.

The Economist, "The subcontinent's own cold war," 25 December 1993-7 January 1994, 329, 44-44.

Feinberg, Richard E., *Economic Reform in Three Giants: U.S. foreign policy and the U.S.S.R., China and India*, Overseas Development Council, 1990.

Ghosh, Partha S., *Foreign Policy and Electoral Politics in India: Inconsequential Connection, Asian Survey*, September 1994, 34, 807-18.

Goldmann, Kjell, *Changes and Stability in Foreign Policy: The Problems and Possibilities of Detente*, (Princeton University Press, 1988).

Hagan, Joe D., "Regimes, Political Oppositions, and the Comparative Analysis of Foreign Policy," in *New Directions in the Study of Foreign Policy*, ed., Charles F. Hermann, Charles W. Kegley, Jr., and James N. Roseanu, (Allen and Unwin, 1987), pp. 339-65.

_____, "Domestic political regime change and foreign policy restructuring: A framework for comparative analysis," in *Foreign Policy Restructuring*, eds., Jerel A. Rosati and Joe D. Hagan, and Martin W. Sampson, III, (University of South Carolina Press, 1994).

The Hindu, "Rao Administration Confrontations," May 19, 1994, pp. 4, 24.

,Holsti, K.J. (ed.), *Why Nations Realign: Foreign Policy Restructuring in the Postwar World*, (Allen and Unwin Publishers, 1982).

Jha, Nalini Kant, "Reviving U.S.-India Friendship in a Changing International Order," *Asian Survey*, December 1994, 34, 1035-47.

Kapur, Harish, *India's Foreign Policy (1947-92) Shadows and Substance*, (Sage Publication Inc., 1994).

Manchando, Rita, "A turn in the South: Rao Strengthens His Grip at Congress Plenum," *Far Eastern Economic Review*, 30 April 1992, 155, 13.

McDonald, Harnish, "Coterie Capers: Rao's New Cabinet is Stacked with Rajiv Loyalists," *Far Eastern Economic Review*, 4 July 1991, 153, 10-11.

_____, *Far Eastern Economic Review*, 23 July 1992, 155, 14-15.

_____, "Still on the Rails: Rao Signals Indian Reforms Will Continue," *Far Eastern Economic Review*, 21 January 1993, 156, 53-54.

_____, "Dissident Backlash: Rao Under Fire for Ayodhya Failure," *Far Eastern Economic Review*, 18 February 1993, 156P, 16+.

_____, "Opening Salvo (Rao's Rival Resigns, to Challenge Him Later)," *Far Eastern Economic Review*, 12 January 1995, 158, 18-19.

Rosati, Jerel A. and Joe D. Hagan, and Martin W. Sampson, III (eds), *Foreign Policy Restructuring*, (University of South Carolina Press, 1994).

Roy, Ramashray, "India in 1992," *Asian Survey*, 33, 119-29.

Roy, Ramashray, "India in 1993: The Struggles of Economic Reform," *Asian Survey*, February 1994, 34, 200-08.

Salmore, Barbara G., and Stephen A. Salmore, "Political Regimes and Foreign Policy," in *Why Nations Act*, ed., M.A. East, S.A. Salmore, and C.F. Hermann, (Sage Publishers, 1978), p. 103-22.

Thornton, Thomas P., "India Adrift: The Search for Moorings in a New World Order," *Asian Survey* December 1992, 32, 1063-77.

Volgy, Thomas J. and John E. Schwartz," Foreign Policy Restructuring and the Myriad Webs of Restraint," in *Foreign Policy Restructuring*, eds., Jerel A. Rosati, Joe D. Hagan, and Martin W. Sampson III, (University of South Carolina Press, 1994).

United Nations Development Program, *Human Development Report 1994*, Human Development Index, Profile of Human Deprivation and Demographic Profile.

World Development Report 1989-94, Text figures: GDP growth rates; Export earning of developing countries; Debt and exports; Share of developing-country exports in the consumption of manufactured goods, agricultural products; Income distribution; and Population growth.

UNITED STATES MIDDLE EAST POLICY IN THE AFTERMATH OF THE COLD WAR AND THE PERSIAN GULF WAR:

A RESPONSE TO A DYNAMIC AND CHANGING MIDDLE EAST SYSTEM?

David H. Johns
Department of Political Science
San Diego State University
San Diego, CA 92182

Abstract—States in the Middle East, somewhat independent of changes in the international political system--but also as a consequence of these changes, have turned increased attention to bilateral and multilateral relations across the region. As a result, a "New Middle East Order" may be emerging which challenges academics and policy-makers to revise the prevailing concept of a Middle East system. For the foreseeable future, the Middle East region will be more diverse, pluralistic, and multipolar--pulled in different directions by regional and extra-regional centrifugal forces. This necessitates that the United States rethink its Middle East policy.

I. UNITED STATES FOREIGN POLICY IN THE POST COLD WAR ERA

The so-called "New World Order" has proven to be more illusory than real. In terms of United States foreign policy, it has proven to be more rhetoric than substance. Nevertheless, the international political system is substantially different in the 1990s. One can debate whether the system is simply altered from the 1980s or is undergoing more substantive change, such as occurred after the Second World War or following the First World War (Waltz, 1993). Alternatively, one can argue whether international politics is in the midst of a systemic change of a magnitude that last occurred around the time of the French and American revolutions, at the beginning of the state system in the mid-seventeenth century, or with the rise of capitalism in the fifteenth and sixteenth centuries (Chirot, 1994; Wallerstein, 1993).

A few critical developments which affect the framing and implementation of United States foreign policy in the post Cold War era need to be mentioned. First, with the end of the Cold War and the collapse of the former Soviet Union, the international political system can no longer be characterized as a bipolar system. It is unlikely that a unipolar system, with the United States as the single superpower, will replace bipolarity. It is possible that a new bipolar system may emerge, perhaps between the North and the South (Klare, 1991), or between two blocs of developed countries, such as the United States and the European Union (EU) against Japan and a wider Asian bloc. Most probable, however, is the emergence of a multipolar system, composed of at least three and perhaps up to five or six more or less equal great powers (Kegley and Raymond, 1994).

It needs to be emphasized that the end of the Cold War and the collapse of the former Soviet Union have affected United States policies toward the Middle East. For more than forty years policies were subordinated to the broader policy of containment and defined according to perceptions of threats from the Soviet Union. As the Soviet Union was contiguous with the Northern Tier states, including Turkey and Iran, a disproportionate amount of United States attention, military assistance and aid, was concentrated in the region. The primary American allies in the region in the anti-communist alliance--most importantly Israel, but also

Turkey and, until 1979, Iran received more or less unconditional support. Saudi Arabia and the Gulf States, and after Camp David, Egypt--states seen by the United States as being opposed to communism and fearful of "radical" change in the region, were drawn increasingly close to the United States. With the end of the Cold War, it became possible to look at the Middle East on its own terms rather than from within the broader framework and sometimes distorted focus of East-West relations.

Additionally, the dynamics of extra-regional involvement in the Middle East have changed. Former Cold War allies, both in the Middle East and outside of the region, now have a number of options to choose from and need not necessarily defer to United States strategic considerations. In a multipolar system the United States finds itself engaged in competition with a number of blocs or states, such as the EU, Japan, Russia and increasingly China. Each has somewhat different interests as well as different perceptions regarding the region. In some instances, a Middle Eastern country, such as Iran, may be able to play one extra-regional actor off against another to its advantage. In other circumstances, as perhaps in Bosnia, admittedly at (or beyond) the region's edge, the extra-regional actors may, in effect, mutually veto each other's involvement or deadlock with one another regarding collective action.

Second, the international political system is more concerned with and increasingly interdependent with the international economic system. The international economic system is best characterized by a global, rather than international, economy. States are not only dependent upon imports and exports for their economic well-being as in an international economy, but they are also part of a global production system and supply and demand network over which they have limited control (Castells, 1993). Hence, economic concerns have joined, if not replaced, military and security concerns as "high politics." The United States, while clearly a superpower in terms of military power, finds itself unable to easily apply or transfer this power into the economic arena. Security and economic concerns can be joined together in curious ways, as, for instance, in linking Middle East arms shipments to United States national security through the shipments' impact on the United States economy (Vartagbedian and Broder, 1994). Such arguments aside, there are limits to the military power of the United States, especially as it is pressed to provide military support in various regional and global crises. For the hegemon to maintain a high level of military preparedness and assistance undermines its economic power and resources (Kennedy, 1987).

The United States is being forced to adjust to the new realities of interdependency within the global economy. This has led, among other things, to calls for a reduction of foreign aid, for the imposition of import tariffs and quotas, for "free and fair" trade and for faster privatization. The concern about the economy has also led to the United States turning inward with a possible return to a more isolationist foreign policy. Those calling for greater United States activity are put on the defensive by demands for utilizing limited resources at home and by the growing recognition of the increased complexity of international relations in the 1990s (Marr, 1994).

Another aspect of this sharpened focus on the economic realm is the broadening and deepening of the revolution of rising expectations. Across the Middle East, as elsewhere in the Third World, there is an awareness of the increased disparity between the rich and the poor and there is a corresponding demand that governments take measures to end it. Demands for an improved standard of living have a direct impact upon the survival of the embattled governments and, in turn, political stability across the region. As a protest against the continuing status quo, there are calls for a greater Islamic presence in the domestic political arena. As a consequence, the United States is open to criticism for supporting the status quo and the more secular regimes across the region and for refusing to provide assistance to alter the growing economic disparity between the North and the South.

Third, the international political system is increasingly characterized by regionalism, particularly the efforts to establish more integrated and more exclusionary economic trading blocs. This economic regionalism has led to growing competition and conflict between regions, thereby affecting political relations at the global level. Alternatively, it has led to greater attention being devoted to regional matters, including more political and ostensibly non-economic concerns, with the consequence of decreased attention to international relations elsewhere.

Over the past few years this has been readily apparent in United States policy. The United States has moved decisively to establish the North American Free Trade Agreement (NAFTA) which sets the region in potential conflict with the EU and the Pacific regions, whether within North America, across the Middle East or elsewhere. Also, as the economic crisis in Mexico in late 1994 and early 1995 confirmed, regionalism has drawn the United States into issues that were not of direct concern earlier. Hence, the United States has become more directly involved in Mexican politics and has put itself at risk economically because of the "bailout" of the Mexican economy. Corresponding less attention has been given to international relations at the global level, particularly issues confronting the Middle East.

Each of these developments--the end of bipolarity, the emergence of a global economy and the increased focus on regionalism--within the international political system has affected United States foreign policy in the post Cold War era. Others, such as the growing concern about human rights, the issue of democratization and the role of Non-Governmental Organizations (NGOs) might be mentioned as well. But regardless of the length of the list, these changes have implications for United States policies toward the Middle East.

II. THE MIDDLE EAST IN THE POST COLD WAR ERA

The changes in the international political system just outlined have affected the Middle East region. The Middle East has changed as a consequence of and in response to these changes in the international political system. In addition, quite independent of extra-regional and global politics, there have been changes taking place within the Middle East itself. Some changes were perhaps occasioned by the Persian Gulf War (PGW). Some are more pronounced as a consequence of the War. Still others are quite independent of the War. Taken together, these changes may signal a "New Middle East Order," one not necessarily stable and peaceful, but more characteristically diverse, pluralistic and multipolar, and one pulled in different directions by regional and extra-regional centrifugal forces.

The Middle East system, as perceived by states within and outside the region, provided some predictability and set certain parameters for intraregional relations, particularly regarding regional issues, such as Arab-Israeli relations. The system itself emerged at the same time as the onset of the Cold War, even if the system had its own dynamics quite independent of the Cold War (Binder, 1964). The jury is still out as to whether the PGW will prove to be a seminal event in Middle East politics (Tschirgi, 1994; see especially Dawisha, 1994). However, the PGW itself and analyses of the region in the aftermath of the War tend to support the argument that there has been a breakdown of the Middle East system and that its norms are no longer operative. Hence, regional or extra-regional policies based on assumptions regarding the existence of the system and its rules require reexamination and reevaluation (Awad, 1994).

First, the region itself has undergone change in its size, measured in geographical expanse and by number of state actors. Given its location in and/or at the edge of three continents, it has always been difficult to define the Middle East. Recent events have made it even more difficult. With the collapse of the Soviet Union, a case can be made that the Middle East region now extends further east into Central Asia. The history, culture, religion and languages of many of the new states which have emerged out of the Soviet Union suggest an eastward expansion of the boundaries of the Middle East. With the breakup of Yugoslavia, Middle East interests are more intimately involved with Europe, particularly with reference to the Muslim populations in Central Europe. In addition, the borders between the Middle East and North Africa or between North and sub-Saharan Africa appear increasingly less meaningful. In sum, the region may be defined more extensively and, in any event, it must be viewed differently than heretofore.

Second, rather than envisioning the Middle East as a region, it is perhaps more accurate to refer to the Middle East as an area constituting a number of regions (or subregions). Increasingly, countries are relating to one another more so in terms of common and shared interests which do not include a majority, let alone all, of the states in the area. The most obvious example is the Persian Gulf region, narrowly defined, which includes the six member states of the Gulf Cooperation Council (GCC), namely Saudi Arabia, Kuwait, the United Arab Emirates, Qatar, Bahrain and Oman. Alternatively, the Persian Gulf region can be defined more broadly so as to include Yemen and even more broadly to bring in Iran and Iraq, for the individual GCC states as well as the GCC states collectively respond to events in Yemen and in Iran or Iraq. This, of course, is the point, namely, that certain states and sets of states interact with one another within their region and across the different regions more so than they interact in an overall Middle East system-wide pattern.

The Persian Gulf region is but one region within the area. Another is the Magreb, which includes the members of the Arab Magrebi Union

(AMU), namely Morocco, Algeria, Tunisia, Libya and Mauritania. Another includes the states in the "core" of the area, Egypt and Israel, together with Palestine, Jordan, Lebanon and Syria, a critically important region in terms of potential economic cooperation. A fourth region is in Central Asia, constituting the countries of Kazakhstan, Kyrgyzstan, Tajikistan, Turkmenistan and Uzebekistan. Here, most dramatically, the emergence of the region pulls other Middle East states, such as both Turkey and Iran, and in different ways Saudi Arabia and even Israel, in a myriad of directions and into possible conflict with one another, thereby further complicating Middle Eastern politics ("Central Asia," 1994; Dawisha and Parrott, 1994; Fuller, 1992a; Fuller, 1992b).

Thus, whether or not these or other regions meet various criteria for regionalism, the dynamics of the Middle East region have changed significantly. The Middle East contains a larger number of states. Many of these states have concluded that their national interests can be met neither on a unilateral basis nor by Middle East-wide efforts, but at best and most likely through joint actions involving a limited number of neighboring states. These developments, in certain respects, parallel similar developments at the global level which have led to the trend towards regionalism.

Third, as already implied, regional norms are changing and, in many respects, changing dramatically. The traditional and long-standing norms of the region revolved around such issues as pan-Arab unity, pan-Islamism, Palestinian recognition and non-recognition of Israel, as well as anti-colonialism and anti-imperialism. These date from the onset of independence which coincided with the start of the Cold War. The dynamics and parameters of each of these regional norms have been substantially altered across time and increasingly so in the past few years.

The norm of pan-Arab unity, while seemingly resilient and flexible, is also more elusive than ever. It seems that the longer the time since independence for each of the Arab states, the less likely Arab unity. In addressing many Middle East issues over the past decade, such as the Iran-Iraq war, the Lebanese civil war and the PGW, the Arab states have been divided more than they have been united. In the PGW an Arab state attacked another although Iraq defended its action under the rhetoric of pan-Arabism. Even when there were efforts to rationalize decisions using the norm of pan-Arab unity, the response of the different Arab states varied, dependent on the analysis of their respective national interests (Tibi, 1994).

Pan-Islamism, while a factor which affects each Middle State (including Israel, but admittedly in a different manner), is another norm subject to challenge across time and increasingly so at present. Pan-Islamism shifts the focus away from pan-Arab unity as it brings Turkey and Iran, among other non-Arab states, into regional politics. It also draws attention to developments taking place beyond the region, given that the majority of Muslims live outside the Middle East. Even if there is a greater commitment to increasing the role of Islam in the political realm in virtually every Muslim state in the area, there are sharp disagreements within states, between states and across the region as to what is required for a modern Islamic state. Furthermore, apart from such disagreements, there are sharp differences regarding the role of regional states, such as Iran or Saudi Arabia, in encouraging and assisting other states within the Middle East to become more Islamic.

The pro-Palestinian and anti-Israeli norms are also being challenged and becoming increasingly irrelevant. In signing the Camp David Accords, Egypt threatened these norms. The Madrid Conference marked another significant turning point with respect to the norms. For all practical purposes, they were no longer viable after the Israeli-PLO Declaration of Principles, with the PLO's acceptance of Israel. The Declaration, in turn, provided Jordan with the necessary rationale for signing a separate Israeli-Jordanian agreement, further diminishing the anti-Israeli norm and, in certain respects, setting aside the pro-Palestinian norm.

Fourth, among the many other changes across the Middle East, as elsewhere in the Third World, is the growing preoccupation with security in the domestic political arena (Ayoob, 1995). The end of the Cold War and the changed dynamics of the regional system have led to a sense of heightened insecurity on the part of the incumbent leadership in the region. Political pressures are building up to a breaking point, whether from within the countries, such as the revolution of rising expectations mentioned above, or from the outside, such as the Structural Adjustment Programs (SAPs) mandated by the International Monetary Fund and the World Bank. The room for maneuver, even in the oil-exporting states, is limited and the outlook for meaningful and necessary structural economic changes is at best problematic (Richards, 1994).

Increased concerns regarding security are reflected in shifts in ideology, which, as before, changes from time to time and differs across the region at any given point in time. Arab socialism, as articulated by Egypt's Nasser, was the dominant ideology in the region by the late 1950s. Subsequently, Arab radicalism, as espoused by Syrian and then Iraqi Baathists in the late 1960s, came to compete with Arab socialism. In turn, Islamic activism came to challenge Arab radicalism following the 1979 Iranian revolution and especially during the Iran-Iraq war. More recently, Islamic activism has been joined by demands for political accountability and perhaps political liberalization. This changed focus in ideology--and its accompanying concerns regarding security--has occurred independent of the PGW, but in some measure has also been furthered as a consequence of it.

Across the Middle East, then, there is an increased awareness of the need to address domestic problems. To do so requires a turning inward away from the region. But, paradoxically, there is an increased awareness that what is happening elsewhere in the region, as earlier in 1979 in Iran and presently in Algeria, may foreshadow changes or be seen as a model to be (or not to be) followed in other states. More generally, the "wall of fear" of authoritarian and corrupt regimes has been breached (Norton, 1992), requiring leadership to respond and react. Ironically, while the problems manifest themselves internally, the solutions require not only appropriate domestic restructuring, but simultaneously call for relevant regional and even extra-regional policies as well.

These and other changes notwithstanding, there remains a dynamic, if changing, Middle East region (Cantori, 1994). Indeed, the region may be the most turbulent of all the world's regions, as the post-PGW transfer of arms suggests. The area still constitutes a system with a set of semi-autonomous relations, with a power hierarchy which may change from issue to issue, and with varying and competing leaderships over time. The broadening of the area, its effective "atomization" and "fragmentation" (Joffe, 1994) into a number of smaller regions, its challenged and changing norms and the growing urgency and complexity of domestic politics all contribute to end and suggest a "New Middle East Order."

III. THE UNITED STATES AND THE MIDDLE EAST IN THE POST COLD WAR ERA

United States policies toward the Middle East in the post Cold War era need to be examined in the context of the changes outlined above. To oversimplify, but not distort, the Middle East has seen too little peace, too little democracy and too little development (Riedel, Quandt and Falk, 1994, p. 5). How to realize these goals and the proper role, if any, for the United States is the pressing policy issue. Should the United States policies follow the path of "benign neglect," "constructive disengagement," "intervention" as more generally defined (Schraeder, 1992, p. 3), or "a more restrictive concept of intervention" (Falk, 1993, p. 756)? Inevitably, on any given issue, there are proponents and opponents in the United States and in the Middle East to any policy proposed or adopted.

The PGW has been seen as the first post Cold War crisis even if it did not introduce a "New World Order" (Ismael and Ismael, 1994). Clearly the PGW led to a heightened and overwhelming United States presence in the region, but it did not lead to a large scale, continuing United States presence in the region. The PGW also led more or less directly to the convening of the Madrid Peace Conference in October, 1991. However, the convening of the Conference did not presage a highly visible and ongoing United States activity in regional issues.

What followed has been an unevenness in United States involvement in the region. One of the infrequently mentioned conclusions from "Operation Desert Storm" was the diminished utility of offensive force in bringing about political change (Amirahmadi, 1993, p. 20). Moreover, by the mid-1990s the feasibility of utilizing the United Nations to address various world crises was being seriously questioned. Nonetheless, there has been a determination by the United States to "stay the course" with the United Nations sanctions against Iraq, although there are significant disagreements between the United States and its allies as well as among the allies themselves (Joffe, 1994, pp. 254-55). On the other hand, after Madrid there was caution and circumspection regarding the peace process between Israel and the Palestinians and between Israel and its immediate Arab neighbors. Elsewhere, there was either disinterest at first and more recently a distancing towards Algeria in response to cancelled elections and the onset of civil war. There was an obvious lack of visible diplomatic pressure put upon Saudi Arabia to open up its political system. Perhaps what has been called "oblivious engagement," in response to contradictory objectives and interests, but with a general view towards dominance, can be replaced by a more reasoned and selective set of policies (Amirahmadi, 1993, p. 7). Overall, United States policies suggest prudence with less activism, realism over idealism and an increased emphasis on trade (Marr, 1994, pp. 216-18).

What is instructive about the PGW, then, is that each crisis in the Middle East needs to be understood on its own terms and that the response of the United States depends on a myriad of factors involving its perceptions of its interests, the feasibility of intervention, and the various options open to the United States in each specific crisis. This applies to regional states as well; that is, each crisis needs to be understood on its own terms and the responses of the various actors will depend on a myriad of factors involving their perceptions of their interests, the feasibility of involvement, and the various options open to states in the specific crisis. Lessons purportedly learned from the recent past may be applied, but the ongoing situation is most likely to be sufficiently dissimilar to the ones in the recent past to provide certain or specific guidelines for responding to the situation.

For the foreseeable future the United States more than likely faces increased resentment from the majority populations in many states. Following Iraq's invasion into Kuwait, many persons across the Middle East felt a certain empathy for Iraq (or at least Iraqis), not in support of Saddam Hussein and his policy, but rather as a consequence of Iraq becoming the underdog vis-à-vis the United States. Such empathy increased when the United Nations, seen as being controlled by the United States, began the wholesale bombing of Iraq as part of "Operation Desert Storm." With the perpetuation of the sanctions against Iraq this identification by the masses with Iraq and resentment toward the United States has been furthered.

Resentment toward the United States follows also from its being identified so closely with the status quo in the Middle East. For instance, close U.S. ties with President Mubarak in Egypt and with King Fahd in Saudi Arabia--regimes seen as corrupt or alien to the local populations, support the contention that the United States backs the status quo without "conditionality" because the United States fears an unfriendly government may come into power, whether through democratic reform or a movement espousing a greater Islamic presence. It may prove to be the case, however, that to try to preserve the status quo may, at best, only postpone changes and, at worst, may make these changes, when they do occur, more threatening to United States interests.

It can be argued whether greater or lesser activity and whether more extensive or limited involvement by the United States is advantageous for the United States and/or the Middle East. Such titles as *Into the Labyrinth* (Brands, 1994), *Quagmire* (Hadar, 1992) or *Payback* (Cooley, 1991) suggest the difficulty and, indeed, the dangers to the United States of growing entanglement in the area. Depending upon the issue and the time (and, of course, the point of view of the protagonist), less activity and more limited involvement by the United States may be seen as advantageous for states in the region. A diminished United States presence may facilitate--rather than prevent--conflict management or resolution.

The 1993 Israeli-PLO Declaration of Principles illustrates this point. United States inactivity after Madrid forced the interested parties to address the issue of Palestinian nationalism on its own terms. Perhaps the significant decrease in United States activity was attributable to the elections in Israel and the United States and to the ensuing changes in each country's leadership. It might also be related to the growing realization, however belatedly, that the Arab-Israeli peace process would not by itself bring a wider regional peace to the area (Riedel, in Riedel, Quandt and Falk, 1994, p. 1). Nonetheless, the inactivity and disinterest of the United States persuaded both the Israeli government and the PLO, albeit for different reasons, that it was in their mutual interest to secretly negotiate the Oslo agreement (Heller, 1994; Khalidi, 1994).

If United States policies towards the region in the past were a function of the Cold War, then with the end of the Cold War policies should change more or less automatically. Since the perceptions which the United States had about the Middle East reflected and mirrored its concerns about the Cold War, she put Middle East issues in the context of the Cold War. With the end of the Cold War, there is less concern about the Middle East simply because the outcomes of various Middle East issues are seen as less critical to United States interests.

Without a preoccupation on "strategic consensus," there is more likelihood of recognizing the proliferation of problems confronting the Middle East. Heretofore the United States had a propensity to focus on a single Middle East problem, typically the Arab-Israeli conflict, as if its resolution was critical to United States interests in the region. The United States became so preoccupied with the problem that other issues were relegated to the back burner or basically ignored. With the revolution in Iran in 1979 and then the Iran-Iraq war in the 1980s, it became difficult to ignore the existence of multiple problems in the Middle East and problems other than those tied in with the Arab-Israeli problem. Therefore, even if one issue were to be addressed so as to bring about a positive policy outcome, other problems would remain. As this is understood, there is less incentive to address an issue that might otherwise appear to be amenable to United States involvement.

Finally, there is the growing realization regarding the intractability of various issues confronting the different Middle East states. Because problems are more complex, this reduces the options and lowers the probability of a positive policy outcome through United States activity. As a consequence there is likely to be more hesitation and less of a sense of urgency to commit the United States. While it may be countered that United States policies have not changed, but rather that the levels of activity have lessened, diminished activity, like its opposite, increased activity, has either positive or negative consequences for individual Middle East states, for regional relations between the states as well as for the extra-regional powers.

In sum, global politics and Middle East politics have both changed. Changes within the former have affected the level of commitment and the potential impact of United States policies toward the Middle East generally and in specific issue areas. Changes within the Middle East itself have altered the nature of the Middle East system. Whether or not there is a "New Middle East Order," the region is more fractured, traditional norms are suspect, and competition for influence and hegemony is more intense. For the decision-maker, the consequences of a move toward multipolarity, both across the Middle East region and within the global system generally, make the formulation and implementation of United States foreign policies more difficult. Similarly, for the academic, the implications of these changes make analysis and prediction into even the immediate future more difficult. Regardless, it seems more than likely that the United States will become less active in the Middle East. Whether or not this proves correct, it also seems more than likely that United States policies will be less influential than in the earlier, seemingly simpler, Cold War era.

REFERENCES

Amirahmadi, Hooshang, ed., *The United States and the Middle East. A Search for New Perspectives*, (Albany: State University of New York Press, 1993).

Awad, Ibrahim, "The Future of Regional and Subregional Organization in the Arab World," in *The Arab World Today*, ed., Dan Tschirgi, (Boulder: Lynne Rienner Publishers, 1994), pp. 147-60.

Ayoob, Mohammed, *The Third World Security Predicament. State Making, Regional Conflict, and the International System*, (Boulder: Lynne Rienner Publishers, 1995).

Binder, Leonard, "The Middle East as a Subordinate International System," in *The Ideological Revolution in the Middle East*, (New York: John Wiley & Sons, Inc., 1964), pp. 254-78.

Brands, H. W., *Into the Labyrinth. The United States and the Middle East, 1945-1993*, (New York: McGraw-Hill, Inc., 1994).

Cantori, Louis J., "Regional Solutions to Regional Security Problems," *Middle East Policy*, 1994, 3(3), 20-30.

Castells, Manuel, "The Information Economy and the New International Division of Labor," in *The New Global Economy in the Information Age. Reflections on Our Changing World*, ed., Martin Carnoy et al., (University Park: The Pennsylvania State University Press, 1993), pp. 15-43.

"Central Asia," *Current History*, 1994, 93(582), 145-86.

Chirot, Daniel, *How Societies Change*, (Thousand Oaks, CA: Pine Forge Press, 1994).

Cooley, John K., *Payback. America's Long War in the Middle East*, (Washington: Brassey's (US), Inc., 1991).

Dawisha, Abeed, "The Gulf War: A Defining Event?" in *The Arab World Today*, ed., Dan Tschirgi, (Boulder: Lynne Rienner Publishers, 1994), pp. 123-34.

Dawisha, Karen and Bruce Parrott, *Russia and the New States of Eurasia. The Politics of Upheaval*, (Cambridge: Cambridge University Press, 1994).

Falk, Richard, "Hard Choices and Tragic Dilemmas. Intervention Revisited," *Nation*, 1993, 257(21), 755-64.

Fuller, Graham E., *Central Asia. The New Geopolitics*, (Santa Monica, CA: RAND, 1992a).

Fuller, Graham E., *Turkey Faces East. New Orientations Toward the Middle East and the Old Soviet Union*, (Santa Monica, CA: RAND, 1992b).

Hadar, Leon T., *Quagmire. America in the Middle East*, (Washington: CATO Institute, 1992).

Heller, Mark A., "The Israeli-Palestinian Accord: An Israeli View," *Current History*, 1994, 93(580), 56-61.

Ismael, Tareq Y. and Jacqueline S. Ismael, *The Gulf War and the New World Order. International Relations of the Middle East*, (Gainesville: University Press of Florida, 1994).

Joffe, E. G. H., "Relations Between the Middle East and the West," *Middle East Journal*, 1994, 48(2), 250-67.

Kegley, Charles W., Jr. and Gregory Raymond, *A Multipolar Peace? Great-Power Politics in the Twenty-first Century*, (New York: St. Martin's Press, 1994).

Kennedy, Paul M., *The Rise and Fall of Great Powers: Economic Change and Military Conflict from 1500 to 2000*, (New York: Random House, 1987).

Khalidi, Rashid, "A Palestinian View of the Accord with Israel," *Current History*, 1994, 93(580), 62-66.

Klare, Michael T., "North vs. South in the 1990s: A New Cold War?" Typescript, 1991.

Marr, Phebe, "The United States, Europe, and the Middle East: An Uneasy Triangle," *Middle East Journal*, 1994, 48(2), 211-25.

Norton, Augustus Richard, "Breaking Through the Wall of Fear in the Arab World," *Current History*, 1992, 91(561), 37-41.

Richards, Alan, "Oil Wealth in the Arab World: Whence, to Whom, and Whither?" in *The Arab World Today*, ed., Dan Tschirgi, (Boulder: Lynne Rienner Publishers, 1994), 67-76.

Riedel, Bruce, William Quandt and Richard Falk, "U.S. Policy Issues Symposium--The Middle East: What Is Our Long-term Vision?" *Middle East Policy*, 1994, (3), 1-19.

Schraeder, Peter J., ed., *Intervention in the 1990s: U.S. Foreign Policy in the Third World*, 2nd ed., (Boulder: Lynne Rienner Publishers, 1992).

Tibi, Bassam, "Redefining the Arab and Arabism in the Aftermath of the Gulf Crisis," in *The Arab World Today*, ed., Dan Tschirgi, (Boulder: Lynne Rienner Publishers, 1994), 135-46.

Tschirgi, Dan, ed., *The Arab World Today*, (Boulder: Lynne Rienner Publishers, 1994).

Vartabedian, Ralph and John M. Broder, "U.S. Weighs New Arms Sales Policy," *Los Angeles Times*, November 15, 1994.

Wallerstein, Immanuel, "Focus On: The World-System After the Cold War," *Journal of Peace Research*, 1993, 30(1), 1-6.

Waltz, Kenneth N., "The Emerging Structure of International Politics", *International Security*, 1993, 18(2), 44-79.

ECONOMIC DEVELOPMENT IN MUSLIM COUNTRIES: A COMPARATIVE EMPIRICAL ANALYSIS

Abbas P. Grammy
Department of Economics
California State University, Bakersfield
9001 Stockdale Highway
Bakersfield, CA 93311

Abstract—This chapter argues that capitalistic development based on private property rights, economic ventures, and profit motive is compatible with Islam. Islamic economic principles encourage individuals to accumulate wealth and direct the state to improve income and wealth distribution. Empirical results indicate that (1) a neoclassical model explains economic development in Muslim countries well; (2) Muslim countries are not any less developed than the developing countries; (3) Muslim countries need to reduce labor force growth and improve labor force productivity to become comparable with non-Muslim developing countries; and (4) Islam exerts a positive effect on economic development.

I. BACKGROUND

Effects of Islam on politico-economic development have been subject to controversy. To many Muslim scholars, development is unthinkable without Islam and to many Orientalist scholars, Islam is an impediment to political change and economic progress.

The Orientalist view refers to the "nature" of the Islamic culture to predispose that Islam and development are incompatible. For example, Sutcliffe (1975) subscribes to the Weberian view (1963) that the Islamic belief system and behavioral pattern have resulted in the underdevelopment of Muslim countries. Similarly, to Parkinson (1967) socio-economic underdevelopment is mainly due to the Muslim people's resistance to change and certain Islamic belief that make them fatalistic in their approach to life. Morris and Adelman (1980) find that the majority of Muslim countries experience "low" level of development, and express the idea that Islam has been capable of reforming a great diversity of cultural behavior to limit the growth of Western-type individualism. Such limitation acts unfavorably to the betterment of the social, political, and economic environment.

Huntington (1984) argues that Islam has not been particularly hospitable to the development of Western-type democratic institutions as there exist no clear distinction between religion and politics or between the spiritual and the secular, and non-religious political affiliation and participation are alien concepts. He demonstrates that Muslim countries are mostly nondemocratic and the majority of Muslim people is deprived of political freedom and civil liberties. Like Sutcliffe, Huntington argues that the structure of Islam is such that intermediate and ultimate ends are closely connected and extreme deference to the politico-religious authority is strongly preserved. He asserts that the Islamic belief system has resulted in a passive and fatalistic approach to life, establishing a serious barrier to political development. Hence, the Islamic form of government is inevitably autocratic in order to closely enforce the divine law.

Challenging the Orientalist view, Hourani (1962) asserts that Islam exalts reason and freedom, encourages progress, and rejects all intermediaries between man and God. In particular, he views Islamic property rights as the basis for ensuring social justice and economic progress. Islam defines property rights in such a way that there are limits to man's claim to natural resources (i.e., *Towhid*: absolute ownership is limited to God). Although private ownership of resources is clearly recognized, it carries with it such socio-religious responsibility as providing fair factor payments and paying property and income taxes.

Rodinson (1966) finds no essential incompatibility between Islamic economic doctrines and capitalistic development. He demonstrates that

Islam favors commercial profit making motive and views merchants as people who should enrich themselves so as to be able to assist the less fortunate members of the society. Behdad (1989) argues that Islam approves economic ventures, profit motive, and private property rights that are all characteristics of a capitalist society, at least, as much as, and maybe more than other major religions. Cummings *et. al.* (1980) discuss that although Islamic economic principles are compatible with the basic principles of *laissez faire* capitalism--especially those which uphold private ownership of resources and moral validity of profit--there are critical differences between them. In Islam, capitalistic practices are accepted only to the extent that they conform to overall social goals. Islamic economic principles (e.g., *Zakat*: giving alms to support the community and to sustain the poor) direct the state to interfere with the operation of markets in order to correct imbalances in the distribution of income and wealth.

Hudson (1980) argues that the Islamic polity constructs a lawful society. As a religion of worldly as well as divine concern, Islam is preoccupied with the regulation of man's conduct according to the *Kur'anic* principles of justice and equality.

Hanafi (1987) demonstrates that revolt against the human law is inherent in Islam. Indeed, Islam means submission to the will of *God*, not to the *Taghut*: the obscurantist and repressive human power. In this respect, Islam is not only a doctrine, it is also a law; not only a belief system, but a life style in which the human power is believed to be the source of oppression and the human law preserves the socio-economic class structures and interests. He argues that submission to the will of *God* means accepting his Word, the *Kur'an*, and acting according to the path he has delineated for man. Submission to the divine rulings, Hanafi argues, will liberate man from submission to exploitative principles created by any human authority. Hence, individuals are free to choose and conduct activities within the general Islamic framework so long as the rights of others are highly respected. Thus, the Islamic type of government must provide the "right" type of institutions that can manage social, economic, and political arrangements under which people live and function. Although the *Shari'a* (Islamic law) specifies consensus as the just basis for making community decisions, no specific form of government is recognized. Islamic rule is reinforced by *Shura* (consultation), *Bay'a* (delegation of power), and *Ikhtiar* (free choice), and is legalized by an *'Aqd* (social contract). Hence, not only is an Islamic community "justly balanced," but it also ideally is imbued with a moral mission and an activist posture. In fact, there are many *Kur'anic* passages like (Sura II, Verse 143) *"Verily never will God change the condition of a people until they change it themselves"* that exhorts Muslims to work actively to improve their conditions and dispels the Orientalist view of fatalism as an Islamic trait.

To explain the underdevelopment of contemporary Muslim countries, Ragab (1980) argues that neither the unique institutional nature and belief system of Islam nor the behavioral pattern and mass conception of Muslim people are unbiased and appropriate explanations. He asserts that the relative underdevelopment of Muslim countries relates to the historical phenomenon of foreign domination of the Muslim World by Ottoman imperialism and European colonialism that has resulted in stunned institutional development of the former territories and colonies, and also by the inherent conflict structure that colonialism has left behind in dividing the land to form independent nation states.

Likewise, Tuma (1987) argues that although the colonial powers introduced the idea of *change,* they did not allow this idea to germinate and grow in the Middle Eastern countries. On the contrary, they implemented *change* only when it benefitted them and those in the native population who collaborated with them. The colonizing powers contributed to the development of agriculture, industry, infrastructure, education, and commerce. Colonialism, however, disrupted the economic, social, and political structures of the occupied areas, subordinated native cultures, and drew territorial boundaries to divide the region into spheres of control and influence. In addition, colonialism created dualistic cultural, financial, and technological institutions that have weakened the native economies ever since.

An alternative, and somewhat correlated, assertion for the politico-economic underdevelopment of contemporary Muslim countries, proposed by Hudson, is that these nations have suffered from prolonged periods of *internal political illegitimacy* and *external military conflict.* In the post-independence era of political experimentation of many Muslim countries, the basic rightness of political leaders, regimes, and systems has not been widely and deeply accepted, and sometimes forcefully rejected by the masses. Regimes fearful of the instability that illegitimacy can cause, have compounded their problems by denying or restricting political rights and civil liberties. Instead of disseminating democratic norms (norms which, as observed above, can be perceived as compatible with Islamic ideas of equality and consultation), leaders have attempted to build a satisfactory legitimacy formula. Such a formula, which invariably includes an Islamic element, has forced the opposition movements into structural and ideological isolation and militancy. Authoritarian and repressive behavior of the political elite has magnified the depth and breadth of the opposition, forcing them into greater reliance on quasi-military activity, mass mobilization capability, and ideological absolutism. Increased antigovernment activity resulting in greater instability has required higher military expenditure to assure regime security and maintain regime stability. Furthermore, a built-in territorial conflict structure, caused by the decomposition of Ottoman Empire and formation of independent nation states and fueled by the Cold War ideological and military rivalry, has required even greater reallocation of resources in favor of military growth and modernization.

This chapter will investigate comparative economic development in Muslim countries in order to (1) examine the compatibility of Islam with capitalistic development; (2) investigate the extent of underdevelopment in Muslim countries; and (3) identify their possible areas in need of improvement. Results of this study can point out the direction of development for Muslim countries, especially during the post-Cold War era when ideological orientations have proven to hinder economic development. The paper is organized as follows. Section II will present the neoclassical growth model. Section III includes comparative data analysis and empirical results. Section VI contains the concluding remarks.

II. MODEL

The neoclassical theory of economic growth by Solow (1956) employs a production function with decreasing returns to capital to investigate the determinants of the steady-state equilibrium level of per capita income. Accordingly, the level of per capita income is determined by the rates of saving and population growth as well as technical progress. Since saving and population growth rates vary across countries, the neoclassical growth theory yields predications on how countries reach steady-state equilibrium. It asserts that countries that have higher rates of saving tend to have higher levels of per capita income, and countries with higher rates of population growth are likely to have lower levels of per capita income. To augment growth and explain development, several empirical studies like Mankiw, Romer, and Weil (1992) and Grammy and Assane (forthcoming) add variables representing human capital formation to the textbook Solow model. They predict that countries which invest in human capital to improve labor force productivity and participation are likely to have higher levels of per capita income.

To model economic development, I write the augmented Solow model as a Cobb-Douglas production function formulated by the above-mentioned studies. In this model, Y is real output, K and L are capital and labor inputs, and A represents the level of technology. L and A are assumed to grow exogenously at rates n and g:

$$L(t) = L(0)e^{nt}$$
$$A(t) = A(0)e^{gt}$$
(1)

Thus, the number of effective units of labor, A(t)L(t), grows at rate n + g. Also, H stands for investment in labor force productivity and Z stands for investment in labor force participation

$$Y_t = K(t)^{\alpha} H(t)^{\beta} Z(t)^{\gamma} (A(t)L(t))^{1-\alpha-\beta-\gamma}$$
(2)

We let s_k be the fraction of income invested in physical capital, s_h the fraction of income invested in labor force productivity, and s_z the fraction of income invested in labor force participation. The change in the stock of capital overtime is determined by

$$k(t) = s_k\, y(t) - (n + g + \delta)k(t)$$
$$h(t) = s_h\, y(t) - (n + g + \delta)h(t)$$
$$z(t) = s_z\, y(t) - (n + g + \delta)z(t)$$
(3)

where y = Y/AL, k = K/AK, h = H/AL, and z = Z/AL. Equations (3) imply that the economy converges to a steady-state defined by

$$k^* = \left(\frac{s_k^{1-\beta-\gamma}\, s_h^{\beta}\, s_z^{\gamma}}{n + g + \delta}\right)^{\frac{1}{1-\alpha-\beta-\gamma}}$$
(4)

$$h^* = \left(\frac{s^{1-\alpha-\gamma} s_k^\alpha s_z^\gamma}{n+g+\delta}\right)^{\frac{1}{1-\alpha-\beta-\gamma}}$$

$$z^* = \left(\frac{s_z^{1-\alpha-\beta} s_k^\alpha s_h^\beta}{n+g+\delta}\right)^{\frac{1}{1-\alpha-\beta-\gamma}}$$

Substituting equations (4) into the production function and taking natural logs give an equation for income per capita

$$\text{insert equation here} \tag{5}$$

This equation shows how income per capita depends on population growth and physical and human capital formation.

III. DATA AND RESULTS

To estimate this model, I will use data collected by Mankiw, Romer, and Weil to construct a database on the purchasing power parities real Gross Domestic Product (GDP) per working-age population, the ratio of Gross Domestic Investment to Gross Domestic Product (I/GDP), steady-state rate of working-age population growth (n + g + δ). In addition, I will use data on two human capital variables collected by Grammy and Assane. They are the Human Development Index (HDI) and Economic Liberty Index (ELI).

HDI measures investment in labor force productivity. It is constructed as an unweighted average of the relative distances measured in longevity (life expectancy at birth), educational attainment (adult literacy and average years of schooling), and access to resources (real per capita income adjusted for the differing purchasing power of each country's currency and the assumption of diminishing marginal utility of income), where the measure of distance is the difference between the actual value of the variable in a country and its minimum value divided by the range of the variable (*Human Development Report*, 1993, pp. 100-8).

ELI represents investment in labor force participation. It is based on an overall ranking of economic liberty by Scully and Slottje (1991), who combine information provided by fifteen attributes of economic liberty (e.g., freedom of information and freedom of peaceful assembly) to construct several summary indexes based on principal component and hedonic weighting techniques. Their overall ranking of economic liberty summarizes the information content of all the summary indexes and appears to be very robust with respect to all of them. To measure economic freedom, Grammy and Assane use the same relative distance formula as HDI to - construct cross-national index values for ELI.

As listed in the Appendix, a sample of 110 countries (WORLD) is divided into 91 less developed countries (LDCs) and 19 more developed countries (MDCs). The LDCs consists of 30 Muslim countries (M-LDCs) and 61 non-Muslim nations (NM-LDCs).

Table 1. Descriptive Statistical Analysis of Sample Means

	GDP Per Capita	I/GDP	n+g+δ	HDI	ELI
M-LDCs	4,525	14.28	2.76	0.37	0.39
(n=30)	(5,915)	(5.77)	(0.96)	(0.26)	(0.23)
NM-LDCs	3,421	16.82	2.47	0.48	0.45
(n=61)	(3,342)	(7.81)	(0.68)	(0.27)	(0.24)
	[1.15]	[-1.59]	[1.70]^c	[-1.86]^c	[-1.15]
LDCs	3,785	15.98	2.56	0.44	0.43
(n=91)	(4,359)	(7.27)	(0.77)	(0.27)	(0.24)
	[0.74]	[-1.17]	[1.18]	[-1.25]	[-0.82]
MDCs	12,077	24.24	1.25	0.91	0.84
(n=19)	(4,475)	(5.84)	(1.00)	(0.09)	(0.10)
	[-4.98]^a	[-6.04]^a	[5.59]^a	[-9.31]^a	[-8.65]^a
WORLD	5,400	17.60	2.31	0.54	0.51
(n=110)	(5,467)	(7.72)	(0.97)	(0.31)	(0.27)
	[-0.77]	[-2.27]^b	[2.25]^b	[-2.79]^a	[-2.22]^b

Note: Numbers in parentheses are sample variances and in brackets are student-t values for the test of difference between sample means of M-LDCs vs. a relevant group of countries. Levels of statistical significance are (a) 0.01, (b) 0.05, and (c) 0.10 for two-sided tests.

Table 1 presents summary descriptive statistics for sample countries and test results for the difference between population means of the M-LDCs versus other groups of countries. Muslim countries exhibit a significantly higher rate of labor force growth, but a lower value of HDI than non-Muslim countries. Compared with the LDCs, all mean differences become statistically insignificant. Except for GDP per working-age population, the M-LDCs lag behind the WORLD. They also lag behind the more developed countries with respect to all indicators of economic development.

Table 2. Results of the Augmented Solow Growth Model

	Constant	ln(I/GDP)	ln(n+g+δ)	ln(HDI)	ln(ELI)	ISLAM	R^2
M-LDCs	5.91	0.53	-1.57	0.47	0.34	-	0.85
	(6.46)ᵃ	(2.32)ᵇ	(-3.91)ᵃ	(3.29)ᵃ	(2.61)ᵇ		
NM-LDCs	7.70	0.44	-0.32	0.82	0.10	-	0.75
	(14.51)ᵃ	(2.95)ᵃ	(-1.85)ᶜ	(7.14)ᵃ	(1.16)		
LDCs	7.32	0.39	-0.37	0.69	0.20	-	0.70
	(14.18)ᵃ	(2.76)ᵃ	(-1.67)ᶜ	(7.08)ᵃ	(2.47)ᵇ		
MDCs	8.90	0.25	-0.08	2.99	0.64	-	0.78
	(10.17)ᵃ	(0.97)	(-0.84)	(4.79)ᵃ	(1.39)		
WORLD	8.00	0.40	-0.21	0.79	0.22	-	0.77
	(18.23)ᵃ	(3.02)ᵃ	(-2.13)ᵇ	(8.97)ᵃ	(2.78)ᵃ		
WORLD	8.05	0.39	-0.30	0.88	0.21	0.47	0.80
	(19.70)ᵃ	(3.14)ᵃ	(-3.14)ᵃ	(10.37)ᵃ	(2.89)ᵃ	(4.23)ᵃ	

Note: Numbers in parentheses are student-t values. Levels of significance are (a) 0.01, (b) 0.05, and (c) 0.10 for two-sided tests.

Table 2 presents results (corrected for heterosedasticity, if necessary) of the augmented Solow model. I observe here that all variables enter significantly in the model of Muslim countries, and that this model has a high explanatory power of eighty-five percent. The model performs well for the NM-LDCs, LDCs, and WORLD, but not so well for the MDCs. Reason for the poor performance of the model for MDCs may stem from a small sample size. When compared to results from other countries, the M-LDCs exhibit the largest negative coefficient for the labor force growth variable, $\ln(n + g + δ)$, but the smallest positive coefficient for the variable representing human capital formation, $\ln(HDI)$. Noticeably, however, the

M-LDCs record the largest statistically significant coefficient for the variable representing economic liberty, ln(ELI).

Finally, to investigate the impact of Islam on economic development, a binary variable ISLAM that takes the value of one for Muslim countries and zero for other countries is added to the entire sample (WORLD). All variables in the model have expected signs and significant coefficients. In particular, ISLAM has a positive and significant effect on GDP per working-age population. Inclusion of variable ISLAM increases the explanatory power of the WORLD model from seventy-seven to eighty percent.

IV. CONCLUSION

Empirical results suggest that (1) the neoclassical model explains economic development in Muslim countries well, supporting the assertion that Islam is compatible with capitalistic economic development; (2) Islam exerts a positive effect on economic development; and (3) although Muslim countries lag behind the more developed countries, they are not any less developed than the developing countries.

Compared with non-Muslim countries, empirical results identify two areas in need of improvement in Muslim countries: labor force growth and labor force productivity. In many M-LDCs, the rate of population growth exceeds the rate of economic growth, causing the per capita income to decline. For instance, the 1980-92 annual growth rate of the labor force averaged 3.9 percent in Saudi Arabia, 3.6 percent in the United Arab Emirates (UAE), and 3.2 percent in Iran, all of which represent some of the highest in the world. In the meantime, their real GDP grew at an average annual rate of 0.4, 0.3, and 2.3 percent in the respective countries. As a result of labor force growth faster than GDP growth, GDP per capita declined at an average annual rate of 3.5 percent in Saudi Arabia, 3.3 percent in the UAE, and 0.9 percent in Iran. Likewise, life expectancy averages 55 years in Muslim countries, which is nearly 6 years lower than that in non-Muslim countries. Also, the average rate of adult literacy is about 40 percent in the M-LDCs compared with nearly 66 percent in the NM-LDCs. In addition, Muslim countries consistently average lower enrollment ratios in primary, secondary, and tertiary education (*World Development Report*, 1994).

The key to reducing labor force growth and increasing labor force productivity is greater investment in human capital so that all productive members of the labor force find opportunities to freely and actively participate in the economic process, thus contributing to long-term growth of per capita real income. An effective strategy to achieving this objective is to improve female education and labor force participation in an attempt to increase opportunity costs of participating in non-market transactions (e.g., home-making and child-rearing), thus decreasing fertility rate and family size. In addition, improved education and health help increase the infant survival rate and decrease the demand for replacement children. As a result, an educated and healthy labor force gains productivity to earn larger income.

Furthermore, human resource development will help Muslim countries achieve socio-political cohesion, particularly in the post Cold War era when the failure of the Soviet-style central planning system has given rise to capitalistic transition in regions like Eastern Europe, Central Asia, Central America, and South Asia. As empirical results indicate, Muslim countries exhibit a significant level of economic liberty, which can be instrumental in achieving sustained economic development. The realization that Islam is compatible with capitalism and supportive of development must facilitate the transition to efficiency-based market practices. These practices must be supplemented by coherent public policies to correct market failure and achieve the overall social goals of prosperity and equality.

In conclusion, empirical results falsify the Orientalist view that Islam is an impediment to economic development. Islamic economic principles based on private property rights approve profit making, mutually beneficial trade, wealth accumulation, and income distribution. Islamic civic laws insist on consultation, free choice, and consensus in the making of public decisions. Consequently, Islam constructs an infrastructure for economic progress and democratic decision making. If so, why Muslim countries are not as developed and democratic? As argued by Ragab, Tuma, and Hudson, colonialism has left behind inherent conflict structures and dualistic organizations that have resulted in stunned institutional development. Such institutional underdevelopment has created conditions of *internal political illegitimacy* and *external military conflict*, where a small and powerful elite group control resource allocation and make public decisions to enrich themselves at the expense of the majority of people. The anti-government sentiment in many Muslim countries stem from political repression, economic inequality, social injustice, and involvement in external military conflict. The high opportunity cost of autocracy increases people's deprivation to fuel anti-government opposition and causes resentment toward the foreign countries (e.g., United States) that help the elite regimes to stay in power.

REFERENCES

Behdad, S., Property Rights in Contemporary Islamic Economic Thought: A Critical Perspective," *Review of Social Economy*, 1989, XLVII, 2, 185-211.

Cummings, A. T., H. Askari, and A. Mustafa, "Islam and Modern Economic Changes," in J. L. Esposito, ed., *Islam and Development: Religion and Sociopolitical Change*, (Syracuse: Syracuse University Press, 1980), pp. 25-47.

Grammy, A.P. and D. Assane, "New Evidence on the Effect of Human Capital on Economic Growth," forthcoming, Applied Economics Letters.

Hanafi, H., "Fundamentalism: Origin of Violence in Islam," *Development*, 1987, 1, 56-61.

Hourani, A., *Arabic Thought in the Liberal Age, 1798-1939*, (London: Oxford University Press, 1962).

Hudson, M.C., "Islam and Political Development," in J. L. Esposito, ed., *Islam and Development: Religion and Sociopolitical Change*, (Syracuse: Syracuse University Press, 1980), pp. 1-24.

Huntington, S. P., "Will More Countries Become Democratic?", *Political Science Quarterly*, 1984, 99, 193-218.

Human Development Report, 1993,(Oxford University Press, Cambridge).

Mankiw, N. G., D. Romer, and D. N. Weil, "A contribution to the Empirics of Economic Growth," *The Quarterly Journal of Economics*, 1992, 107, 408-37.

Morris, C. T. and I. Adelman, "The Religious Factor in Economic Development," *World Development*, 1980, 8(7/8), 491-501.

Ragab, I. A., "Islam and Development," *World Development*, 1980, 8(7/8), 514-21.

Rodinson, M., *Islam and Capitalism*, (London: Penguin Books, 1966).

Scully, G. W. and D. J. Slottje, "Ranking Economic Liberty Across Countries," *Public Choice*, 1991, 69, 121-52.
Solow, R., "A Contribution to the Theory of Economic Growth," *Quarterly Journal of Economics*, 1956, 19, 65-94.
Sutcliffe C. R., "Is Islam an Obstacle to Development? Ideal Patterns of Believe versus Actual Patterns of Behavior," *The Journal of Developing Areas*, , 1975, 10, 77-82.
Tuma, E.H., *Economic and Political Change in the Middle East*, (Palo Alto: Pacific Books, 1987).
Weber, M., *The Sociology of Religion*, translation by E. Fischoff (Boston: Beacon Press, 1963).
World Development Report 1994 (New York: Oxford University Press, 1994.

APPENDIX

Sample Countries (WORLD)

More Developed Countries (MDCs):
Australia, Austria, Belgium, Canada, Denmark, Finland, France, Germany, Ireland, Italy, Japan, Netherlands, New Zealand, Norway, Spain, Sweden, Switzerland, United Kingdom, United States.

Less Developed Countries (LDCs):

Muslim (M-LDCs):
Afghanistan, Algeria, Bangladesh, Chad, Egypt, Ethiopia, Gambia, Guinea, Indonesia, Iran, Iraq, Jordan, Kuwait, Malaysia, Mali, Mauritania, Morocco, Niger, Nigeria, Oman, Pakistan, Saudi Arabia, Senegal, Somalia, Sudan, Syria, Tunisia, Turkey, United Arab Emirates, Yemen.

Non- Muslim (NM-LDCs):
Angola, Argentina, Benin, Bolivia, Botswana, Brazil, Burkina Faso, Burma, Burundi, Cameroon, Central African Republic, Chile, Congo, Costa Rica, Dominican Republic, Ecuador, El Salvador, Gabon, Greece, Guatemala, Guyana, Haiti, Honduras, Hong King, India, Israel, Ivory Coast, Jamaica, Kenya, Korea (Republic of), Liberia, Madagascar, Malawi, Mauritius, Mexico, Mozambique, Nepal, Nicaragua, Panama,

Papua New Guinea, Paraguay, Peru, Philippines, Portugal, Rwanda, Sierra Leone, Singapore, South Africa, Sri Lanka, Suriname, Swaziland, Tanzania, Thailand, Togo, Trinidad and Tobago, Uganda, Uruguay, Venezuela, Zaire, Zambia, Zimbabwe.

Note:
Results from the Chow-test of structural equality indicate that the corresponding regression coefficients are not statistically different from each other for groups of LDCs and MDCs. Here, the model can be estimated for the entire sample countries (WORLD).

THE PEACE PROCESS AND THE PALESTINIAN REFUGEES

Elias H. Tuma
Department of Economics
University of California
Davis, CA 95616

Abstract—Now that conflict is in the process of being resolved the refugee status has become anachronistic. A solution has to be found that will do at least two things: enhance the peace process, and give the Palestinians refugees the opportunity to rehabilitate themselves as citizens and productive people. I propose, first, that without resolution of the refugee problem the peace process may be seriously handicapped. Second, resettlement of the PR outside Palestine is the only viable option. Third, If given viable alternatives to returning to Palestine, the majority will choose another option. Fourth, the Gulf countries should be a mutually most attractive destination for resettlement. Finally, resettlement would most successful if the PR take personal economic responsibility; therefore, financing resettlement should be by interest-free loans rather than by grants.

I. INTRODUCTION

September 1993 was the beginning of the end of the Israeli-Palestinian conflict. Prime Minister Rabin and Chairman Arafat signed a statement of principles on that occasion to guide the negotiations of a peace agreement between the two parties. It was logical then to bring up all the dormant issues between them, especially the issue of the refugees whose fate had been virtually ignored while attention was focused on military and political matters. However, as these two areas of conflict have been brought under control, it has become evident that the viability of any peace agreement will depend heavily on resolution of the refugee problem. This study, therefore, may be viewed as an attempt to contribute to the resolution of that conflict.

Solution of the Palestinian refugees (PR) is integral to the ongoing peace process between the Arab countries and Israel as well as the negotiations between Israel and the Palestine Liberation Organization (PLO). The refugee issue is politically significant because a majority of the Palestinians are classified as refugees. They form large conglomerations in the host countries in which they reside and therefore can have a political impact if they were to participate in political activity. Furthermore, the Palestinians have become politically alert especially since the *intifada* and it would be unwise to ignore them in any solution to the Arab Israeli conflict that may be pursued.

The refugee question, however, is important in economic and social respects as well. The Palestinian refugees embody a large stock of human capital which is underutilized primarily because of their political status in the countries of current residence and because of the ongoing conflict with Israel. Their mobility is restricted in most cases, their economic decisions are not free and their opportunities are not based on merit. As a result their product is presumably far below their capabilities. This underutilized capital is reflected in the quality of life they experience, the level of unemployment they suffer, and the inequality of opportunity they face wherever they reside in the Middle East compared with the citizens of those countries. The loss, however, is shared by the Palestinians themselves and the countries in which they reside.

The PR are in an almost unique situation also because of the apparent common conviction that even after a peace settlement with Israel has been concluded, they will not be able to return to their homes or country--a similar situation has been evolving for the Bosnian Muslims who are being evicted in the process of what has become known as ethnic cleansing. The PR are therefore threatened with the permanent loss of identity as Palestinians and of their homes and country. The loss, however, would not be as devastating as it sounds if it were the result of a voluntary decision by Palestinians to migrate or assume another national identity. The critical nature of this status is clearly reflected in the ambivalent attitude of the Palestinians of Jordan. While they have acquired citizenship, or the right to citizenship, form a majority of the population of Jordan, elect and get elected, and travel on Jordanian passports, they still call themselves Palestinians rather than Jordanians, and act as if the Israeli-Palestinian conflict is their own. Even those who were born in Jordan and have never set foot on Palestinian soil behave as if they were only recently displaced and turned into refugees.

Another feature that adds gravity to the refugees situation is that a high percentage of those registered as refugees live in camps, in very crowded houses, with few of the amenities of life enjoyed by others. They depend on the good will of the host country, aid from the United Nations, and employment opportunities that cannot be filled by citizens of the employing countries.

These conditions have prevailed as long as the Israeli Palestinian conflict has continued. Now that conflict is in the process of being resolved the refugee status has become anachronistic. A solution has to be found that will do at least two things: enhance the peace process, and give the Palestinians refugees the opportunity to rehabilitate themselves as citizens and productive people. I propose, first, that without resolution of the refugee problem the peace process may be seriously handicapped. Second, resettlement of the PR outside Palestine is the only viable option. Third, If given viable alternatives to returning to Palestine, the majority will choose another option. Fourth, the Gulf countries should be a mutually most attractive destination for resettlement. Finally, resettlement would most successful if the PR take personal economic responsibility; therefore, financing resettlement should be by interest-free loans rather than by grants.

In the next section we shall look at the size and distribution of the refugee population; next I shall explore the possible solutions which have been discussed in the literature; In the final section I shall propose what I consider to be most viable solutions or approaches to the problem and the steps to take in the immediate future.

II. PROFILE OF THE PALESTINIAN REFUGEES

The PR are a relatively small segment of the total refugee population. As of 1993 there were 18.2 million people registered as refugees around the world. Another 24 million people were recorded as displaced within their own countries. The largest single group are Afghans, followed by the Palestinians, Yugoslavs, and Mozambiquis. Refugees and displaced people exist in all continents, in virtually all cases as a result of civil wars and therefore hope to return to their homes once such wars come to an end--as noted above the Palestinians and Bosnian Muslims are exceptions. The Palestinians have been scattered around the world, but those holding a refugee status are concentrated in Middle Eastern countries, as follows: North Africa, 9,400; Syria, 299,200; Lebanon, 319,400; West Bank, 459,100; Gaza Strip, 560,200; Jordan, 1,010,700.[1] Others may be regarded as refugees but are not registered as such with UNRWA and therefore may not be included in these statistics, though any decision made regarding refugees would effect them as well. The PR have acquired fairly high levels of education through UNRWA, generosity of the host countries, and aid from international foundations. Their level of skill is above average for any country in the Middle East, with the exception of Israel. Their ability to participate in productive economic life has varied according to the country in which they reside, ranging from full equality of opportunity, as in Syria, to highly restricted activities as in the Gulf countries. The same variation applies to their freedom of mobility, educational and health privileges, and social status. However, except in Jordan, the Palestinians have no political freedom. They cannot participate in the political affairs of the country of residence, regardless how long they have been in that country. This is the symbol of statelessness since they became refugees. The assumption is that a resolution of the Israeli-Palestinian conflict will also resolve their refugee problem and restore to these stateless people full political rights as commensurate with the national status of free people.

The economic and political status of the PR is complicated by a number of conditions. First, they are concentrated in relatively resource-poor

---

1. World Refugee Survey, 1993, as reported in the *Britannica Book of the Year, 1994*, Chicago: Encyclopaedia Britannica, Inc., 1994, p. 254

countries and regions such as Jordan, Lebanon, and the Gaza Strip. Second, because of their concentration they dominate in the localities in which they reside in the respective countries and hence can make a difference if they were active participants in the politics of the country. Third, their numbers continue to rise rapidly through natural growth--though not much more rapidly than the growth of the native population. Fourth, in addition to their stateless status, the PR are still considered outsiders by the citizens of the countries in which they reside. Their refugee status is actually reinforced by the attitude of the people of the host country. Hence, resolution of the refugee problem must cope with all these conditions and make it possible for the Palestinians to free themselves of the refugee status, both technically and behaviorally.[2] Before proceeding to explore solutions we should distinguish between two groups of refugees, those within the Occupied Territories (OT) and those outside it. The former group already resides within the Palestinian territory and, therefore, once the political conflict has been resolved, the solution to its problems will be primarily economic and social. The political solution is part of the peace process. Those who reside outside the OT face territorial, political, as well as social and economic problems that await resolution. These distinctions will be elaborated in the next section.

III. POTENTIAL RESOLUTIONS OF THE REFUGEE PROBLEMS:

A. *Territorial and Political Solutions.* The question of territory and political status has in effect been resolved for the two groups of refugees, those who reside in the OT but have been displaced from their homes and live in camps and those who have been displaced but do not live in camps. These groups, which number around one million, are within the Palestinian territory and will enjoy the same rights as the Palestinians who have remained in their homes in the OT. Their problem is primarily social and economic.

Another group whose resettlement and political status have been essentially resolved includes those who are considered potential returnees

---

2. For a vivid detailed description of the refugee conditions see Don Perez, "Palestinian Refugees and Middle East Stability," Washington, D.C.: DARSP, Nov. 1992.

to the OT by the PLO leadership, estimated at about 750,000 people.[3] These potential returnees will probably be involved in the administration of the Palestinian entity and their families, coming from various parts of the diaspora. How they will be chosen remains for the Palestinian authorities to determine. For our purposes, however, this group can be removed from the status of refugees from the political and identity standpoints.

Another assessment of potential returnees has been made in the *Masterplanning the State of Palestine*.[4] According to this estimate between 250,000 and 750,000 refugees will return during each of the first five years of statehood. If 1.5 million refugees were to return from the outside in addition to the refugees who are already within the OT, then the total refugee population will be virtually resettled within the Palestinian entity. In that case, the remaining problems would be economic and social rehabilitation and development. However, it is doubtful that that many will return.

In my previous study, with Haim Darin-Drabkin, we proposed an economic plan that would absorb all the refugees within the state.[5] We believed then as I do believe now that the Palestinian economy can absorb all the refugees. However, I am not as confident that the road to economic viability with all the refugees returning would be as smooth now as it seemed then, nor do I believe that as large a percentage of refugees would be as eager to return now as were then. As to the economic viability question, the population has increased dramatically in the meantime, but the resources have not; actually the resources have declined because of capital destruction and deterioration of the infrastructure under occupation. Furthermore, I suggest that refugee expectations have changed both on account of political development and divisionism among Palestinians, and because of the passage of time and potential prospects elsewhere. Therefore I would estimate the potential returnees to be no more than those estimated by PLO leaders (750,000). I adopt this estimate on the assumption that the PLO will play a central role in facilitating the return of refugees in due course, facilitate employment and housing, and ease their in-

---

3. A statement to that effect was made by Nabeel Shaath at the Carnegie Mellon University conference ...; See also George Abed, ed., *The Economic Viability of a Palestinian State*, Washington, D.C.: Institute for Palestine Studies, p. 6.
4. Ramalla, West Bank: The Center for Engineering and Planning, March 1992, pp. 3, 134.
5. *The Economic Case for Palestine*, Croom-Helm, 1978.

tegration in the community. Without PLO approval, those who return on their own will probably face risks of unemployment, housing shortage, and difficulty of fitting in the community. Therefore, the decision to return or not to return will be made on the basis of comparison between available options and the better the alternative option, the fewer refugees will opt to return to Palestine.

The non-returning refugees will form the crux of the PR pending territorial and political status problem. These are concentrated in Lebanon, Syria, and Jordan. Although the Jordanian authorities have expressed little displeasure towards integration of the Palestinians in Jordan, they have shown concern regarding the capability of the Jordanian economy to absorb them. More indirectly, however, there has been concern regarding the role the Palestinian may play in the politics of Jordan once they are convinced that Jordan is their ultimate home country. Such concern is significant for the majority of Palestinians in Jordan, those who reside in refugee camps or who have not become integrated in the Jordanian society and polity.[6]

However, some of those returnees will also come from Lebanon and Syria. In any case, the fate of those who are not accounted for so far, a little over one million people, is crucial to a successful peace settlement. It is with these refugees that I shall be concerned in the rest of this paper.

Several options have been recurrent in the literature as hypothetical solution though only some of them are feasible. Probably the most desirable though not evidently feasible solution is for the refugees to return home to Palestine, either to their original homes or at least to the Palestinian entity. However, this solution has been acknowledged as physically and political unfeasible, as has been apparent for a long time. Therefore, substitute solutions have been discussed. One of these is a formal recognition of the right of the refugees to return home as per UN Resolution 194 but not its implementation; instead viable alternative options for resettlement would be provided. Thus the refugees would have the formal right to return but practical difficulties would be allowed to preclude implementation. The argument for this proposal is that it resolves the political

---

6. Some of these people will be among the potential returnees to the Palestinian entity.

identity crisis of the PR and reduces the problem to the securement of territorial space for resettlement outside Palestinian territory.[7]

Resettlement outside the Palestinian entity may be planned according to one of several possibilities. Probably the easiest solution from a logistical standpoint is resettlement in the host country. In that case the refugee camps will be dismantled and their occupants will be encouraged to seek their place of residence anywhere in the respective country. Though in some countries new communities are established to house resettled refugees, it is important that freedom of choice of residence and community be respected. Such a solution, however, is replete with political, economic, and social difficulties. For instance, transforming the refugees into citizens with full political rights could alter the shape of the polity in the respective countries to an extent that the citizens would not be comfortable with that transformation, as may be the case in Lebanon. Another obstacle to this solution is the limited absorptive capacity of most countries of the region, unless large sums of capital are invested in them. Lebanon provides a good illustration of this handicap. A third obstacle is social in the sense that the Palestinian refugees have not always been welcome in the host countries and resettlement on a permanent basis may create social conflict with the native people. Therefore, while this solution may seem most logical, other options must be considered.

Another option is to encourage or plan resettlement in Arab countries which have sufficient absorptive capacity and political maturity and stability to be able to stand the shock of large numbers of newcomers to the country to share citizenship and participate in the polity. Syria is one such country; Iraq is another; Sudan is a third. Although these countries have political troubles of their own, the resettlement of a few hundred thousand Palestinians within their territories will not make much difference to the stability of the political system in the country; on the contrary, such resettlement may help to create stability by bringing in new ideas and human resources. A variation of this option is to offer the Palestinian

---

7. I discussed one version of this solution in my *Peacemaking and the Immoral War. Arabs and Jews in the Middle East*, Harper and Row, 1972, pp. 97-100; for a recent explicit statement of this approach to the Palestinian right of return see Ziad Abu Zayyad, "The Palestinian Right of Return: A Realistic Approach," *Palestine-Israel Journal*, # 2, Spring 1994, pp. 74-8; for changing interpretations of that right see Rashid Khalidi, "Observations on the Right of Right of Return, " *Journal of Palestine Studies*, vol. 21, # 2, Winter 1982, pp. 20-40.

refugees a place for resettlement while at the same time allowing them to obtain a Palestinian citizenship and thus retain their Palestinian identity. This option, however, is unstable since a Palestinian citizenship away from Palestine can have only a symbolic meaning and may not be adequate to substitute for the political and psychological benefits inherent in active citizenship within a country.

My preferred resettlement option outside the current host countries is to resettle most refugees *as citizens* in the oil exporting countries which suffer from labor shortage, especially the Gulf states. Such a program of resettlement would have mutual benefits to the refugees and the adopted countries. First, the Gulf states need labor to keep their economies fully functional; having citizens employed is more desirable than having migrant labor. Second, as citizens, the new settlers can be selected so as to maximize the benefits to both parties, including loyalty to the new home state. Third, the benefits these countries can offer should be a sufficient incentive for the new citizens to integrate in society and avoid any activity that might threaten these benefits, especially in view of the fact that the return to Palestine is no longer an option. Finally, the Palestinian settlers will offer the new home countries large stocks of human capital at little or no cost; they will come with training and skills to put to work in the economy. This is how the New World has been built, and how Israel has managed to develop its economy as an island within an underdeveloped region. Kuwait, Saudi Arabia, and the United Arab Emirates jointly have the capacity to absorb and the need for all the non-returning refugees who might opt to settle in those countries.

Still another option is to encourage mobility and resettlement outside the Arab countries and the Middle East region. A million people can be easily absorbed in the new world, the United States, Canada, Latin America, Australia, and New Zealand. This solution is most attractive from the standpoint of the opportunities it offers to the individuals who take advantage of it. It is, however, costly to those who desire to retain their Palestinian or Arab identity beyond one generation or who believe that they have a role to play in the creation and nourishment of the new Palestinian entity. Resettlement outside the region implies willingness to be assimilated into the new community one joins. These various solutions are not mutually exclusive. They may all be applied according to the place and resources available to make them successful. This leads us to the social and economic solutions.

B. *Social and Economic Solutions.* In order to be successful these various solutions have certain requirements in common. First and foremost the Palestinian refugees, as groups and as individuals, must have a say in the choice of the solution applied to them. Second, whatever solution is opted for, it must give sufficient promise that the living conditions of the resettled family will be improved socially and economically and that its members will become more productive, independent, and free. A third prerequisite is the provision of sufficient resources for viable resettlement according to the new environment. Probably a major source of success would be the ability to match resource availability with potential occupations and skills of the settlers to the extent possible.

On the other hand, there are certain conditions to be avoided if resettlement is to succeed and the refugee status is to be abolished. For example, there should not be a single hint or implication that the resettled people are undesirable in the Palestinian entity. A second condition to be avoided is the selection of country or region for resettlement according to ethnic, religious, or economic class background of the settlers. To suggest that one's religious beliefs or affiliation or that economic wealth will be the determining factor in the choice of resettlement destination can be a source of instability and threaten a backlash against resettlement outside the Palestinian entity. Another implication to dispel is that resettlement outside the Palestinian entity is evidence of Israel's victory or Palestine's defeat in the conflict. Resettlement should be projected as the best possible solution of a conflict, reached through negotiation, and implemented through cooperation between the refugees themselves and the respective agencies involved in the resettlement operation. Finally, it is imperative that no implication of charity, pity, or aid to helpless people should be allowed to filter through to the potential settlers and threaten their self respect and needed cooperation. Their self respect must be safeguarded so that their potential abilities can be mobilized in the resettlement process. Having stated the conditions to encourage and those to avoid in the resettlement process, I shall point out certain steps that seem imperative in resolving the PR problem as part of the peace process.

IV. Imperative Steps to Take

The following steps are premised on the assumption that wherever resettlement occurs the receiving country will be fully cooperative to facilitate mobility and integration of the new settlers into the community. We assume also that the Palestinian authorities and the United Nations will be directly involved in implementation of the resettlement plan. International agencies should be involved as facilitators but not as decision makers as to who goes where for resettlement. We assume further that the resettlement program and the resources made available for it are independent of the issue of compensation for Palestinian properties left behind in Palestine. The issue of compensation for such properties must be isolated from the process of resettlement; compensation is an accounting matter; resettlement is a political, social, and economic process whose success depends primarily on cooperation of the settlers and the receiving country. Given these assumptions, we recommend the following steps as soon as possible in the peace process.

First and foremost is the need to survey the refugees to find out what attracts them most among the feasible solutions. The PR issue has been on a backburner for a long time. Interest in the refugee problem has been limited to the provision of basic needs and containment of their political activity. The highly qualified and enterprising among them have freed themselves of the refugee environment though not always the status, but these are relatively small in number. Those who have remained as refugees, the majority of the dislocated, are nationalistic and ambitious for freedom and identity as political solutions. To reconcile those expectations with feasible solutions is probably the most serious obstacle to tackle. However, regardless of the solution attempted, the objective is bound to be removal of the refugee status and rehabilitation of the social and economic life of the dislocated people.

The success of the solution will probably depend on the degree of freedom of choice and voluntary cooperation of the refugees. To impose a resettlement program will no doubt meet stiff resistance and can easily cause political disorder. Imposition would be considered akin to the occasional suggestions by certain Israeli leaders to conduct population transfers to get rid of Arabs in the OT. It would also be as hateful as the so-called ethnic cleansing in former Yugoslav states.

A different approach is to entice the PR to move out of the camps on their own in order to get economic and civic benefits and avoid being forced to move out or at least abandon the refugee status. This approach will no doubt be branded as blackmail but could succeed. Other approaches with lesser degrees of imposition may be applied but all such approaches will be seen as imposed solutions. Therefore, to avoid such an obstructive stigma it would be constructive to survey the preferences of the PR from among the feasible solutions, coopt leaders and skilled Palestinian refugees to help in the implementation of the selected solution, and tailor programs to fit expectations to the extent possible.

To my knowledge no survey of the rank and file of the PR has been conducted. Negotiations regarding PR future and proposals for resolution of their problem have been carried out by political leaders and academic experts with little explicit or systematic consideration of the refugees' desires or preferences. The leaders and politicians do not necessarily represent the refugees. Academicians who might or might not have visited refugee camps are not better qualified to reflect refugee preferences. Though surveying refugee preferences might have been difficult while a liberation movement underway, the question of the refugee preferences can no longer be ignored, given that an agreement has been signed for peaceful solutions of the Palestinian-Israeli conflict, including the refugee problem.

It is imperative for policy makers to find out what the PR prefer, what it takes to gain their cooperation, and how best any selected program can be administered to assure its success. A well-designed survey would go a long way toward answering these questions. The results will have strategic significance in the peace process. While the survey would give the PR some say in their future affairs, it would also make them aware of the difficulties and constraints that must be overcome to resolve their problem. It would help in the design of the appropriate program and thus increase the probability of its success. Finally, it would enhance the position of the Palestinian leaders among their constituents and internationally, promote harmony between the PR and the communities in which they eventually integrate, and give the refugees who will not return to Palestine a certain degree of self-respect as having participated in choosing the solution.

A second and connected step is to coopt the Palestinians in the formulation and implementation of the various options that are feasible. Once the survey results are known it would be most effective to recruit qualified administrators and staff from among the refugees so as to give them both employment and responsibility for the success of the program. Coopting the PR should serve as a major first step in their rehabilitation and restoration of their self confidence as self-reliant citizens wherever they happen to reside. Cooptation of PR leaders and staff should serve also to highlight the wealth of human capital they represent and can potentially use in building their economic and social future. This measure should also prove to be less costly than other approaches of leadership and staffing, given the social savings that can be realized by utilizing local talent and gaining confidence of the PR community.

A third step which overlaps both of the above steps is to embark on a campaign of reeducation of the refugees regarding their future as citizens, not dependent refugees. The PR have lived in refugee camps or in other communities as refugees believing that they have a right of return to their home and country. They have built expectations to that effect, even as it has become more and more unlikely that they will be able to enjoy that right. Therefore it should be a big shock to them to face a fact that after such a long wait they have no "guaranteed" right of return nor any reason to hope that some day they will be able to return to home or country. The PR are bound to be angry enough to cause instability in the region. Reeducation is a way to smooth the transition. The PR should be fully informed about the negotiation process, the feasible and infeasible, the costs and benefits of different alternatives, and the prospects that lie ahead.

The PR need to be convinced that they are not being abandoned or sacrificed by their own people, the Palestinians who are settled, that their status is not uncommon, and that solutions are never exactly as one desires. They need to be convinced also that the chosen solution or solutions are the best under the circumstances. Illustrations of how other refugees have had their problems resolved and how they have been rehabilitated would be helpful. Literary explanations, videos, and organized visits to resettled communities can be highly useful to strengthen PR cooperation, reduce opposition, and provide models for implementation of the chosen solutions.

The process of reeducation is long and energy consuming, but its functions can hardly be overestimated. The most important benefit is to strengthen the confidence and determination of the PR to succeed outside the refugee camp or without the refugee status and help of others, in spite of the hardships they are bound to face. If successful the transformation through reeducation can also be a preventive measure against a backfire by the PR who are denied their most desired solution while other Palestinians enjoy theirs. The sooner the PR begin to identify with their future country or community, the more fruitful will be reeducation and the more promising its results.

These three steps are tied closely to the availability of adequate resources, the method of utilization of these resources, and the amount of economic freedom the individual gains by sharing them. The needed resources are of two types: economic opportunity, and capital or purchasing power. Economic opportunity means that the PR will enjoy the same economic freedoms enjoyed by other members of the communities they join, including freedom of enterprise, residential and occupational mobility, rights of ownership, and security of investment. The resettled PR should be able to pursue any economic activity, public or private, enjoyed by the community members without discrimination against them because of their newness, former national identity, or previous refugee status.[8] Equality of opportunity for the resettled citizens or residents will help to assure them that resettlement as a solution embodies equality status in the economies in which they become integrated. It also enhances their incentives to perform and excel for their own benefit. They should now be able to buy homes, become owner farmers, shopkeepers, business leaders, and crafts people and professionals according to their qualifications and merits. Only then can they be fully integrated in the new communities and can the refugee status be fully obliterated.

Resettlement capital is the other form of indispensable resources. The PR have depended on the United Nations resources for a long time. It is time for them to depend on their own resources. Therefore, the resources made available to them should be in the form of interest-free loans drawn from a revolving fund established for their resettlement. The fund, capitalized from all available international sources, would extend loans to individuals and families to cover moving and transportation costs to their

---

8. Reeducation of the receiving community becomes essential in this regard; though Palestinians in Jordan have the right to Jordanian citizenship and some have acquired it, there are charges of economic discrimination against them, even against those born in Jordan, Voice of America, Arabic broadcast, Oct. 7, 1994.

new communities, sustenance and shelter for a given period of time, say six months, and an additional sum to invest in a business or other project if requested. Repayment begins a year and a half after settlement in the new community in small enough instalments to be affordable and not threatening to the new business or the borrower. Given that the value of an interest-free loan will diminish over time because of inflation, it means that its burden will also diminish. At the same time the need for the revolving fund will also diminish because the number of PR to be resettled will decline and eventually vanish.

One argument against a program of lending to the PR instead of giving them outright grants is that they have suffered a lot and have lost land and property and therefore should not be burdened with loans. Two points should be emphasized in this regard: the loss of land and property left behind in Palestine is a separate issue and should be negotiated separately from solution of the residence and political status of the refugees. It is safe to assume that compensation will be paid to those who qualify for compensation as resolved by the negotiating teams of the respective parties. On the other hand, an interest-free loan can hardly be a burden and yet it can be a major source of self-respect, a positive factor in building self-reliance, probably an advantage over the benefits enjoyed by the citizens, and a mechanism to assure availability of resources for other refugees who will need them in the future.

An important financial issue is the burden resettlement of PR may entail on the receiving communities. Given that a sudden increase of population will increase the demand for services and uses of the infrastructure, it should be possible to contribute to those communities adequate funds to offset the costs of absorbing the new members of the community. These sums, however, should be in the form of grants rather than loans, both to entice them to cooperate and to free them from the burden of absorbing relatively large population increments from the outside. Rapid expansion of the schools, transportation systems, utilities, sanitation and public health requires funds that usually are beyond the means of most communities in the Arab countries. Provision of funds for those purposes will not only make absorption possible but it will reduce any negative sentiment against the new members of the communities because of increasing burdens on their public budgets. Such expenditure will also serve to inject capital, create jobs, and help to integrate the newcomers into their new communities.

V. SUMMARY AND CONCLUSIONS

Given the imminent peace agreement between Israel and its Arab neighbors, it has become imperative to address the refugee problem and search for a final solution. In this study I have addressed four aspects of the problem: first, economic and social rehabilitation of the Palestinian refugees is an integral part of the peace process. Second, a survey of the feasible options leads to the conclusion that resettlement outside Palestine is the most viable option to satisfy political as well as social and economic objectives, and resettlement in the oil-exporting Gulf states can be mutually beneficial to the refugees and to the receiving states. Third, success of resettlement options and other solutions depends much on the degree of choice the refugees have and the input they contribute to those solutions. Fourth, resettlement resources should be dispensed in two ways, as interest-free loans to the settlers from an internationally financed revolving fund, and as grants to the receiving countries to help them absorb the new settlers. Finally, to advance resolution of the refugee problem and enhance the peace process it is imperative to conduct a survey of refugee preference, explore ways to coopt them in the design and implementation of feasible solutions, and establish an international fund to extend interest-free loans to settlers and grants to the countries as soon as resettlement becomes possible.

REFERENCES

Abed, George, ed., *The Economic Viability of a Palestinian State*, (Washington, D.C.: Institute for Palestine Studies).

Abu Zayyad, Ziad, "The Palestinian Right of Return: A Realistic Approach," *Palestine-Israel Journal*, Spring 1994, 2.

Britannica Book of the Year, 1994, (Chicago: Encyclopaedia Britannica, Inc., 1994), p. 254

Perez, Don, "Palestinian Refugees and Middle East Stability," (Washington, D.C.: DARSP, Nov. 1992).

Khalidi, Rashid, "Observations on the Right of Right of Return," *Journal of Palestine Studies*, Winter 1982, 21(2).

The Center for Engineering and Planning, Ramalla, West Bank, *Masterplanning the state of Palestine*, March 1992

Tuma, Elias H. and H. Darin-Drabkin, *The Economic Case for Palestine*, (Croom-Helm, 1978).

Tuma, Elias H., *Peacemaking and the Immoral War. Arabs and Jews in the Middle East*, (Harper and Row, 1972).

THE GEO-ECONOMICS OF THE IRAQ-KUWAIT CONFLICT:

A RETROSPECTIVE COMPARATIVE ANALYSIS

Abbas P. Grammy
Department of Economics
California State University, Bakersfield
9001 Stockdale Highway
Bakersfield, CA 93311

Richard G. Quiring
Department of Social Sciences
Highland High School
2900 Royal Scots Way
Bakersfield, CA 93306

Abstract—In this chapter, we will explore the geo-economic motives of the Iraqi invasion of Kuwait. We will provide a comparative data analysis to demonstrate the economic conditions which prompted Iraq to annex Kuwait in an attempt to emerge as a regional super power. Then, we will analyze the historical trends of the level of per capita real GNP for Iraq and Kuwait, and investigate the convergence possibilities of their future trends under two retrospective scenarios of *status quo* and *war*.

I. BACKGROUND

Iraq is virtually a *land-locked* nation and has historically remained a *river-state* economy. It has a narrow window to the Persian Gulf, the Shatt al-Arab: a common 100 mile channel connecting the Tigris and Euphrates

Rivers that restricts the country's coastline to a mere 37 miles without any deep water port.[1] In addition to the slender physique of the Shatt al-Arab, Iraq's access to open water became even more limited by the Algiers Agreement of 1975 which shifted the Iran-Iraq boundary from the east bank of the Shatt al-Arab to the deepest part of the channel.[2]

Such geographical constraints have forced Iraq to depend highly on several infrastructural arrangements with neighboring countries of Jordan, Saudi Arabia, Syria, and Turkey to accommodate systematically its rapidly expanding flow of foreign trade. Highways and railways parallel to the rivers connect Iraq to Kuwait, Saudi Arabia, and Iran in the south and Syria and Turkey in the north. The transdesert Baghdad-Agabah Highway through Amman has become Iraq's back door to facilitate the importation of a wide range of consumer and producer goods and the exportation of oil in a return flow.[3] In addition, Iraq has expanded its oil export capacity by constructing successive pipeline systems to the Mediterranean coasts through Syria and Turkey and by connecting across northern Saudi Arabia to intersect with Saudi's petro-line.[4] Consequently, Iraq has become immeasurably more dependent on the goodwill of its neighbors to expedite the exportation of petroleum and the subsequent earnings of foreign exchange. In addition to damages to Iraq's oil export facilities during the Iran-Iraq War, a series of disputes between Syria and Iraq and the recent Iraq-Kuwait conflict have forced indefinite closure of all Iraqi pipeline systems, thus depriving its economy of desirable foreign currency.[5]

Kuwait, on the other hand, is a *maritime city-state* economy. It has taken advantage of its geographical location on a deep coastal indentation to build a rapidly expanding economy which has exclusively relied on maritime activities. Its superb harbor on Kuwait Bay provides the greatest port potential in the northern Persian Gulf coastal area by accommodating fishing, pearling, boat handling, and trade.[6] Oil discovery in 1938 brought

---

1. Colbert C. Held, *Middle East Patterns: Places, Peoples, and Politics* (Boulder: Westview Press, 1989), p. 262.
2. Ibid., pp. 180-181.
3. Ibid., pp. 269-270.
4. ibid., pp. 112-113.
5. Ibid., p. 203.
6. Ibid., pp. 293-294.

immense wealth and rapid socio-economic development to Kuwait in a few decades. Since its independence in 1961 from Great Britain, Kuwait has achieved economic viability amongst the Gulf states. The major thrust of Kuwait's affluence rests on four pillars: favorable geographical location, small population, enormous petroleum reserves, and large foreign investments. With 225 miles of coastline and a deep water port, population of less than 3 million, the second largest proven oil reserves in the Middle East of 92 billion barrels in 1987 with an average daily production of over 1.3 million barrels during 1976-85, and more than 85 billion dollars in foreign investments in 1987, Kuwait has emerged as a consumer-oriented economy with one of the highest per capita incomes in the world.[7]

Historically, Iraq has claimed sovereignty over Kuwait based on Ottoman territorial arrangements which included parts of northern Kuwait. By 1915, the expansion of Kuwaiti influence and preeminence of the Al-Sabah family enabled Kuwait to double its size. However, it was not until the respective signators inked the Treaty of Uqayr in 1922 that Kuwait's British protectors negotiated half of the principality's enlarged territory back to Saudi Arabia and Iraq. In 1961 when Kuwait gained full independence from the British, Iraq claimed sovereignty over the emirates and made several threatening gestures. The crisis subsided when Britain sent troops to Kuwait. In 1973, Iraq laid claim to the Kuwaiti islands of Warbah and Bubiyan (two mud flats blocking Iraq's access to the Persian Gulf and command the approaches to the Iraqi naval base at Umm Qasr) and then occupied the Kuwaiti border post of Semite in the mainland. A military clash ensued. Although Iraq withdrew from Kuwait in 1974, additional border incidents continued. Iraq's offer to lease the islands was rejected by Kuwait because of national security considerations. Relations between the two states remained tense during the decade of the 1970s due to differences in territorial and ideological issues. In the 1980s, however, Kuwait politically supported and financially assisted Iraq in its war against Iran. During the war, Iran's ideological and military aims included the intimidation of Kuwait in order to facilitate a cessation of the conduit for money and materials for the Iraqi war efforts.[8]

---

7. Ibid., pp. 292-297.
8. David E. Long and Bernard Reich, *The Government and Politics of the Middle East and North Africa*, (Boulder: Westview Press, 1986), pp. 117-119.

The recent Iraq-Kuwait crisis was fueled by the Iraqi claim that Kuwait was helping lower the world crude oil prices by exceeding the Organization for Petroleum Exporting Countries (OPEC) prescribed quota. Reduced oil prices would obviously lower the export proceeds to Iraq and subsequently cripple the Iraqi economy at a time when it was struggling to reconstruct its war-torn economy and pay off 80 billion dollars of war debts. Moreover, Iraq complained that Kuwait had "stolen" 2.4 billion dollars of oil from its Rumaila Field by slanting wells down from the small Kuwaiti corner of the field. Iraq demanded that Kuwait should pay between 13 and 15 billion dollars in reparations, forgive 10 billion dollars in war debts, rectify its border line 45 miles to the south, give up its corner of the Rumaila Oil Field, and grant a long lease on the two islands of Warbah and Bubiyan. Negotiations between the two countries failed even after Kuwait agreed to reduce oil production and OPEC raised oil prices. The Iraqi geo-economics calculations, which led to the invasion of Kuwait and the ensuing Persian Gulf War, demonstrated that by combining the OPEC quotas of Iraq and Kuwait and by forcing oil prices up to 30 dollars per barrel, Iraq would earn 60 billion dollars each year to double its reconstruction budget, pay-off its war debts, and considerably expand its coastlines to include a deep water port.[9]

This chapter will explore the economic motives and consequences of the Iraqi invasion of Kuwait. Section II will provide a comparative data analysis to demonstrate the socio-economic motives and conditions which prompted Iraq to annex Kuwait in an attempt to emerge as a regional super power. Section III studies militarism in Iraq and the historical trends in its military expenditures. In section IV, we simulate the prospective economic trends of Iraq and Kuwait based on two retrospective scenarios of the *status quo* and *war*. The final section will include deductions made from the data provided in the previous sections.

---

9. Tom Mathews, "The Road to War: A Behind-the-Scenes Account of Gross Errors and Deft Maneuvers," *Newsweek* (January 28, 1991), pp. 54-65 and Hermann F. Eilts, "The Persian Gulf Crisis: Perspectives and Prospects," *The Middle East Journal*, 45(1), 1991, pp. 7-22.

II. COMPARATIVE ECONOMIC DEVELOPMENT

We argue that Iraq's militarism and expansionism, coupled with rapid economic deterioration with no anticipated positive trends in the future, motivated the invasion of Kuwait and perhaps Saudi Arabia. Iraq attempted to justify its military aggression against its former allies and Muslim "brothers" on the basis of its territorial claim over Kuwait, the border dispute, oil exploration and pricing policies. However, gaining access to the upper Persian Gulf coastlines and control of the enormous Kuwaiti wealth were to be more probable motives for Iraq to invade Kuwait.

Data presented in Table 1 demonstrate the differentials between resource endowments and socio-economic conditions of the two countries. Iraq is nearly 25 times larger than Kuwait and Iraq's population is virtually 7 times greater. But, Kuwait's population is more urbanized and more rapidly growing. With such high rates of population growth, both Iraq and Kuwait are expected to double their populations in less than twenty years.

Although quite diminutive in size, Kuwait is credited with nearly twice the proven petroleum reserves of neighboring Iraq. In 1987, the reserves were estimated to be 91.9 billion barrels for Kuwait compared to 47.1 billion barrels for Iraq. In fact, the combined Iraq-Kuwait proven oil reserves of 139.0 billion barrels would have enabled Iraq to effectively challenge Saudi Arabia with her 166.5 billion barrels as the world's dominant oil exporting nation. A combination of Iraq-Kuwait proven oil reserves would have amounted to more than 34 percent of the world's proven reserve with significant leverage on pricing formulas.[10] If Saudi Arabia became entangled in the Iraq-Kuwait web, regardless of circumstances, this *trio* would have controlled an imense 75 percent of the world's known reserves. During 1976-85, daily petroleum production in thousands of barrels averaged 1,872 in Iraq and 1,341 in Kuwait. The combined Iraq-Kuwait average daily production of 3,212 thousands of barrels would have been slightly larger than that of Iran, but considerably smaller than that of Saudi Arabia.[11]

---

10. Held, pp. 115-7.
11. Ibid., pp. 117-8.

Table 1. Comparative Socio-economic Development

Indicator	Kuwait	Iraq	Kuwait as percentage of Iraq
Area (thousands of square miles)	6.9	169.2	4.1
Population (millions, mid-1990)	2.7	18.9	14.3
Population growth rate (%, 1963-88)	4.4	3.5	118.9
Population doubling time (years)	17	19	119.0
Urban population (% of total, 1989)	95	71	133.8
Proven petroleum reserves (billions of barrels, 1987)	91.9	47.1	195.2
Petroleum production (thousands of barrels average daily output, 1976-85)	1,341	1,872	68.4
GNP per capita (constant 1988 U.S. dollars, 1988)	13,811	3,738	369.5
GNP growth rate (%, constant 198 U.S. dollars, 1963-88)	-5.0	-4.6	87.0
GDP share of industry (%, most recent years)	56	46	121.7
GNP share of military (%, 1985)	6.1	30.7	19.9
Physical Quality of Life Index (1985)	84	53	158.5
Disparity Reduction Rate (%, 1980-85)	7.3	1.9	384.2
Life expectancy (years, 1989)	74	63	117.5
Adult literacy (%, 1985)	70	89	78.7
Infant mortality (per 1000 live births, 1989)	15	67	22.4
Population per physician (1984)	640	1,740	36.8
Birth attended by medical staff (%, 1985)	99	50	198.0
Daily calorie supply (per capita, 1988)	3,132	2,962	105.7
Primary school enrollment (% of age group, 1988)	93	96	96.9
Secondary school enrollment (% of age group, 1988)	81	47	172.3

Source: *World Development Report*, various issues, *World Military Expenditures and Arms Transfer* (Washington, D.C.: United States Arms Control and Disarmament Agency, 1989) and *Worldfact Book* (Washington, D.C.: The Central Intelligence Agency, 1987).

Compared with Iraq, Kuwait has enjoyed a higher standard of living. In 1988, the per capita real Gross National Product (GNP) of Kuwait was nearly four times larger than that of Iraq. During the 1963-1988, however, both Kuwait and Iraq recorded large negative GNP growth rates. A higher Gross Domestic Product (GDP) share of industry indicated that the Kuwaiti economy was more industrialized, whereas a higher GNP share of military spending suggested that the Iraqi economy was more militarized.

The Physical Quality of Life Index (PQLI) in 1985 was 84 for Kuwait, 31 points higher than that of her counterpart. Compared with Iraq, Kuwait's life expectancy was eleven years higher, while its infant mortality rate was much lower. However, adult literacy was higher in Iraq. The Kuwaiti population had better access to medical facilities as indicated by a lower number of the population per physician and higher percentage of births attended by medical staff. Also, the standard of nutrition as measured by daily per capita calorie supply was higher in Kuwait. Although, the primary school enrollment was considerably high in both countries, the secondary school enrollment ratio was almost twice as large in Kuwait. As a consequence of improved standards of health, nutrition, and education, Kuwait enjoyed a much higher rate of social development than Iraq, as measured by the Disparity Reduction Rate (DRR).[12]

Our comparative data analysis suggests that although Iraq is better endowed with a larger area and population, Kuwait has been able to achieve a higher level of socio-economic development. Of the 21 development indicators examined above, 13 favor Kuwait. They are proven petroleum reserves, urbanization rate, per capita real GNP, GDP share of industry, GNP share of military spending, life expectancy, infant mortality, population per physician, births attended by medical staff, daily per

---

12. The PQLI is an unweighted mean of the index of infant mortality, index of life expectancy, and rate of adult literacy. The DRR measures the change in the PQLI during a certain time interval by the following formula:

$$DRR = 1 - (\frac{100 - PQLI_{t+n}}{100 - PQLI_t})^{\frac{1}{n}}$$

where t indicates the initial time period and n is the time interval (see Morris 1979). For detailed explanation, see Morris D. Morris, *Measuring the Conditions of the World's Poor: The Physical Quality of Life Index*, (London: Frank Gass, 1979).

capita calorie supply, secondary school enrollment ratio, the PQLI, and the DRR.

III. MILITARISM IN IRAQ

Iraq has been ruled by successive military governments since July 1958 when King Faysal II and his closest advisors and relatives were murdered in a coup d'etat by General Abd Al-Karim Qassim. The Qassim government fell, in turn, to a coup in 1963 that initially brought power to the Baath (Arab Renaissance Party). Soon the Baath was ousted. After coup attempts failed in 1965 and 1966, a decisive Baath coup succeeded in July 1968. It has since retained power with a one-party political system under the leadership of General Hasan Al-Bakr until July 1979, with the chief executive role falling to Saddam Huysayn Al-Takriti.

Since the mid 1960s, Iraq has allocated an ever-increasing amount of public expenditure to expand and modernize its military industry. Militarism served the state to overcome both internal and external security threats and challenges. The government, which represents the Sunni Arabs (21.9 percent of the 1988 population) has frequently used force against the Shiite Arabs and Persians (53.5 percent of the 1988 population) and Kurds (19.0 percent of the 1988 population) in order to maintain dominance and control. Military growth and modernization have been also justified to support the Arab-Israeli conflict and the on-going territorial and ideological disputes with Iran and Syria. Furthermore, favorable budgetary conditions, especially in the 1970s due to exorbitant oil price increases, enabled Iraq to allocate more resources to expand its armed forces.

Table 2 presents income and military expenditure in Iraq during 1970-88. Two distinct trends can be identified in Iraq's income and military data. First, one notes a pre Iran-Iraq War expansionary period of 1970-80 during which Iraq's per capita real GNP rose from 4,250 to 9,440 dollars, at an average annual growth rate of 6.3 percent. Meanwhile, her per capita military expenditure rose at an average rate of 7.5 percent from 829 to 2,123 dollars; the share of military expenditure increased from 19.5 to 22.5 percent; the number of members of the armed forces rose from 10.4 to 32.6 per 1,000 population. Iraq became a major importer of armaments as

Table 2. Income and Military Expenditures in Iraq

Year	GNP per Capita (constant 1988 US $)	Military Spending per Capita (constant 1988 US $)	GNP Share of Military Spending (percentage)	Import Share of Arms (percentage)	Armed Forces (per 1,000 people)
1968	4,250	829	19.5	57.7	10.2
1969	4,272	1,015	23.7	28.9	9.9
1970	4,213	929	22.0	18.0	10.1
1971	4,218	887	21.0	10.8	10.8
1972	4,500	883	19.6	36.1	10.5
1973	4,860	1,130	23.2	124.6	9.9
1974	4,875	1,309	26.8	48.7	10.2
1975	5,905	1,198	20.3	25.3	10.4
1976	6,174	1,172	19.0	43.3	10.9
1977	6,467	1,169	18.1	48.7	11.8
1978	7,114	1,368	19.2	57.0	29.4
1979	9,242	1,380	14.8	44.6	35.0
1980	9,440	2,123	22.5	17.2	32.6
1981	5,140	2,319	45.1	20.3	28.6
1982	4,780	2,141	44.8	33.0	28.5
1983	4,429	2,007	45.3	57.5	29.5
1984	4,516	1,921	42.5	83.0	51.8
1985	4,268	1,312	30.7	44.5	49.9
1986	3,468	1,204	34.7	55.9	48.9
1987	3,890	1,064	27.3	74.2	52.9
1988	3,738	933	25.0	37.1	56.8

Source: *World Military Expenditures and Arms Transfers* (Washington, D.C.: United States Arms Control and Disarmament Agency, 1989).

its import share of arms sharply increased during the energy boom of the 1970s, reaching an all time high of 124.6 percent in 1973 before declining to 17.2 percent in 1980.

During the Iran-Iraq War period of 1980-88, Iraq's per capita real GNP declined from 5,140 to only 3,738 dollars; this represented an average annual decay rate of 3.4 percent, while the per capita military expenditure reduced from 2,319 to 933 dollars. In spite of such rapid economic decline, the GNP share of military expenditure climbed from 22.5 percent in 1980 to its highest value of 45.3 percent in 1983 before declining to 25 percent in 1988. The import share of arms increased from 20.3 percent in 1981 to 83 percent in 1984, declined to 55.9 percent in 1986, rose to 74.2 percent in 1987, and then finally dropped to 37.1 percent in 1988. In the meantime, the number of the armed forces continued to increase to an all time record of 56.8 per 1,000 people in 1988. Indeed, by the end of the Iran-Iraq War, Iraq became the sixth largest military force in the world with nearly 1 million soldiers. Nevertheless, Iraq's inability to permanently annex Iran's oil-producing province of Khyuzistan across the Shatt al-Arab coupled with its rapidly deteriorating economy and mounting war debts created conditions conducive to military occupation of Kuwait, which politically and financially supported Iraq in its war against Iran.

IV. Retrospective Economic Forecasts

As argued above, Iraq's decision to invade Kuwait was motivated by geo-economic and military considerations. The following prospective analysis is an attempt to investigate possible trends in the Kuwait-Iraq per capita GNP gap in the 1990s when their economies greatly declined during the Iraqi invasion of Kuwait and the ensuing Persian Gulf War. For comparative purposes, we apply two retrospective scenarios of the *status quo* and *war* to predict values of the per capita GNP for each country.

Kuwait has always had a higher level of real per capita GNP than Iraq. However, data indicate that their per capita income gap continuously narrowed prior to their recent military conflict in 1990. As depicted in Figure 1, their *absolute* income gap, $\left| Y_t^I - Y_t^k \right|$, in constant 1988 United States dollars gradually declined from 62,800 in 1960 to 9,700 in 1989. On average, their *absolute* income gap narrowed from 42,600 dollars in the 1960s to 23,500 dollars in the 1970s and 15,500 dollars in the 1980s. Likewise, as shown in Figure 2, their *relative* income gap, $\left[(Y_t^I / Y_t^k) * 100 \right]$, gradually narrowed from 5 percent in 1960 to 28 percent in 1989. Their average *rela-*

tive income gap narrowed from 9 percent in the 1960s to 20 percent in the 1970s and 24 percent in the 1980s.[13]

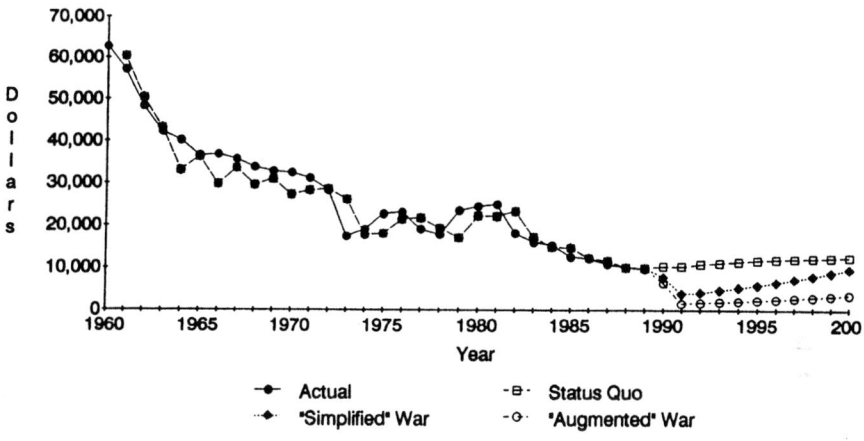

Figure 1. Absolute Income Gap

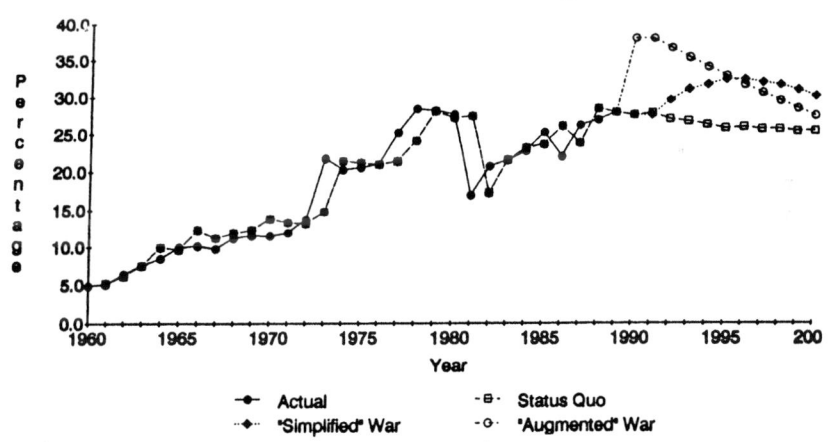

Figure 2. Relative Income Gap

The narrowing of their per capita GNP gap resulted from demographic and economic growth differentials that favored Iraq. During 1960-89, Kuwait's population increased at an average annual rate of 8 percent from

---

13. Calculated from *International Financial Statistics Yearbook*.

0.25 to 2 million. Meanwhile, its GNP grew at an average annual rate of 3 percent from 15 to 27 billion dollars, reaching a peak level of 46 billion dollars in 1980. As a result of population growth faster than economic growth, Kuwait's per capita GNP declined at an average annual rate of 5 percent from 65,900 dollars in 1960 to 13,500 dollars in 1989.

During the same time period, Iraq's population grew at an average annual rate of 3.3 percent from 7.2 to 18.2 million. In the meantime, its real GNP grew at an average annual rate of 4.9 percent from 22 to 69 billion dollars, reaching a peak level of 125 billion in 1980. Iraq's per capita GNP grew at an average annual rate of 1.7 percent from 3,000 dollars in 1960 to 3,800 dollars in 1989. By 1980, Iraq achieved its highest level of per capita GNP of nearly 9,500 dollars. In the 1980s, however, its per capita GNP rapidly deteriorated at an average rate of 7.3 percent.[14]

To focus on the narrowing tendencies in the income gaps between Kuwait and Iraq, we examine the convergence hypothesis: the long run tendency for a "lagging" economy to catch up with the productivity level of a "leading" economy at a rate which is inversely related to the initial productivity level of the "lagging" economy. The rationale for income convergence is that capital formation in the "leading" economy contributes to productivity growth by embodying recent advances in technology, whereas investment in the "lagging" economy can draw upon a larger pool of technology that includes these recent advances plus a larger reserve of previously available but unused technology. This hypothesis suggests productivity growth in the "lagging" economy must be higher than that in the "leading" economy in order for their income gap to close.

To investigate time-series convergence, we note the study by Alam (1991) who estimated a linear regression model $GY_t = a + b\, RY_t + u_t$, where GY is the annual growth rate of per capita real income of the "lagging" economy (i.e., Iraq) minus that of the "leading" economy (i.e., Kuwait), RY is the ratio of per capita real income of the "lagging" economy to that of the "leading" economy (i.e., the relative income gap) for the same year and u is a random error term. Here, $b<0$ indicates income convergence. Estimation results suggest no convergence tendency since the coefficient of RY is statistically insignificant.

---

14. Ibid.

$$GY_t = 10.27 - 0.06\ RY_t$$
$$(0.31) \tag{1}$$
$$r^2 = 0.03 \qquad d = 1.95 \qquad sse = 0.46$$

To model the historical trends of the per capita GNP, we note studies by Nelson and Plosser (1982) and Todd (1984) that found evidence that macroeconomic time-series behave like *random walks with drift*. To investigate the behavior of the per capita GNP time-series, we test for random walks. Following Pindyck and Rubinfeld (1991, pp. 455-6), we observe that the per capita GNP series are nonstationary as their autocorrelation functions barely decline, even up to a 5-period lag. They are, however, first-order homogeneous since their first-differenced series are stationary and appear to resemble white noise. To determine whether the differenced series are indeed white noise, we calculate the Box-Pierce Q-statistic for up to the first 5 lags. The computed values of the Q-statistic are all insignificant at the 0.10 level. We can, therefore, conclude that the differenced series are white noise and that the original per capita GNP series can be modeled as random walks (i.e., $Y_t = Y_{t-1} + e_t$). In addition, values of the Dickey-Fuller statistic from the *unit root* tests less than the MacKinnon critical value at the 0.01 level fail to reject the hypothesis that the per capita GNP follows a random walk (Pindyck and Rubinfeld, 1991, pp. 459-62).

Results from extrapolation models suggest that the natural logarithmic linear regression has the best fit for the per capita GNP time-series. Regression models estimate slope coefficients significantly different from zero but insignificantly different from one, with uncorrelated residual:[15]

$$\ln Y = 0.17 + 1.24 \ln Y_{-1} - 0.67 \ln Y_{-2} + 0.40 \ln Y_{-3}$$
$$(0.19) \qquad (0.28) \qquad (0.40) \tag{2}$$
$$r^2 = 0.91 \qquad\qquad sse = 0.31$$

$$\ln Y = 1.63 + 1.01 \ln Y_{-1} - 0.25 \ln Y_{-2} + 0.04 \ln Y_{-3}$$
$$(0.20) \qquad (0.29) \qquad (0.20) \tag{3}$$
$$r^2 = 0.72 \qquad\qquad sse = 0.52$$

---

15. The number of lags is determined by using the FPE criterion. The Lagrange Multiplier test for first order serial correlation indicate the absence of serially-correlated residuals.

In the *status quo*, we reexamine the convergence hypothesis using the predicted per capita income values from the above equations for the period of 1960-2000. Estimation results identify a convergence tendency between the per capita GNP

$$GY_t = 12.06 - 0.40\, Ry_t$$
$$(0.23) \quad\quad\quad\quad\quad (4)$$
$$r^2 = 0.07 \quad\quad d = 2.00 \quad\quad sse = 0.47$$

of Iraq and Kuwait since the estimated coefficient of RY is significant at the 0.10 percent level when first degree serial correlation is corrected.

Although the war-torn economies of Iraq and Kuwait have greatly declined, reconstruction began--though at a different pace and direction--shortly after the war that ended in March 1991. Still, the full extent of damages to human, physical, and social-overhead capital are hard to access. Since prognostication is not exact, one-year decay rates of 25, 50, and 75 percent for the years of 1990 and/or 1991 are considered. Per annum recovery rates of 2.5 to 7.5 percent are also cause for deliberations. From all combinations, a scenario of *war* applies selected decay and recovery possibilities. The "simplified" *war* scenario assumes a decay rate of 50 percent in 1991 and an annual recovery rate of 3 percent beginning 1992 for both economies. The "augmented" *war* scenario assumes decay rates of 25 percent in 1990 and 75 percent in 1991 for Kuwait and 75 percent in 1991 for Iraq, and annual recovery rates of 7.5 percent for Kuwait and 3.75 percent for Iraq beginning 1992. The rationale for variable decay rates is due to the extent of damages inflicted upon Kuwait by the Iraqi invasion in 1990 and near full devastation of both economies during the ensuing Persian Gulf War. The reason for variable recovery rates is due to assistance from the global community to rebuild Kuwait, but the imposition of the United Nations sanctions on Iraq. These high recovery rates may not seem unrealistic after such large declines have occurred.

Estimation results of both the "simplified" and "augmented" *war* scenarios indicate

$$GY_t = 10.95 - 0.30\, RY_t$$
$$(0.20) \quad\quad\quad\quad\quad (5)$$
$$r^2 = 0.06 \quad\quad d = 2.00 \quad\quad sse = 0.46$$

and
$$GY_t = 10.10 - 0.27\, RY_t$$
$$(0.20) \tag{6}$$
$$r^2 = 0.05 \quad d = 1.96 \quad sse = 0.48$$

insignificant convergence tendencies between the level of per capita incomes of the two countries.

We make three inferences from the empirical results and graphical presentations: (1) although their per capita GNP gap was narrowing, there was no significant evidence of income convergence during 1960-89; (2) should the historical trends continued, their per capita GNP gap would have continued to narrow to warrant significant convergence; and (3) the *war* scenarios suggest no evidence of income convergence. In retrospect, therefore, *war* prevented Iraq to continue to narrow its income gap with Kuwait.

V. CONCLUSION

Considering that the demographic and economic trends favored Iraq, a rational choice for Iraq should have been the implementation of policies of long-term growth to further bridge its per capita income gap with Kuwait, rather than becoming involved in a military invasion and an international war. When the Iran-Iraq War ended, Iraq's deliberate policies of economic development could have aimed at attracting additional petro-dollars of investment funds to reconstruct its war-torn economy. Consequently, Iraq would have been able to achieve a reasonably higher real GNP growth rates to close its gap with Kuwait. Unfortunately, though, Iraq relied on militarism and expansionism to overcome its geographical constraints and to improve its economic conditions. Incorrect policy choices leading to the Iran-Iraq War and the Persian Gulf War have resulted in rapidly declining standards of living in Iraq. Such devastating economic declines indicate that external military conflicts have ruined the benefits of rapid growth experienced prior to 1980, thus leaving Iraq with several decades of economic reconstruction.

REFERENCES

Alam, M.S., "Convergence Tendencies: Some Time-Series Results," *Southern Economic Journal*, 1991, 57(3), 841-7.

Eilts, H. F., "The Persian Gulf Crisis: Perspectives and Prospects," *The Middle East Journal* 45(1), 1991, 7-22.

Held, C. C., *The Middle East Patterns, Peoples, and Politics* (Boulder: Westview Press, 1989).

International Financial Statistics Yearbook, (Washington, D.C.: International Monetary Fund, various issues).

Long, D. E. and B. Reich, *The Government of Politics of the Middle East and North Africa* (Boulder: Westview Press, 1986).

Mathews, T., "The Road to War: A Behind-the-Scenes Account of Gross Errors and Deft Maneuvers," *Newsweek*, January 28, 1991, 54-65.

Morris, M.D., *Measuring the Conditions of the World's Poor: The Physical Quality of Life Index* (London: Frank Gass, 1979).

Nelson, C.R. and C.I. Plosser, "Trends and Random Walks in Macroeconomic Time Series: Some Evidence and Implications," *Journal of Monetary Economics*, 1982, 10, 139-62.

Pindyck, R. S. and D. L. Rubinfeld, *Econometric Models and Economic Forecasts*, (New York: McGraw Hill, 1991).

Todd, R. M., "Improving Economic Forecasting with Bayesian Vector Autoregression," Federal Reserve Bank of Minneapolis *Quarterly Review*, Fall 1984.

World Development Report (Washington, D.C.: World Bank, various issues).

World Military Expenditures and Arms Transfer, (Washington, D.C.: U.S. Arms Control and Disarmament Agency, 1989).

World Factbook, (Washington, D.C.: The Central Intelligence Agency, 1987).

ORTHODOX STRATEGIES IN A "DISENABLING" ENVIRONMENT: POLITICO-ECONOMIC DECLINE IN SUB-SAHARAN AFRICA

Marlyn A. Madison
Department of Political Science
and Criminal Justice
California State University, Fullerton
Fullerton, CA 92634

Abstract—Structural adjustment policies have failed to restore growth significantly in Sub-Saharan Africa after more than a decade. The major responsibility for the current malaise rests with orthodox approaches to Africa's economic problems enhanced by the ideals of the New World Order. Democratization, liberalization and limited government involvement has contributed to political instability. Further application of macroeconomics under the auspices of New World Order will do little to improve the fundamental challenge of development--human development.

I. INTRODUCTION

The post-Cold War era held the promise of creating an order more conducive to growth in the developing world. Elimination of tensions between the East and West should have reduced the ideological conflict and released resources for constructive purposes. Unfortunately, the emerging unipolar environment held some reason to be skeptical about the willingness of major actors to commit themselves to bettering the conditions of the weaker and less powerful actors in the world. Without superpower competition, what was a significant reason for advanced industrial countries to assist developing countries in Sub-Saharan Africa or elsewhere was replaced by other short-run, self-serving priorities. Two ideals exemplify the basic focus of the New World Order and illustrate this type of behavior in the African context: democratization and liberalization.

During the last decade the World Bank has publicly espoused a commitment to sustainable growth and development in the African region as its highest priority (Jaycox, 1996, p. 50). In spite of these pronouncements, the development prospects of Sub-Saharan Africa remain problematic. Africa's troubled development trajectory was initially documented in the World Bank (IBRD) study, *Accelerated Development* (1982). As the debt crisis emerged throughout the African region, the International Monetary Fund (IMF) administered "shock therapy" through its stabilization programs; meanwhile, the Bank encouraged states in the region to undertake medium-range structural adjustment. These orthodox solutions were supposed to turn the situation around. They did not.

As the post-Cold War era began, structural adjustment was already in trouble in the African region. Continued economic stagnation was increasingly being accompanied by political instability. Weak or negative economic growth rates, combined with austerity measures, fueled noisy protests against debt burdens. Economic stagnation also encouraged internal challenges to stabilization programs and economic liberalization (Nelson, 1990). Nevertheless, consistent with the logic of the New World Order, the Bank and IMF encouraged countries to democratize and liberalize as solutions to the problems. Why have structural adjustment policies and the ideals of the New World Order failed to deliver the prescribed results? What are the implications of the region's predicament for United States policy makers and the New World Order?

This paper will argue that environmental constraints make it unlikely that structural adjustment efforts will assist Sub-Saharan Africa in producing economic growth given current donor priorities. The situation becomes even more precarious as orthodox policy solutions concentrate on limiting as opposed to enabling states. In a "disenabling economic environment" (Jaycox, 1995, p. 50) calls for increasing democratization and liberalization undermine stability in Sub-Saharan Africa. Promoting stability requires alternatives emphasizing human development and institution-building rather than either democratization or liberalization.

II. THE CONTEXT OF STRUCTURAL ADJUSTMENT

Barbara Stallings argues that the post-Cold War era has spawned a massive rivalry among major capitalist trading states (Stallings, 1993, p. 4). One of the key elements in this rivalry is the ability to develop or improve on technology. Developing the type of commercial technology needed to maintain comparative advantage in trade is based on having an independent, resourceful, technological base. John Zysman argues that both Europe and Japan are seeking and increasingly establishing independent R & D bases through purposeful political strategies in their economies and through industrial development. The United States however, remains the country with "the deepest and broadest technological and scientific capacities." (Zysman, 1991, p. 85). Newly industrialized countries are also creating their own fledgling technological bases.

Another important feature of trading relations in the post-Cold War era is increased regionalism. Barbara Stallings suggests that differentiation of developing countries will occur in the context of regional spheres of influence established by rival capitalist powers: the European Community, Japan and the United States. Developing countries associated with the most dynamic advanced countries stand to gain at the expense of developing countries associated with less dynamic industrialized countries (Stallings, 1993). East and Southeast Asian exporting countries are seen as integrally linked to Japanese and financial networks. The European Community, or more specifically Germany, is expected to have a similar relationship with Eastern Europe. Mexico may benefit from U. S. investment under the North American Free Trade Agreement. The developing countries left out of the scenario have the weakest prospects. Where does this leave the countries of Sub-Saharan Africa?

"Marginalization" is the concept used frequently by analysts to describe the African region's position in the international economy of the post-Cold War era (Ravenhill 1993; Callaghy 1993). Lacking technological bases, dynamic regional partners, or strong industrial infrastructures, these states face the possibility of being limited to primary product exporters in the post-Cold War order (Nelson 1990). The international economy is logically perceived as a generally inhospitable environment by African states.

Meanwhile, the failure of the socialist model in the Soviet Union and Eastern Europe has encouraged Western policymakers to accept the virtues of democracy and the market as fact and support widespread application of these principles. These attitudes are strongly reflected in the World Bank and the International Monetary Fund. Asymmetrical power relations between Northern donor countries and African recipients, apparent in the early 1980s, have become more pronounced in the post-Cold War era. In spite of continued economic stagnation under structural adjustment, African leaders have no alternatives except to continue with problematic policies.

III. Assessing the Reforms

After nearly a decade of structural adjustment in Sub-Saharan Africa, the Bank is on the defensive. The Bank's response is largely due to the poor growth rates in the area. In the Bank's *Adjustment in Africa:Reforms, Results, and the Road Ahead* (1994) only six African countries out of the twenty-nine surveyed demonstrate positive rates of economic growth due to improved macroeconomic policies. The median increase in the growth rate of the six states is almost two percent of gross domestic product (GDP) per capita. The increase reflects a shift from negative growth to an average 1.1 percent a year during 1987-91 (IBRD, 1994). Although growth resumed, the rate clearly is not impressive.

Many of the remaining African states displayed negative growth rates and continued inappropriate macroeconomic policies. In light of this situation, the Bank argues:

> However, reforms remain incomplete. No African country has achieved a sound macroeconomic policy stance--which in broad terms means inflation under 10 percent, a very low budget deficit, and a competitive exchange rate. In a third of the countries, macroeconomic policies actually deteriorated over the decade. Furthermore, countries are still taxing their farmers heavily, through marketing boards and/or overvalued exchange rates.

Most countries have further to go in eliminating nontariff barriers and adopting a moderate, tariff-based level of protection. Social spending, while not showing an overall decline during the adjustment period, is misallocated within the health and education sectors. And the politically difficult reform of the public enterprise and financial sectors lags well behind (IBRD 1994, pp. 1-2).

In spite of the obvious reasons for concern, the Bank remains committed to structural adjustment packages based on orthodox policy prescriptions. It recognizes the need for "rethinking" in light of some clear-cut problems: inadequate levels of consensus or insufficient resources in finance and the public sector. But the Bank is unwilling to admit that its policies are poorly designed for the African region because of donor priorities.

It should be noted that all of the Bank's empirical studies on Sub-Saharan Africa (except *Africa's Adjustment and Growth in the 1980s* in 1989) have indicated that structural adjustment is not working. In terms of growth and other domestic indicators, Sub-Saharan African countries implementing bank programs performed worse on average than countries not undertaking adjustment (Weeks, 1995). The situation has encouraged the Economic Commission on Africa (ECA) and several other agencies to issue strong criticisms of the reforms. Meanwhile, the original consensus within Washington has dwindled in the face of the results. Thus, the search is on for policies that may or may not be more heterodox in nature (Kahler, 1990). As for Africa's development prospects, they seem to have been put on hold while the policymakers wrestle with the impact of the following constraints on Africa's development.

IV. DEBT AND GROWTH

Sub-Saharan African countries have serious problems producing growth because of their external debt load. There are opportunity costs associated with an excessive debt burden; thus, its impact on development prospects must be considered. The average ratio of external debt to exports of the region was 362 percent of total exports in 1989. More than half of the countries in the region are considered highly indebted. And it is not unusual to see countries with debt burdens above 500 percent of total exports, particularly in countries having experienced civil strife (IBRD, 1991).

While the Bank notes the fact that these states have been able to continue making payments, the African states have only been able to avoid cash flow problems because of short-term lending from the IMF. The lending helped temporarily, but it added to the overall external debt burden (Nelson, 1990). The Bank is aware of other policy costs associated with constant efforts to renegotiate debts in African countries. Frequently, African policymakers find themselves involved in debt renegotiations when they are needed for other pressing matters (IBRD, 1994). In a region where bureaucracies are frequently short on technical expertise, constant renegotiations are an unwise use of scarce resource capacity.

One problem reducing the effectiveness of the reforms is inadequate investment and savings levels (IBRD, 1994). In the low-income countries of Sub-Saharan Africa, inadequate levels of investment present a real dilemma for a growth-oriented strategy. Median gross domestic investment in Africa's adjusting countries declined from more than 21 percent of GDP in the second half of the 1970s to 17 percent in the early 1980s. By the second half of the 1980s, it had slipped to 16 percent. Investment actually fell in thirteen of twenty-eight adjusting countries during the same period (IBRD, 1994,154). The Bank concedes that structural adjustment has a negative impact on investment. But it dismisses the problem as negligible because of the increased efficiency of the lower levels of investment (Weeks, 1995).

Denial of access to credit in the international market is another difficulty haunting African countries because of their heavy debt burdens. In theory, the international markets are open to everyone. In practice, they have traditionally excluded states considered uncreditworthy. They also excluded countries that are very poor. Sub-Saharan Africa clearly suffers from both of these problems. An "implicit bargain" between the African states and the international aid agencies was struck when the African states agreed to attempt economic reforms. If the African countries used orthodox approaches to reform their economies, under the guidance of the IMF and the Bank, international capital from the private sector would become available to them once again. The "implicit bargain" of increased foreign investment has not materialized (Callaghy, 1993). In essence, excessive debt burdens have contributed to the "marginalization" of the region in the international economy. The debt burden makes it difficult for the government or the people to help themselves by investing in their own development and attracting private capital.

Another critical area of concern is imports. The region's inability to purchase needed imports due to lack of foreign exchange is a serious constraint on development. During the period 1980-86, the volume of African imports fell on average by eight percent each year. The years of 1987 and 1988 saw further declines in the volume of imports in Sub-Saharan Africa. One of the most significant declines was registered in imports of capital goods. Machinery and transport equipment declined by 40 percent from 1981 to 1985-86.

The growth in export volumes during the first part of the 1980s was offset by deteriorating terms of trade. Movements in the terms of trade have cost African countries close to 25 percent of the purchasing power of their exports in the last decade (Ravenhill, 1993, p. 31). This loss was compounded by the fact that African states used between 10 to 50 percent of their export receipts to pay external debts in such circumstances (IBRD, 1991, pp. 251-2). There was no money for vital inputs for industrialization, for paying farmers higher prices for their goods through the marketing boards, or for investing in development per se.

Acknowledging the impact of debt on development, the Bank has supported debt reduction. From its perspective, debt reduction alone will not cure the problems of the countries in Africa. Current debt reduction efforts under Trinidad terms have not helped many African states. Only six of the twenty-one severely indebted low-income African states have sustainable debt loads under the Trinidad guidelines (IBRD, 1994). Clearly, more thorough and innovative approaches to eliminating the burden in Africa must be found before development can proceed.

V. EXPORTING AS THE KEY TO GROWTH

Traditionally, exporting the goods in which a state has a comparative advantage has been one of the main themes of the Bank's structural adjustment efforts. The Bank argues that Sub-Saharan Africa's inward-oriented policies failed to provide appropriate incentives for exporting; thus the sector was not able to help shift the region's economies toward sustained economic development as was the case in East Asia (IBRD, 1994). In this perspective, exports are "so beneficial", Sub-Saharan African countries are encouraged to apply an "exporters first rule" (IBRD, 1994)

This logic has been questioned by critics who argue that exporting does not naturally translate into rising national income. Latin America's experience in the 1980s suggest that the Bank's logic is flawed, particularly if the countries are heavily indebted and relying on the export of primary products (Kuczynski, 1988). Not surprisingly, Sub-Saharan Africa has not fared as well as Latin America using an export-led strategy.

The Bank recognizes that Sub-Saharan Africa faces an uphill battle because it relies on six agricultural exports to earn the bulk of its foreign exchange. Because these products are produced by other countries, the producers may not get favorable prices in the market. As for Africa's exports, from the Bank's perspective, this "adding-up" situation is "not serious in most cases". The elasticities can be managed (IBRD 1994, p. 90).

In practice, the Sub-Saharan African countries have not been able to escape the realities of a weak market in raw materials. For two of Africa's principal agricultural exports, cocoa and coffee, prices fell by 48 and 55 percent respectively between 1986 and 1989. Although the market was generally weak for raw materials, the "fallacy of composition" in the Bank's policy prescriptions suggests that Africa may not have a comparative advantage in agriculture at all (Ravenhill, 1993, p. 32).

If the region is "lucky" enough to increase production of its agricultural exports, the market may not yield the kind of rewards needed to support a viable export-led strategy without diversification. While the Bank feels that Africa needs to diversify its exports, it has no illusions about Africa's inability to follow the East Asian model of hi-tech industrial exporting. Current Bank policies suggest textile production as a possible alternative to primary product exports (IBRD, 1994). Unfortunately, the prices for low-value added products such as textiles may also be affected by an overcrowded market as many countries diversify using the same type of manufactured commodity directed to Northern markets.

The risks of the current international marketplace have encouraged some development experts to warn against excessive reliance on export-led strategies for development. These strategies subject a country to the fluctuations of the international marketplace. Tendencies towards protectionism, slower rates of growth in the global economy, and the emergence of exclusive trading blocs all suggest the need to look beyond exporting to produce an economic take-off in the region (Griffin and McKinley, 1994). Thus far, the Bank's "rethinking" has not moved towards reassessment of this aspect of structural adjustment.

The external constraints facing the states in Sub-Saharan Africa have clearly made it difficult for it to "get the basics right" (IBRD, 1993). Although the Bank has noted that the region is peculiarly vulnerable to external shocks, the success of countries in East Asia and the priorities of the post-Cold War era, have seemingly obfuscated reality. Reducing Africa's problems to "politics" and "commitment" has become commonplace. Meanwhile, the inefficiencies of public sector serve to justify ignoring the principal factor inhibiting effective development strategies: inadequate state capacity to enhance people's capabilities to live full, rich lives (Sen, 1992).

VI. ADJUSTMENT WITH LIMITED CAPACITY

The ability of African governments to implement adjustment reforms is dependent on the existence of adequate state capacity. Interestingly enough, state capacity is needed for implementing sound macroeconomic policy as well as managing external constraints such as reducing debt burdens and pushing exports in a precarious international economy. State capacity is identified with the existence of a significant number of well-trained and experience analytical staff in the central government or a technocratic elite (Nelson, 1990). This capacity is generally limited in most African states. According to some experts, it is not enough for a state to possess this expertise. It must be able to insulate its technocratic elite from special interests in order to effectively manage economic development (Haggard and Chung-in Moon, 1994). The ideals of the New World Order mitigate against this type of management in Sub-Saharan Africa.

> How does the Bank evaluate Africa's current level of technocratic expertise?

> Technical capacity is weak. Accountability and transparency are lacking. And all too often, the power of the state is used to further narrow political objectives through favoritism toward one constituency or another (IBRD 1994, p. 183).

Even if markets fail or do not work correctly, the Bank makes it clear that it does not believe African governments should involve themselves in state intervention (IBRD, 1994). In this case, what was good for South Korea is not good for promoting development in Africa.

While it may be true weak capacities hamper policymaking in the African setting, the Bank is interested in building the power of the private sector and coalitions that will support donor objectives and policies. This effort logically conflicts with the interests of former beneficiaries of state policies; thereby creating potential adversaries to economic adjustment programs. Blinded by orthodox ideology, the Bank argues that the state's already too limited capacity should only be used to perform activities that the market cannot perform alone (IBRD, 1994). A tremendous opportunity to build is therefore wasted.

Providing infrastructure and basic human services, running the legal and judicial institutions supportive of market economies, and protecting the environment in Sub-Saharan Africa requires the capacity of a modern state just as providing the basis for entitlements does ie. "infrastructural power". Infrastructural power is created by a state doing and providing specific services for the people (Mann, 1991). Enabling the African state to perform the tasks associated with a modern state more efficiently is essential if development is to occur. In the face of external constraints in Africa, enabling the state may be a prerequisite to building anything, including a private sector, at a time when the African state has too little capacity to govern (Francis, 1995).

In formulating development policies, programs and plans, it is more important to put people first and to specify objectives in terms of the enhancement of human capabilities. In this area, the state must necessarily play a leading role. A state need not be large, in the sense that it accounts for the bulk of total expenditures in a society. By saying this, neither does it imply a state be small and limited to providing only minimal services and leaving the rest to the private sector. The functions a state performs and how well they perform them is what matters most (Griffin and McKinley, 1994).

In Sub-Saharan Africa, the nature of external constraints and deficits in technocratic expertise make it imperative that some basis for learning be established. Learning by doing is a logical process of generating technocratic expertise to manage external shocks as well as direct macroeconomic policy. Knowledge can be gained by a state's doing as South Korea has ably demonstrated.

Not surprisingly, most structural adjustment efforts have not led to noticeably enhanced state capacity in the African context. Comparing data from the United Nation's Development Program's (UNDP) Human Development Index (HDI) provides some insights on technocratic capabilities in the African region. The HDI is an indicator of a state's ability to provide and administer resources in areas such as education and health care in a society.

Sub-Saharan African states have some of the lowest HDI rankings as one might expect given limited technocratic expertise. Noting that the highest ratings are 1.00, almost all Sub-Saharan African countries have aggregates below 0.500 on the index indicating limited or weak capacity. Nearly thirty African states have levels of 0.250 or below. The indices provide some insight into why this region has fared so poorly in terms of promoting economic takeoffs using any strategy. It also explains the slow pace of economic reform.

On this index, low national income is not necessarily the major problem. A state's ability or inability to use resources to provide the means to help its people enhance improve their lives--education, health care, and nutrition--is the main issue. (Griffin and McKinley, 1994). States without capacity may also suffer from legitimacy problems. Regimes may suffer from the political dilemmas that naturally stem from the absence of important ingredients of state sovereignty.

The index reveals a condition that can be changed with appropriate priorities. The UNDP has noted that other developing countries have started with low indices on the HDI in the last three decades. Some have managed to increase their rankings over time. The *Human Development Report* (1993) identifies the Gulf States in the Middle East as having made the greatest strides in enhancing the quality of life of their people. After acquiring resources from steep increases in oil these Arab states have made rapid progress. Saudi Arabia demonstrated the greatest change in its HDI value--from 0.386 in 1970 to 0.688 in 1990 (UNDP, 1993, p. 16)

Africa in the 1990s has a number of states with HDI values in the general range of Saudi Arabia's in 1970. The example of the Saudi experience seems to suggest that resources, a suitable amount of time, and some technocratic expertise are required to shift upward on the HDI ranking.

Nigeria has had the resources and the time, but it lacked adequate technocratic expertise to make these factors contribute significantly to its long-term economic health.

The only African case where structural adjustment reforms have been completed is Mauritius. It "graduated from adjustment in the mid-1980s" (IBRD, 1994). This African country has HDI rankings placing it at the top of the medium human development category. Table 1 presents HDI values of several states that have successfully implemented stabilization policies and adjustment reforms in comparison with some less successful African states.

Table 1. 1990 HDI Values/ Capacity Africa and East Asia

Developing States	HDI Value	HDI Level	Capacity
Hong Kong	0.913	High	High
Singapore	0.849	High	High
South Korea*	0.872	High	High
Mauritius*	0.794	Medium	Medium/High
Nigeria	0.246	Low	Low
Kenya	0.369	Low	Low
Ghana	0.369	Low	Low

Source: 1993 *Human Development Report* p.14. * State has succesfully managed reforms.

Note the strong correlation between HDI and structural adjustment as evidenced by Mauritius. Ghana, as one of the first African countries to attempt structural adjustment reforms, does not show significant differences in HDI values from other African countries (Kenya or Nigeria) in spite of the fact that reforms have continued. Limited capacity has undoubtedly affected the timing and sequencing of its reforms (IBRD, 1994). Herein lies the basis for concentrating on a human development strategy as opposed to standard structural adjustment.

VII. Consequences: Regime Instability

Structural adjustment reforms in Africa operate in an environment shaped by external and internal constraints. Meanwhile, the same reforms have also shaped the African environment. Reforms aim to lay the foundations for sustained economic growth in the region. Their failure only contributes to the problems of the region. There is increasing evidence that the reforms are self-defeating because of their association with a dismal economic climate and the political consequences of hard-times on downwardly mobile groups. Solutions suggest changing a "disenabling economic environment" or developing a capability to cope with the environment within individual states. The latter is far more feasible than the former.

The Bank acknowledges the difficulties suffered by many groups in the wake of structural adjustment. Programs to develop human resources should be protected during the adjustment process (IBRD 1994, p. 14). Unfortunately, the realities of budgetary constraints do not always allow such an option. In spite of pronouncements that governments are maintaining social spending, education and health care services in the region have declined. Thus, segments of the African people have been willing to strike, to demonstrate and to follow demagogues (Darnton, 1995).

To create better environments for undertaking reforms and to offset emerging political difficulties, the Bank and Fund have called for political liberalization in the African setting. New World Order principles are therefore justified in terms of African conditions. The agencies hope that the emerging beneficiaries of the economic reforms will mobilize and support their interests within the government. From the Bank's perspective, it is simply creating an enabling environment (Callaghy, 1993).

Unfortunately, the political and economic realities of the region argue otherwise. The Bank acknowledges the fact that structural adjustment produces both losers and winners in the economic game (IBRD, 1994). In Sub-Saharan Africa, some of the most apparent losers have been workers, students, civil servants and the lower ranks of the military. Urban communities generally have been hurt by reform efforts; thus, they are more politically volatile than usual. The groundwork for political struggles along either class or ethnic lines is emerging to threaten the long-term viability of both reforms and many African regimes.

For African regimes shifting regime priorities to comply with donor preferences at a time when resources to coopt or pacify opponents are scarce is politically risky. Democratization under the auspices of the New World Order only exacerbated the difficulties of the African elites. Experts note that the African country progressing most rapidly with its reforms did so under a military dictatorship-- Ghana under Jerry Rawlings.

Orthodox policy prescriptions have been criticized because they can produce perverse and destabilizing effects (lowered growth and increased inflation) in some developing countries (Kahler, 1990). In fact, sound economics may clash with what is politically sensible. In January 1994, the value of the French-backed currency of the African Financial Community (C.F.A.) was cut in half. While financial analysts hailed the move as long overdue, it destabilized 14 countries in West and Central Africa (Darnton, 1995). Thus, serious stress was placed on weak regimes. Two cases highlight the central role of structural adjustment reforms and New World Order ideals in the political difficulties African countries are experiencing in recent years-- Ghana, the Bank's success story and Nigeria, the Bank's failure.

In Ghana, where Jerry Rawlings' military regime was firmly in control, political challenges to the regime followed its adoption of specific economic reforms. Urban workers were hostile as the Rawlings' regime announced 25,000 labor cutbacks in 1984-85. These cuts were followed by 32,000 layoffs the next year. Ghana's well organized trade union movement moved onto the offensive, criticizing the regime for the layoffs. Rawlings responded with repression. After jailing several outspoken union leaders, his regime was forced to use nearly 1,000 policemen backed by armored cars to quell a protest by workers in Accra at the headquarters of the Trade Union Congress (Walton and Seddon, 1994).

Given the Ghanaian military's support of Rawlings, his opposition concentrated on pressuring the regime and protesting economic reforms by calling for greater participation. After greater economic difficulties emerged in 1989, Rawlings conceded and made tentative moves to open up his regime consistent with the Bank's support for political liberalization. Urban groups hostile to the reforms were allowed to form new political parties. One of leaders, a former civilian President overthrown by Rawlings, openly attacked the economic reforms, specifically the devaluation, as a "terrible disaster" that the "dictatorship" of the IMF and World

Bank had imposed on Ghana in order to "stuff their own pockets" (Callaghy, 1993).

As the election progressed, Ghana's structural adjustment packages became the central focus of the first major multiparty election held in years. Rawlings eventually won the presidential election, and his party gained control over the legislature. But the political circumstances were questionable. While the reforms continue, the political consensus supporting them and the Rawlings' regime in Ghana remains fragile.

Meanwhile, in Nigeria, the effects of structural adjustment efforts almost immediately generated opposition from the Nigerian Labour Congress. By 1988 when the Bank and Fund put on pressure for the abolition of fuel subsidies, a major riot erupted in Jos involving students, workers, and school children. Rioting claimed twelve lives and involved the burning of several government buildings. Following this particular incident, the Nigerian government was faced with protests in cities across the country. Civil servants, hospital workers, tanker drivers and others came out in spite of government bans on such activity (Walton and Seddon, 1994).

This series of protests was a reflection of the growing discontent of segments of the population with the demands of structural adjustment. Devaluation of the naira had substantially raised the price of imported inputs and spare parts for Nigerian industry. As a result, there were numerous closures and cut-backs. In Kano, 19 companies were forced to close in 1987. That year 60 percent of the industries were operating at 20-25 percent of capacity. Living standards of Nigerian industrial workers had dropped prior to the onset of the New World Order.

A logical response to this situation is to call for greater participation in governing by losing groups. The Bank's calls for democratization in line with the New World Order allows these forces to be taken more seriously; although this did not make it easier for the African government to respond. Nigeria is a case in point. One former Nigerian Head of State, General Obasanjo, contended that adjustment reforms had drastically reduced the living standards of all productive workers except "speculators" and "commission agents". Meanwhile, dissatisfaction with the Nigerian regime increased. Eventually there was an attempted coup. The London *Financial Times* argued that public antipathy to the hardship created under the reforms reached the point that it fed into the attempted coup against the Babangida regime in 1990 (Walton and Seddon, 1994).

The Babangida regime seems to have reconsidered its relationship with key segments of the population after this event. A windfall of oil money also helped. Fiscal restraint to buying support for the regime. Additional revenues from oil wealth garnered after the Persian Gulf crisis, in addition to other funds, were used to purchase "toys" for the Ghanaian military. The purchases included 150 new Vickers tanks from Britain, twelve Czech fighters and 300 new Peugeot sedans for the military officers. The regime also decided to make payoffs to opponents of economic reform, major societal groups and to anyone else in Nigerian society willing to upset the status quo.

Further calls for political liberalization by the Bank and the IMF only intensified the regime's behavior in this respect. Political liberalization under the auspices of the New World Order by itself came with an additional price tag. Continued spending without "accountability or transparency" effectively reduced any chances of Nigeria pursuing economic reform and seriously upset Bank officials (Callaghy, 1993).

The reforms have "hollowed out" and the Nigerian government eventually reneged on its promise to return Nigeria to civilian rule. But the problems remain and solutions for coping with them are in short supply. As in so much of Sub-Saharan Africa, the short-run disadvantages of adjustment exacted their toll before the long-run benefits could be reaped and the goals of the New World order came at an inauspicious time.

The failure of orthodoxy in the African setting has encouraged some reexamination of the policies advocated by the Bank in recent years. But there is little evidence that the priorities of democratization and liberalism inherent in the policy prescriptions of the New World Order have been abandoned in favor of more feasible approaches. The balance of power within the specialized agencies of the United Nations has not been altered in spite of post-Cold War changes. It has actually been reinforced. Thus reform of these critical agencies is unlikely.

Weighted voting continues to allow U.S. policymakers to dominate the IMF and the World Bank in spite of Japan and Germany's increased financial presence in the international arena. There is speculation that Japan's prominence as the leading donor country might give it greater voice in advocating development strategies (Stallings, 1993; Weeks 1995); but there is nothing conclusive here.

For years developing countries in Africa and elsewhere have discussed the need for reforming United Nations' agencies to generate increased development. In spite of these calls the situation remains essentially as asymmetrical as ever. Robert Mugabe of socialist Zimbabwe commented in a 1991 conference of nonaligned states in Caracas "The current..order continues to accentuate poverty in the developing countries... Developed countries are continually manipulating international systems to their benefit yet purporting to be *democratic*" (Ollapally, 1993, 175). While some things change; others remain the same.

VIII. CONCLUSION

Economic stagnation in Sub-Saharan Africa has not been alleviated by structural adjustment policies, particularly in the wake of the New World Order. Imposing the values of the New World Order has only complicated an already complex situation. Orthodoxy has frequently been correlated with the strongest countries in the international political economy (Spero, 1990). A state must be able to absorb immediate costs in the short-run to reap the benefits of long-run economic growth (Krasner, 1995). Whether a state is large or small, weak or strong there is no exception due to size or position in the hierarchy. Having political capacity to absorb costs is one of the important lessons derived from the experiences of the transitional economies in Central Europe as far as market oriented reforms and democracy are concerned (Nelson, 1992).

Macroeconomics encouraged broad scale use of orthodox solutions in Africa where states and institutions have long been recognized as weak. Consequently, the political adaptations of these states to deteriorating politico-economic climates associated with structural adjustment were not successful. More importantly, the New World order ideals of democratization and liberalization added insult to injury in the African context. Without resources and supporting institutions neither ideal has any real prospects. Structural adjustment has not done anything to either principle in Africa.

Washington's role in pushing these policies and ideals in the New World Order cannot be ignored. The United States' profile within the international development agencies has been too high. If political strife intensifies in parts of Sub-Saharan Africa, the international community will be faced with the task of restoring order in addition to alleviating poverty. In other words, the task will be more complicated that it was a decade or more ago.

Orthodoxy did not create all of the problems plaguing the African region, but it added to them by concentrating on a type of development emphasizing Western goals such as growth, liberalization and democratization without institutions or capacity. The Bank is aware of this fundamental problem: " ... the fundamental development challenge of improving Africa's human resource base requires more than policy change--it also requires sustained investment and institution-building" (IBRD, 1994, p. 14). Unfortunately, current policies contribute to "disenabling" in both these areas.

The need for defining development in terms of expanding capabilities (Sen, 1992) and enabling the African state to engage in these efforts can now be justified precisely because the Cold War has ended. Some of the lessons of the interwar period should be noted. States, which are already weak, do not need reasons to engage in repression or warfare. It is it not in any state's interest to help another state do poorly. States, like people, can accomplish this task all by themselves.

REFERENCES

Callaghy, Thomas, "Political Passions and Economic Interest: Economic Reform and Political Structure in Africa," in *Hemmed In: Responses to Africa's Economic Decline*, eds., Thomas M.Callaghy and John Ravenhill, (New York: Columbia University Press) pp. 463-519.

Darnton, John, "Africa Tries Democracy, Finding Hope and Peril," in *Developing Areas*, ed., Robert J. Griffin, (Sluice Dock Guilford, Connecticut: Dushkin, 1995), pp. 46-49.

Francis, Michael J., "A Response to 'Rethinking Development,' in *Developing Areas*, ed., Robert J. Griffin, (Sluice Dock Guilford, Connecticut: Dushkin, 1995) pp. 38-40.

Griffin, Keith and McKinley, Terry, *Implementing a Human Development Strategy*, (New York: St. Martin's Press, 1994).

Haggard, Stephan and Chung-in Moon, "The South Korean State in the International Economy: Liberal, Dependent or Mercantile?", in *International Political Economy: Perspectives on Global Power and Wealth*, (New York: St. Martin's Press, 1995), pp. 47-60.

I.B.R.D., *Adjustment in Africa: Reform, Results and the Road Ahead*, (New York: Oxford University Press, 1994).

I.B.R.D., *East Asian Miracle: Economic Growth and Public Policy*, (New York: Oxford University Press, 1993).

I.B.R.D., *World Development Report 1991: The Challenge of Development*, (New York: Oxford University Press, 1991).

Jaycox, Edward, "The World Bank View: The Benefits of Adjustment," in *Developing World 95/96* (Guilford, Connecticut: Dushkin Publishing Group, Inc., 1995), pp. 50-52.

Kahler, Miles, "Orthodoxy and Alternatives" in *Economic Crisis and Policy Choice*, ed. Joan M. Nelson, (Princeton: Princeton University Press, 1990), pp. 33-61.

Kennedy, Paul, *African Capitalism: The Struggle for Ascendancy*, (Cambridge: Cambridge University Press, 1988).

Krasner, Stephen D., "State Power and the Structure of International Trade," in *International Political Economy: Perspectives on Global Power and Wealth*, (New York: St. Martin's Press), pp. 19-36.

Kuczynski, Pedro-Pablo, *Latin American Debt*, (Baltimore, Maryland: Johns Hopkins University Press, 1988).

Mann, Michael, "The Autonomous Power of the State," in *Comparative Politics*, eds., Roy C. Macridis and Bernard E. Brown, (Belmont, California: Wadsworth Publishing, 1990), pp. 67-74.

Nelson, Joan M., "Introduction: The Politics of Economic Adjustment in Developing Nations," in *Economic Crisis and Policy Choice*, ed., Joan M. Nelson, (Princeton: Princeton University Press, 1990), pp. 4-32.

Nelson, Joan M., "The Politics of Economic Transformation: Is Third World Experience Relevant in Eastern Europe?", *World Politics*, April 1993, 45, 433-63.

Ollapally, Deepa, "The South Looks North: The Third World in the New World Order," *Current History*, April 1993, pp. 175-179.

Ravenhill, John, "A Second Decade of Adjustment: Greater Complexity, Greater Uncertainty," in *Hemmed In: Responses to Africa's Economic De-*

cline, eds., Thomas M. Callaghy and John Ravenhill, (New York: Columbia University Press, 1993), pp. 18-52.

Sen, Amartya, "Development: Which Way Now," in *The Political Economy of Development and Underdevelopment*, eds., Charles K. Wilber and Kenneth P. Jameson, (New York: McGraw-Hill, 1992), pp. 5-26.

Spero, Joan E., *The Politics of International Economic Relations*, (New York: St. Martin's Press, 1990).

Stallings, Barbara, "The New International Context of Development," *Items: Social Science Research Council*, March 1993, 1(1), 1-6.

United Nations Development Program, *Human Development Report*, (1992) and (1993), (New York: Oxford University Press).

Weeks, John, "A Critic's View: Credit Where Discredit is Due," in *Developing Areas*, ed., Robert J. Griffiths, (Sluice Dock Guilford, Connecticut: Dushkin, 1995), pp.46-49.

Walton, John and Seddon, David, *Free Markeets and Food Riots: The Politics of Global Adjustment*, (Cambridge: Blackwell, 1994).

Zysman, John, "U.S. Power, Trade and Technology," *International Affairs*, 1991, 67(1), 81-106.

MARKET REFORMS AND STRUCTURAL ADJUSTMENTS IN THE NEW WORLD ORDER: THE CASE OF CÔTE d'IVOIRE

Abel Konan
International Economics
and Politics Program
East-West Center
1777 East-West Road
University of Hawaii, Manoa
Honolulu, HI 96822

Djeto Assane[*]
Department of Economics
University of Nevada, Las Vegas
Las Vegas, NV 89154

Abstract—Despite sobering conditions and developmental disappointments, the post-Cold War era has brought reasons for hope in Africa. Today, more than ever in the history of the continent, a large number of countries has held free elections to facilitate democratic transition. Furthermore, several governments have initiated reforms to liberalize their economies and ease state regulations. This chapter offers the experience of Côte d'Ivoire as a case study. It examines efforts of the country to strengthen democratic political institutions and to liberalize economic arrangements.

---

[*] We wish to thank Hailu Abatena and Suad Cox for comments and suggestions on a preliminary draft. Assane is grateful to the First Interstate Bank for Leadership for partial funding.

I. INTRODUCTION

It has become widely accepted that Africa is a continent "on a precipice" and threatened by significant marginalization in an increasingly global market. The post-Cold War period has, by and large, added very little to Africa's circumstances that are difficult. Yet despite sobering conditions and developmental disappointments, the new era also brought reasons for hope. In recent years, several Sub-Saharan African countries have attempted to adapt to the New World Order. The most visible challenge in this setting is characterized by the building of democratic institutions and the implementation of market-oriented reforms that are compatible with local culture and tradition.

Using the recent experience of Côte d'Ivoire as a case study, this chapter attempts to examine how the country embarked sweeping economic reforms to adjust to profound and complex global changes. It must be emphasized, however, that reforms in Côte d'Ivoire share a great deal with those advocated elsewhere in developing countries and Eastern Europe. Broadly presented, they aim at promoting market economy and democratic polity in an environment that reinforces aspirations for greater freedom and global independence.

Since the late 1980s, a series of politico-economic demands exerted powerful pressures for democratization, which transformed Côte d'Ivoire from a one-party to a multi-party political system. In 1990, the first ever contested election became wide open and competitive at all levels, which provided the opposition with a representation in the parliament, controlled by the incumbent *Democratic Party of Côte d'Ivoire* (PDCI). On the economic front, key reforms were initiated to keep the federal budget deficit under control and to provide the framework for a more liberalized economy.

The rest of the analysis will focus on the Côte d'Ivoire's attempts to develop an economic environment to boost private initiatives and reduce government involvement in economic activities. The first section of the analysis provides an overview of the structure of the economy by stressing salient economic performances of the country over the past two decades. This setting is then used as a background to investigate economic reforms launched by the government.

II. STRUCTURE OF THE ECONOMY

Since its independence in 1960, Côte d'Ivoire has emphasized liberal economic policies as a way to expand its growth potential. The policy attracted investment, technology, and managerial skills, mostly from Europe, while unskilled labor from neighboring Sahelian countries was employed in the export crop plantations of coffee, cocoa, rubber, palm, coconut, pineapple, and banana. In the financial market, banks and insurance companies were essentially subsidiaries of European and American institutions.

To remedy the shortage of domestic capital and insufficient participation of nationals in the economy, the government took upon itself the task of investing systematically in most sectors of the economy. It not only created public enterprises, but also took minority or majority participation in existing private enterprises. Hence by the end of the 1970s, the liberal coexistence of an overwhelming para-statal sector with the private sector, created an economic environment overly dependent on the public sector. The country was able to carry its ambitious economic development plans largely financed by export earnings derived from favorable international prices of primary commodities. These export windfalls allowed the government to finance capital expenditures in the para-statal sector as the economy grew at an average annual rate of 7 percent during 1960-80. This favorable period of continuous growth helped develop modern financial and telecommunication infrastructures, equip the country with a second deep water port, build airports, hospitals, and schools. During this initial period of rapid growth, the government was successful in building the foundations of a modern economy (World Bank, 1978).

By the 1980s, however, the "miracle" growth came abruptly to an end as the country's economic strength became its weakness. Stagnation, to a large extent, was attributed to sharp declines in the primary commodity prices, the debt crisis fueled by high international interest rates, and an overvalued CFA franc currency which impeded the competitiveness of the economy.

Indeed, a 50 percent decline in export earnings during 1986-90 contributed to the country's financial fragility. Consequently, Côte d'Ivoire stopped servicing its foreign debt and part of its domestic debt, thereby spreading in the process, the fiscal woes to the financial market. The primary deficit (calculated after deducting interest payments from total expenditures) compounded by an inefficient, poorly managed, heavily subsidized, and highly protected para-statal sector, reached 7.6 percent of the Gross Domestic Product (GDP) by 1989. Likewise, the current account deficit worsened to reach 10 percent of the GDP during 1988-89, which accentuated the inability of the country to compete in international markets. As a result, Côte d'Ivoire experienced both fiscal and liquidity crises resulting in negative growth rates that induced the government to embark on structural adjustments and market reforms.

The next section of this chapter analyzes the necessary adjustment policies initiated by the Ivorian government to implement market based reforms in accordance with the New World Order. These market reform and structural adjustment policies are supported by the United States and Western Europe as manifested through assistance from the World Bank and International Monetary Fund (IMF). The Ivorian experience may not be fully replicated, but some useful policy reform lessons may be learned from.

III. CORRECTING MACROECONOMIC IMBALANCES

Stagnation of Ivorian economy can be attributed to cyclical and structural factors. Cyclical factors resulted from fluctuations in world price of primary products, which affected more than 50 percent of its export earnings. To lessen the economic impact of price fluctuations, the nation's agricultural policy was designed to complement the existing crop policy with a more aggressive policy of promoting food crop production (e.g., rice, maize, cassava) to reduce the dependency on food imports.

Federal budget deficit reduction required structural reforms dealing with privatization of the para-statal sector in order to end inefficient and subsidized public enterprises that have contributed to the worsening of fiscal deficits. Reform included the revision of the tax system and the need to cut government expenditures. It still remains, however, that the initial step toward fiscal discipline requires a reduction in spending and the development of a revenue enhancing tax system.

A. Expenditures Reduction

To reduce public expenditures, the government had in mind what is politically safe, socially acceptable and economically tolerable. Accordingly, benefits of civil servants (housing subsidies, administrative cars, gasoline allowance) were drastically reduced or eliminated to the top echelon of the administration, military, and paramilitary. Government excess vehicles and houses were sold. Telephone, electricity, and water usage were rationed. Maintenance expenditures including government buildings, roads, schools, and hospitals were postponed; capital expenditures were reduced; wages and salaries were frozen until a 5 to 20 percent adjustment that followed the 1994 devaluation. As a result, non-wage operating expenditures were reduced from 261 billion CFA francs in 1989 to 182 billion in 1991 or to 70 percent of the 1989 level and stabilized at that level in the following years. The primary deficit was reduced gradually from 7.6 percent of the GDP in 1989 to 2.1 percent in 1990, 0.8 percent in 1991. The budget was balanced in 1992 and thereafter.

B. Tax Reform

The tax policy was guided by a quest for fiscal stability that is compatible with the need for increasing tax revenues and stimulating economic growth through tax incentives. Accordingly, the corporate income tax rate was reduced from 50 to 35 percent; the tax on services was replaced by a value added tax (except for banks) and reduced from 25 to 20 percent; several sales tax rates were reduced and the collection process was simplified, and the payroll tax for national workers was eliminated. Property tax was reinstated and new procedures to collect unpaid taxes were put into effect. To further reform the tax system, exemptions were gradually removed to eliminate the difference between the value added tax rate on domestically produced goods and imports. Although it is too early to assess the impact of these fiscal innovations, there are indications that the adopted measures have had positive budgetary effects.

C. Exchange Rate Adjustment

Côte d'Ivoire is a member of the West African Monetary Union (WAMU) whose central bank, the *Banque Centrale des Etats de l'Afrique de l'Ouest* (BCEAO) issues the CFA franc, pegged to the French franc. Participation in the Monetary Union provides Côte d'Ivoire with several advantages. It tends to minimize the uncertainty surrounding the volatility of the nominal exchange rate. Also, it circumvents the hardship of having an unconvertible local currency and guarantees access to international trade and finance in today's generalized floating system. Finally, it imposes a monetary discipline that enables the country to contain monetary expansion and inflationary pressures. The monetary discipline, however, has limited options against likely macroeconomic disturbances.

The assurance of a currency union has made the member countries better-off in terms of low inflation in a stable monetary union. But, by the same token, the very nature of the union may have encouraged member countries to delay appropriate adjustment measures which limited their ability to cope with external shocks (Assane and Konan, 1994). Indeed, the lack of flexibility to adjust may have further accentuated the implied costs of (1) growing external debt, which has impeded the ability of the country to meet its financial obligations; (2) sharp declines in the terms of trade, that have worsened of the current account, and importantly; (3) foreign exchange rate disequilibria, which has affected directly external competitiveness of the country. The effect of an overvalued exchange rate can be devastating on small open economies. It can, for example, weaken the export sector and trigger massive capital flight due to speculative behavior toward devaluation.

A WAMU member country's inability to cope with domestic and external shocks was made transparent, as dismal economic growth rates beset even a traditional overachiever like Côte d'Ivoire. Figure 1 shows the reversal of fortune for WAMU countries when comparing their growth performances with those of other Sub-Saharan (SSA) countries. While during 1975-85 WAMU countries recorded superior economic growth relative to their counterpart SSA countries, such advantage evaporated in the latter period of 1986-93. Hence, by the early 1990s it became evident that attempts to boost economic growth by reducing

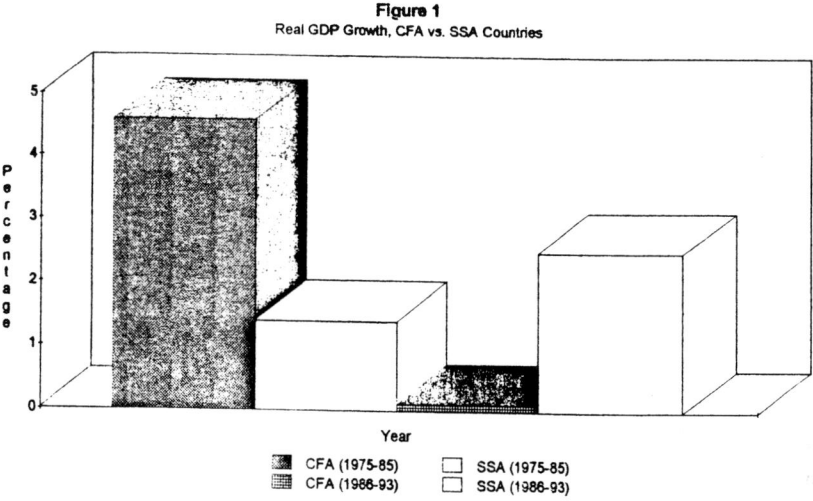

Figure 1. Real GDP Growth, CFA vs. SSA Countries

domestic expenditures and liberalizing domestic and trade policies would remain ineffective without an appropriate readjustment of an overvalued CFA franc. Throughout the 1980s the effect of an overvalued CFA franc greatly contributed to the loss of WAMU's international competitiveness against non-franc major partners. For example, through large and successive devaluation, Ghana and Nigeria, two neighboring SSA countries, witnessed heavy depreciation in their respective currencies, which enabled them to improve competitiveness.

A number of studies have imputed that an overvalued CFA currency was due to a rigid fixed parity rule between the CFA franc and French franc. Devarajan and Rodrik (1991) outlined a formal framework presenting the trade-off facing WAMU countries. The critical choice being between alleviating the cost of external shock due to the deterioration in terms of trade and the goal of maintaining lower inflation rates relative to non-CFA neighboring countries. They concluded that setting the CFA franc immutable fixed to the French franc was a "bad bargain" for WAMU countries and that allowing for flexibility in the exchange rate regime would ease adjustments to external shocks. Referring to the trade-off between economic growth and monetary stability, Nascismento (1987) found the trade-weighted basket a superior alternative exchange rate regime to the single peg. Addressing this issue along the same line, Gilles and Nöel (1984) suggested periodical modification of the parity within the franc zone, without necessarily affecting the institutional framework of the zone. According to the World Bank (1994), a 60 percent devaluation of the CFA franc would have been necessary to restore the competitiveness of WAMU countries. In January 1994, the CFA franc was finally devalued, from the 1948 parity of 50:1 to 100:1 French franc. This measure came four years later than when most comparable SSA countries had completed their real exchange rate adjustments.

Devaluation alone cannot be a panacea to guarantee healthier economic growth. But, for Côte d'Ivoire this measure proved to be the missing link between successive and fruitless adjustment policies and economic recovery. To some extent, important factors contributed to the recognition that the country would benefit from the enforced adjustments. This measure couldn't come at a better time than during a rise in the price of exportables such as coffee, cocoa (the pillar of the economy). This favorable environment rightly contributed to jump-start the sluggish export sector. Meanwhile, the government resisted temptations of allowing prices and wages to increase too rapidly which could hamper growth. Accordingly, pessimistic expectations of high inflation, high wage demand or even social unrest which tend to accompany devaluation measures in most developing countries, never quite materialized in this case. The first quarter following devaluation was marked by an inflation rate of 21 percent, while nominal wages rose by 5 to 20 percent. Meanwhile, government revenues increased by 100 billion of CFA francs and the trade balance improved by 140 billion CFA franc, as export grew by 13 percent. Table 1 highlights and contrasts trends in the real GDP, inflationary pressures, and current account deficit for the period of 1993-95. The findings in Table 1 appear to be consistent with the anticipation that Côte d'Ivoire would rank high among CFA franc countries to restore trade competitiveness and move along a faster growth path. By stimulating export while keeping inflation low, adjustment policies may have paved the way to a more optimistic economic outlook.

Table 1. Economic Growth, Price Inflation, and Budget Deficit

Year	Real GDP Growth Rate (percentage)	Inflation Rate (percentage)	Current Account Deficit (percentage of the GDP)
1993	-0.8	2.1	-10.1
1994	1.7	25.8	- 2.4
1995*	6.4	8.0	- 2.2

Source: IMF, *World Economic Outlook*, 1995, p. 37.

IV. MARKET REFORMS

We now focus on Côte d'Ivoire's effort to build a sound regulatory environment that promotes private enterprises, competition, and free trade. Likewise, there is a genuine willingness for the government to divest from production and service activities by privatizing state-owned enterprises.

A. FINANCIAL REFORM

Until the mid 1980s, credit allocation policy was the driving force of financial activities. In practice, the policy was used to direct domestic credit toward sectorial activities as determined by government economic plans (Fry, 1988). State-owned banks or banks with state majority participation, carried instructions according to the nature and direction of loans. Preferential lending rates were assigned to projects qualified as priority according to predetermined objectives, irrespective of market criteria. Poor management of state-owned banks, bad loans especially to the para-statal sector and to special groups, and the negligence of prudential norms precipitated a financial crisis.

The clean up led to the liquidation of eight state-owned financial institutions, and with support from France, the World Bank, and the African Development Bank-- four major Ivorian commercial banks were recapitalized and the state participation in these respective institutions reduced. Credit allocation was abandoned and preferential lending rate regime was eliminated. Consequently, the government had to raise special funds through domestic borrowing, foreign aid, and taxation to promote and finance appropriate development programs. As the grip of the government on the economy lessened, the emerging financial system was strengthened through competition and diversified services offered by financial institutions. Hence, the number of private banks almost doubled from five to nine banks, and by 1992, only one bank was state-owned (World Bank, 1994). An independent supervisory commission, the *Banking Commission of the WAMU*, was empowered to supervise the activities of financial institutions.

The final aspect of the financial reform focused on transforming the *Bourses des Valeurs d'Abidjan* (BVA), the stock market, into a vital regional financial center, capable of handling diverse financial instruments, to raise capital and offer investment opportunities for dealing with domestic, regional, or international markets. Accordingly, access and registration to the stock market was facilitated by the reduction of quotation fees and registration fees. The first regional bond was issued in 1993 and the potential for establishing a mutual funds market seemed great. Moreover, brokerage transactions were no longer exclusive function of commercial banks, because a distinct brokerage profession was created in 1994 and is opened to candidates who meet the required qualifications. Finally, through privatization a large number of private enterprises have been enlisted on the stock market and it is likely that this market will extend as more state-owned enterprises become private.

B. Trade Reform

Domestic and foreign trade liberalization are important components of the market reform strategy. Since 1991, significant efforts have been made to liberalize all forms of trade. On the domestic side, the policy of price control, in effect since 1978, was abandoned in 1992, except for a short list of 25 essential goods.

Likewise, foreign trade policies were drastically altered to promote free flow of goods and services. The number and tariff rates were reduced to 20 to 25 percent, with a maximum rate not to exceed 35 percent. Tariff barriers were dismantled, with 1995 as the target year for their complete elimination. Furthermore, import licenses and pre-authorization procedures were eliminated with the provision that importers must register their command for identification, inspection and custom formalities.

Similarly, export license and pre-authorization were suppressed except for the protection of the environment and the national patrimony. Finally, the country became more active in the World Trade Organization which facilitates free trade.

C. LABOR MARKET REFORM

The first step toward a flexible labor market began with the introduction of laws that facilitated hiring and firing decisions. The state employment office was dismantled and replaced by privately organized employment agencies. Restrictions on hiring "temporary workers" were relaxed and collective layoff related to unfavorable economic conditions were made possible. Finally, the status of the state workers was reformed to limit civil servant categories to seven, and regulations regarding career mobility, employment contracts, and incentives in the public sector were drafted.

D. PRIVATIZATION

Privatization is the bridge between structural adjustments and market reforms pursued by the government. It embodies the government willingness to disengage from production activities whenever the private sector can measure up to the challenge and take up the slack. In 1989, the para-statal sector comprised 140 enterprises, partially or totally owned by the public sector, represented accumulated investments of approximately 50 percent of the 1992 GDP. According to the government's newsletter, *La Lettre de la Primature* of April 1992, the 120 billion CFA francs invested in the para-statal sector during 1982-88, generated less than 2 percent return and public enterprises accumulated 85 billion CFA francs in losses. Moreover, enterprises with state majority participation lost 20 billion CFA francs, while those with state minority participation accumulated 144 billion CFA francs in profit (\$US 1 = 363 CFA francs, average over the period of 1982-88). These findings reinforced the idea that privately-owned enterprises perform relatively better than their public counterparts, and that they are invaluable to sustain economic growth and generate considerable amounts of tax revenue for the government.

The privatization committee was organized under the direct supervision of the Prime Minister Office, assisted by a *Technical Cell* in charge of the execution of the actual privatization operations. In 1994, The National Assembly passed the Privatization Law to replace the 1990 decree under which, only 10 of the 54 enterprises were required to initiate privatization measures. Overall, privatization has touched a wide range of firms in the agricultural, transportation, energy, telecommunication, financial, and hotel and hospitality sectors. The ensuing investment opportunities were made available to domestic as well as foreign private investors and privatization transactions were transparent and subject to competitive bidding.

In adopting the privatization program, the goal of the government was to minimize its intervention in the economy and allow the private sector to provide goods and services efficiently and competitively. By the same token, it was believed the government would gain by reducing subsidies to inefficient public enterprises to eliminate a major source of budgetary deficit. Hence, as mismanaged and wasteful public enterprises were transferred to the private sector, the economy would gain productivity and competitiveness to accelerate growth.

In 1994, 12 of 54 enterprises scheduled for privatization have successfully passed through the transitional step to becoming private. The remaining companies are at different stage of transition process. Although the privatization program is in its infancy, it has so far impacted positively on government finance, improved the current account position, and contributed to gain in economic efficiency.

V. Conclusion

It has become fashionable to dub Africa as a continent in crisis, with headlines dominated by war, famine or calamities overshadowing the other side of Africa that, despite the difficult circumstances, has undergone momentous political and economic reforms in the post-Cold War era. Today, more than ever in the history of the continent, several countries held free elections or facilitated the implementation of democratic rules. Furthermore, many governments have initiated reforms to liberalize their economies and eased state regulations. Also, though still limited to a handful of nations, Africa's emerging stock markets have become the most recent place to invest money.

We have highlighted the experience of Côte d'Ivoire in an attempt to overhaul its politico-economic systems in order to adjust to the reality of the New World Order. The late 1980s saw the country embark on the democratic political process and adopt strategies to further liberalize the economy and minimize previous government intervention.

As the role of the private sector expands, the need for a safety net arises to alleviate the social cost of the adjustments and reforms (Groortaert, 1993). Since efforts to build sustainable reforms stand little chance without changes in individuals attitudes, the consensus is that government intervention is not the solution to all problems. This attitude fits the ongoing market reforms and helps promote private initiatives. The challenge on the horizon points to the ability of a newly elected government to maintain political stability and accelerate economic growth.

REFERENCES

Assane, Djeto and Abel Konan, "Exchange Rate Variability and Imports in the WAMU Countries: Is this Relationship Relevant," *World Development*, 1994, 22 (5), 795-801.

Devarajan, Shantayanan and Dani Rodrik, "Do the benefits of Fixed exchange Rates Outweigh their Costs? The Franc Zone in Africa," paper presented at CEPR/OECD Conference on International Dimensions to Structural Adjustment: Implication for Developing Country Agriculture, (Paris, April 22-23, 1991).

Fry, Maxwell, *Money and Banking in Economic Development*, (Baltimore, Md.: John Hopkins University Press, 1988).

Gilles, Michael and Michael Noël, "The Ivorian Economy and Alternative Trade Regimes," in Zartman, William and Christopher Delgado, (eds.), *The Political Economy of the Ivory Coast*, (New York: Praeger, 1984).

Grootaert, Christian, "The Evolution of Welfare and Poverty under Structural Adjustment and Economic Recession in Côte d'Ivoire, 1985-1988," *World Bank Policy Research Paper*, 1993, 1078.

IMF, *World Economic Outlook*, (Washington D.C., 1995).

Nascismento, Jean Claude, "The Choice of an Optimum Exchange Currency Regime for a Small Open Economy: An Econometric Analysis," *Journal of Development Economics*, 1977, 23, pp. 149-165.

Primature, *La Lettre de la Primature*, various issues, (Abidjan, 1992-1994).

World Bank, *Ivory Coast: The Challenge of Success*, (Baltimore, Md.: John Hopkins University Press, 1978).

World Bank, *Adjustment in Africa, Reforms, Results, and the Road Ahead*, (Oxford University Press, 1994).

THE ECONOMICS OF POLITICAL CHANGE

Abbas P. Grammy
Department of Economics
California State University, Bakersfield
9001 Stockdale Highway
Bakersfield, CA 93311

Abstract—Should authoritarian governments reform or repress in response to increased people's deprivation? If the government reallocates resources to reduce deprivation (the *reform* option), preferences of the households and government will converge to maintain the status quo and sustain economic growth. If the government reallocates resources to increase deprivation (the *repression* option), preferences of the households and government will diverge to create inducements for political discontent and economic decay. Thus, authoritarian governments seeking growth and stability must reform rather than repress.

I. INTRODUCTION

Since the Second World War, many developing countries have experimented with systems of government. This era of political experimentation consists of two interdependent processes: (1) *externally-induced transition to autocracy* mainly in response to the Cold War politics and regional security considerations and (2) *internally-induced transition to democracy* largely in response to economic inefficiencies caused by the commend and control approach of the authoritarian rule.

In the post-World War II era of decolonization, developing nations were induced by the East-West conflict to establish authoritarian governments that could protect the benefits of ruling elites and a super-power in return for economic and military assistance. Consequently, states were required to participate in a global strategic "plan" to help maintain regional security and promote super-power ideology in a highly bi-polar politico-economic environment. In doing so, authoritarian governments maintained power by (a) adopting a development "plan" to facilitate economic growth which, they hoped, would "trickle-down" eventually to benefit the segment of population not directly involved in the growth process, and (b) enlarging and modernizing their security forces to defend against external aggression and internal unrest. In the case of the United States, as Fattahi and Fattahi (1996, pp. 3-4) argue, the intended plan of democratization was reversed to help install military-led authoritarian regimes in the Middle East (e.g., Iran) to contain Soviet expansionism and to ensure the flow of oil to the West. Also, the Soviet-type autocracy emerged throughout the Third World (e.g., Cuba) to establish centrally planned economies.

In the post-Cold War era, however, authoritarian governments had to adjust to rapidly changing internal and external conditions in one of two ways: economic *reform* in an attempt to sustain growth and maintain power, or political *repression* in an effort to clamp down the opposition and preserve the status quo. In the New World Order era of increased aspirations for politico-economic change, self-interested authoritarian governments seeking growth and stability are induced to *reform* to satisfy a growing public demand for economic goods and political freedom (e.g., Côte d'Ivoire). Authoritarian governments unable to *reform* have continued to *repress* to try to maintain power. Repression resulting in political unrest and economic decay may facilitate the emergence of even more repressive governments (e.g., Nigeria), or the transition to democratic rule (e.g., Chile). Governments that *repress* so very swiftly have remained in power at enormous human costs (e.g., Iraq).

This chapter will focus on the *internally-induced transition to democracy* to demonstrate that *reform* can bring about growth and stability, whereas *repression* will result in decay and discontent. Section II presents the thesis for a politico-economic interaction model, constructed in section III, in which deviation from a *trigger* level of economic deprivation causes political change. Section IV presents the main policy choices, *reform* or *repress*, facing authoritarian governments in response to increased deprivation. The final section includes the summary and conclusion. In the concluding remarks, we will reformulate the politico-economic interaction model to apply to the post-Cold War experiences of the developing countries.

II. BACKGROUND

Should authoritarian governments *reform* or *repress* in response to increased people's deprivation? To address this question, Bloch (1986) constructs a politico-economic interaction model to demonstrate that in autocracy, like democracy, governments are constrained by preferences of households toward resource allocation, and that authoritarian rulers are under a continuing threat of being overthrown if their preferences are in significant variance with those of the people. He measures a *trigger* level of economic deprivation above which households question the allocative outcomes of public policies, thus opposing the government. Bloch also demonstrates that economic growth can increase deprivation above its *trigger* level to induce political discontent (pp. 118-9, 24).

Here, we will extend Bloch's politico-economic interaction model to analyze policy choices facing authoritarian governments in response to increased deprivation caused by economic growth. In particular, it will investigate politico-economic outcomes of the government's resource reallocation choices to alter people's deprivation. If the government reallocates resources to reduce deprivation to its *trigger* level, preferences of the households and government will converge to maintain the status quo and sustain economic growth. If the government reallocates resources to increase deprivation above its *trigger* level, preferences of the households and government will diverge to create inducements for political discontent and economic decay.

III. A POLITICO-ECONOMIC INTERACTION MODEL

To construct a politico-economic interaction model, Bloch asserts that both households and government derive utility from production of goods that create economic welfare (hereinafter Q-goods) and goods that create internal and external security for the government (hereinafter S-goods). He also asserts that households derive utility from production of S-goods since they do value political stability and national security, even if its provision requires a lower level of economic welfare. Given a social preference function that exhibits positive and diminishing marginal utilities and an economy-wide product transformation curve that exhibits standard characteristics of smoothness and factor specialization, equilibrium is achieved at the tangency of the highest attainable indifference curve and the production possibilities frontier (p. 122; also Mansfield, 1994, pp. 515-6).

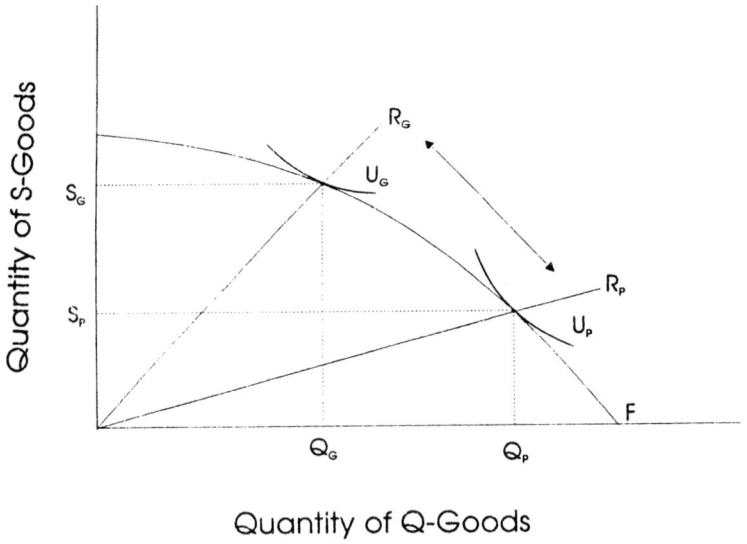

Figure 1. Equilibrium with Divergent Perferences

But, preferences of an authoritarian government tend to diverge from those of the people since the government values S-goods more highly than the people do. Here, Bloch draws similarities with the theory of the demand for public goods to reason that households are likely to prefer less S-goods and hence more Q-goods out of a given economic pie than the government. In Figure 1, we assume the government is powerful enough to impose its preferred output combination (Q_G, S_G) on the people who prefer the output combination (Q_P, S_P). Consequently, households feel deprived since the amount of Q-goods desired (Q_P) exceeds the amount actually available (Q_G). Meanwhile, households negatively value any amount of S-goods in excess of what they desire. They view the difference between the amount of S-goods desired (S_P) and actually available (S_G) as increasingly malign (e.g., excess police and security protection and frivolous offensive weapons). Thus, any additional positively valued S-goods above S_P are canceled by the negatively valued ones. Here, Bloch asserts that the imposition of the government's preferred output combination (Q_G, S_G) represents the maximum sustainable deviation from preferences of the households (pp. 121-4).

The value of people's absolute (or relative) deprivation, $D = Q_P - Q_G$ (or $d = \frac{Q_P - Q_G}{Q_P}$), is potentially a factor in predicting the probability that the government will maintain power. The value of D (or d) is thus a constraint to the optimizing behavior of the government. This constraint will be binding if $D > D^*$ (or $d > d^*$), where D^* (or d^*) is the *trigger* level of deprivation, which is defined as "the extent of deprivation deemed by the government to be sufficient to galvanize the people in revolt." It will not be binding if $D \leq D^*$ (or $d \leq d^*$). Applying the standard programming theory, production takes place at $D = D^*$ (or $d = d^*$), unless the government is to some extent altruistic (p. 123).

Furthermore, Bloch demonstrates that economic growth, when proportional in favor of resources capable of producing both goods, makes households more deprived in absolute terms, but no more or less deprived in relative terms. Growth in favor of factors specialized in production of Q-goods makes households more deprived in both absolute and relative terms. Whereas, growth in favor of factors specialized in production of S-goods makes people less deprived, at least in relative terms (pp. 124-6).

To extend the above politico-economic interaction model where economic growth results in increased deprivation, we use Bloch's illustration of non-proportional growth in favor of factors specialized in production of Q-goods in which people feel more deprived in terms of both the absolute and relative shortfalls in the availability of Q-goods.[1] As depicted in Figure 2, the optimizing behavior of the households and government along a higher production possibilities frontier causes deprivation to increase. With D>D* (or d>d*), households oppose outcomes of resource allocation policies of the authoritarian rule. The government must now decide whether to defuse the opposition by reducing the people's sense of deprivation: the *reform* option, or to clamp down the opposition: the *repression* option (p. 120; also Tullock, 1974, p. 59).

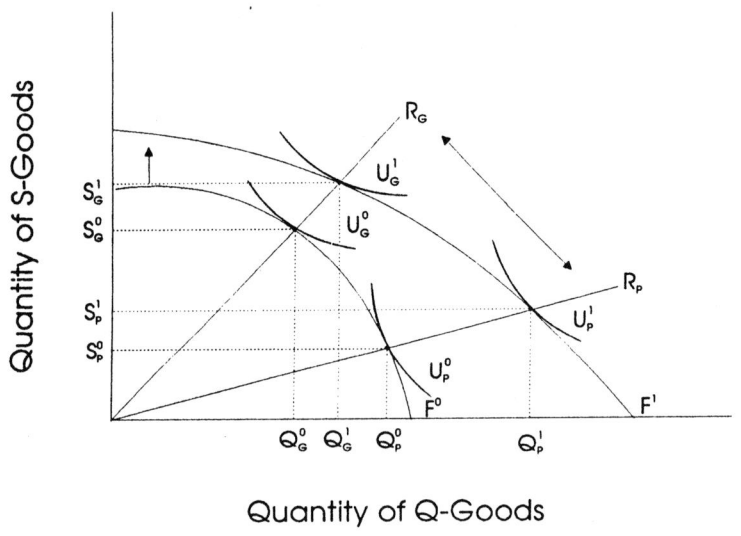

Figure 2. Growth with Divergent Perferences

The *reform* option is illustrated in Figure 3 by a rightward rotation of the ray from the origin R_G to R_G^D as the government revises its valuation of

---

[1]. This case of growth is used for the purpose of consistency between absolute and relative changes in the level of economic welfare. It also conforms with the "inverted U-hypothesis" by Kuznets (1955) and Adelman and Morris (1973) who suggest that in an early stage of growth, income distribution will tend to worsen, while at a later stage it will improve if the government plays an active economic role to invest in human capital. As we shall see below, we focus our attention on the post-growth public policy choices.

S-goods toward that of the people. Now, utility maximization for the government moves to southeast of its post-growth equilibrium to reduce deprivation toward its *trigger* level. The willingness of the government to improve resource allocation in favor of Q-goods will enhance its interactions with households in an effort to maintain power and sustain growth.

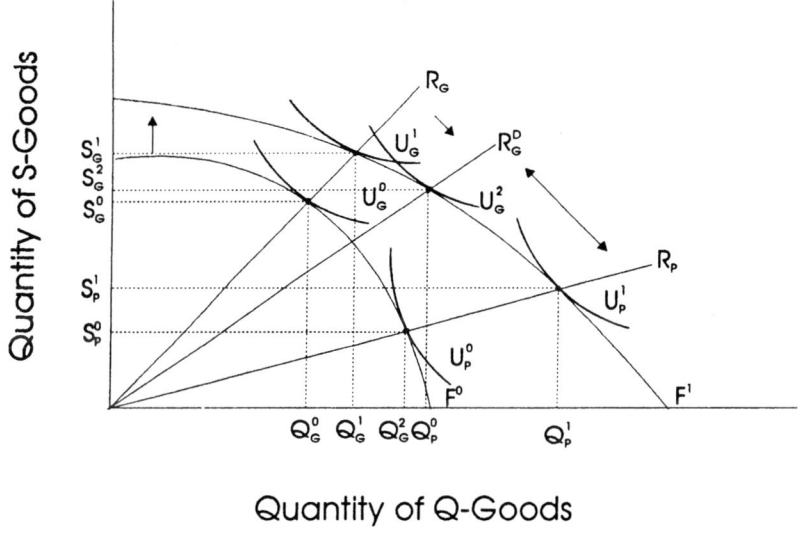

Figure 3. Growth with Convergent Perferences

Another case of shifting preferences is when the government initiates an economic *mobilization* plan to produce more S-goods at the expense of Q-goods to respond to an external security threat. As depicted in Figure 4, armament requires a leftward rotation of the ray from the origin R_G to R_G^D which will increase deprivation. To support *mobilization*, households will too desire more S-goods and less Q-goods. This revision will cause the ray R_P to rotate to R_P^D. Now, utility maximization for the government and households move to northwest of their post-growth equilibrium, thus reducing deprivation toward its post-growth level. However, prolonged external conflict that sustains deprivation above its *trigger* level will induce households to question the welfare consequences of *mobilization*, thus desiring more Q-goods.

Figure 4. Growth with Shifting Perferences

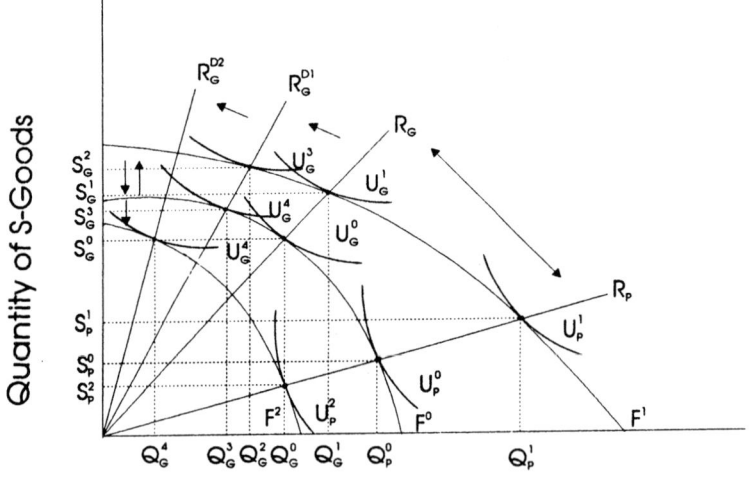

Figure 5. Growth with Divergent Perferences

The *repression* option is illustrated in Figure 5 by a leftward rotation of the ray from the origin R_G to R_G^{D1} as the government chooses an output combination that yields more S-goods and hence less Q-goods. Now, utility maximization for the government moves to northwest of its postgrowth equilibrium to further increase deprivation above its *trigger* level. Increased deprivation will give rise to the probability that households oppose the government. Active opposition of households to increased deprivation is costly to the government in terms of additional resources needed to keep people repressed (e.g., more prisons, more police, more censorship, and more arrests). Reduced productivity due to restricted information flows and lower labor force contribution will cause the production possibilities frontier to shift inward. Economic decay may not necessarily reduce deprivation since, as Bloch argues, a decrease in real income is asymmetrical with an increase in real income. Negative growth generates new types of deprivation (e.g., lower life expectancy) as the people lose the means to sustain themselves because of reduced economic welfare measured by a decline in the amount of Q-goods actually available (p. 126). Status quo conditions may continue if economic decay and political repression make the people feel deprived of the means to revolt.

Otherwise, households will stage an uprising against the government. To respond to the people's revolt, the government chooses an output combination that yields even more S-goods and less Q-goods. This situation is depicted also in Figure 5 by another leftward rotation of the ray from the origin R_G to R_G^{D2}. Violent confrontations between people and government security forces will inflict damages to human, social-overhead, and physical capital. The resulting deterioration in economic conditions will move equilibrium to the tangency of lower indifference curves and a greatly reduced production possibilities frontier to further reduce the availability of Q-goods and increase deprivation.

V. SUMMARY AND CONCLUSION

Economic consequences of the trade-off between civilian and military goods influence political behavior of authoritarian governments. As depicted above, utility maximization for the government in the *reform* option occurs at the tangency of a higher production possibilities frontier and higher indifference curves compared with those of the *repression* option. Growth with convergent preferences reduce deprivation, whereas growth with divergent preferences induce unrest and decay to increase deprivation. Because of economic welfare and political stability considerations, it is beneficial to an authoritarian government to *reform* than *repress*. It is to the benefit of self-interested politicians to *reform* inegalitarian policies of the authoritarian rule in an effort to gain popular acceptance and sustain growth, instead of destabilizing the economy, which will aggravate deprivation and create discontent. Consequently, states seeking political legitimacy must implement a broad-based development strategy to improve efficiency and equity instead of resorting to *repression* to keep commend and control.

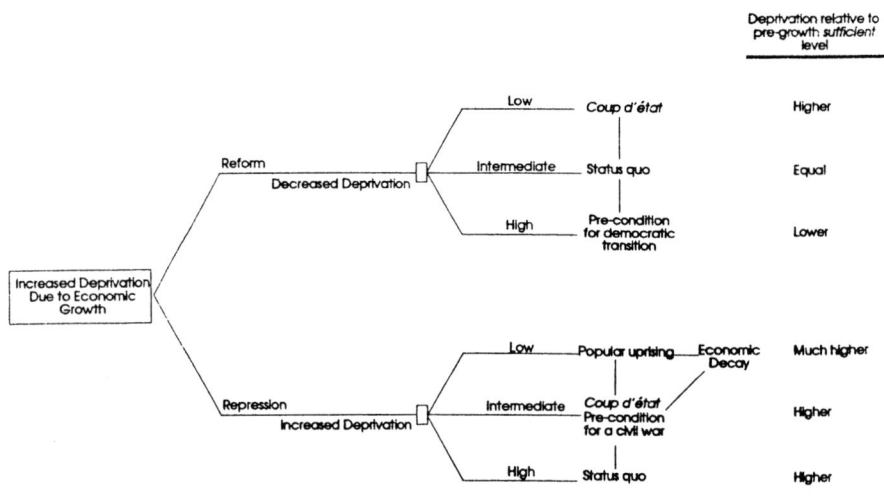

Figure 6. Politico-economic Interaction Model

To conclude, we expand and apply our politico-economic interaction model in Figure 6 to consider several possibilities caused by non-proportional growth that results in increased deprivation.

Path: reform-intermediate-status quo. Economic *reform* to reduce deprivation results in the convergence of the government's preferences toward those of the people. As the government provides less military goods and more civilian goods, it reduces deprivation toward its *trigger* level in order to maintain power and sustain growth (e.g., South Korea, Costa Rica).

Path: reform-high-democratic transition. Autocratic governments, as Bloch concludes, do not behave so differently from democratic governments in that they must improve economic conditions if they desire popular acceptance. The fulfillment of economic rights will, in turn, enable households to gradually gain political rights (p. 127). Rapidly growing countries where growth results in increased availability of civilian goods are expected to further improve income distribution and political participation (e.g., Singapore, and Taiwan). In rapidly growing, but non-democratic countries (e.g., Indonesia, Thailand, and China), economic *reform* should lead to political *reform* if the government facilitates a transition process in which benefits of economic progress spillover into the political arena.[2]

Path: reform-low-coup d'état. Failure of economic *reform* to sufficiently reduce deprivation will increase the probability that power shifts from one political faction to another. This political shift can take place in one of two directions. One direction points to autocratic transition in which unsuccessful democratic governments are overthrown by authoritarian (usually military) regimes (e.g., Nigeria, Ghana, and post-World War II Latin America). The second direction can bring about democratic transition in which unsuccessful authoritarian regimes are replaced by democratic governments (e.g., South Africa, Côte d'Ivoire, and post-Cold War Latin America). In addition to internal pressures to lower deprivation, democratization of the polity and liberalization of the economy in these countries are also externally-induced in response to increased global interdependence (see e.g., Konan and Assane, 1996).

Path: repression-high-status quo. Repression leads to increased deprivation as preferences of the households and government greatly diverge. People will have to accept the status quo if *repression* is so severe that they lose the means to revolt [The people of Iraq dominated by a repressive military regime and suffering from increased deprivation after the Iran-Iraq and

---

2. A growing number of empirical studies suggests that economic development, measured by such indicators as real per capita income, life expectancy, education, health, and culture, is positively linked with the propensity to experience democracy, and that democracy induces growth [e.g., Pourgerami (1988) and Barro (1994)].

Persian Gulf Wars (Horwitz, 1991 and Grammy, 1996) have virtually no resources to reverse the status quo].

Paths: repression-low-popular uprising and *repression-intermediate-coup d'état*. Repression can induced the people to stage a popular uprising (e.g., Iran, 1978-79) or an armed struggle (e.g., Nicaragua, 1978-86) to overthrow the regime. Under these conditions, *repression* is not too severe to fully eliminate the opposition who resort to collective violence. Confrontation between the government security forces and the people causes economic decay and increased deprivation [During 1980-92, both Iran and Nicaragua suffered greatly from prolonged stagflation as indicated by negative real Gross National Product per capita growth rates and high inflation rates (-1.4 and 16.2 percent in Iran) and (-5.3 and 656.2 percent in Nicaragua)][3].

The New World Order of greater economic interdependence necessitates political change in the developing countries. Authoritarian regimes capable of implementing broad-based *reform* will help pave the way to participatory democracy as people whose economic rights are satisfied demand greater political freedom. Initially though, the reforming leaders are likely to face a range of conflicting pressures which will test their commitment to change and influence the success or failure of their *reform* efforts (White, 1993, p. 8). Repressive regimes, on the other hand, will continue to suffer from mounting efficiency costs resulting from the command and control system of politico-economic management. These inefficiencies will require inevitably a shift in the system of government whose outcome may be uncertain: status quo under the existing regime, a new and perhaps more repressive autocratic rule, or transition to participatory democracy.

REFERENCES

Adelman, I. and Morris, C. T., *Economic Growth and Social Equity in Developing countries*, Stanford: Stanford University Press, 1973.

Barro, R., "Democracy: A Recipe for Growth?" *Wall Street Journal*, 1 (December), A24, 1994.

---

3. See *World Development Report 1994: Infrastructure for Development*, pp. 162-3.

Bloch, P., "The Politico-economic Behavior of Authoritarian governments." *Public Choice*, 51(2), 117-28, 1986.

Fattahi, B. and Fattahi, O., "The Political Economy of Oil: United States and Middle East Post-World War II Relations," in A. Grammy and C. K. Bragg, eds., *United States-Third World Relations in the New World Order*, NOVA Science Publishers, 1996.

Horwitz, T., "In Iraq Today, Children Scavenge for Food, Economists Drive Cabs," *Wall Street Journal*, 15 (July), A1, 1991.

Grammy, A. "The Geo-Economics of the Iraq-Kuwait Conflict: A Retrospective Comparative Analysis," in A. Grammy and C. K. Bragg, eds., *United States-Third World Relations in the New World Order*, NOVA Science Publishers, 1996.

Konan, A. and Djeto, A., "Market Reforms and Structural Adjustments in the New World Order: The Case of Cote d'Ivoire," in A. Grammy and C. K. Bragg, eds., *United States-Third World Relations in the New World Order*, NOVA Science Publishers, 1996.

Kuznets, S., "Economic Growth and Income Inequality," *American Economic Review*, (March), 1-28, 1955.

Mansfield, E., *Microeconomics*, New York: W. W. Norton, 1994.

Pourgerami, A., "The Political Economy of Development: A Cross-National Causality Test of Development-Democracy-Growth Hypothesis," *Public Choice*, 58(2), 123-41.

Tullock, G., *The Social Dilemma: The Economics of War and Revolution*, Blacksburg, VA: University Publications, 1974.

White, G. *Riding the Tiger: The Politics of Economic Reform in Post-Modern China*, Stanford: Stanford University Press, 1993.

World Development Report 1994: Infrastructure for Development, (New York: Oxford University Press, 1994).

FACTORS AFFECTING THE DEVELOPMENT OF FOSSIL ENERGY RESOURCES OF DEVELOPING COUNTRIES

Muhammad Sahimi
Department of Chemical Engineering
University of Southern California
Los Angeles, CA 90089

Abstract—We analyze and discuss various factors that affect the development of fossil energy resources, and in particular those of oil and gas, of developing countries. We identify *five* factors which are, (1) the geopolitical factor, (2) the social dynamics of these countries, (3) the state of international economy, (4) the environmental issues and concerns, and (5) the scientific and technological advances. The role of each of these factors is discussed in detail. We argue that these are interrelated and cannot be ignored or isolated from one another.

I. INTRODUCTION

Nearly two hundred years ago, Thomas Malthus composed one of the most famous works on demography that has ever been written. Published in London in 1798, and usually known as Malthus's first *Essay on Population*, the work focussed upon the rapidly-increasing population of England, France, and their neighbouring states in northwest Europe. Malthus regarded it as inconceivable that food supplies could keep up with a population that was doubling every 25 years. He therefore predicted a gloomy future for Europe: One characterized by malnutrition, *giant inevitable famines*, social, economical, and military wars, and vast deaths, all of them the result of a population outstripping its surrounding resources. However, although famine and death did afflict many countries (for example, Ireland during the so-called potato famine) in the following decades, Malthus's gloomy picture of the future turned out to be mostly wrong. Emigration to the "new" worlds of America, Australia and elsewhere, coupled with significant and steady increase in agricultural products, kept pace with food demand. But perhaps the most important reason for Malthus's predictions not materializing was the fact that he failed to see the power of new technologies for altering human fate. The steam-driven Industrial Revolution created huge increases in productivity, trade, and national wealth of many of the countries that he was concerned about. As a result, living standards were raised for decade after decade, social expectations were altered, and the size of families was reduced. In short, technology provided a solution to the challenge of over-population.

Why is it important to remind today's social scientists, economists and other scholars, and *politicians* of this historical case-study, especially since we know that Malthus's predictions were mostly wrong? What is the relation between Malthus's work and the energy outlook of the contemporary world? There are two chief reasons why we should be concerned. One is that after the Oil Embargo of 1973 and the Iranian Revolution of 1979, and the subsequent huge increases in the price of oil, a gloomy future for much of the world was also predicted that was characterized by stagnant or recessionary economies, social turbulence (some of which, at a small scale, did in fact occur in the United States in 1979), and the dependence of much of the world for its energy supplies on a relatively few developing countries with unstable political structures. The second reason is that today, nearly two hundred years after the appearance of Malthus's *Essay*, the world is again witnessing a population explosion, *not* in Japan, Europe, and North America, regions that can cope with a large increase in their population (although their population will actually decrease over the next 40 years; see below), but in the poor and energy-resource depleted countries of Central and South America, Africa and much of the Indian subcontinent, and in energy-resource rich countries of the Middle East (or Near East, as some would like to call this region). For example, the annual rate of population growth (ARPG) in Iran is well over 3 percent, and since the 1979 Revolution her population has nearly doubled. Nigeria, with a population of over 90 million, has an ARPG of 3.1 percent. Even in China that appears to have a successful program for birth control, the population is already enormous. This population explosion profoundly affects the social fabrics, and economical and political policies of every country of our planet in which energy export or import plays a prominent role in its economy. We need only remember the 1990-91 Gulf war, in which ideological foes participated in a grand coalition, to see how energy resources are still the driving force for major policies of every country, both internal and external. It is also important to remember that when Malthus's European countries confronted the challenge of their demographic explosion, they possessed certain advantages: strong state structures, rapidly-growing economies, large amounts of investment capitals, numerous entrepreneurs, engineers and inventors, and infrastructres that were reasonably advanced for their times. Few, if any, of such strengths are evident in many of the energy-resource depleted or energy-resource rich but undeveloped or underdeveloped countries mentioned above. In sharp contrast, we live in a world in which technology resources and capitals are in one side of our planet, the so-called "North", which is energy-hungry, whereas the population growth and social and political turbulence are in the other half of the planet, the so-called "South", where one finds vast energy resources, and in particular those of oil.

In order to understand the role of energy in today's world, especially in the developing countries that have vast oil reservoirs, we must understand that in the world of energy, three facts remain inescapable:

1. Oil and gas still are the most important sources of energy.

2. It is generally believed that oil will remain the most important source of energy for many years to come, unless either technological advances can develop a viable alternative energy source, or the impact of oil and other types of fossil energy on the environment will become so severe as to render their usefulness or practical use. One goal of this article is to argue that if the current trends continue, one or both of these will be realized by the end of this decade.

3. The third, and perhaps the most important, fact is that much of the known oil and gas reservoirs of the world are in the Middle East

and in a few other developing countries which have a long history of social and political upheaval and instability. In particular, the Middle East, which has reshaped the history of oil in the twentieth century, will continue to be the most important source of oil supply for the rest of this century and, even more critically, in the first few decades of the next century as well. With the collapse of the Soviet Union and the monoumental changes in Europe, these facts are more evident than ever.

II. FACTORS AFFECTING THE DEVELOPMENT OF FOSSIL ENERGY RESOURCES

Given these facts, how should fossil energy resources, and in particular those of oil and gas, be developed? Oil is the *non-renewable* national wealth of many developing countries. Once it is produced and exported, it can never be regenerated. Of course, the simplistic view of a layman in the Western hemisphere or in the "North" is that oil must be produced as much as possible and sold as cheaply as possible, so that his standards of living can be preserved. Unfortunately, this is also the view of some influential right-wing figures in the United States, who even have advocated the take over of the Middle East oil fields for fifty years or more, until their oil is completely depleted. But this view does not have any practical or *moral* value, and cannot be taken seriously. Since most of the oil resources are in the developing countries, many factors influence their development, none of which can be ignored by the producers. One should not expect the oil-exporting countries to deplete their non-renewable national wealth without getting any lasting products or benefits in return. What would happen after all the recoverable oil and gas of these countries are gone? Without a reasonable political and economical infrastructure, these countries will need massive aid just to barely survive, and this would be a huge burden for the "North". Moreover, what would happen to the huge chemical industry in the West that uses oil- and gas-derived materials for its production, and is an important source of jobs? Where would the German plastic factories and the American polymer producers get their raw materials from, if oil and gas resources are quickly depleted? What would happen to the huge petrochemical complexes in many countries, such as South Korea, that are allied with the West? Thus, rapid depletion of oil and gas resources of developing countries also has serious implications for the "North".

The history of the oil industry in the producing countries chronicles stormy relations between them and the multinational corporations and the political establishments of the consumer countries, some of which are the most powerful in the contemporary history. The history of oil is inseparable from that of colonialism, imperialism, regional, ethnic and ideological conflicts, and the quest for a new international economic order and justice. The producer countries, especially those that are in the Middle East, often have inflicted damage on themselves by succumbing to the consumers' tactics of divide-and-rule, with the result being devastating losses to their economies and their oil production capacities on one hand, and the establishment of a political and military presence by the powerful consumer countries in the region on the other hand, a most undesirable situation as far as almost all of the oil-producing countries are concerned. Iran's turbulent contemporary history provides a classical example of this phenomenon. From the CIA-backed coup of 1953 which toppled the national democratic government of Dr. Mohammad Mosaddegh, and was the direct response of the United States and Britain to Mosaddegh's nationalization of Iran's oil industry, to the direct roles that the Shah played in the large increase in the oil price after the 1973 Oil Embargo, and in putting down the leftist insurgency in Oman in 1975, the 1979 Revolution, and the eight-year war with Iraq, we see the direct and undisputable role of oil. Thus, no oil-exporting country, especially one in the Middle East, that is trying to develop her oil resources can ignore such political realities. This fact, which we call the *geopolitical factor*, influences deeply the development of oil resources of the developing countries.

The second factor is the *social dynamics* of the oil-producing countries. The ultimate goal of any oil exporting country is to use the income for developing her infrastructure, raising the living standards of her citizens, and laying the foundations for a sound future *without* any oil and gas to export. However, there are important differences between a country like Iran or Nigeria, with a young, large and rapidly increasing population, and, e.g., Kuwait, a sparsely-populated country with gigantic oil reserves. The development of oil and gas resources in these countries is a strong function of their social dynamics.

The third factor, *the state of the international economy*, manifests itself in the interdependent nature of the economies of the producing and consuming countries. No country can isolate her economy from the rest of the world. What affects the economic growth of the Western European countries, Japan and the United States also influences that of the oil-exporting countries, and vice versa.

The fourth factor is what we call the *environmental issues and concerns*. While we may all know the current *market* price of oil, gas or coal, most of us ignore, or are unaware of, the *hidden costs* of fossil energy. These hidden costs do not appear in our energy bills, yet we have to pay for them directly or indirectly, because such costs are the result of the health problems caused by air and groundwater pollution, damage to the nature as the result of mining operations, global warming, the greenhouse effect and depletion of the ozone layer in the atmosphere, acid rains, etc.

The fifth and final factor is the *scientific and technological advances*. While oil may currently be one of the most economical forms of energy, this may not be so in the relatively near future, especially if one adds the indirect costs of cleaning the environment. Moreover, a study of the history of science indicates that progress in any research field is not usually made with a constant rate, but rather in a *sporadic manner*. There are periods when a problem looks so difficult that we do not even know where to start attackingit, and periods when some epoch-making discoveries or inventions remove an obstacle to progress and thus enable a great advance. Thus, what may look like a favorable situation for the continued use of oil as the main energy source may drastically change in the near future, if alternative sources of energy, or novel methods of energy conservation, are developed. Moreover, technological advances in instrumentations and measurments, and increasing understanding of the impact of oil usage on the environment have greatly improved public awareness of the dangers that threaten our planet.

Thus, a developing country with oil-exporting capabilities has to accept and confront the fact that there are several important factors that influence the development of her oil resources. These factors are *not* independent of each other, but are interrelated through a set of complex interactions, and therefore one cannot take some of them into consideration while ignoring others. What follows is a detailed discussion of the role of each of them.

1. THE GEOPOLITICAL FACTOR

Political realities of our world directly influence the world energy outlook, and in particular, the oil market. Political rather than market forces dictate the broad direction of oil prices, and to some degree, supply and demand. Under the Bush Administration the United States, whose predominance in the energy world and in the international political arena was boosted by the Gulf war, opposed any dialogue between oil producing and consuming countries and asserted that oil production and prices should be determined by *market forces alone*. The Clinton Administration has not taken any clear position on this matter. But it is naive, and indeed ridiculous, to think that geopolitical considerations have no impact on the oil price. If the oil price is allowed to be determined solely by market forces, then it will be completely dominated by chaos and large fluctuations, since every oil-exporting country would attempt to "steal" other oil producers' market. We recall that one of the main Saddam Hussein's excuses for invading Kuwait in 1991 was that Kuwait was stealing Iraq's foreign oil market by overproducing oil and selling it cheaply. Moreover, in 1985-86 when there was a price war between major members of the Organization of the Petroleum Exporting Countries (OPEC), we witnessed a spectacular drop in the price of oil, from around 30 dollars per barrel to about 8-10 dollars. This dramatic drop in the price of oil caused considerable hardship for many oil-exporting countries *and* corporations. One of the main reasons for the collapse of the oil price at that time was the fact that Saudi Arabia, the most important member of OPEC, was deeply worried about the gains that Iran's armed forces had made in the war with Iraq, and thus she decided to pressure Iran by drawning the market in cheap oil (remember that every barrel of Saudi's oil costs only about 40 cents to produce). However, the damage went well beyond Iran's borders, so much so that George Bush, the then Vice President, and the former Texan oil man, had to travel to Saudi Arabia to urge her government to stop the price war, since even large American oil corporations such as ARCO and Mobil were also suffering greatly from this price war. A barrel of oil that ARCO produces in Alaska (its main source of oil) costs about 8 dollars, so that a very low oil price would be very harmful to ARCO.

On the other hand, over the past few years the political map of the world has changed dramatically. The spectacular collapse of the Soviet

Union, the dramatic changes in Eastern and Central Europe, the unification of Germany, the rising economic power of Japan and the declining power of the USA, the rapid development of the *Four Tigers* in the Asia-Pacific region, namely, Hong Kong, Singapore, South Korea, and Taiwan, the end of the apartheid regime in South Africa and the independence of South West Africa, the Gulf War, the conflict in the former Yugoslavia, and many more developments have given rise to a world virtually unrecognizable from what we knew only a few years ago. Among these the collapse of the Soviet Union and the Gulf War have undoubtedly affected the energy outlook of the world, and will have a profound influence on the future development of the oil resources, and thus deserve detailed discussion.

To better comprehend the significance of the collapse of the Soviet Union to the oil market, we have to remember that the highest levels of proven oil reserves outside the Persian Gulf area lie in the territories of the old USSR. Therefore, the energy outlook of the world has to be influenced by the collapse of the USSR, and this influence manifests itself in two different ways.

(1) The first is the fact that vast oil fields in some of the old Soviet Republics are no longer under Moscow's control. What used to be vast operations in different climatic and time zones, ranging from Sakhalin Island in the far east to Kaliningrad region in the west, from Barents and Karsks seas in the Arctics to the southern republics of Azerbaijan and Kazakhstan, making the USSR the largest oil producing country of the world, have shrunk considerably. Before the collapse of the Union, even the most optimistic scenario considered by the USSR Academy of Sciences predicted only very modest increases, about 0.4 percent per year, in the production of oil, gas, and coal through 1995. However, the internal strife in Russia and lack of capital for development of her oil and gas fields have considerably reduced the production capabilities of Russia. Even by 1991, just before its collapse, oil production in the Soviet Union had already decreased from the 1988 peak of 12.7 million barrels per day. Moreover, some of the oil fields, such as those in Azerbaijan, are in politically unstable areas, while some others are in decline, as a result of lack of capital for their further development.

Azerbaijan is a country of seven million people with *one million* refugees. Her war with Armenia in the Nagoro-Karabakh area is not only about the religious and ethnic rights of the Armenians in a region that was controlled by Azerbaijan, it also has to do, to a very large extent, with the control of the some of the largest oil fields in the world that are in Azerbaijan. Equally important is the strategic location of Azerbaijan, sitting in the middle of a region drawned in oil that starts from the Russian city of Tyumen and ends on the shores of the Persian Gulf, where Iran's oil fields are located. Moreover, if one wishes to ignore the territories of Russia, then Azerbaijan provides the only outlet for another region with huge oil fields, one that starts from the small northern Caucasus Republic of Chechnya and extends to the Kazakhstan Republic in Central Asia.

In 1993, the government of Azerbaijan reached an agreement with British Petroleum for developing three of her oil fields. These are the Azeri and Chirag fields and the deepwater portion of the Guneshli field, located about 120 miles offshore Azerbaijan in the Caspian Sea. A new pipeline was also to be built that would transport oil from Azerbaijan to a port in Turkey. The government of Azerbaijan wanted the pipeline to pass through Iran, thus completely bypassing Russia and Armenia. Britain, Turkey, and the United States preferred a route through Armenia, while Russia, fearing a complete loss of her influence in the region, proposed a third route that would pass through her territory and end in Novorossiysk on the Black Sea. However, the route proposed by Britain, Turkey and the United States would require an end to Nagoro-Karabakh war. Hence, in July 1993 Mario Rafaeli, Chairman of the Council on Security and Cooperation in Europe's group on the war visited Baku and Yerevan, Azerbaijan's and Armenia's capitals, respectively, trying to arrange a cease fire and a peace agreement. The two countries at war were prepared to sign a peace agreement that had been proposed by Russia, Turkey and the United States. However, the coup in Azerbaijan that ousted President Ebulfez Elichibey and brought to power Gaidar Aliev, the former KGB general and General Secretary of Azerbaijan's Communist Party, postponed the peace effort. In August 1993, Armenia's army from Karabakh attacked and captured a key region in Azerbaijan, near her border with Iran, that was to be part of the oil pipeline route. Thus, the conflict that has continued to date, has a direct, deep, and little-noticed link with oil.

Another geopolitical aspect of Azerbaijan's oil has to do with her relation with Iran. Originally, Azerbaijan was going to sell a part of her portion of the consortium to Iran. But under huge political pressure by the

West, and particularly the USA, Azerbaijan changed her position and decided against selling that portion to Iran. Iran has retaliated by cutting off the supply of electricity to Azerbaijan, under the pretext that Azerbaijan has not paid her old bills yet, and the relation between Tehran and Armenia has also warmed up. The third aspect of the deal has to do with Russia's response to it. Russia has contended that the Caspian Sea should be considered a lake, which is what it really is, not a sea, which is what Azerbaijan claims it to be. If the Caspian Sea is considered a sea, then every bordering country has some territorial waters that she solely controls. If it is considered a lake, then coastal states, which are Azerbaijan, Russia, Iran, Kazakhstan, and Turkmenistan would have to reach joint agreements in all resource exploitation deals, thus diluting Azerbaijan's control on the offshore fields. Russia cites two Soviet-Iran treaties in 1921 and 1940 to support her position, which is also supported by the other coastal states, except Azerbaijan. The matter has remained unresolved.

Some of the old Soviet Union's potentially huge fields, such as the Tengizski field, are in Kazakhstan which, after Russia, is the largest country to emerge from the collapse of the Soviet Union. It is a country of nearly 3 million square killometers and 17 million people, 40 percent of whom are Kazakh, another 40 percent Russian, and the remaining 20 percent consist of 130 different nationalities. It is run by a maverick and independent-minded government led by President Nursultan Nazarbaev. In 1992, the Kazakh government signed agreements with Chevron and Elf Aquitaine, with Chevron exploring the Tengizski field, and Elf Aquitaine the Temir plot in the Aktiubinski area. A British-Italian joint venture was the winning bidder for exploring the Karachaganakski region. In June 1993, an agreement was signed in Almaty (formerly Alma-Ata), Kazakhstan's capital, for creating a consortium of international oil companies to explore Kazakhstan sector of the Caspian Sea, which is believed to have oil reserves several times larger than those of Tengizski fields. Members of this consortium include a government company, Kazakhstankaspijski Shelf, British Gas, Statoil (an alliance of British Petroleum and the Norwegian Oil Company), Mobil, Shell Oil of Holland, and France's Total. However, even Kazakhstan is not completely stable. The war in neighboring Tajikistan (another Central Asian country that emerged from the collapse of the Soviet Union), the unsettled status of nuclear warheads of the old Soviet Union that are still in Kazakhstan, and the internal turmoil all contribute to this relative instability, although Kazakhstan is certainly in much better conditions than Azerbaijan.

The emergence of these countries, the regional conflicts in or around them, and the decline in oil production from the territories of the old Soviet Union have created opportunities for other oil producing countries, especially for those members of OPEC that are in or near the Middle East. Total oil production from the old Soviet Union is not expected to reach its 1988 level for several years to come. Although the decline in the oil production from the old Soviet Union has so far been compensated by a drop in the domestic demand and the exports to Eastern Europe, it does not follow that the situation will remain the same in the future.

(2) The second effect of the collapse of the Soviet Union is the elimination of the superpowers rivalry. Even before this collapse, the cold war had effectively ended, and a period of cooperation between the two superpowers had started. With the collapse and the subsequent internal political strife and economic chaos, Russia, the heir to the old Soviet Union, will not be able to provide effective competition for the West for several years to come. The Third World, some of whose members are major oil producers, benefited from the superpowers rivalry. This lack of competition between the superpowers, or at least lack of two *competing* superpowers, has also given rise to unusual phenomena. For example, the coalition that defeated Iraq in the Gulf War was unthinkable only a few years ago. The coalition was of course led by the United States in an attempt to influence and secure oil supplies, and *not* because Kuwait had to be rescued, or Saddam had to be taught a lesson. During the Iraq-Iran War, the United States had "tilted" toward Iraq, and together with Britain, France, and the Soviet Union, had supplied Iraq with the most modern weapons. Moreover, for over three years we did not see any such grand coalition, led by the Western powers, for helping the Muslims of Bosnia. The United Nations mandated arms embargo only benefitted the Serbs. The United States intervention during Summer and Fall of 1995 only took place *after* the political cost of the war in Bosnia became unbearable for the Clinton Administration.

Another lesson of the Gulf War was that the only alternative to the oil from the Middle East, and the compensation to any possible disruption in supplies from it, lie within the region itself. When during the war oil supplies from Kuwait and Iraq were cut off, more than 90 percent of the shortfall was quickly compensated by the other countries in the region, notably by Iran and Saudi Arabia. Thus, although the oil price rose in August and September of 1990 and reached 34 dollars per barrel, it decreased again in the subsequent months, and even the start of the war itself in early 1991 did not cause any major increase in the price of oil. An ironic result of this war was the fact that it restored Iran as the second most important member of OPEC after Saudi Arabia, a position that she had lost because of her war with Iraq.

The rapid growth of the *Four Tigers* of East Asia and of Japan also has geopolitical consequences. These countries are widely considered as models of successful economic growth. Their success has resulted in their dominance of some markets, and reduced economic influence of the United States and some Western European countries. Their success has also meant some economic dislocations in other countries, even in the United States, which have provoked friction and protectionist cries. Examples include "voluntary" export restraints and the USA-Japan Strategic Impediments Initiative. Hence, although superpower rivalry and the Cold War have ended, economic wars between some of the former allies may very well replace them, which will surely include fierce competition for access to the oil resources of the world, and in particular those of the Middle East. We see that despite the heavy pressure exerted by the United States, and President Clinton's executive order banning all commercial links with Iran announced on April 30, 1995, Japan, Germany and many other European countries have close commercial ties with Iran, and one major factor for this is their desire for having access to Iran's oil. None of these countries has joined the USA in the embargo ordered by Preseident Clinton. Close commercial links with Iran not only gives them access to her oil and satisfies their energy needs, but also gives them access to the large market that Iran provides for their industrial products. Although after the oil crisis of 1979-1980 Asian oil production, notably in Indonesia, Australia, Malaysia, and China increased rapidly, and by 1985 regional reliance on the oil imports from the Middle East was at an all-time low, most analyses predict a long-term decline in production, particularly in South East Asia, and thus more dependence on the Middle East oil.

Given these political realities, it is clear that the oil producers and consumers are dependent on each other. If there is no meaningful interaction and cooperation between the two sets of countries, the global energy outlook, and in particular that of oil, will be fragmented to serve parochial interests. Some may seek short term gains at the expense of those whose interest lies in long-term growth and stability. However, history can testify that short term gains have usually led to long-term harms. Higher energy prices, and in particular oil, can lead to lower prices, giving rise to a vicious cycle. Thus, the recognition of the interdependence and the promotion of global integrative linkages are imperative, without which there can be no stability in the energy supply of the world. Viewed this way, the political realities of today's world also become part of the interdependence between the suppliers and consumers of oil, gas, and other forms of energy. This interdependence should then give rise to *mutual security*. However, security in this context has different meanings for the suppliers and consumers, which may or may not be compatible with each other. Security for the consumers implies the steady supply of oil at a reasonable price, such that it can foster their economic growth. On the other hand, security for the producers means continued access to the market of oil-importing countries, a steady share of oil in total energy consumption over the long term, fair and stable prices that allow their development over the next many decades and, most important of all, absence of any military threats or invasion, economic blackmail, and attempts to dominate the oil producing countries: in short *respect for their independence and national sovereignty*. If this interdependence is not recognized, protectionism will rise, regional conflicts such as those in the Middle East will frequently arise which are destabilizing and difficult to resolve, and oil prices may suffer large fluctuations, all of which may result in a stagnant global economy which will not be in anybody's interest.

2. THE SOCIAL DYNAMICS OF THE PRODUCING COUNTRIES

As discussed in Introduction, one of the greatest pressures exerted on the world is the continuing growth in population of the developing countries, some of which are important oil producers. Consider, for example, three major oil producing countries in the Persian Gulf area, namely, Iran, Iraq, and Saudi Arabia. As of July 1994, Iran's population was estimated to be close to 65 million with an ARPG of about 3.5 percent, while Iraq's population was estimated to be about 20 million with an ARPG of about 3 percent. Finally, Saudi Arabia's population is about 16 million with an ARPG of about 3 percent. These ARPGs represent some of the highest rates in the world today. Their significance may be better understood if we compare them with those of some industrialized nations. For example, according to World Bank Report, *World Population Projection 1994-95*, it is predicted that between 1995 and 2035 the population of Germany will *decrease* by about 9.4 percent, and that of Japan by about 2-4 percent. According to the same report, over the same period the population of Angola (which has rich oil deposits) will increase 175 percent. In addition to Iran, many other OPEC members have large populations and ARPGs. Examples include Nigeria (with a population of over 90 million) and Indonesia (with a population of over 150 million). Population growth leads to greater energy needs in these countries as they develop their resources and industrial bases. However, producing energy, and in particular oil, is, of course, not an end in itself but a means of providing services. It is these services, not oil, that directly satisfy people's needs. Thus, one needs to consider the effect of energy resources, in particular oil and gas, of developing countries on their development programs. Let us discuss this in more detail.

One common phenomenon among most of the developing countries with rich energy resources is that, within most of them a giant internal population migration is taking place as peasants seeking employment stream into shanty-cities of several million people with completely inadequate infrastructures and utilities. At the same time, according to several reports, including United Nations's *World Urbanization Prospects* (1992 Revision) and *Population and the Environment*, published by the UN Population Fund, the urban population of developing countries, including those of many oil-exporting countries such as Iran, will nearly *triple* by the year 2025. Moreover, these are demographically *adolescent* societies in which over half of the population is under the age of 30, and in some countries under 20 - ideal prescription for social and political turbulence - should the masses of frustrated and energetic young people fail to obtain food, education and employment. According to the same reports, developing countries must create 30 million new jobs *each new year* just to maintain their current employment levels, and many of these countries are already suffering from high levels of unemployment. No developing country can ignore this fact. All aspects of national policies of every oil-exporting country is dictated by oil itself. Consider, as an example, higher education in these countries, whose institutions have to service the petroleum industry. Historically, the petroleum industry has been run by chemical and petroleum engineers. Therefore, to maintain the level of production and development at a reasonable level, the oil-rich countries have to train a large number of such engineers. Thus, since 1985 all Iranian universities with engineering schools have had large chemical and petroleum engineering programs, and have accepted a large number of new students every year. Moreover, Abadan Institute of Technology has been converted to a full fledge university, most of whose programs concentrate on chemical and petroleum engineering. The same is true about Saudi Arabia which has 7 universities, and Iraq which has 6 universities. In fact, two of Saudi Arabia's universities exclusively train chemical and petroleum engineers, and all of her 60 colleges provide support, at least in part, for the oil, gas, and petrochemical industries.

The interdependence of the development of oil resources and social policies of the developing and oil-exporting countries manifests itself to an even greater degree in their general development plans. In the first 5-year development and reconstruction plan carried out by Iran after the Revolution, 400 billion dollars was to be spent, of which roughly 120 billion dollars was to come from the oil and gas income. The first two development plans that were carried out in Saudi Arabia in the period 1970-80 were totally dominated by oil, gas, and petrochemicals. Two new industrial cities were created, one in Jubail on the Persian Gulf coast, and another one in Yanbu on the Red Sea coast. It took ten years and 80 billion dollars to construct these cities, in which 5 refineries, 7 petrochemical plants, and one natural gas processing plant were built. Although in the third plan the emphasis was on manpower training, to make the country less dependent on expatriate population, and on agriculture, oil, gas, and petrochemicals continued to play important roles, since a significant portion of the expatriate population help maintain and run these industries. On the other hand, the fourth development plan for the period 1985-90 fell short of its targets, mainly because of the steep decline in oil revenue after 1986. The implementation of many projects were delayed, or cancelled altogether.

The emergence of Islamic Fundamentalism in the Middle East after the 1979 Revolution in Iran, as a potent socio-political force, is another important factor that has to be considered in this context. The dominant religion in all the oil-producing countries of the Middle East is Islam. Moreover, the vast majority of the population in Azerbaijan and Kazakhstan is also Muslim. Instead of trying to understand its roots and reaching an accomodation with it, the West has been very hostile toward Islamic Fundamentalism. There would not have been such a movement, if the West had not tried to dominate the Islamic world both economically and culturally. There would not have been such a movement in the Islamic world, if the West had not supported such corrupt and anti-democratic regimes as those of the Shah of Iran and President Mubarak in Egypt. There would not have been such a movement, if the West had not falsified many facts about Islam and its social, political and economical teachings, presenting it in the most reactionary and anti-progress fashion imaginable.

The impact of oil on the social dynamics of the developing countries with vast oil resources must also be of concern to the rich, but energy-hungry of the "North", because, as a result of the interdependence discussed above, social instability in these countries will inevitably affect the oil-importing countries. One result of social instability and chaos in the developing countries is the mass migration of their population to the rich countries of the "North", a problem that has already caused considerable stress and tension in several European countries, and is beginning to affect the United States as well. Note that such massive migrations are *not* restricted to the people who come from poor, energy-depleted and undeveloped countries such as African countries, Bangladesh, Pakistan, or Brazil. Oil-rich countries such as Indonesia, Russia, Mexico, and Iran have also seen a significant fraction of their population migrate to the West. If the oil-exporting nations cannot get a fair price for their oil, if the rich and oil-importing countries of the "North" move toward protectionism and close their markets to the oil-producing nations, and if they attempt to control or dominate the oil-producing countries through military threats or invasion, then social conditions in the oil-producing countries will detoriate, nationalism and anti-foreign tendencies will rise, leading to revolutions, wars, and disruption of energy supplies. The same phenomenon can occur if some of the oil-exporting countries, such as Saudi Arabia, are somehow favored by the West or the "North", while others like Iran, Nigeria and Iraq are constantly pressured. The result of such a bias can be catastrophic. If in the eyes of most people in the Middle East a country like Saudi Arabia is doing well because of the support that she receives from the West, while their own countries are not doing as well, as a result of being pressured by the outside forces, the resulting resentment can lead to huge conflicts. Ayatollah Khomeini did use this fact skillfully to advance Islamic Revolution's cause among Muslim masses.

Another aspect of the social dynamics of the oil-exporting countries and its effect on energy supplies is the role of oil in the environment, which is discussed separately below.

3. THE STATE OF THE INTERNATIONAL ECONOMY

A number of important factors tie the development of oil reserves of developing countries to the international economy. For these countries it is vital to maintain a high level of revenue from their oil, and more generally their energy exports, if they are to continue developing their infrastructure and industrial basis, and satisfying the needs of their growing population, and at the same time investing in their oil industry in order to maintain and develop its resources to meet world wide demand. Exporting oil at an acceptable level, and for a reasonable price, requires a stable and growing international economy with increasing demand for energy. Maintenance and further development of oil resources in developing countries require huge capital and transfer of technology from the developed and energy-importing countries to the developing ones. This also requires a stable and growing international economy; otherwise the scarcity of the required capital will impede this, as a result of which the developing countries will suffer heavily. As the world economy and the energy market are becoming larger and more interdependent, the role of the international economy in the development of the developing and energy-producing countries is becoming more evident.

Even if we ignore the damage that the oil industries of Kuwait and Iraq suffered during the Gulf war, it is generally estimated that the OPEC countries need to invest about 60 billion dollars in their oil industries in the period 1991-95, if they are to expand their oil production capacity to meet the growth in the world wide demand. It is estimated that the demand for OPEC oil will rise to about 27.8 million barrels per day in 1995, and to 31.5 million barrels per day by the year 2000 (*Oil & Gas Journal*, Dec. 1994, p. 35). If we assume that the OPEC countries use between 80 to 90 percent of their installed capacity for producing oil, they would need to expand their production capacity from the present capacity of about 27 million barrels per day to about 35 million barrels per day by the year 2000. This expansion requires huge capital investment the bulk of which has to be provided by the developed and energy-importing countries of the "North". However, unless the economy of these countries is growing and robust, they will not be able to provide such a huge amount of capital to the developing countries. The destruction of the oil installations of Kuwait and Iraq during the Gulf war, and the damage that those of Iran suffered during its war with Iraq, have made this an even more important problem, since it is estimated that an additional 40 billion dollars is needed for repairing and upgrading their oil installations. In addition to these, significant capital investment, totalling billions of dollars, will be necessary for expanding the refining capacity of both the importing and exporting countries, and for developing the necessary technology for reducing CO_2 emission which damages the environment (see below), and for cleaning up the pollution already caused by the oil usage. Given that the economies of the Western countries and Japan, the most important oil-importing countries, are currently entrapped in relatively slow growth cycles, the uncertainties surrounding such capital investments are higher than any other time over the past two decades.

In addition, the energy policy of the United States weighs heavily on the oil market, and hence on the development plans of oil-exporting countries. In 1989, and for the first time since 1977, the gross crude oil imports of the United States exceeded her domestic production, and was equivalent to 42 percent of her national energy consumption. It is predicted that, if current trends continue, by the year 2000 the net imports of the United States will be equivalent to 55-60 percent of its consumption. Clearly, the energy policy of a country with such a huge thirst for oil can have a profound effect on oil market, which in turn depends to a large extent on her domestic economy and the demand for more oil. Thus, although over the past few years the need for cooperation between the oil producing and importing countries has become more evident than ever, strangely enough the Bush Administration opposed any *global* dialogue between oil producing and importing countries, but was in favor of the meaningless *bilateral* negotiations. The same President (George Bush) that talked about a *new world order*, presumably a world of cooperation, was opposed to any international dialogue between oil-exporting and importing countries. Even more strange was the Bush Administration's assertion that the oil price should be determined solely by *market forces*. The energy policy of the Clinton Administration is not completely clear and there is no firm indication about its general goals, as the US Department of Energy has been primarily preoccupied by the nuclear weapons and the clean up of the nuclear wastes dumping sites, although one may argue that the gasoline tax hike of 1993 might lead to energy and oil conservation.

Several studies have indicated that there is a negative correlation between the fluctuations in the oil price and those in the gross national products, or gross domestic products of many industrialized countries. For example, these studies have shown that the economies of Japan, the United States, France, Germany, and Canada show negative correlations with oil-price increases. However, such a negative correlation is not a very good indicator of the effect of the oil price on the international economy. We recall that while the price of oil was relatively high in the first half of the 1980-90 decade, the economies of the United States, Japan, and most of the Western European countries were expanding, whereas the second half of the same decade, which was characterized by the collapse of the oil price, was marked by recessionary economies, the effect of which presists even today. At the same time, although the oil-exporting countries, and in particular members of OPEC, increased their oil production by about 36 percent between 1985 and 1990, during the same period their net income *fell* by about 8 percent. This decrease in the oil income had a significant effect on the domestic policies and development program of these countries, which in some cases sparked social and political tensions. Those affected most were the most heavily populated countries, such as Nigeria and Egypt. At the same time, lower oil prices has *increased* the dependence of most of the oil-importing industrialized nations, and in particular the United States, on the foreign oil imports, resulting in larger trade deficits. But most important of all, it has resulted in the *loss* of over 500,000 jobs in the oil and related industries of the United States, perhaps permanently, and bankruptcy of hundreds of small and independent oil companies and oil equipment suppliers. In 1863, two years after the discovery of the first oil field in Pennsylvania, the price of oil was 13.75 dollars per barrel (D. Yergin, *The Prize*, Simon and Schuster, New York, 1991). Today, after over 130 years, the oil price is about 17 dollars per barrel. Over the same time period, the price of practically every commodity has increased by 10-20 folds. A cheap oil is not only harmful to the producer, it is also damaging to the consumer, because it impedes meaningful development of alternative energy sources.

Given these realities, it is absolutely essential to have international cooperation between the exporting and importing countries, and in particular, between the industrialized nations of the "North" and the oil-exporting countries of the "South". This cooperation should result in stable income for the developing and oil-exporting countries, so that they can further develop their resources and domestic economies, diversify their production, and build the necessary infrastructure for the post-oil era. As for the oil-importing countries, this should result in secure supply of energy at a reasonable price. At the same time, rich and oil-importing countries have to be sensitive to the economic development and improved social welfare of the developing and oil-exporting nations. The oil crises of 1956, 1967, 1973, 1979-80, and 1990-91 have demonstrated that the threats constantly weighing on world oil supplies are less associated with the physical availability of oil than with the economic difficulties, social infrastructure and political instability of the exporting countries. No real progress can be made in bringing about the harmonization of the national interests of the energy-producing and importing countries, if one loses sight of the crucial fact that the producing countries are entitled to a fair compensation for depleting their *non-renewable* national resources such as oil.

4. ENVIRONMENTAL ISSUES AND CONCERNS

To someone like this author who has lived in two of the largest metropolitan areas in the world -- Los Angeles and Tehran -- the sunsets in these two cities are quite spectacular. Colors blaze across their skies as the sun sinks and disappears. However, an aerial view of these cities during the day reveals another spectacular scene. Instead of the beautiful colors, one finds a layer of dark haze hanging menacingly over these cities. The sun light filters through the polluted air, giving rise to the spectacular scene at the sunset. However, polluted air can also cause health problems every year for millions of people living in these cities.

What is the main cause of air pollution in cities such as Los Angeles and Tehran? The main reason is the fossil fuels, mainly oil, and to some extent coal, the primary sources of energy that we burn every day in our vehicles, power plants, etc. In the USA alone fossil energy accounts for 85 percent of the current fuel use. But this dependence on fossil energy has serious implications for the future, and air pollution is but one of the problems caused by this kind of energy.

How much do we pay for using oil? 20 dollars per barrel? This price only reflects the cost of producing oil (including the costs of of labor and materials used for its extraction from underground reservoirs), and of transporting it to the consumer. But some of the costs of using fossil energy, and in particular oil, are not directly included in our energy bill, nor are they paid for by the companies that sell us energy. These are *hidden costs* of fossil energy that we pay indirectly for the health problems caused by air pollution resulting from using oil, gas, and coal; environmental degradation caused by global warming, acid rains, and water pollution. Since the producers and consumers do not pay directly for such costs, society as a whole must pay for them. Thus, although such costs are hidden, they are real. According to the American Lung Association, health costs, including, for example, lost potential income, of air pollution *alone* are estimated to be about 50 billion dollars a year. Moreover, although it is difficult to put a price on the damage to nature, acid rain has done significant harm to such ecosystems, especially in the industrialized countries of Europe and the USA.

How does fossil energy damage the environment? The Union of Concerned Scientists (UCS) carried out a comprehensive study of this issue, and what follows is a summary of its findings (*Nucleus*, 15, Summer 1993). When fossil fuels, especially oil, are burnt they emit several pollutants, such as nitrogen oxides (NO_x), sulfur oxide (SO_2), carbon monoxide (CO), hydrocarbons, and particulate materials. These pollutants cause environmental damage and severe public health problems, can irritate the lungs, cause bronchitis and pneumonia, decrease resistance to respiratory infections, promote the growth of cancerous tumors, lead to the formation of smog and precipitate out to form acid rain, and can affect visibility. These oxides combine with water vapor and form sulfuric and nitric acids, which become part of rain, snow, and clouds. After precipitating, they accumulate in lakes and rivers and harm plants and animal life. They also damage forests, crops, and even buildings.

Hydrocarbons are a broad class of pollutants, most of which react in the atmosphere with NO_x to form tropospheric (ground-level) ozone, a major constituent of smog. In the stratosphere (the upper atmosphere), ozone proctects the earth from sun's ultraviolet rays, which are harmful to humans. However, ozone in the trotosphere, in which we live and breathe, is harmful because it injures plant tissues, inhibits photosynthesis, and increases the susceptibility of crops to other pollutants, diseases, and drought. It also damages lung and respiratory systems in humans and animals, natural and synthetic rubbers, and fades certain dyes. Over a long period oftime, it can also lead to chronic lung disease and cancer.

In addition to these, oil-derived fuel emissions are also implicated in a threat to the future of humans and our planet: global warming. Emission of large amounts of CO_2, which is the major heat-trapping gas, and its build up in the atmosphere can cause an unprecedented rise in the earth's temperature. It has been suggested that such a warming would cause the sea levels to rise, forcing coastal communities to spend large sums of money to proctect against flooding. Such a warming would also affect agricultural output because of increased summer dryness and a higher frequency of droughts and heat waves. These emissions mostly are from motor vehicles and fossil fuel power plants. The rest come from industrial and residential sources. In the United States transportation alone consumes roughly 13 million barrel of oil a day, nearly 75 percent of the petroleum use and 40 percent of all the energy used each year. According to the UCS report, in 1988, 5.6 *billion tons* of CO_2 were emitted in the USA, 20 percent of which were from motor vehicles, while 37.6 million tons out of a total of 67.3 million tons of emitted CO came from motor vehicles. Fossil fuel power plants were responsible in 1988 for 10.7 million tons of CO emissions (16 percent of the total); 1.9 billion tons of CO_2 (35 percent of the total); nearly 12 million tons of NO_x (55 percent of the total); and 18 million tons of SO_2 (79 percent of the total sulfur dioxide emissions in the USA).

There are other harms done to the society and nature by oil and gas. Oil spills can leave waterways and their surrounding shores uninhabitable for some time and result in the loss of plants and animal life. According to the UCS report, with the 1989 *Exxon Valdez* spill alone an estimated 400,000 birds were killed in the months immediately following the spill, and others died later or suffered reproductive damages. Mammals and fish suffered as well, both with deaths and long-term injuries to the species. These spills can also affect humans, economically, socially, and even psychologically. The presence of oil in the environment can create a deep sense of uncertainty about the present and the future among the local residents. In Alaska, where Exxon Valdez spill occured, the spread of oil prevented normal fishing activities for 72 percent of people, resulting in strong feelings of economic uncertainty.

Finally, we should point out that as part of the "bottom-up" review that was carried out by Les Aspin, the first Defence Secretary of President Clinton, four threats to the national security of the United States were identified which were, (1) regional security; (2) *environmental problems*; (3) nuclear proliferation; and (4) economic stagnation. Thus, environmental problems, one of the main source of which is oil-related energy, have found a prominent role even in the national security of the United States.

So, after learning about the damage that fossil energy, especially oil, is inflicting upon us, we should ask ourselves again: How much is oil really costing us? Although it is notoriously difficult to estimate the costs of the damages caused by fossil fuels, most indications are that they are very large. According to the UCS report, for example, it is estimated that in the United States every ton of SO_2 that is emitted into the atmosphere costs society about 3500 dollars in health-related damage alone, and in 1988 the USA emitted 22.8 million tons of sulfur dioxide. If health care and other costs from all emissions were factored into the price of energy, the actual cost of a barrel of oil to the society may be at least *twice* as large as its nominal price of 17-20 dollars per barrel. It is also difficult to quantify the loss of historical monuments, lands of agricultural significance, plants, wildlife, etc. Estimating the possible cost of global warming to the earth is currently *impossible*.

To deal with this dangerous situation and its grim outlook, many governments have taken actions. In the United States, the Clean Air Act, amended by Congress in 1990, requires that automobile manfacturers install pollution control devices to reduce the emissions of hydrocarbons and NO_x; the polluted cities and suburbs meet federal air quality standards by certain deadlines; and that certain industries limit emissions of chemicals and air toxics. Japan has devised stringent specifications on sulfur in oil products, and Taiwan and Korea have tightened sulfur specifications of fuel oil and diesel. Even Thailand, which is considered a developing country, is tightening control on sulfur emissions. Thus, demand for low-sulfur oil is increasing in these countries, and as local resources for such fuels is scarce, the dependence of these countries on the Middle East,

North Africa, and Latin America oil is also increasing. This establishes a close connection between environmental concerns and the geopolitical factor already discussed. Capital constraints are also a concern in the planning and constructing critical projects that are necessary for developing clean fuel technologies, thus connecting environmental concerns to the international economy discussed above.

However, the Clean Air Act and similar initiatives are not enough for eliminating all pollutants, nor do they address greenhouse-gas emissions. For example, it is generally accepted that in the industrialized nations substantial reduction of CO_2 emission over the next 50 years will be difficult to achieve, unless alternative energy sources, other than oil, are developed and adopted. Thus, it has been proposed that a more comprehensive way to deal with the damage to society from fossil energy is to change the way it is priced, so that it can compare the real, total costs of fossil fuels with those of alternative sources. Although changing the energy pricing system is politically difficult and unpopular to implement, the hidden costs of oil, and more generally fossil energy, must be, and will eventually be, brought out of the closet, because such fuels represent a very damaging package. The environment, the economies of many countries, and the human health are all suffering because of our reliance on these fuels. Thus, as the public pressure mounts, drastic actions may be taken in many rich and oil-importing countries, which in turn will have deep and far reaching implications and consequences for the oil-exporting countries which rely, almost exclusively, on the income from the export of their oil.

5. SCIENTIFIC AND TECHNOLOGICAL ADVANCES

Scientific advances have also influenced the development of energy resources, and in particular those of oil, and their influence will even be greater in the future. This influence is exerted in several different ways.

(1) Technological advances in instrumentation and measurement equipments, together with the progress made in many branches of science have enabled us to gain a much deeper understanding of the effect of fossil energy, and in particular oil, on the environment, which we already discussed above.

(2) Significant scientific progress made over the past few years has provided us with a wealth of information about the geological formations that may contain oil, or have provided definitive clues to where they might be found. As a result, the estimated remaining recoverable oil and gas reserves of many countries have increased significantly. For example, the remaining recoverable oil in the United States is now estimated to be about three times larger than the estimated of a decade or fifteen years ago. Reservoir simulation, the mathematical and computational models for predicting flow of oil and gas in the underground reservoirs, has also benefitted greatly from such advances, giving us much higher levels of confidence for developing new onshore and offshore oil and gas resources, and more efficient development of the old reservoirs. It is at least partly based on such advancements that, for example, Shell Oil Company is willing to spend over 1.5 billion dollars on its offshore field in the Gulf of Mexico. Clearly, with adequate investment and a sound strategy the domestic oil production of the United States can be increased very significantly, which in turn will affect the oil market and the development of oil and gas resources in the world, and in particular those of the developing countries.

(3) Scientific advances can make alternative sources of energy competitive with fossil energy. What are these alternatives? Some of them are nuclear power, biomass and hydropower, solar thermal electric, photovoltaics, wind, geothermal resources, ocean thermal, wave and tidal power, and nuclear fusion. In terms of their cost, or the power they provide, most, if not all, of them are not currently competitive with fossil energy. Nuclear power can provide significant amounts of energy, but its significantly expanded development has been hampered by concerns over the safety of the nuclear reactors, accidental reactor damage, problems associated with nuclear wastes and their management and, in some developing countries, by the possible diversion of nuclear fuel to weapons. It is estimated that in the 1990s in the United States improvement of nuclear power requires nearly 400 million dollars a year. However, scientific advances should enable us to demonstrate the utility of at least one new type of reactor. This is an advanced light water reactor which features passive safety features. Successful operation of this reactor provides safe sources of energy. If the problems associated with the management of nuclear wastes are also solved, as expected, then nuclear power will also be an

energy source which does not harm the environment, and as such it will become the preferred source of energy.

Although there are also problems associated with other alternative sources of energy, it does not necessarily follow that they cannot be solved. For example, solar thermal electric, photovoltaics and wind sources of energy are still expensive. According to the report by the Electric Power Research Institute in Palo Alto, California, in 1980 in the United States the costs of generating electric power per killowatt-hour were 0.06, 0.30, 2.0, and 0.25 dollars, using gas and coal, wind, photovoltaics, and solar thermal methods, respectively. The corresponding costs in 1990 were 0.05, 0.08, 0.4, and 0.11 dollars, while the projected costs for the year 2000, according to the Electric Power Research Institute, are 0.05, 0.04, 0.20, and 0.08 dollars. Thus, by the end of this decade, and as a result of scientific and technological advances, the cost of generating electric power by wind and solar thermal methods will be fully comparable with that of fossil energy. These sources of energy do not generate any pollution, and they are also *limitless*. Moreover, they are not vulnerable to many factors that affect the development of oil-based energy, and thus are a stable and dependable source of energy. It is also estimated that in the United States solar and other forms of renewable sources of energy require about 200 million dollars a year for the rest of this decade for their full development, much lower than the necessary capital for the development of new oil and gas fields and upgrading their present infrastructure. Thus, by the end of this decade solar and other forms of renewable energy resources may contribute very significantly to the energy needs of the United States. Obviously, by proper technology transfer, the same renewable energy resources may be utilized in many other countries, especially in the developing countries that lack fossil energy resources.

(4) Finally, scientific advances can contribute to the development of materials and technologies that will help us *save* energy, and thus decrease our net energy consumption and reliance on oil. For example, up until 1986, it was generally believed that it would be very difficult, if not impossible, to develop materials that become *superconducting* at temperatures above 420 degrees F. These are materials that pass electrical current *without* any resistance, and thus do not dissipate (waste) any energy. However, beginning with the Nobel Prize winning work of Georg Bednorz and Karl-Alex Muller at IBM laboratories in Zurich in 1986, several

new classes of materials have been discovered that become superconducting at up to 220 degrees F. Magnetometers operating at low temperatures have already been used to make magnetocardiograms, and they are now available commercially. The detection of magnetic anomalies associated with oil deposits and other geological features will also benefit tremendously from superconduting gradiometers in the near future. Most important of all, there are bright possibilities for power transmission lines made of superconducting materials, resulting in huge energy savings.

Thus, we may conclude that scientific and technological advances have contributed to the development of alternative energy resources and better understanding of the effect of oil-based energy on the environment, and will contribute to the development of materials and technologies that will save energy and also result in a cleaner environment.

III. CONCLUSIONS

In this article, we analyzed various factors that we believe affect the development of fossil energy resources of developing countries. Based on our analysis, we conclude that

1. Fossil energy is an international commodity, and the development of its resources is affected by geopolitical factors as well as the international economy, and the social dynamics of the developing countries with rich resources of this kind of energy.
2. The rapid growth of the population in many of the oil-producing countries, and the emergence of Islamic Fundamentalism in the Islamic world, some of whose members possess vast resources of oil and gas, are two important social factors that will have profound effect on the oil market and politics. As long as the needs of this population are not met, and so long as many corrupt and antidemocratic governments in the Islamic world are supported by the West and the "North", there will be mass resistance to the West, and Islamic Fundamentalism will continue to trive. These in turn will give rise to a turbulent energy outlook for the foreseeable future.

3. Oil is a *non-renewable* national wealth of many developing countries. It cannot be squandered cheaply so that the "North" can maintain its standards of living, while leaving very little for the future generations in the developing countries. Its price has to be reasonable, and there has to be a transfer of technology from the developed countries to the developing and oil-exporting nations, so that the latter countries can build their economical and political infrastructures and prepare for a future, which is not too distant, in which there is no oil to export.

4. Environmental, safety, and health considerations can, and will, dominate technical and economical factors in the future.

5. Because of the public awareness about the environmental hazards of fossil energy, the development of new sources of energy is imperative and is already underway. Public acceptance of such new energy resources and technologies is critical to their effective utilization, and this acceptance depends on their effect on their cost *and* their effect on the environment.

In his now famous, and in my opinion arrogant and baseless, article in the *New York Times* in 1990, Francis Fukuyama, a high ranking State Department official in the Bush Administration, claimed that *history is ending*, because the Soviet Union, her empire, and communism have all collapsed, and thus have ceased to provide the West with competition. I believe that not only history is not ending, but if anything, it is more vibrant than ever before, since the most humane values and principles, namely, elimination of exploitation, fair and just redistribution of wealth, peace, and freedom in all forms and shapes for all *the engines of history* not only have not died, but are alive and thriving more than any other time throughout the history of mankind. These are exactly what the rapidly growing population of many oil-producing countries, that the West has tried to dominate for over a century, as well as that of many poor and energy-hungry countries of our planet, are demanding today. If these demands are not met, oil and rapid population growth (and the social, political and environmental problems that they create), and socio-political movements such as Islamic Fundamentalism, that are the direct result of not paying attention to these needs and demands, will guarantee that history will continue for at least many more decades, if not centuries, to come.

Acknowledgments

This work is partly the result of numerous stimulating discussions with many colleagues, a list of whom is too long to be given here. I am grateful to all of them. Preliminary versions of this article were first presented at the Gustave E. von Grunebaum Center for Near Eastern Studies of the University of California, Los Angeles, and in the International Non-Renewable Energy Sources Congress, December 1993, Tehran, Iran.

THE ROLE OF POLITICAL RISK IN FOREIGN DIRECT INVESTMENT THE CASE OF EIGHT ASIAN COUNTRIES

Harinder Singh
Department of Economics
Grand Valley State University
1 Campus Drive
Allendale, MI 49401

Abstract—In the present post-Cold War era, punctuated with sporadic political tensions and globalization of economic production, the positive influence of political stability on different dimensions of economic performance needs to be investigated more intensively. This paper provides sample evidence of the benefits of political stability for one international dimension of economic performance: the ability to attract foreign direct investment. The influence of political instability on Foreign Direct Investment (FDI) flows is analyzed for eight developing countries. The results of previous empirical work are mixed, partly because the proposed proxies for political instability capture only some aspects of a complex phenomena. This investigation finds a broad-based subjective evaluation index of political stability to be a significant determinant of FDI flows in eight Asian countries. An alternative index of political risk as it relates to business operating conditions is statistically significant in some specifications.

I. INTRODUCTION

In this chapter, the role political instability in determining Foreign Direct Investment[1] (FDI) flows to developing countries is analyzed. Political instability can manifest in a variety of events ranging from splintering of political parties, smoldering ethnic tensions, to demonstrations, riots and assassinations. Before we analyze the precise role different aspects of political instability can play in determining FDI flows, some background about recent global trends is in order.

The period after the Cold War is often characterized as the beginning of a New World Order. Different interpretations of the term New World Order have been made. For the purpose of this paper, I regard the New World Order to consist of a fundamental change in both our political and economic constraints. First, in the political domain, after the demise of the Cold War between the super powers, the contours of the new world lack definition. The disciplining and policing role by the two super powers has decreased greatly. Consequently, the propensity for political strife and instability within and across countries may have increased. In this context, the influence of political instability on economic activity in general and FDI flows in particular has assumed greater importance.

The second fundamental change in the New World Order has been evolving over sometime: the integration of national economies and the internationalization of the stages of production. This trend toward globalization in the New World Order has escalated in recent years. One aspect of integrated economies is that different countries compete with each other for the same global supply of capital resources. Taken together, I take the term New World Order to imply two fundamental forces: the lack of political definition/discipline and the globalization of economic production.[2]

---

1. Foreign Direct investment is defined as at least 10% controlling interest in a local enterprise with a view to influencing management decisions.
2. The impact of the New World Order is not directly tested in the economic model because the evolution of this new reality is continuous and uneven. Consequently, a shift dummy variable will not capture the gradual and uneven evolution of the new order. However, a time trend variable is included to capture **all** time-varying factors which are not explicitly in the model. Some evolution of the new order is probably picked up by this time trend variable.

In the context of this New World Order, the stakes for developing countries are high for two reasons. First, they are attempting to catch up with the developed economies and their expectations have been raised by some recent success stories, particularly in East and South Asia. Second, the traditional sources of capital are drying up. The World Debt Tables (WDT), 1994-95, indicate that official development finance to developing countries has only increased marginally from 42.6 billion dollars in 1989 to 54.5 billion dollars in 1994. Moreover, commercial bank lending has resulted in an outflow of capital, from a positive 0.8 billion dollars in 1989 to negative 2.2 billion dollars in 1993.

In contrast to these traditional sources of foreign capital, there are two channels of capital flows which have shown a dramatic increase. Portfolio equity investment to developing countries has jumped from 3.5 billion dollars in 1989 to 39.5 billion dollars in 1994. However, as the recent events in Mexico demonstrate, equity portfolio investors may have a short term outlook and sustainability may be an issue. The second channel of external capital flow involves a relatively long term commitment: Foreign Direct Investment. FDI has also increased dramatically from 25.7 billion dollars in 1989 to 77.9 billion dollars in 1994. Moreover, the WDT Report indicates that FDI has been harnessed by developing countries at different income levels, although middle income countries are relatively more successful than low-income countries.

Compared to alternative sources of external finance, FDI generally has some inherent advantages for the development effort. First, the foreign investor is sharing the risk of successfully launching an enterprise, consequently he/she will have an incentive to monitor the implementation of the project quite closely. Second, there is potential for sharing new technology and training with the industries from the host countries. Third, the influx of FDI can be tied toward developing a dynamic export sector, although in some cases FDI is obtained at the cost of exporting natural resources (i.e., "extractive" FDI). Finally, FDI flows unlike official development assistance is governed by market discipline and the need to be successful in a competitive environment. Consequently, there is an in built premium for efficiency.

The paper is organized as follows: In Section 2, we discuss previous empirical research on the effect of political instability on FDI flows. Section 3, discusses previous empirical findings on other factors besides political instability that have shown to determine FDI flows. In Section 4, details of the sample data for testing the influence of political instability in a sample of eight South Asian countries are discussed. Section 5 analyzes the empirical results. Section 6 follows with conclusions, policy implications and suggestions for future empirical work.

II. THE ROLE OF POLITICAL INSTABILITY

Although "political risk" is generally mentioned as influencing decisions to invest in another country, previous empirical results do not always support the hypothesis. Subjective surveys by Aharoni (1966) showed that executives rank political instability as the most important variable, apart from market potential. On the other hand, Bennett and Green (1972) found that U.S. direct investments are not affected by political instability in the recipient countries.

Levis (1979) employing two proxies for political stability obtained conflicting results. He found "the absence of aggressive domestic behavior within the political system against groups or officeholders" to be a significant determinant of FDI for the current period but not for the lagged period. An alternative variable (the legitimacy of the regime) was found to be significant for the lagged period but not significant for the current period.

Root and Ahmed (1979) performing a discriminant analysis of 58 developing countries found that "the number of regular (constitutional) changes in government leadership between 1956 and 1967" was significant. However, other political variables such as number of internal armed attacks, degree of nationalism and colonial affiliation did not show significant results.

The COBDAB data base was employed by Nigh (1985) to construct aggregate measures of intra-country and inter-country conflict and cooperation. He found that for developed countries inter-nation political events were more significant determinants of FDI. On the other hand, for developing countries intra-nation political events had a more robust relationship with FDI. Another extensive study by Schneider and Frey (1985) found a negative relationship between "number of political strikes and riots in host countries" and "the inflow of foreign direct investment".

A recent investigation by Wheeler and Mody (1992) found a principal component measure of administrative efficiency and political risk to be statistically insignificant. An empirical investigation of South East Asian developing countries by Lucas (1993) did not directly incorporate proxies for sociopolitical risk, although he found dummies for "good events" such as the Asian and Olympic games in Korea, Acquino's accession in the Philippines to be positively related to FDI. Conversely, "negative events" such as Park's assassination in South Korea and Marcos's martial law in Philippines had a negative influence on FDI flows.

III. POLITICAL RISK INDEX (PRISK)

The results of previous empirical studies diverge because of differences in samples (both time period and countries analyzed) and the precise way in which the proxy for political instability is operationalized. As stated earlier, political instability can be represented by a range of political events which could be either violent or non-violent. Clearly, political instability is a complex, multi-dimension phenomena. Most proxies that are available, may capture only some aspects of this complex determinant.

Within the context of FDI flows, however, what is critical is how political events are perceived to change the overall risk configuration for the host country. These events have to be evaluated within the historical and institutional context of each host country within the context of the New World Order. For this reason, an over-arching proxy we employ for political instability is a subjective risk index based on an unbiased judgment of experts in the field. These judgments are "unbiased" in the sense that the decision makers do not have a personal axe to grind.

Due to these considerations, a Political Risk Index (PRISK) developed by Business Environment Risk Intelligence, S.A. (BERI) is employed in the empirical model[3]. Approximately 60 Political Specialists from around the world, evaluate each country with respect to a range of indicators of political instability. Six causes of political risk, such as fractionalization of the political spectrum, linguistic, ethnic and religious fractionalization, coercive political risk (dependence on and\or importance to a hostile

---

3. I am very grateful to Dr. F.T. Haner, President, Business Environment Risk Intelligence, for graciously allowing me to use the data for this investigation.

power) and two symptoms of political risk (societal conflict involving demonstrations and street violence) are evaluated by the judges. The qualitative index based on these criteria ranges from 0 (prohibitive risk) to 100 (complete stability). The values determined by 60 political specialists are averaged for each country on a annual basis. This single averaged index for each host country provides a comprehensive indicator for potential political risk. Consequently, our first hypothesis is:

Hypothesis I: Does political instability (proxied by a comprehensive judgment index) independently influence FDI flows to developing countries?

IV. POLITICAL BUSINESS INDEX (BRISK)

In 1981 Stephen Kobrin pointed out that "The term 'political risk' thus appears constrained from both an analytical and operational viewpoint. What we are, or should be, concerned with is the impact of events which are political in the sense that they arise from power or authority relationships and which affect (or have the potential to affect) the firm's operation. Not the events, qua events, but their potential manifestation as constraints upon foreign investors should be of concern." (p. 71)

It appears that the empirical evidence on the impact of political risk may be mixed because political risk is not evaluated within the context of business operating conditions. Helleiner (1989) has shown that investment incentives created by the government, such as tax holidays are not effective in inter-country investment decisions. Most surveys support the notion that specific incentives do not have a major impact, particularly when these incentives are perceived to compensate for other comparative disadvantages. On the other hand, it is generally believed that low political risk within the context of good business operating conditions will exert a positive effect on FDI flows.

Again this paper employs a qualitative index developed by BERI representing the judgments of experts in the field. The Operation Risk Index makes judgments not only on political risk and continuity but also on how the political establishment controls the general business environment. Besides political risk, additional factors considered include potential for nationalization, currency convertibility, trade flow performance, enforceability of contracts, infrastructure availability and local management skills. Following Stephen Kobrin's advice this qualitative judgment made by 105 experts incorporates political risk within the context of business operating conditions.

Based on these considerations our second hypothesis is:

Hypothesis II: Does political risk as reflected in the general business operating conditions significantly influence FDI flows in developing countries?

V. OTHER FACTORS INFLUENCE FDI FLOWS TO DEVELOPING COUNTRIES

In order to analyze the role played by political risk, we need to control for other factors that are known to influence FDI flows. In this section, we briefly discuss previous work to determine the appropriate control variables.

Dependent Variable: Relative FDI Flows

A relative measure of FDI is employed to control for any large country effects. The dependent variable is FDI flows in constant dollars (normalized by the import price deflator), relative to real GDP (henceforth referred to as PFDI). PFDI is "net" in that it excludes repatriated profits. However, the fact that some developing countries have become exporters of capital is a positive sign, so outward bound FDI is not excluded from FDI flows.

GDP Growth Rate

The size of the market, (typically proxied by the level of GNP) or potential market size (proxied by GDP growth rate) appears to be an important determinant of FDI flows. Bandera and White (1968) found market size to be a significant determinant for United States FDI. For developing countries, Root and Ahmed (1979), Torrisi (1985), Schneider and Frey (1985), and Wheeler and Mody (1992) all find market size to be significant.

An extensive survey by UNCTC (Pearce et al., 1992) on FDI flows cites evidence for potential market size (growth rate of GDP). Based on a forward looking model, one would expect potential market size to be a more relevant variable rather than actual market size. Lunn (1980) found the growth rate of output to be statistically significant. Since our dependent variable is FDI relative to the level of GDP, it is more appropriate to employ the growth rate of GDP to avoid spurious correlation. Consequently, we include GROWTH RATE to control for potential market size.

Relative Wage Index

Another likely candidate is wage costs, the hypothesis being that lower relative wage costs will encourage FDI flows to minimize costs of production. Extensive empirical investigations of the relative wage costs in Canada and the U.S. seem to indicate that for developed countries, wage differentials are not a significant determinant [Owen (1982), Gupta (1983)]. However, recent results for developing countries seem to indicate that relative wage costs are a significant determinant of FDI flows.

Flamm (1984), Schneider and Frey (1985), Lucas (1993), and Wheeler and Mody (1992) all find a wage cost variable to be significant. This difference in results could be due to structural differences between developed and developing countries and the fact that relative wage differentials in developing countries are more divergent. We include a real earnings index as a control for real wages (WINDEX).

Exchange Rate

Although all the variables are converted to dollars, Lucas (1993) has contended that the exchange rate may have " a residual role with respect to exchange rate risk, for example, in determining the value of repatriated profits or in threatening restrictions on such remittances." (p. 393). In order to control for this possibility the real exchange rate is included as a control variable (ERATE).

Supply Side Factors

The inclusion of home country factors is another possibility. When Culem (1988) analyzed the bilateral flows of direct investment for six developed countries (United States, Germany, France, U.K., the Netherlands and Belgium), he found that the characteristics of the home country of the investing firm (e.g., growth rates and labor costs) did not improve the performance of the model. We cannot control for home country factors of specific countries since our dependent variable is global FDI flows to host countries.[4] A general increase in the opportunity costs of the home countries would influence the size of the overall flow of FDI to developing countries but not its specific allocation to different countries. Consequently, in order to control for aggregate supply side effects, we include the average industrial production index of the G-7 countries [computed from IMF's International Financial Statistics (1993)] as a control variable (IPIndex).

Lagged PFDI

FDI flows are likely to take time to adjust to desired levels, depending upon the specific constraints faced by a transnational corporation. A simple partial adjustment process can incorporate the speed of adjustment. If the lagged dependent variable is included on the right hand side of the regression equation, a partial stock adjustment model is represented, [see Pindyck and Rubinfeld (1991), pp. 208-209 for details].

There are two other persuasive reasons for including lagged dependent variable. First, it controls for any residual autocorrelation which may exist. Second, the lagged dependent variable indirectly incorporates other "omitted" relevant factors which may have influenced FDI in the previous period. Consequently, a lagged dependent variable is employed as a control variable (PFDI1).

Based on the above considerations our estimated equation (MODEL 2 in the table) can be represented as:

$$PFDI = D_1 + D_2(\text{GROWTH RATE}) + D_3(\text{WINDEX}) + D_4(\text{ERATE}) \quad (1)$$
$$+ D_5(\text{PFDI1}) + D_6(\text{IPINDEX}) + D_7(\text{PRISK}) + E_t.$$

Where, E_t is a random error term and all other variables have been defined in the discussion above.

---

4. Data on country specific FDI is not available in a comprehensive manner. One possible source is the U.S. Department of Commerce data of Outward bound FDI. This data is disaggregated at the sectoral level.

VI. Data Specifics

The empirical results are based on a pooled model. In order to keep the data set manageable and to minimize inter-regional differences, the sample study is performed on eight Asian countries: India and Pakistan (South Asia), S. Korea (East Asia), and Indonesia, Malaysia, Philippines, Singapore and Thailand (South East Asia). The time period of analysis is 1978-1992, governed basically by the availability of the data for the BERI qualitative indices.

Table 1. Descriptive Statistics

Variable	Mean	Range	Source
Real FDI as a % of GDP (PFDI)	2%	-0.33% to 19.89%	World Debt Tables World Bank
Annual GDP % (Growth Rate)	6.31%	-7.33% to 13.43%	World Tables World Bank
Real Earnings (1970 =100) (WINDEX)	173.84	65.09 to 436.66	World Tables World Bank
Political Risk Index (PRISK)	48.27	27 to 80	Beri, S.A.
Industrial Production Index (IPINDEX)	98.78	88.71 to 114.57	International Financial Statistics, IMF[*]
Operation Risk Index (BRISK)	52.17	29 to 78	Beri, S.A.
Exchange Rate Foreign Currency Per $ (ERATE)	241.05	1.81 TO 1842.81	World Tables World Bank

Notes: (1) Range gives the minimum and maximum values in the sample. (2) The sample data spans from 1978 to 1992, with the exception of WINDEX which is available only from 1978-90.

Table 1 shows the definition, mean, range and the source of each variable employed in the model. There is considerable variation in the relative

---

[*] Note that the International Monetary Fund (IMF) reports the real effective exchange rate for most developed countries only for the 1980s and 1990s, but not for the 1970s.

FDI flows to the eight countries and in the independent variables. In particular, the qualitative indices for political and business risk range from the twenties to the eighties, indicating considerable differences in risk perceptions for different countries over time.

Table 2. FDI and Political Risk Index (PRISK)

Variable	Model 1	Model 2
Dependent Variable	PRFDI	PFDI
CONST.	-2.26	-5.35
	(-2.49)	(-2.62)
PRISK	0.034	0.033
	(2.43)	(2.19)
TIME	0.058	-
	(1.76)	
GROWTH RATE	0.026	0.022
	(.74)	(.58)
PFDI1	0.92	0.93
	(15.98)	(13.08)
ERATE	-0.00043	-0.00027
	(-1.44)	(-.55)
WINDEX	-	-0.0019
		(-.64)
IPINDEX	-	0.044
		(2.27)
F	185.83	104.45
D.W.	2.67	2.11
Adj R^2	0.88	0.86
Observations	120	101

Notes: (1) T-values are in parenthesis. (2) The Alternative Durbin Statistic for Model 2 indicates a t-statistic of 0.68 for the lagged error term.

Table 3. FDI and Business Risk Index (BRISK)

Variables	Model 1	Model 2
Dependent Variable	PRFDI	PFDI
CONST.	-2.05 (-2.18)	-4.54 (-2.33)
BRISK	0.032 (2.05)	0.031 (1.81)
TIME	0.037 (1.20)	-
GROWTH RATE	0.023 (.64)	0.017 (.46)
PFDI1	0.94 (17.66)	0.95 (14.08)
ERATE	-.00021 (-0.77)	-0.00014 (-0.29)
WINDEX	-	-0.0013 (-.42)
IPG7	-	0.034 (1.84)
F	182.77	102.59
D.W.	2.70	2.12
Adj. R^2	0.88	0.86
Observations	120	101

Notes: (1) T-values are in parenthesis. (2) The Alternative Durbin Statistic for Model 2 indicates a t-statistic of -0.69 for the lagged error term.

VII. Empirical Results

Having described the variables and discussed the rationale for including various control variables, we now proceed to test each hypothesis. The hypothesis testing can be represented by a simple equation:

$$PFDI = F(HV, CV) \qquad (2)$$

Besides the proxy for the hypothesized variable (HV), the specification of the vector of control variables (CV) is important for correctly estimating the equation. Here we have taken previous empirical work as a guide to what should be included (Section 3). All models are estimated with Ordinary Least Squares. Since higher income countries may attract more absolute flows, all variables are in real and relative terms.

Political Risk (PRISK)

Hypothesis I: Does political instability (proxied by a comprehensive evaluation index) independently influence FDI flows to developing countries?

In order to analyze the influence of PRI on FDI flows, two different specifications are employed. One general problem with the data is some missing observations. As a general rule, if data is not available for a specific variable and time period, the observation is excluded from the regression estimation[5]. All results are reported after White's (1980) correction for heteroscedasticity.

A major issue in estimation is the problem of autocorrelation. The inclusion of the lagged dependent variable reduces autocorrelation considerably. Since we have a lagged dependent variable on the right hand side, the Durbin Watson statistic is not strictly applicable, although it does give some indication of the extent of autocorrelation. Consequently, for each hypothesis the Alternative Durbin statistic is estimated for Model 2.

Model 1: In the initial model, relative FDI flows are regressed with growth rate, lagged FDI, exchange rate, a time dummy and the political risk index. The high t-value of RFDI1 (15.98) and the low value of the adjustment coefficient (0.08)[6] indicates that the stock adjustment model should be employed. GDP growth rate has the expected positive sign but is not statistically significant. Similarly, the exchange rate and time trend have the expected sign, with the time trend being significant at the 10 percent level.

---

5. The alternatives of either interpolating for the missing values or employing the mean values as a proxy are regarded as less desirable.
6. The adjustment coefficient is obtained by subtracting the beta coefficient of the lagged dependent variable from unity. Please see Pindyck (1991, p. 208-209) for details.

The political risk index (PRISK) has the expected positive sign and is significant at the 1% level. Approximately 88% of the variation in relative FDI flows is explained by the independent variables.

Model 2: In the alternative specification, we include the supply side variable about the industrial production of the G7 countries (IPINDEX) and the real earnings index (WINDEX). The sample size is reduced since the earning index is only available until 1990. Indeed, this is the primary reason for estimating an alternative specification. The results from model 2 indicate that the political risk index remains significant at the 5 percent level.

The alternative Durbin test for autocorrelation in a "lagged dependent variable model" indicates that first order autocorrelation is not statistically significant (the residuals of model 2 regressed against lagged residuals results in a t-value of -0.68). Results of these two specifications reveal that a comprehensive qualitative index of political risk is a significant determinant of FDI flows to developing countries.

Business Risk (BRISK)

As discussed earlier, it may be useful to analyze the influence of political risk as it affects business operating conditions. Besides political risk, BRISK captures a wide range of antecedent conditions which affect business environment. These factors include potential for nationalization, currency convertibility, trade flow performance, enforceability of contracts, infrastructure availability and local management skills. In order to test the significance of BRISK, the same specifications of Model 1 and Model 2 are employed.

In Model 1 specification, BRISK is significant at the 5 percent level. When the hypothesis is tested for Model 2 specification, BRISK is significant only at the 10 percent level. This result could be because of the fact that business operating conditions are correlated with economic performance variables.[7]

---

7. The Pearson correlation between the GDP growth rate variable and BRISK is 0.28, the corresponding correlation between growth rate and PRISK is 0.23. Consequently, multicollinearity resulting in higher standard errors reduces the significance of BRISK.

XIII. Concluding Remarks

Since socio-political instability is a complex phenomena, it appears that there are significant differences in previous research when different proxies are employed to capture the relationship between FDI flows and political instability. The results indicate that a broad based, qualitative Political Risk Index significantly influences relative FDI flows. Since this index is the average of the subjective evaluations of experts in the field, it captures different dimensions of political instability in a more comprehensive manner than specific data related to one or few aspects of political instability. This difference may partially explain why the proxy for political instability is significant in this investigation and previous results have been mixed.

A qualitative index for political risk reflected in general business conditions is a significant factor for FDI flows, although the results are not as robust as for the political risk index. This may be due to the confounding influence of economic performance variables (such as GDP growth rate) which are correlated with business operating conditions.

In the New World Order after the demise of the Cold War, political tensions and conflicts have become sporadic if not endemic. The time trend variable in the regressions, picks up some of the evolutionary trends in the New World Order which are not captured by other explanatory variables. The stakes are progressively increasing over time because every country is competing for the same global resources. Within this context, developing countries are attempting to improve the economic conditions of the general masses. It is important to realize that political policies that foster stability and continuity have discernible economic implications. In this investigation, we have shown that at least on dimension of economic activity (FDI flows) is positively influenced by stable political conditions. In general, the dynamic linkage between political policies and economic performance is difficult to ignore and needs intensive scrutiny.

A number of general caveats are in order. First, country-specific data can mask a great deal of complexity and variation within the country. Consequently, only broad trends can be inferred. Second, the proxies we utilize to test the hypothesis may not have captured the entire complexities of the phenomena. Third, there are some missing observations is some of the explanatory variables, which are excluded in the estimation process. Fourth, this investigation is confined to eight Asian countries. The results indicate that in the New World Order, the impact of political instability on FDI flows continues to be significant. It remains to be seen if the results can be generalized to other countries. Due to these limitations, the results should be regarded as tentative.

Future empirical work needs to develop alternative proxies for political instability, for a wider set of developing countries with a different set of control variables to confirm the robustness of these results.

REFERENCES

Agarwal, J.P.,"Determinants of Foreign Direct Investments: A Survey", *Weltwirtschaftliches Archiv*, 1989, Vol. 116, pp.739-773.

Aharoni, Y.,*"The Foreign Investment Decision Process,"* Cambridge, Mass.: Harvard Graduate School of Business,1966.

Bandera, V.N. and White, J.T., "US direct investments and domestic markets in Europe", *Economia Internazionale*, 1968,21, pp. 117-133.

Barro, R, "Economic Growth in a Cross Section of Countries", *Quarterly Journal of Economics*, 1991, CVI(2), 407-444.

Bennett, P.D. and Green, R.T.,"Political instability as a determinant of direct foreign investment in marketing", *Journal of Marketing Research*,1972, 9, 162-186.

Browns, R.L., Durbin, J. and Evans, J.M.,"Techniques for testing the constancy of regression relationships over time", *Journal of Royal Statistical Society*, 1975, 37, 49-73.

Buckley, P.J. , Casson, M.,"A long-run theory of the multinational enterprise", in Buckley, P.J. and Casson, M.C. (Eds.) *The Future of Multinational Enterprise*, (London: Macmillan, 1976), pp. 32-65.

Casson, M "The Theory of Foreign Direct Investment"in *International Investment*, Buckley, P., Ed., (Aldershot, England: Edward Elgar Publishing Ltd., 1990), pp. 244-273.

Caves, M.C., *Multinational Enterprise and Economic Analysis*, (Cambridge: Cambridge University Press, 1982).

Caves, M.C., Porter, M.E. and Spence, A.M.,, *Competition in the Open Economy*, (Cambridge: Harvard University Press, 1980).

Chen, Edward, "Foreign Direct Investment and Trade as a vehicle for Rapid Economic Growth: The NIE Experience" Working Paper presented in Colombo, Feb. 1994.

Culem, C.G.,"The Locational Determinants of Direct Investment among Industrialized Countries", *European Economic Review*, 1988, 32, 885-904.

Dipak, G., *The Economics of Political Violence: The Effect of Political Instability on Economic Growth*, (New York: Prager, 1990).

Dollar, D.,"Outward-oriented Developing Economies Really Do Grow More Rapidly: Evidence from 95 LDC's 1976-1985", *Economic Development and Cultural Change*, 1992, 40,3, 523-544.

Dunning, J.H., "The Determinants of international production," *Oxford Economic Papers*, 1973, 25, 289-336.

_____, *International Production and the Multinational Enterprise*, (London: Allen and Urwin, 1981).

Gooptu, S., "Portfolio Investment Flows to Emerging Markets, Policy Research Working Papers, *International Economics Department, World Bank*, 1993.

Flamm, K., "The Volatility of offshore investment, *Journal of Development Economics*, 1984, 16, 231-248.

Fry, M.J., "Foreign Direct Investment in a Macroeconomic Framework: Finance, Efficiency, Incentives and Distortions." WPS 1141, *International Economics Department, World Bank*, 1993.

Green, R., "Political Instability as a Determinant of U.S. Foreign Investment", *Bureau of Business Research*, University of Texas at Austin, 1972.

Gupta, V.K., "A Simultaneous determination of structure, conduct and performance in Canadian manufacturing", *Oxford Economic Papers,1983*, 35, 281-301.

Helleiner, G.K., "Transnational Corporations and Direct Foreign Investment", in *Handbook of Development Economics*, (Elsevier Publishers, 1989), Vol. II, pp. 1441-1480.

Hein, S., "Trade Strategy and the Dependency Hypothesis: A comparison of Policy, Foreign Investment, and Economic Growth in Latin America and East Asia, *Economic Development and Cultural Change*, 1992, 40(3), 495-521.

Hymer, S., "The International Operations of National Firms: A Study of Direct Foreign Investment", (Cambridge, MA: MIT Press, 1966 (published in 1976)).

Hymer, S., "The Efficiency (Contradictions) of Multinational Corporations", *American Economic Review*, 1971, 110, 2.

International Finance Corporation, "Trends in Private Investment in Developing Countries, World Bank, 1992.

Kobrin, S., "Political Risk: A Review and Reconsideration," *Journal of International Business*, Spring 1981, pp. 67-80.

Leamer, E., "Sensitivity analysis would help", *American Economic Review*, 1985, 73(3), 308-313.

Levis, M., "Does political instability in developing countries affect foreign investment flow? An Empirical examination," *Management International Review*, 1979, 19, 59-68.

Lim, L.Y. and Fong, P.E.,"Foreign Direct Investment and Industrialization in Malaysia, Singapore, Taiwan and Thailand",Development Center of the Organization for Economic Co-operation and Development (OECD Paris, 1991).

Lucas, R.,"On the Determinants of Direct Foreign Investment: Evidence from East and Southeast Asia", *World Development*, 1993, 21(3), 391-406.

Lunn, J.L., "Determinants of US direct investment in the EEC", *European Economic Review*,1980, 13, 93-101.

Nigh, D.,"The effect of political events on US direct foreign investment: A pooled time-series cross-sectional analysis", *Journal of International Business Studies*, 1985, 16, 1-17.

Pindyck, R and Rubinfeld, D, "Econometric Models and Economic Forecasts," (New York: McGraw Hill, 1991.

Pearce, R., Islam, A. and Sauvant, K., "The Determinants of Foreign Direct Investment, A Survey of empirical evidence, "*United Nations Centre on Transnational Corporations*, (New York: United Nations, 1992).

Root, F. and Ahmed, A., "Empirical Determinants of Manufacturing Direct Foreign Investment in Developing Countries", *Economic Development and Cultural Change*, 1979, 27, 751-767.

Schneider, F. and Frey, B., "Economic and Political Determinants of Foreign Direct Investment", *World Development*, 1985, 13(2), 161-175.

Torrisi, C.R., "The determinants of direct foreign investment in a small LDC"' *Journal of Economic Development*, 1985, 10(2), 29-45.

Vernon, R., "International investment and international trade in the product cycle", *Quarterly Journal of Economics*, 1966, 80, 190-207.

_____, "The Product Cycle Hypothesis in a new international environment", *Oxford Bulletin of Economics and Statistics*, 1979, 41, 255-67.

Wheeler, D. and Mody, A., "International investment location decisions, The case of U.S. firms", *Journal of International Economics*, 1992, 33, 57-76.

White, H., "A Heteroscedasticity-consistent covariance matrix and a direct test for heteroscedasticity, *Econometrica*, 1980, 48, 817-838.

THE MACROECONOMIC EFFECTS OF OIL PRICE SHOCKS

Mohsen Bahmani-Oskooee
Department of Economics
The University of Wisconsin-Milwaukee
Milwaukee, WI 53201

Margaret M. Malixi
Department of Economics
California State University
Bakersfield, CA 93311

Abstract—The near doubling of oil prices in the United States in 1990 was commonly viewed to be a result of Iraq's maneuvers to raise oil prices and her eventual invasion of Kuwait less than a week later. This event led to major revisions in the forecasts of the economic outlook for the U.S. and also renewed interest in the impact of oil price shocks on important macroeconomic variables. This chapter investigates potential channels of impact of oil price shocks on the U.S. economy during the last quarter of a century. We investigate both the demand and supply side effects of such shocks. The nature and significance of the impact of oil price variations on inflation and output is estimated and analyzed using modern methods of cointegration.

I. INTRODUCTION

The near doubling of oil prices in the United States in 1990 was commonly viewed to be a result of Iraq's maneuvers to raise oil prices and her eventual invasion of Kuwait less than a week later.[1] This event led to major revisions in the forecasts of the economic outlook for the U.S. and also renewed interest in the impact of oil price shocks on important macroeconomic variables such as production and the general price level.

It is still widely believed that the primary and most immediate impact of a price shock would be the onset of a recession which would then trigger various policy responses such as the easing of monetary policy. Hamilton (1983) investigated the statistical relation between the incidence of recessions and significant oil price increases in the post World War II period. His empirical results led to the conclusion that:

> "All but one of the U.S. recessions since World War II have been preceded, typically with a lag of around three-fourths of a year, by a dramatic increase in the price of crude petroleum..." (Hamilton, p. 228).[2]

Hamilton cautions, however, that although oil price shocks are an apparent contributing factor, this should not be interpreted to mean that they caused the recessions.

Paramount to the determination of an appropriate policy response or non-response is the identification of the specific transmission mechanism by which oil price shocks impact the macroeconomy. Two major arguments are prevalent in the literature. One argument focuses on the fact that energy resources are an indispensable factor in any production process. An energy price shock would therefore impact the quantity of goods produced and potentially alter the combination of resources used in their production. This supply side argument further suggests that losses in output resulting from energy price shocks are permanent, implying further that policy actions or the manipulation of market prices are ineffective in replacing the lost output. This explanation is generally used to characterize the 1973-74 and 1978-79 energy price shocks and, as some argue, is relevant in explaining the 1990-91 price shock as well.

---

1. Oil prices increased from 16.16 dollars per barrel in the second quarter of 1990 to 30.00 dollars in the final quarter.
2. This statement was true for seven out of the eight recessions during the postwar period, the single exception being the 1960-61 recession. The period of Hamilton's study (1948 to 1981) does not include the most recent oil shock episode of 1990-91.

A second explanation is often used to characterize the transmission path of the oil price shocks of the fifties and sixties. According to this view, a rise in energy prices raises the oil import bill and therefore reduces aggregate demand through the negative impact on net exports. It is further suggested that the resulting output losses are cyclical or transitory and are therefore reversible through appropriate economic policy or wage and price adjustments. Thus, the appropriateness and potential success of economic policy in the face of an oil price shock are dependent on the nature of the transmission channel.

More recent discussions center around the nature of the effect of the 1990-91 oil price shock and its relation to the coincident recession. One hypothesis is that the most recent oil price increase has a significantly smaller impact on the U.S. economy than previous price shocks for one of the following reasons. First, is the argument that the adverse impact of an oil price hike is proportional to the share of oil imports in the Gross National Product (GNP) and that share has fallen since previous price shocks. Second, this effect is proportional to energy use per unit of output and this usage has fallen as well. Fieleke (1990) provided data on the amount of energy used to produce each billion dollars of the Gross Domestic Product (GDP) for a sample of developed countries. As a group, industrialized countries improved their efficiency by almost 40 per cent while the United States made efficiency gains of about 34 per cent: from 271,000 metric tons of oil per billion dollars of GDP in 1973 to 179,000 metric tons of oil per billion dollars of GDP in 1988 (Fieleke, p.5).

Yet a third reason emphasizes the persistence of the price shock. It appears that although oil prices rose in August and September of 1990 to a high of 34 dollars per barrel, prices declined in subsequent months because more than ninety per cent of the shortfall from Kuwait and Iraq were compensated for by increased supply from other countries in the region (Sahimi, p.11). The opposing argument is that the 1990-91 oil price shock is comparable in both magnitude and macroeconomic impact to the earlier price shocks.

Dramatic changes in the world political map, especially the Gulf War and the dissolution of the former Soviet Union which eventually ended the Cold War, have led researchers to question the impact of the New

World Order on oil resources and energy policy.[3] According to Sahimi (1996) three significant observations on the role of energy persist in the new world order. These are that: (1) oil and gas are still the most important sources of energy; (2) unless either technological advances lead to the development of viable alternatives, or the environmental harm caused by oil and other types of fossil energy become so severe as to render them useless as energy sources, it is generally believed that oil will continue to be the most important energy source in the future; and (3) known world oil and gas reserves are heavily concentrated in the Middle East and a few other developing countries which have long histories of social and political instability. It appears that despite significant world developments, oil will continue to retain its prominent position in U.S. national policy.

The primary purpose of this chapter is to investigate the potential long-run impact of oil price shocks on the U.S. economy in the light of recent world developments. It investigates both demand and supply side effects of such shocks. The nature and significance of the impact of oil price variations on inflation and output are estimated using modern methods of cointegration analysis. The focus of the empirical analysis is the impact of oil price shocks on the U.S. economy during the last quarter of a century including the most recent 1990-91 price shock. The remainder of the paper is organized as follows: section II provides a simple model that is used to assess the long-run relation between domestic production and oil prices; section III introduces a simple model of inflation; section IV discusses the study's empirical methodology; and section V reports the results supporting the notion that an oil price shock is inflationary and contractionary, in the long-run. Data sources and variable definitions are listed in the appendix.

II. OIL PRICE SHOCKS AND DOMESTIC OUTPUT

The reduced form of the output model to which cointegration analysis is applied, includes the oil price as a supply-side variable, in addition to

---

3. Sahimi (1996) provides an extensive discussion on the factors that affect the development of fossil energy resources, particularly that of oil and gas. These are: (1) the geopolitical factor, (2) the social dynamics of these countries, (3) the state of the international economy, (4) the environmental issues and concerns, and (5) the scientific and technological advances.

demand-side factors. The literature on the contractionary or expansionary effects of currency depreciations is relevant to our discussion of the impact of oil price shocks on domestic output. The consensus among economists is that depreciation could stimulate aggregate demand by expanding its net export component and it could contract aggregate supply by raising the cost of imported inputs. Thus, the net effect of depreciation on domestic production is dependent upon the relative size of the shift in aggregate demand and aggregate supply. If the expansion in aggregate demand exceeds the contraction in aggregate supply, then a depreciation could result in increased domestic output. If, however, the contraction in aggregate supply is more extensive than the expansion in aggregate demand, then a depreciation could result in a decline of domestic production. In the first case, depreciation is said to be expansionary and in the latter case depreciation is said to be contractionary.

Theoretical support for the above arguments are found in the studies of Diaz-Alejandro (1963), Guitian (1976), Krugman and Taylor (1978), Hanson (1983), Wijnbergen (1986), Lizondo and Montiel (1989) and Baumol and Blinder (1991). The more recent studies by Lizondo and Montiel (1989, p.182) and Baumol and Blinder (1991, p.423) come to the conclusion that on analytical grounds, the direction of the impact of devaluation on real output is ambiguous.

The results of empirical studies are rather mixed and appear to be focused on the experiences of less developed countries (LDCs). Gylfason and Schmidt (1983) estimated the parameters of a simple macro model for a group of five LDCs and five developed countries (DCs) and demonstrated that for most of the countries in the sample, devaluations are expansionary in the short to medium run. Contradictory results were obtained by Solimano (1986) who investigated the experience of Chile and concluded that devaluations are contractionary in the short to medium run. Edwards (1986) estimated a reduced form real output equation by pooling data from 12 LDCs and concluded that devaluations have a negative short-run impact on output. However, Edwards' results showed that after one year, devaluations are expansionary with no effect on output in the long-run.[4] When a similar procedure of pooling data was used by

---

4. Note that the exogenous variables in Edwards' model were money growth surprises, government expenditure, terms of trade and real exchange rates.

Agenor (1991), it was concluded that contractionary effects of anticipated depreciations remain significant even after a year.[5]

To analyze the effects of oil prices on U.S. domestic output we adopt a modified version of Edwards' (1986) reduced form model. Edwards' model related output to a measure of fiscal policy, monetary policy, commercial policy, and the exchange rate. In addition to these measures, we include the oil price in the output model, equation (1) below:

$$\text{Log } Y = F [\text{ Log RBUD, Log RM, Log REX, Log POIL }] \qquad (1)$$

where Y = real domestic output measured by real GDP. RBUD is the real full-employment budget as a measure of fiscal policy. It should be noted that during the entire period under study, 1973.I to 1992.II the RBUD variable was negative and we were, therefore, unable to calculate its logarithm. Our solution was to multiply the budget data by -1 to make them all positive. Thus, we now interpret an increase in RBUD as an increase in budget deficits. A deficit reflects either a tax cut or an increase in government spending (an expansionary fiscal policy). A measure of monetary policy is denoted by real money supply, RM measured by the real M2 monetary aggregate. As a measure of commercial policy, Edwards included the terms of trade as well as the nominal exchange rate. However, since the terms of trade is inclusive of oil price changes, we replaced it with the real effective exchange rate (REX) to avoid potential multicolinearity between the terms of trade and oil prices. Finally, POIL denotes the price of oil. As far as the expected signs on the coefficients are concerned, an increase in RBUD or an increase in the budget deficit which is an indication of expansionary fiscal policy, is expected to stimulate domestic output yielding a positive sign. An expansionary monetary policy or an increase in real money supply is also expected to have a positive effect on Y. As the appendix indicates, the REX variable is defined as units of foreign output per unit of U.S. output. Thus, if real depreciation is to expand domestic production, we would expect REX to carry a negative coefficient. Finally, if an oil price hike is to be recessionary, we would expect POIL to carry a negative coefficient.

---

5. The conflict between Edwards' and Agenor's results could be due to the fact that while Edwards pooled time series data from 12 LDCs, Agenor pooled data from 23 LDCs.

III. OIL PRICE SHOCKS AND DOMESTIC INFLATION

In investigating sources of inflation some have relied upon the structuralist approach in which many macroeconomic variables, including the inflation rate, are linked through a system of relationships. Otani (1975), Lipschitz (1984), and Anderson et. al. (1988) are examples of studies that have used the structuralist model of inflation. However, once again due to the methodology of cointegration, we need to identify a reduced form model of inflation such as the monetarist model of inflation. In the original monetary model, Harberger (1963) related the domestic inflation rate to the rate of change of the nominal money stock in excess of the rate of change of domestic output. This model has been applied to many countries by Bomberger and Makinen (1979), Sheehey (1979), Nugent and Glezakos (1979), Ize and Salas (1985), and McNelis (1987). Three other studies by Rana and Dowling (1985), Darrat and Arize (1990) and Bahmani-Oskooee and Malixi (1992), have applied the monetarist model augmented with imported inflation and exchange rate depreciation, to some LDCs. Following either Rana and Dowling (1985) or Bahmani-Oskooee and Malixi (1992), we employ the augmented monetarist model outlined in equation (2) below:

$$P_t = a + b(NM - Y)_t + c\, PXW_t + d\, NEX_t \quad (2)$$

where P is the rate of change of the price index; NM is the rate of change of the nominal money supply, Y is the rate of change of real output, PXW is the rate of change of world export prices as a proxy for imported inflation, and NEX is the rate of change of the nominal effective exchange rate.

Previous studies which employed equation (2) or one of its variants are methodologically flawed in that they employed the rate of change of each variable without verifying whether these variables contained one, two, or more unit roots. The determination of the stationarity of variables is now fundamental in time series analysis. Following Bahmani-Oskooee (1995), in the context of cointegration analysis, we must include the level of each variable rather than its rate of change. Furthermore, equation (2) is modified by the addition of a measure of fiscal policy (RBUD) and by replacing imported inflation by the oil price variable (POIL), as in equation (3):

$$\text{Log } P_t = F[\text{LogNM}_t, \text{Log } Y_t, \text{Log RBUD, Log POIL, Log NEX}_t] \quad (3)$$

In (3) it is expected that the nominal money supply (NM) will carry a positive coefficient indicating that an increase in the money supply results in an increase in the general price level (P). An increase in domestic output (Y) is expected to cause a decline in the domestic price level, yielding a negative coefficient for Y. If an increase in the budget deficit is to be inflationary, RBUD should carry a positive coefficient. If imported inflation, proxied by an increase in oil prices, is to contribute to domestic inflation, POIL must carry a positive sign. Finally, if a depreciation is to contribute to domestic inflation, NEX defined as the number of foreign currency per U.S. dollar, must carry a negative coefficient.

IV. THE METHODOLOGY

As indicated above, the focus of our study is the long-run equilibrium relationship among a set of macroeconomic variables. The appropriate methodology is based on the cointegration technique of Johansen (1988) and Johansen and Juselius (1990) who suggest a maximum likelihood estimation procedure that provides two test statistics for the determination of the number of cointegrating vectors as well as estimates of all cointegrating vectors which could exist among a set of variables.

Johansen (1988) defines a distributed lag model of a vector of variables, X as

$$X_t = \pi_1 X_{t-1} + \pi_2 X_{t-2} + \ldots + \pi_k X_{t-k} + \varepsilon_t \quad (4)$$

where X is a vector of N *stationary* variables. In case variables in X are non-stationary and achieve stationarity after being differenced once, equation (4) can be rewritten in first difference form similar to the Augmented Dickey Fuller (ADF) test as indicated by (5):

$$\Delta X_t = \Gamma_1 \Delta X_{t-1} + \Gamma_2 \Delta X_{t-2} + \ldots + \Gamma_{k-1} \Delta X_{t-k+1} - \pi X_{t-k} + \varepsilon_t \quad (5)$$

where $\quad \Gamma_i = -I + \pi_1 + \pi_2 + \ldots + \pi_i \ (i=1, \ldots k)$

and $\quad \pi = -(I - \pi_1 - \pi_2 - \ldots - \pi_k).$

The long-run or cointegrating matrix is given by p which is an NxN matrix and includes r cointegrating vectors which is the rank of p. If we define two matrices a and b (both Nxr) such that p = ab', the rows of b will form the r cointegrating vectors. Johansen and Juselius prove that one can test the hypothesis that there are at most r cointegrating vectors by calculating the two likelihood test statistics known as the *trace* and the *l-max* tests.

V. THE EMPIRICAL RESULTS

The output model outlined in equation (1) and the price model outlined in equation (3) are subject to empirical analysis in this section. Quarterly data over the period 1973.I-1992.II are employed to carry out the empirical analysis. As indicated in the previous section, we first need to determine whether all variables in both models are stationary. To do this, we apply an Augmented Dickey-Fuller (ADF) test that includes a trend term. For a variable Z_t the ADF test is formulated by equation (6) below:

$$Z_t = \alpha + \beta t + \sigma Z_{t-1} + \sum_{i=1}^{k} \gamma_i \Delta Z_{t-i} + w_t \quad (6)$$

where w is an error term. The ADF test statistic is calculated as the ratio of the estimate of s-1 to its standard error. The cumulative distribution of the ADF test statistic is provided by Mackinnon (1991). If the calculated statistic is less than its critical value, then Z is said to be stationary or integrated of order zero denoted by I(0). If a variable achieves stationarity after being differenced once, that variable is said to be integrated of order 1 or I(1). The results of the ADF test appear in Table 1.[6]

Comparing the calculated ADF statistic to its critical value reported at the bottom of Table 1, we conclude that none of the statistics is less than the critical value for the level of the variables, indicating that none of the variables are stationary. However, when we consider the first differenced variables, all achieved stationarity except Log P. Although, the ADF statistic of -2.78 for the stationarity of ΔLog P variable is not less than the

---

6. In accordance with the literature, the choice of lags in the ADF test was determined by the level of the significance of the estimated lag coefficients using the standard t-test.

Table 1 The results of ADF test applied to the level as well as first differenced variables: 1973I-1992II

Variable	Calculated ADF Statistic[a]
Log P	-1.21[3][b]
Log NM	0.87[1]
Log Y	-2.60[2]
Log NEX	-1.99[3]
Log POIL	-1.61[4]
Log RBUD	-2.78[4]
Log RM	-1.85[2]
Log REX	-2.19[4]
ΔLog P	-2.78[1]
ΔLog NM	-6.88[1]
ΔLog Y	-4.60[1]
ΔLog NEX	-3.94[2]
ΔLog POIL	-6.09[3]
ΔLog RBUD	-4.68[4]
ΔLog RM	-5.47[2]
ΔLog REX	-3.51[4]

Notes: a. The Mackinnon (1991) critical value of the ADF statistic for 78 observations (when a trend term is included in the test) is -3.46 at the 5% level of significance and -3.15 at the 10% level of significance.

b. Numbers inside the brackets are number of lags.

critical value, it is much less than the -1.21 for Log P. The implication is that we can still assume on this basis that the first differenced Log P is stationary or it is an I(1) variable. Therefore, we use first differenced variables in the Johansen-Juselius cointegration procedure. We are now in a position to apply the cointegration procedure to the variables of the output equation. First, a decision must be made about the optimum number of lags. A common practice when working with quarterly data is to use four lags. However, in order to determine whether the results are sensitive to the choice of the number of lags, we also experimented with five lags. The results of λ-*max* and *trace* tests are reported in Table 2.

Table 2. Johansen's Maximum Likelihood Procedure Results for the Variables of Output Equation

Null	Alternative	A: 4 Lags in the Procedure			
		l-max Statistic	95% Critical Value	Trace Statistic	95% Critical Value
r = 0	r = 1	38.78	33.32	102.96	70.59
r ≤ 1	r = 2	24.24	27.13	64.18	48.28
r ≤ 2	r = 3	19.55	21.07	39.93	31.52
r ≤ 3	r = 4	16.08	14.90	20.38	17.95
r ≤ 4	r = 5	4.29	8.17	4.29	8.17

Null	Alternative	B: 5 Lags in the Procedure			
		l-max Statistic	95% Critical Value	Trace Statistic	95% Critical Value
r = 0	r = 1	47.46	33.32	110.97	70.59
r ≤ 1	r = 2	32.23	27.13	63.51	48.28
r ≤ 2	r = 3	14.62	21.07	31.28	31.52
r ≤ 3	r = 4	9.54	14.90	16.66	17.95
r ≤ 4	r = 5	7.11	8.17	7.11	8.17

Consider first the results in panel A where four lags are imposed in the procedure. The null hypothesis of no cointegration, i.e., r=0 is rejected because the calculated λ-max statistic is greater than its critical value. Thus, there is at least one cointegrating vector among the variables of the output equation. The null of r≤1 versus r=2, however, cannot be rejected suggesting that there is one cointegrating vector. The same is true for the null of r≤2 versus r=3, but not for the null of r≤3 versus r=4, which suggests that there are four cointegrating vector whereas r≤1 versus r=2 suggests that there is only one vector. Due to this inconsistency we shift to panel B where five lags are employed in the procedure and where there is no inconsistency in the results. In this panel no matter which test we consider, the null of r=0 is rejected in favor of r=1 and r≤1 is rejected in favor of r=2. However, the null of r≤2 cannot be rejected in favor of r=3. Thus, both the λ-max and the trace tests support the evidence of two cointegrating vectors among the variables of output equation.[7]

Table 3. Estimates of Cointegrating Vectors for Output Model

	Variables				
	Log Y	Log RM	Log REX	Log RBUD	Log POIL
Vector 1	-1.0000	2.2015	0.4789	-0.3245	-0.0659
Vector 2	-1.0000	0.8091	-0.0604	0.0248	0.0469
χ^2 stat.	16.4000	20.4300	14.4600	31.7600	14.4400

Note: Since there are two cointegrating vectors, the χ^2 statistic in this case has two degrees of freedom. The critical value of $\chi^2 = 5.99$, at the 5% level of significance.

The next step is to report the two cointegrating vectors. These vectors are associated with maximum eigenvalues, which are reported, in Table 3. Furthermore, convergence toward a long-run equilibrium could be due to a strong relation among some of the variables but not all of the variables in the output equation. To determine which variable(s) should be excluded from the cointegrating space, we apply the likelihood ratio (LR) test for the exclusion of each variable in each case. Johansen (1988, p.237) and Johansen and Juselius (1990, p.194) show that the LR test for excluding a variable (or restricting the coefficient of that variable to zero) is based on the estimates of eigenvalues of unrestricted and restricted cointegrating space according to (7):

$$-2 \operatorname{Ln}(Q) = T \sum_{i=1}^{r} \ln\{(1-\lambda_i^*)/(1-\lambda_i)\} \qquad (7)$$

---

7. Cointegration analysis involves vector autoregressions, where all equations have the same lag length and all polynomials, $A_{ij}(L)$, are the same degree. This is necessary in order to preserve the symmetry of the system. In this case because of this cross-equation restriction, an equation by equation test such as the FPE criterion, is not an appropriate method of selecting the number of lags. Instead, a likelihood ratio test such as that suggested by Engle and Granger (1987) and Enders (1995), employed in this chapter and called sensitivity analysis, is an appropriate and accepted method of determining whether cointegration results are sensitive to the choice of lags (see Bahmani-Oskooee, 1995).

where r is the number of cointegrating vectors, λ^* is the eigenvalue of the ith vector from the restricted space and l is the eigenvalue of the ith vector from unrestricted cointegrating space. They show that quantity (7) is distributed as χ^2 with r(p-s) degrees of freedom where r is the number of cointegrating vectors, p is the dimension of unrestricted cointegrating space and s is the dimension of restricted space. In each case, since we are restricting one of the coefficients to zero, s = p - 1 which implies that the degrees of freedom for each χ^2 statistic is actually equal to r(p-p+1)=r, i.e., the number of cointegrating vectors in each case. In Table 3 we report the cointegrating vectors for each case and inside the bracket, the calculated χ^2 statistic. Note that it is common practice to normalize the coefficients by setting one of them to -1. We normalize each vector by setting the coefficient of Log Y to -1.

As can be seen from Table 3, the oil price variable (POIL) carries its expected negative sign, at least in the first vector, indicating that an oil price hike results in a contraction in output. Monetary policy seems to be expansionary in both vectors, since RM carries its expected positive sign. Fiscal policy seems to be expansionary in the first vector and real depreciation of the dollar is also expansionary in the second vector. Furthermore, the null hypothesis of excluding any of the variables from cointegration space is rejected. This is because all calculated χ^2 statistics are larger than the critical value. We now turn to the analysis of the price equation. All results corresponding to the cointegration among the variables of the price model where 5 lags are employed in the procedure, are reported in Table 4.

Table 4. Cointegration Results for the Price Model

		A: 4 Lags in the Procedure			
Null	Alternative	l-max Statistic	95% Critical Value	Trace Statistic	95% Critical Value
r = 0	r = 1	54.79	39.42	152.08	95.17
r ≤ 1	r = 2	37.36	33.32	97.29	70.59
r ≤ 2	r = 3	29.21	27.13	59.92	48.28
r ≤ 3	r = 4	12.85	21.07	30.70	31.52
r ≤ 4	r = 5	9.81	14.90	17.85	17.95
r ≤ 5	r = 6	8.04	8.17	8.04	8.17

	B: Estimates of Cointegrating Vectors					
	Log P	Log NM	Log Y	Log NEX	Log RBUD	Log POIL
Vector 1	-1.0000	0.7051	0.4957	0.2530	-0.1607	0.0159
Vector 2	-1.0000	0.7403	-0.4960	-0.0481	-0.0018	0.0943
Vector 3	-1.0000	1.6180	-2.2686	0.0717	-0.0478	-0.0809
χ^2 stat.	14.6000	16.9600	18.0300	14.9700	39.2400	8.4900

Note: Since there are 3 cointegrating vectors, the c^2 statistic in this case has 3 degrees of freedom. The critical value of $\chi^2 = 7.81$, at the 5% level of significance.

From panel A in Table 4 we gather that no matter which test we use, the null of no cointegration is rejected. Both tests support the existence of three cointegrating vectors among the variables of the price model. The estimates of all three vectors are reported in panel B. It is evident from the results that at least in the first two cointegrating vectors, the oil price increase has a positive effect on domestic inflation. Nominal money expansion also has a positive effect on domestic inflation, as indicated by the positive coefficient of NM in all three vectors. Vectors 2 and 3 support our theoretical expectation that an increase in domestic production reduces the price level in the long-run, as the Y variable carries a negative sign in these two vectors. Nominal depreciation seems to be inflationary only in vector 2. Finally, since all χ^2 statistics for the exclusion of each variable from cointegrating space are larger than the critical value, all variables belong to the cointegrating space. All in all, concentrating on the central theme of this chapter, it is clear that an oil price hike contributes to domestic inflation.

VI. SUMMARY AND CONCLUSIONS

The standard text book argument against an oil price shock is that by raising the cost of production it contributes to domestic inflation. The increased price level, on the other hand, causes different agents in the economy to economize on their spending leading to a decline in production.

In this chapter we applied cointegration analysis to quarterly data over 1973.I-1992.II period to establish the long-run relation between U.S. output and oil prices on the one hand, and the U.S. price level and oil prices on the other. Further analysis of the cointegrating vector revealed that the relation between the variables of concern are, in most instances, in line with our theoretical expectations. The results also lend empirical substance to the notion that there are no significant differences in terms of macroeconomic impact, between the most recent 1990-91 oil price shock and the earlier shocks of the seventies. All three resulted in varying degrees of stagflation for the U.S. economy. The implication is that despite recent world developments, despite significant improvements in oil usage and despite the increased vulnerability of the U.S. and other developed countries to disruptions in the supply of oil; the recessionary and inflationary impacts of oil price shocks cannot be denied. In the 1990s, oil price shocks continue to impact the U.S. macroeconomy in fundamentally the same way as they did in the 1970s.

Certainly, economic fundamentals continue to impact the dynamics of the U.S.-Milddle East economic relationship in the post-Persian Gulf War era. Oil price shocks in industrialized countries motivate energy conservation and the development of alternative energy sources. An attendant recession would result in cutbacks in purchases of domestic, and especially, more expensive imported products such as foreign oil. However, the U.S., like other developed countries, still responds enthusiastically to a fall in world oil prices, increasing its consumption of imported oil and discouraging U.S. production. Petroleum receipts, on the other hand, enhance the ability of Middle Eastern oil exporters to purchase U.S. goods, such as food, beverages and feed.

One other complicating factor is the tenuous nature of the market-sharing agreement among member countries of the Organization of Petroleum Exporting Countries (OPEC). Fieleke (1990) characterizes the OPEC as a "partial market-sharing cartel"[8], which is the weakest form of cartel arrangement and whose behavior is difficult to predict. Nevertheless, U.S. policy experience in dealing with previous price shocks have led to the identification of appropriate economic policies such as those of the strategic petroleum reserve (SPR) release; cuts in domestic excise taxes on oil, refined products and competing energy sources; monetary easing by the Federal Reserve to combat unemployment; as well as widespread international cooperation in matters of energy security.

---

8. A "partial market sharing cartel" is one in which the members usually raise a lower production jointly, although some may make larger percentage changes than others (Fieleke, p. 9).

Recent experience demonstrates that safeguarding what appears to be a mutually beneficial economic relationship between the U.S. and the Middle East will continue to be a challenge in the future. Moreover, the macroeconomic impacts on the U.S. economy will be severe if either technological advances do not lead to the development of viable alternatives or if the social and political instability in the Middle East escalates. Thus, U.S. intervention in the Middle East to promote peace and stability should reduce the stagflationary impacts of future oil price shocks.

REFERENCES

Anderson, R. B., Bomberger, W. A., and G. E. Makinen, "The Demand for Money, the reform Effect, and the Money Supply Process in Hyperinflation," *Journal of Money, Credit and Banking*, November 1988, 635-672.

Bahmani-Oskooee, Mohsen, "What are the Long-Run Determinants of the U.S. Trade Balance?" *Journal of Post Keynesian Economics*, Fall 1992, 15, 85-97.

Bahmani-Oskooee, Mohsen, "Source of Inflation in Post-Revolutionary Iran," *International Economic Journal*, Summer 1995, 9, 61-72.

Bahmani-Oskooee, M. and M. Malixi, "Inflationary Effects of Changes in Effective Exchange Rates: LDCs Experience," *Applied Economics*, April 1992, 465-471.

Bomberger, W. A., and G. E. Makinen, "Some Further Tests of the Harberger Inflation Model Using Quarterly Data," *Economic Development and Cultural Change*, July 1979, 629-644.

Baumol, William J. and Alan S. Blinder, *Macroeconomics: Principles and Policy*, Fifth Edition, (New York: Harcourt Brace Jovanovich Publishers, 1991).

Darrat, A. F. and A. Arize, "Domestic and International Sources of Inflation in Developing Countries: Some Evidence from the Monetary Approach", *International Economic Journal*, Winter 1990, 55-69.

Diaz-Alejandro, Carlos F., "A Note on the Impact of Devaluation and the Redistributive Effect," *Journal of Political Economy*, August 1963, 71, 577-580.

Edwards, Sebastian, "Are Devaluations Contractionary?" *The Review of Economics and Statistics*, August 1986, 68, 501-508.

Enders, Walter, *Applied Econometric Time Series*, (New York: John Wiley & Sons, Inc., 1995).

Engle, R.F. and C.W.J. Granger, "Cointegration and Error Correction: Representation, Estimation and Testing," *Econometrica*, 55, 251-276.

Fieleke, Norman S., "Oil Shock III?" *New England Economic Review*, September/October 1990, 3-10.

Gordon, Robert J., *Macroeconomics*, Sixth Edition, (New York: Harper Collins College Publishers, 1993).

Guitian, Manuel, "The Effects of Changes in the Exchange Rate on Output, Prices and the Balance of Payments," *Journal of International Economics*, February 1976, 6, 65-74.

Gylfason, Thorvaldur and Michael Schmid, "Does Devaluation Cause Stagflation?," *Canadian Journal of Economics*, November 1983, 16, 641-654.

Hamilton, James D., "Oil and the Macroeconomy since World War II," *Journal of Political Economy* April 1983, 91, 228-248.

Hanson, James A., "Contractionary Devaluation, Substitution in Production and Consumption, and the Role of the Labor Market," *Journal of International Economics*, February 1983, 14, 179-189.

Harberger, A., "The Dynamics of Inflation in Chile", in *Measurement in Economics* ed., C. F. Christ, (Stanford: Stanford University Press, 1963).

Ize, Alain and Javier Salas, "Prices and Output in the Mexican Economy: Empirical Tests of Alternative Hypotheses," *Journal of Development Economics*, April 1985, 175-199.

Johansen, Sfren, "Statistical Analysis of Cointegration Vectors," *Journal of Economic Dynamics and Control*, June/Sept. 1988, 12, 231-254.

Johansen, Sfren and Katarina Juselius, "Maximum Likelihood Estimation and Inference on Cointegration-With Application to the Demand for Money," *Oxford Bulletin of Economics and Statistics*, May 1990, 52, 169-210.

Krugman, Paul and Lance Taylor, "Contractionary Effects of Devaluation," *Journal of International Economics*, August 1978, 8, 445-456.

Lipschitz, Leslie, "Domestic credit and Exchange rates in Developing Countries: Some Policy Experiments with Korean Data," *IMF Staff Papers*, December 1984, 595-635.

Lizondo, J. Saul and Peter J. Montiel, "Contractionary Devaluation in Developing Countries: An Analytical Overview," *IMF StaffPapers*, March 1989, 36, 182-227.

Mackinnon, James G., "Critical Values for Cointegration Tests," in *Long Run Economic Relationships: Readings in Cointegration*, eds., R.F. Engle and C.W.J. Granger, (New York: Oxford University Press, 1991).

McNelis, Paul D., "Indexing, Exchange Rate Policy and Inflationary Feedback Effects in Latin America," *World Development*, August 1987, 1107-1117.

Nugent, Jeffrey B., and Constantine Glezakos, "A Model of Inflation and Expectations in Latin America," *Journal of Development Economics*, September 1979, 431-446.

Otani, Ichiro, "Inflation in an Open Economy: A Case Study of the Philippines," *IMF Staff Papers*, Nov. 1975, 750-774.

Pesaran, Hashem M. and Bahram Pesaran, *Microfit 3.0, An Interactive Econometric Package*, (Oxford: Oxford University Press, 1991).

Rana, Pradumma B., and J. Malcolm Dowling, Jr., "Inflationary Effects of Small but Continuous Changes in Effective Exchange Rates: Nine Asian LDCs," *The Review of Economics and Statistics*, August 1985, 496-500.

Sahimi, Mohammad, "Factors Affecting the Development of Fossil Energy Resources of Developing Countries", in *United States - Third World Relations and the New World Order*, eds. A. P. Grammy and C. K. Bragg (Commack, N.Y.: NOVA Science Publishers, 1996), 361-89.

Solimano, Andres, "Contractionary Devaluation in the Southern Cone:The Case of Chile," *Journal of Development Economics*, September 1986, 23, 135-151.

Sheehey, Edmund J., "On the Measurement of Imported inflation in Developing Countries," *Weltwirtschaftliches Archiv*, Heft 1, 1979, 68-80.

Tatom, John A., "Are There Useful Lessons from the 1990-1991 Oil Price Shock," *The Energy Journal*, 1993, 14, 129-150.

Wijnbergen, Sweder Van, "Exchange Rate Management and Stabilization Policies in Developing Countries," *Journal of Development Economics*, October 1986, 23, 227-247.

APPENDIX

DATA DEFINITION AND SOURCES

All data are quarterly over 1973I-1992II period and collected from the following sources.

a. Gordon (1993, Appendix A), Table A-2.
b. International Financial Statistics of the IMF, various issues.
c. Direction of Trade Statistics of the IMF, Yearbook of 1992.
d. Survey of Current Business.

Variables:

P = Price level in the U.S. measured by the GDP deflator (1987=100). Data come from source a.

NM = Nominal money supply measured by M2 monetary aggregate in Billions of Dollars. Data come from source a.

RM = Real money supply. NM is deflated by P.

Y = Real output in the U.S. measured by Gross Domestic Product in 1987 dollars. Data come from source a.

RBUD = Real full-employment federal budget in 1987 dollars. The real natural federal surplus (if positive) and deficit (if negative) in billions of 1987 dollars are from source a.

POIL = Price of oil in index form (1987=100). The price charged for crude petroleum by the largest member of OPEC (Saudi Arabia) is used for this variable. The data comes from the Saudi Arabian page in source b. The missing observations for 1986 and 1989 are proxied by the price of U.S. imported petroleum products which come from source d. Note that these observations were adjusted by an overlapping observation to match the Saudi price.

REX = index of the real effective exchange rate of the dollar (1987=100). Since no source reports the real effective rate for the entire period under analysis, we had to construct this index. In doing so, we followed the four steps suggested by Bahmani-Oskooee (1992).[9] First, we

---

9. Note that the International Monetary Fund (IMF) reports the real effective exchange rate for most developed countries only for the 1980s and 1990s, but not for the 1970s.

needed the bilateral exchange rates between the U.S. dollar and each of its trading partners currencies. These rates, which we denote by EX_i's and define as the number of units of trading partner i's currency per unit of the U.S. dollar are period average rates and are collected from source b. In the second step we calculate the real bilateral exchange rates using EX_i's and CPI indexes (1987=100):

$$REX_i = (CPI_{U.S.} EX_i / CPI_i)$$

where $CPI_{U.S.}$ is the U.S. price level, CPI_i is the price level in trading partner i, and REX_i is the real bilateral exchange rate defined as units of i's currency per unit of the U.S. dollar. Note that the CPI (from source b) is the only price index available for all trading partners. Since we need to calculate the weighted average of real bilateral exchange rates, the third step involves making the real bilateral exchange rates homogenous across all trading partners by setting them in index form. Thus, denoting the index of the real bilateral exchange rates by $IREX_i$ and selecting 1987 as the base year, we have:

$$IREX_i^t = (REX_i^t / REX_i^{87}) * 100$$

Finally, as indicated above, we take the weighted average of $IREX_i$ in order to obtain the *index of real effective exchange rate* which we have denoted by REX in the text. Thus

$$REX^t = \sum_{i=1}^{n} a_i IREX_i^t$$

where a_i is the share of U.S. imports from trading partner i and $Sa_i = 1$. Fixed import shares in the base period (1987) are from source c. Twenty five trading partners (i's) are selected and they are: Australia, Austria, Belgium, Canada, Denmark, Finland, France, Germany, Italy, Japan, Netherlands, New Zealand, Norway, Spain, Sweden, Switzerland, U.K., Ireland, India, Indonesia, Korea, Malaysia, Philippines, Singapore, and Thailand.

NEX = nominal effective exchange rate, 1987=100. This variable is constructed in the same manner as REX where the price levels are excluded from the procedure.

INDEX

A

Advertising, 148
Afghanistan, 40, 59, 277
aggression, 22, 42, 301, 348
agricultural exports, 320
agricultural goods, 201
air force, 46
Algeria, 255, 257, 277
APEC, 173, 187, 202
apparel, 177
Arab states, 255, 256, 323
Arafat, Yasir, 279
Argentina, 54, 88, 92, 101, 102, 104, 105, 106, 108, 109, 110, 111, 112, 113, 114, 115, 116, 119, 121, 122, 277
armed forces, 105, 211, 304, 306, 367
army, 15, 369
Asian countries, 151, 162, 163, 202, 241, 391, 394, 400, 406
Australia, 175, 277, 287, 362, 372, 430

B

balance of payments, 109, 237
balance of power, 328

Bekaa Valley, 59
bilateral relations, 173, 181
black market, 136, 143
Bosnia, 251, 371
Brazil, 54, 66, 68, 74, 75, 76, 84, 92, 105, 106, 110, 111, 112, 113, 115, 116, 277, 376

C

California, 9, 49, 87, 101, 118, 119, 120, 122, 123, 146, 147, 149, 169, 191, 207, 231, 265, 279, 297, 313, 331, 347, 361, 386, 389, 411
Canada, 88, 132, 175, 277, 287, 379, 398, 430
capital goods, 201, 319
capitalism, 144, 209, 250, 267, 275
Central Asia, 254, 255, 262, 263, 275, 369, 370
Chechnya, 369
China, 150, 151, 173, 205, 217, 233, 251, 357, 359, 363, 372
civil war, 255, 259, 282
Clinton, President William, 4, 5, 7, 8, 46, 139, 141, 144, 209, 210, 212, 213, 216, 220, 221, 222, 223, 224,

432 Index

225, 226, 227, 229, 235, 240, 244, 367, 371, 372, 379, 383
Cold War, 1, 2, 3, 4, 5, 6, 7, 8, 9, 10, 15, 16, 22, 24, 38, 47, 49, 50, 54, 55, 56, 57, 58, 59, 61, 62, 63, 64, 69, 70, 83, 85, 87, 88, 97, 99, 125, 191, 201, 207, 209, 210, 211, 214, 215, 217, 231, 232, 233, 234, 237, 240, 249, 250, 251, 253, 255, 256, 258, 260, 262, 263, 264, 269, 275, 313, 314, 315, 316, 321, 328, 330, 333, 334, 344, 347, 348, 349, 357, 372, 391, 392, 405, 413
Colombia, 60, 81, 92, 102, 103, 104, 105, 106, 107, 109, 110, 111, 112, 113, 114, 115, 116, 117, 120, 121
commodities, 171, 335
communism, 3, 30, 31, 35, 36, 41, 50, 54, 70, 83, 123, 124, 209, 251, 388
Communist Party, 369
competition, 1, 5, 26, 127, 128, 134, 151, 163, 193, 222, 233, 234, 251, 252, 261, 314, 341, 342, 371, 372, 388
computer software, 194
Congress, 4, 41, 54, 57, 67, 69, 71, 82, 83, 85, 127, 177, 208, 237, 238, 239, 241, 243, 246, 326, 327, 383, 389
conservation, 44, 200, 366, 379, 425
Consortium, 222
consumer goods, 209
consumption, 28, 32, 34, 44, 130, 153, 160, 161, 163, 244, 247, 373, 378, 386, 425
conventional arms, 234
corruption, 94, 135, 136, 148, 237
countryside, 77
Cuba, 34, 56, 88, 100, 348
cultural barriers, 88, 97, 99

D

decentralization, 242
defense, 4, 7, 17, 40, 42, 51, 52, 53, 54, 242
deterrence, 9, 10, 11, 12, 13, 15, 19, 20
developing countries, 70, 71, 72, 73, 78, 82, 112, 140, 141, 144, 172, 182, 184, 204, 247, 265, 274, 314, 315, 323, 326, 329, 334, 340, 347, 349, 358, 361, 362, 363, 364, 365, 373, 374, 376, 377, 378, 385, 386, 387, 388, 391, 392, 393, 394, 395, 396, 397, 398, 399, 403, 404, 405, 406, 408, 414
domestic market, 108, 406
drug traffic, 57, 113
dual containment, 46

E

East Asia, 6, 8, 149, 150, 151, 161, 162, 163, 164, 165, 166, 171, 174, 186, 188, 203, 209, 215, 216, 224, 225, 241, 320, 321, 324, 331, 372, 395, 400, 407
economic embargo, 211, 218
economic growth, 2, 5, 21, 32, 45, 70, 131, 137, 145, 192, 199, 203, 204, 269, 274, 307, 314, 316, 325, 329, 337, 338, 339, 340, 343, 345, 347, 348, 349, 351, 366, 372, 373
economic management, 240, 358
economic reform, 4, 51, 53, 238, 239, 240, 245, 318, 323, 325, 326, 328, 334, 344, 348, 357
education, 3, 53, 68, 73, 75, 81, 97, 113, 194, 198, 268, 282, 303, 317, 323, 325, 357, 374
El Salvador, 52, 54, 92, 277

elites, 2, 51, 54, 132, 133, 243, 326, 348
emigration, 108, 116
employment, 109, 113, 114, 138, 145, 186, 193, 281, 284, 291, 343, 374, 416, 429
energy consumption, 44, 373, 378, 386
energy resources, 29, 361, 363, 364, 374, 384, 386, 387, 388, 412, 414
engineers, 363, 375
entrepreneurs, 98, 217, 245, 363
Ethiopia, 59, 277
European Union, 250, 251, 252
export earnings, 136, 143, 335, 336

F

factories, 80, 364
family planning, 68, 71, 79
famine, 232, 344, 362
farmers, 7, 107, 292, 316, 319
foreign assistance, 65, 71
foreign debt, 335
foreign direct investment, 5, 141, 191, 192, 241, 394
foreign exchange, 128, 298, 319, 320, 338
foreign policy, 4, 7, 8, 24, 42, 43, 44, 45, 47, 65, 69, 70, 83, 105, 207, 208, 210, 212, 215, 216, 231, 232, 233, 234, 236, 237, 239, 240, 241, 242, 243, 244, 245, 246, 250, 252, 253
France, 5, 8, 88, 211, 214, 215, 226, 277, 341, 361, 370, 371, 379, 398, 430

G

GATT, 164, 173, 178, 179, 180, 182, 183, 184
Gaza Strip, 282, 283
Gaza, 282, 283
General Agreement On Tariff And Trade, 164, 173, 178, 179, 180, 182, 183, 184
Germany, 5, 51, 181, 232, 241, 277, 315, 328, 368, 372, 374, 379, 398, 430
global change, 24, 236, 334
grants, 94, 279, 281, 293, 294
Great Britain, 5, 299
Greece, 25, 277
Gross National Product, 15, 297, 302, 303, 304, 305, 306, 307, 308, 309, 310, 311, 397, 413
Gulf Cooperation Council, 46, 254
Gulf crisis, 37, 46, 328
Gulf states, 42, 287, 294, 299
guns, 15, 16, 17

H

Hawaii, 333
health care, 67, 69, 76, 198, 323, 325, 383
Hong Kong, 150, 151, 215, 324, 368
hostility, 213
housing, 198, 199, 284, 337
human resources, 286, 325
human rights, 4, 54, 70, 75, 236, 244, 253

I

import substitution, 191, 192
India, 25, 57, 233, 234, 235, 236, 239, 240, 241, 242, 244, 245, 246, 247, 400, 430
Indonesia, 54, 149, 150, 153, 156, 157, 158, 159, 160, 161, 162, 169, 170, 171, 173, 176, 196, 200, 202, 217, 277, 357, 372, 374, 376, 400, 430
inflation, 67, 110, 129, 130, 137, 143, 293, 316, 326, 338, 339, 340, 358, 411, 414, 417, 418, 424, 428
infrastructure, 28, 59, 74, 115, 191, 192, 203, 204, 209, 268, 275, 284, 293, 322, 364, 365, 377, 380, 386, 397, 404
intellectual property rights, 179, 181
intellectual property, 177, 179, 181, 182
international organizations, 72, 80, 214
international terrorism, 56
investment, 5, 6, 10, 17, 19, 20, 50, 58, 70, 101, 114, 115, 117, 127, 128, 129, 130, 136, 137, 138, 139, 140, 141, 145, 150, 164, 172, 175, 176, 177, 178, 179, 180, 181, 182, 183, 184, 185, 186, 191, 192, 193, 196, 197, 200, 202, 210, 211, 217, 220, 240, 241, 244, 245, 271, 275, 292, 308, 311, 315, 318, 330, 335, 342, 344, 363, 378, 385, 392, 393, 396, 398, 406, 407, 408, 409
Iran, 3, 23, 25, 29, 30, 31, 33, 34, 35, 36, 39, 40, 41, 43, 46, 54, 56, 57, 60, 164, 250, 251, 254, 255, 256, 257, 261, 274, 277, 298, 299, 304, 305, 311, 348, 358, 363, 365, 367, 369, 371, 372, 373, 374, 375, 376, 378, 389, 426
Iraq, 9, 11, 20, 23, 29, 31, 33, 36, 38, 39, 40, 46, 56, 60, 61, 254, 255, 257, 258, 259, 261, 277, 286, 297, 298, 299, 300, 301, 302, 303, 304, 305, 306, 307, 308, 310, 311, 348, 357, 359, 365, 367, 371, 372, 373, 375, 376, 377, 411, 413
Israel, 29, 31, 35, 42, 45, 46, 255, 256, 258, 260, 263, 280, 282, 286, 287, 288, 294
Italy, 277, 430

J

Japan, 2, 5, 8, 20, 28, 30, 88, 150, 151, 163, 164, 172, 174, 175, 189, 211, 250, 251, 277, 315, 328, 362, 366, 368, 372, 374, 378, 379, 383, 430
Jordan, 29, 38, 39, 46, 47, 255, 256, 277, 281, 282, 283, 285, 292, 298

K

Kansas, 58
Kazakhstan, 44, 255, 368, 369, 370, 376
Korea, 3, 56, 149, 150, 151, 153, 156, 157, 158, 159, 160, 161, 162, 164, 211, 322, 323, 324, 357, 365, 368, 383, 395, 400, 430
Kuwait, 9, 11, 14, 15, 23, 29, 31, 33, 37, 41, 42, 61, 124, 254, 259, 277, 287, 297, 298, 299, 300, 301, 302, 303, 306, 307, 308, 310, 311, 359, 365, 367, 371, 377, 411, 412, 413

L

labor force, 265, 270, 271, 273, 274, 275, 355
land ownership, 94
Latin America, 1, 3, 5, 58, 60, 61, 65, 67, 68, 73, 75, 81, 82, 83, 84, 87, 88, 89, 90, 91, 92, 93, 94, 95, 96, 97, 98, 99, 100, 104, 112, 118, 119, 120, 122, 124, 140, 144, 147, 166, 287, 320, 331, 357, 384, 407, 428
Leadership, 8, 237, 333
Lebanon, 36, 57, 59, 255, 282, 283, 285, 286
legislation, 32
Libya, 46, 56, 59, 60, 255
licensing, 240
life expectancy, 2, 271, 274, 303, 355, 357
living standard, 2, 327, 362, 365
local government, 63
loyalty, 36, 53, 243, 244, 287

M

Madrid Peace Conference, 258
Malaysia, 149, 150, 151, 153, 156, 157, 158, 159, 162, 169, 170, 192, 196, 200, 202, 277, 372, 400, 408, 430
managerial skills, 335
manufactured goods, 247
market access, 176, 179, 185
market forces, 179, 244, 367, 379
medical services, 67
Mexico, 69, 81, 84, 88, 91, 92, 94, 96, 99, 100, 123, 124, 125, 126, 127, 128, 129, 130, 131, 132, 133, 134, 135, 136, 137, 138, 139, 140, 141, 142, 143, 144, 145, 146, 147, 148, 186, 253, 315, 376, 385, 393
MFN, 184
Middle East, 6, 7, 23, 24, 26, 28, 29, 30, 31, 32, 33, 34, 36, 37, 38, 39, 40, 41, 42, 43, 44, 45, 46, 47, 50, 249, 250, 251, 252, 253, 254, 255, 256, 257, 258, 259, 260, 261, 262, 263, 268, 277, 280, 282, 283, 286, 287, 294, 295, 298, 299, 300, 312, 323, 348, 359, 362, 364, 365, 371, 372, 373, 375, 376, 414, 425, 426
military power, 14, 96, 251
MILITARY, 22, 53, 58, 263, 302, 304, 305, 312
missile technology, 235
modernization, 51, 53, 130, 198, 214, 304
monopoly, 199
Morocco, 255, 277
most-favoured national, 184
murder, 132

N

narcotics, 57, 60, 111, 112, 113
NATO, 7
navy, 30
networks, 315
New World Order, 1, 3, 5, 7, 47, 49, 88, 97, 98, 99, 123, 124, 126, 146, 149, 152, 163, 164, 191, 192, 201, 202, 203, 204, 205, 231, 234, 235, 244, 245, 247, 250, 258, 263, 313, 314, 321, 325, 326, 327, 328, 329, 331, 333, 334, 336, 345, 348, 358, 359, 392, 393, 395, 405, 406, 428
New York, 8, 23, 47, 50, 51, 52, 53, 84, 99, 100, 118, 120, 121, 132, 139, 146, 147, 165, 166, 208, 212, 221,

226, 227, 228, 262, 263, 277, 312, 330, 331, 332, 345, 359, 379, 388, 407, 408, 426, 427, 428
New Zealand, 175, 277, 287, 430
newly industrialized countries, 5
North Africa, 25, 254, 282, 299, 312, 384
North Korea, 56
nuclear arms race, 3, 10
nuclear weapons, 57, 61, 232, 234, 235, 379

O

OECD, 5, 6, 8, 167, 188, 345, 408
Oil and gas, 363
oil prices, 32, 33, 34, 35, 36, 37, 45, 300, 367, 373, 379, 411, 413, 414, 416, 418, 424, 425
oil revenues, 32, 26, 27
oil, 7, 23, 24, 25, 26, 28, 29, 30, 31, 32, 33, 34, 35, 36, 37, 38, 39, 40, 41, 42, 44, 45, 46, 47, 96, 114, 116, 137, 256, 287, 294, 298, 299, 300, 301, 304, 306, 323, 328, 348, 361, 362, 363, 364, 365, 366, 367, 368, 369, 370, 371, 372, 373, 374, 375, 376, 377, 378, 379, 380, 381, 382, 383, 384, 385, 386, 387, 388, 411, 412, 413, 414, 416, 417, 418, 423, 424, 425, 426, 429
OPEC, 33, 34, 35, 36, 37, 39, 44, 46, 47, 300, 367, 371, 372, 374, 377, 379, 425, 429
Orange County, 222, 224, 227, 228
ownership, 93, 94, 194, 266, 267, 292

P

Pakistan, 233, 234, 235, 236, 244, 277, 376, 400
Palestine Liberation Organization, 256, 260, 280, 284
peacekeeping, 4
Persian Gulf states, 42
personnel, 59, 60
Philippines, 3, 54, 57, 150, 151, 169, 170, 171, 196, 278, 395, 400, 428, 430
planned economy, 238
police force, 10, 17, 52, 58, 60
political parties, 134, 135, 235, 237, 238, 243, 326, 392
political reforms, 63, 218, 357
political support, 3
population growth, 2, 7, 239, 269, 271, 274, 301, 308, 363, 388
preferences, 290, 326, 347, 349, 350, 353, 356, 357
propaganda, 2, 52
property, 59, 177, 179, 181, 182, 192, 194, 200, 201, 265, 266, 267, 275, 293
Protectionism, 177, 184, 187
public schools, 89
public works, 53

Q

Qatar, 254

R

Rabin, Yitzhak, 279
raw materials, 320, 364
recession, 5, 412, 413, 425

Reeducation, 291, 292
regional security, 42, 202, 235, 244, 347, 348, 383
regional stability, 46, 173
rehabilitation, 284, 289, 291, 294
rural areas, 72

S

Saddam Hussein, 9, 14, 16, 123, 124, 259, 367
sanctions, 16, 74, 97, 217, 224, 258, 259, 310
Saudi Arabia, 29, 30, 33, 41, 42, 43, 46, 251, 254, 255, 256, 259, 274, 277, 287, 298, 299, 301, 323, 367, 372, 373, 375, 376, 429
scholars, 265, 362
security, 3, 7, 24, 38, 39, 42, 44, 45, 46, 47, 50, 51, 54, 55, 58, 69, 70, 83, 112, 123, 124, 140, 170, 192, 198, 202, 209, 215, 232, 234, 236, 237, 240, 241, 244, 251, 256, 257, 269, 292, 299, 304, 347, 348, 350, 351, 353, 355, 358, 373, 383
sex, 68, 69, 72, 75, 76, 77, 78, 79, 80
ships, 154
Simon, Senator Paul, 57, 91, 100, 121, 379
Singapore, 149, 150, 151, 153, 157, 158, 159, 162, 169, 170, 171, 178, 187, 188, 189, 191, 192, 193, 194, 195, 196, 197, 198, 199, 200, 201, 202, 203, 204, 205, 241, 278, 324, 357, 368, 400, 408, 430
smuggling, 114
sovereignty, 104, 105, 141, 244, 299, 323, 373
Spain, 88, 94, 277, 430
Standards, 193

subsidies, 97, 111, 179, 181, 192, 200, 327, 337, 344
suburbs, 383
Sudan, 277, 286
supply and demand, 34, 44, 45, 251, 367
Sweden, 277, 430
Syria, 29, 46, 56, 255, 277, 282, 285,

T

Taiwan, 150, 151, 211, 357, 368, 383, 408
tariff barriers, 179, 181, 184
taxation, 179, 181, 182, 341
telecommunications, 194
terrorism, 52, 53, 55, 56, 57, 62, 63, 64
textiles, 320
torture, 52, 54, 63
trade barriers, 163, 179
trade deficit, 130, 144, 150, 160, 161, 162, 183, 379
trade imbalance, 92
trade surplus, 92, 126, 129, 130, 135, 141, 142, 143, 145, 160
transportation, 53, 96, 97, 110, 115, 194, 292, 293, 344, 382
Tunisia, 255, 277
Turkey, 250, 255, 256, 263, 277, 298, 369

U

United Arab Emirates, 254, 274, 277, 287
United Kingdom, 181, 277
United States, 1, 2, 3, 4, 5, 6, 7, 8, 9, 10, 11, 16, 17, 23, 24, 25, 27, 28, 29, 30, 31, 32, 34, 35, 36, 37, 38, 39, 40,

41, 42, 44, 45, 46, 47, 49, 50, 51, 52, 53, 54, 55, 56, 58, 59, 60, 61, 62, 63, 64, 65, 68, 69, 70, 71, 72, 77, 82, 83, 85, 87, 88, 89, 92, 93, 94, 95, 97, 98, 99, 101, 102, 111, 115, 116, 117, 125, 129, 131, 132, 133, 139, 149, 153, 160, 162, 163, 169, 172, 173, 174, 175, 176, 178, 179, 180, 181, 182, 183, 184, 186, 189, 197, 202, 209, 214, 215, 217, 220, 224, 225, 227, 228, 231, 232, 240, 241, 249, 250, 251, 252, 253, 258, 259, 260, 261, 262, 263, 276, 277, 287, 302, 305, 306, 314, 315, 329, 336, 348, 359, 362, 364, 365, 366, 367, 369, 371, 372, 376, 378, 379, 382, 383, 385, 386, 397, 398, 411, 413, 428
urbanization, 67, 303
Uruguay Round, 173, 181, 183, 184
Uruguay, 106, 108, 109, 110, 115, 116, 173, 181, 183, 184, 278

V

Venezuela, 33, 92, 96, 101, 102, 103, 104, 105, 106, 107, 108, 109, 110, 111, 112, 113, 115, 116, 118, 119, 120, 278
videos, 291

Vietnam, 34, 52, 54, 59, 62, 63, 169, 170, 174, 202, 207, 208, 209, 210, 212, 213, 214, 215, 216, 217, 218, 219, 220, 221, 222, 223, 224, 225, 226, 227, 228, 229, 241
violence, 9, 52, 56, 59, 69, 77, 102, 113, 125, 128, 146, 358, 396

W

wages, 130, 137, 138, 337, 340, 398
warfare, 4, 15, 52, 59, 60, 63, 330
weapons of mass destruction, 56, 57
West Bank, 282, 284, 295
Western Europe, 2, 26, 28, 233, 336, 366, 372, 379
workforce, 67, 80, 138
world economy, 172, 232, 377
world market, 203
World Trade Organization, 4, 173, 343

Y

Yitzhak Peres, 66